W9-AEF-003

THE BUCCANEER KING

THE BUCCANEER KING

The Biography of Sir Henry Morgan
1635–1688

Dudley Pope

WITH ILLUSTRATIONS AND MAPS

DODD, MEAD & COMPANY
NEW YORK

1 2 3 4 5 6 7 8 9 10

The Buccaneer King was originally
published in England as *Harry Morgan's Way*
First published in the United States in 1978

Library of Congress Cataloging in Publication Data

Pope, Dudley.
    The buccaneer king.

    Bibliography: p.
    Includes index.
    1. Morgan, Henry, Sir, 1635?-1688.
2. Buccaneers—Caribbean area—Biography.
I. Title.
F2161.M83P66   972.9′03′0924 [B]   77-17962
ISBN 0-396-07566-5

For Norman
and
Dorothy Boettcher

THE MORGAN

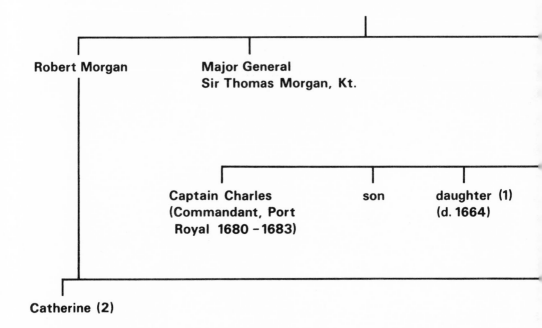

Robert Morgan   **Major General
                            Sir Thomas Morgan, Kt.**

                           **Captain Charles   son   daughter (1)
                           (Commandant, Port   (d. 1664)
                           Royal 1680 – 1683)**

Catherine (2)

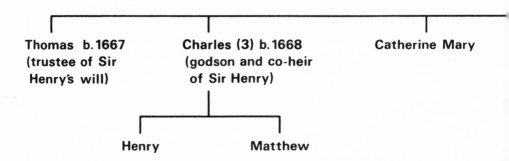

**Thomas b. 1667   Charles (3) b. 1668   Catherine Mary
(trustee of Sir   (godson and co-heir
Henry's will)   of Sir Henry)**

                           Henry   Matthew

(1) Died on voyage to Jamaica.

(2) Her married name is given as 'Loyd' in Sir Henry's will.

(3) Charles Byndloss and Henry Archbold, Sir Henry's godsons, inherited his
     estate on condition they adopted the surname Morgan.

FAMILY

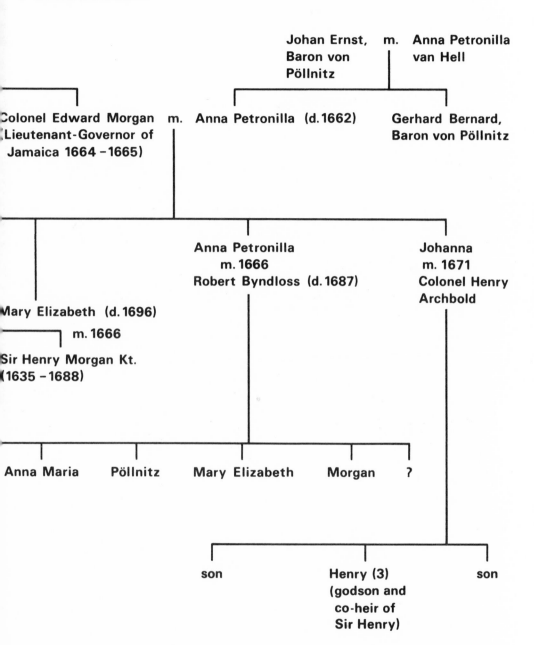

Johan Ernst, m. Anna Petronilla
Baron von van Hell
Pöllnitz

Colonel Edward Morgan m. Anna Petronilla (d. 1662)   Gerhard Bernard,
(Lieutenant-Governor of   Baron von Pöllnitz
Jamaica 1664–1665)

Anna Petronilla   Johanna
m. 1666   m. 1671
Robert Byndloss (d. 1687)   Colonel Henry
                                   Archbold

Mary Elizabeth (d. 1696)
m. 1666
Sir Henry Morgan Kt.
(1635–1688)

Anna Maria   Pöllnitz   Mary Elizabeth   Morgan   ?

son   Henry (3)   son
                   (godson and
                   co-heir of
                   Sir Henry)

Contents

Illustrations

Thus was consumed that famous and antient City of Panama, which is the greatest mart for silver and gold in the whole world, for it receives the goods into it that comes from Old Spain in the King's great Fleet, and likewise delivers to the Fleet all the silver and gold that comes from the mines of Peru and Potosi.

Henry Morgan to the Governor of Jamaica
20 April 1671

WEST INDIES 1670-1680

——————— Coast held by Spain
(The rest unpopulated, or disputed by Buccaneers.)

Morgan's
Major
Raids

— — — —   1663-1665 (Villahermosa, Granada.)

—·—·—·—   1668 (Puerto Principe, Portobelo.)

———————   1668-1669 (Maracaibo)

— — — — —   1670-1671 (Panama)

BAHAMAS

ATLANTIC

OCEAN

incipe
ntiago

Passage

Tortuga

Puerto Plata

aria Windward

rt Royal

Mona Passage

PUERTO
RICO

HISPANIOLA

Ocoa

C. Tiburon

Santo
Domingo

Saona

Mona I.

St. Kitts

LEEWARD
ISLANDS

Île à
Vache
(Cow Island)

Nevis

Guadeloupe

Dominica

(1668-1669)

Martinique

S

E

A

TRADE
WINDS

Barbados

RIBBEAN)

N)

WINDWARD
ISLANDS

Aruba

Bonaire

Curacao

Santa Marta

Ríohacha

Gulf of
Venezuela

Trinidad

Puerto
Cabello

Cumana

Maracaibo

Cartagena

Gibraltar

SPANISH   *MAIN*

Miles

0   100   200   300   400   500   600   700

Foreword

Almost anyone cruising the Caribbean in a sailing yacht for eleven years is going to become fascinated by the legend of the buccaneers and their leader, Sir Henry Morgan, who at various times in his life was a junior officer in the Port Royal militia, admiral of the Brethren of the Coast, governor of Jamaica, lieutenant-general, president of the Admiralty Court, the buccaneer leader who sacked Portobelo, Maracaibo and Panama – and a State prisoner, arrested and sent to England in a leaky frigate, locked up with a condemned pirate.

Sailing among the islands one hears and reads some tales that could not be true and others that only hint at even more startling origins, but beating to windward in a yacht equipped with most of the modern aids to navigation one soon becomes humbled at the thought that buccaneers in boats half the size went off cheerfully to raid fortified cities on the Spanish Main with a cask of water and a sack of boucan for provisions and pikes or decrepit muskets as weapons.

More than half the vessels sailing the breadth of the Caribbean with Morgan to raid the city of Panama were the size of fishing smacks but each was crowded with fifty men or more. And the buccaneers – who were they? They ranged from Cromwell's nephew, Sir Thomas Whetstone, to some of the most murderous blackguards who ever clutched hands to swords. Who were the cow killers and whence came the buccaneers?

Morgan received a knighthood at the hands of Charles II and a commission as lieutenant-governor of Jamaica – but surely he was in England under arrest, a prisoner of State? What is the difference between a buccaneer and a pirate? Why did Spanish pieces of eight suddenly become legal currency in Jamaica? What is the connection between boucan and buccaneer?

Questions fall like spray in a high wind. Within twenty miles of where we are anchored in the British Virgin Islands are Privateer Point and Towing Point, Beef Island (what connection, if any, with the cow killers?), Loblolly Bay, Dead Chest Island, Brandywine Bay, Treasure Point with Privateer Bay next to it, Deadman Bay, Hell Hole and Rogues Point. Between here and Jamaica, 750 miles to leeward, there are scores of places with similar names in various languages.

Names, legends and questions seemed all that remained of the Age of the Buccaneers and eventually it became too much for us (by now my wife and small daughter were equally intrigued), so because I am a naval historian the research began and this book is the result.

One thing is certain about Morgan – he was the product of his time. He could not have flourished as the greatest of the buccaneers had he been born twenty years earlier or twenty years later. The decade during which he was the great buccaneer was also the golden age of privateering, and he is so little understood that he has hitherto been hailed as a great sailor although quite clearly he was in fact a great soldier but an extremely poor seaman.

Morgan and the buccaneers were created by Spain: they would not have existed had not Spain claimed the New World for herself, forbidding any foreigners to cross the Line. The story of Morgan and his men is therefore meaningless without an understanding of the West Indies at the time the Welsh youth arrived as a member of the expedition sent out by Cromwell to capture Hispaniola but which, almost by accident, took Jamaica instead.

For Spain the New World was solely a place to supply her with gold, silver and gems; it was a source of a vast income for very little work or investment. (By 1600, long before Morgan was born, Spain had shipped back more than three times the gold and silver supply in Europe at the time Columbus had sailed.) Spain became wealthy with almost no work, so that trade and industry shrank and inflation increased. Unemployment became so bad that Church and the New World bureaucracy provided the only jobs. In Morgan's day more than a million Spaniards held Church appointments and nearly half a million worked for the government.

The point is made by a comparison: the Spanish island of Cuba, 44,000 square miles, had fewer people and smaller exports than Jamaica, 4400 square miles, but being ten times the size was almost impossible to defend (apart from having its main port at the leeward end of the island).

The French, Dutch and British regarded the New World as an area in which to trade, with new fields to till, plant and harvest. In the face of Spain's refusal to accept any foreigners, the buccaneers' strength was in their unity: they formed the only group who lived, worked and fought together irrespective of a man's religion, colour or politics. They gave their loyalty to successful captains.

It is fashionable today to criticize their barbarity – when, for example, they tortured people to make them reveal where they had hidden their money and valuables, and ransomed people and towns. In the last quarter of the twentieth century there are few cities whose streets are free of footpads savaging pedestrians for their money. Hijacking or sabotaging airliners and ransoming the passengers, attacking crowds in airports with machine guns, setting off bombs in busy streets and buildings – these are commonplace. The difference in three hundred years is that at the time of the buccaneers a person's life was safe the moment he handed over his money...

Very occasionally men emerge from the crowd to leave their mark on history. They are a motley company, including such diverse names as Nelson and Cromwell, Napoleon and Lincoln, Churchill and Lenin, Hitler and Drake, but whether the mark they left was for good or evil they have one thing in common: each was a product of his time, and this narrative shows that Morgan's name should be among them. A Nelson in the twentieth century would have failed the medical examination for the Royal Navy, a nineteenth-century Morgan would have been no more than a hard-drinking planter, an eighteenth-century Hitler is unlikely to have moved out of his Austrian village. They became famous because each man was born in the particular age that allowed him to flourish.

This book answers most of the questions about Morgan and the buccaneers, although a few are beyond a positive answer. I have tried to avoid obvious moral judgments in the text because I believe that if this narrative is to have any value it should describe the period as seen through the eyes of Morgan and his colleagues – the eyes of the 1670s. Using slave labour was then a completely acceptable way of running plantations; casual drowning was a commonplace way for privateers to dispose of prisoners. The Spanish put their prisoners on the rack, made them work in salt mines or locked them up in dungeons for the rest of their lives – the fate of Sir Thomas Whetstone, Cromwell's nephew.

Anyone writing of Morgan's time faces the problem of words not then in use. International, diplomacy, colonial, colonization, expenditure, electioneering – these words did not arrive until many decades later. The Caribbean was then called the North Sea on charts (though rarely in speech) to distinguish it from the South Sea, one being north of the Isthmus of Panama and the other south. The Caribbean area was referred to as the Indies or West Indies, although occasionally Cariby or Carribbee was used to refer to the islands. I have occasionally used the word Caribbean when the sea area is meant, and where the spelling of place names has changed I have given the modern name as well, then continued the old to avoid confusion when quoting from old documents.

British islands such as Jamaica, Barbados, Antigua and Nevis were known as the Plantations; the men in Whitehall administering them were the Lords of Trade and Plantations, comparing in skill and knowledge with the Foreign Office of today. The constant use of the word 'English' seems an affront, particularly in a book whose main character was a Welshman, but the fault is not mine: the Spanish (and in turn the French and Dutch) cursed the 'English' buccaneers and even distraught governors of Jamaica trying to stop privateering and piracy usually wrote to Whitehall complaining of

'English' rogues and villains. English readers might well complain that the English received more than their fair share of the blame.

This voyage through Henry Morgan's life has been as fascinating as the voyage through the Caribbean, but it was a combination of looking at Spanish fortifications and checking through documents that made me first realize that Morgan was a great soldier, not a great sailor. The research has been something like Caribbean weather – one is never quite sure what is about to come over the horizon.

D.P.
Yacht Ramage
Antigua–Nevis–Tortola–Puerto Rico

I

Sunrise in the West

'The most important thing about money is to maintain its stability ...
With paper money this stability has to be maintained by the government.
With a gold currency it tends to maintain itself even when the natural
supply of gold is increased by discoveries of new deposits, because of
the curious fact that the demand for gold in the world is practically
infinite. You have to choose (as a voter) between trusting to the natural
stability of gold and the natural stability of the honesty and intelligence
of the members of the government. And, with due respect to these gentlemen, I advise you, as long as the Capitalist system lasts to vote for Gold.'

George Bernard Shaw

There have been three great and romantic ages of Caribbean history which
can be named the Age of Columbus and Exploration (1493–1550), the Age
of Drake and the Merchant Venturers (1550–1600) and the Age of Morgan
and the Buccaneers (1650–80).

The mundane and unromantic fourth age began as a sick and thwarted
Harry Morgan, knighted, rich and his name already a legend, but dis-
credited and stripped of power by the influence of the merchants he detested,
drank himself to death in Port Royal while a witch doctor smeared him
with magic clay and his beloved Jamaica slid inexorably into the Age of
the Administrators, a period which was to last almost three centuries, until
the island became independent.

The fourth age could not begin until the continual threat of Spanish attacks
had ended; until Jamaica could stop watching the horizon with fearful
eyes for the sails of a hostile Spanish fleet, knowing that the buccaneers were
its only defence. From then on the island's future was bound up in land
taxes and trade balances, Customs returns and acreage yields. Decisions
previously made by lively men of action were then made by mediocre men
whose lives were dedicated to avoiding decisions; officials who needed everything to be codified, whose every action was conditioned by regulations.

In the great days of Sir Harry Morgan's life, when the buccaneers – the
Brethren of the Coast – had elected him their leader with the resounding
title of admiral, Jamaica had grown and prospered as a prize market while
he sacked and looted the great cities on the Spanish Main, making the

Spanish pay a thousand-fold for their twin claims that the West Indies were the monopoly of their king and that there was 'no peace beyond the Line'.

Yet by a bitter irony, although he more than any man smashed the Spanish monopoly of the Caribbean, once he had forced the Spanish to erase the Line from their charts – a Line drawn by the Pope, and beyond which no one but a Spaniard was supposed to venture – the looting and pillaging was bound to give way to peaceful trade among the nations. And the Sir Harry Morgan who was eventually forced by his own government to put down his sword was unable to pick up the pen, the only weapon that from then onwards could have assured him power in Jamaica.

Although recent research has stripped away much of the legend surrounding the activities of Columbus and Drake and their contemporaries at sea in the Caribbean, the later achievements, exploits and shortcomings of Harry Morgan are still generally described in sharply-defined black and white, the constant repetition of absurd legends and half-truths that merely reflect the stories put about by the merchants who engineered his downfall three hundred years ago. New histories of the West Indies frequently quote from predecessors, adding little but more distortion.

This incurious approach to Morgan and the buccaneers has meant, for example, that he is still hailed as a great seaman, whereas quite clearly he was one of the most disastrous seamen sailing out of Port Royal. His skill was as a soldier: he was a brilliant general. His victories on land were remarkable; considering the men he led, those at Granada, Portobelo, Maracaibo and Panama rank with anything before or since in British history. By comparison he rarely went to sea without losing his ship.

More than most controversial figures, the truth about Morgan lies in varying shades of grey, particularly because very few people understand the difference between buccaneering and piracy. Apart from the legal aspect – the buccaneers usually held commissions, or letters of marque, issued by the governor of Jamaica – the buccaneers (as distinct from regular privateers) rarely fought at sea; if they did it was a case of a single ship finding and capturing an enemy privateer or merchant ship. Their admiral was elected to lead them on raids against towns and cities; they attacked forts and castles, savage affairs of patrols and sieges, scaling ladders and petards, with their ships safely anchored somewhere out of the way, merely the necessary transport. Their treasure came from raiding the coffers of Spanish towns, looting houses, extorting ransom; it rarely came from crates and boxes found in the holds of enemy ships.

Morgan was a brave and bold soldier who was never bound by orthodox tactics; he recognized better than most that surprise was usually necessary for victory, and he had the imagination to devise unorthodox tactics and the knowledge of the capacities of his own cosmopolitan troops to achieve it.

During the whole of the time that Morgan led the buccaneers, London's official policy towards Spain had all the consistency and wisdom of a weathercock, but Morgan could have been a lawyer for the skill he showed in always having a regular commission (and usually orders from the governor of Jamaica as well) to prove that any particular attack on the Spanish was legal and duly authorized, even if Madrid and London were at peace.

It is naïve in the extreme to dismiss the buccaneers as licensed pirates; the fact is that for many years, while Jamaica was being threatened by Spain, France or the Netherlands, the successive ministers in London did not send out troops or ships (apart from an occasional frigate) to defend the island. Governor after governor had to rely on the buccaneers and their ships to come to the island's defence, paying for their own powder and shot.

The Caribbean has always been a sea of contradictions. When Columbus, a man of the Renaissance, discovered it for Spain there were Stone Age Indians living on most of the islands, yet in Mexico, only one hundred and fifty miles away across the Yucatán Channel from Cuba, the Aztec and Maya civilizations were in many ways comparable to that of ancient Egypt.

The gigantic and mathematically precise Pyramid of the Sun and nearby Pyramid of the Moon rose up more than two hundred feet in the Valley of Mexico and had been built by the Toltecs (without using the wheel) even before the coming of the Aztecs. To the south, along the Pacific coast of South America, the Incas lived a similar advanced life, and none of them put a great value on gold and silver, the two metals that they had in comparative abundance.

Although they put no great value on them, they had for centuries been making great use of both, particularly gold, because it was both beautiful and so easily worked for ornaments, whether for jewellery or temple decoration. All three peoples were lucky because, until the Spanish arrived, they had no hostile neighbours who wanted their gold and were free to use it in great quantities for what it was, an easily-worked metal useful for mugs and plates and buckles as well as intricate ornaments.

In the Old World, monarch, adventurer and merchant always had the gleam of gold in his eyes; it was one of the very substances from which both dreams and occasional reality were made. From the very earliest days, when men began to advance beyond the stage of straight barter and a token or measure was needed, gold was given a value and became the agreed symbol of permanence in an ever-changing world.

Not only is gold rare but it does not rust, corrode or tarnish. It always stays the same: left at the bottom of the sea for a thousand years it comes out as bright and pure as the day it went in, whereas silver tarnishes, iron rusts and copper corrodes. It can be worked easily – fifty years before Christ Pliny was writing that an ounce of gold could be beaten into 750 thin sheets, each a square the width of four fingers; today the same ounce can be drawn into fifty miles of wire.

From such simple beginnings gold became the currency for trade, ransom and gifts (the Queen of Sheba's present to Solomon of 120 talents of gold weighed more than 6000 lb), and it became a convenient way of measuring the wealth of a nation or an individual. The Lydians first used gold for coins (and thus as currency) some four hundred years before Christ, according to Herodotus, and Croesus minted coins of both gold and silver. However, coins in bulk are difficult to carry or store and gold and silver ingots are still the safest and most convenient way of dealing with basic wealth (an ingot of gold the size of a house brick weighs about 27½ lb).

At the time that Columbus sailed to discover the New World gold had been mined in Europe among the mountains of Spain, the Alps, along a line running north-west through France to the British Isles, and in the Balkans. There were far richer mines in Arabia, Anatolia and Armenia (as well as India, China, Japan and Korea, although the greatest deposits of all, in South Africa and California, were to remain undiscovered for another four centuries).

The Romans began working the mines of Spain, but although from AD 500 to AD 700 very little more gold was mined in Europe, there was so much available that Spain and France (and briefly England) had gold coinage – gold which may once have formed part of the treasure of an Egyptian pharaoh or Alexander the Great, the Queen of Sheba or Solomon 'in all his glory'. Indeed, one of the fascinating things about it is that while the gold of a twentieth-century wedding ring might have come recently from a South African mine it could have been melted down a hundred times after starting out as an Aztec mask brought to Spain as part of the riches of the Indies.

In a stable world the demand for gold always increases. From the time of the Crusades (from 1096 until 1272) more gold was brought back to Europe from the Levant to replenish the treasuries of European kings and princes. Inevitably some countries, notably Portugal, began searching for new mines, and this was, of course, one of the main reasons for the Portuguese voyages of discovery down the west coast of Africa, part of which became known as the Gold Coast.

By the time Columbus sailed westward, gold had for a long time been firmly established as the measure of a country's military and economic strength. Slowly it had changed from being the monopoly of kings and churches, and once it reached private hands certain men quite naturally accumulated quantities of it. Merchant bankers acquired enormous power by their ability to lend large sums to kings at high interest – and foreclose, when necessary.

More important, it was fully realized by then that any single country suddenly finding a new source of gold had also found a new source of power because gold was readily transmuted into larger armies and navies, as well as extending trade and subsidizing more exploration, expenses previously paid for by taxing an unwilling population.

Portugal's discoveries along the Gold Coast led to Lisbon becoming a centre for gold, and this naturally disturbed Ferdinand and Isabella, who could see that Portugal's growing financial and trade strength based on West African gold and markets was a potential threat to Spain. It was an important factor in their decision to finance Columbus's expedition: they hoped the judicious outlay of a small amount of money to send the *Santa Maria* and two small caravels on their way westward would reveal gold in far greater quantities than found by the Portuguese.

In an age when it was not uncommon for the Pope to settle international disputes, the Portuguese had · already taken the precaution of securing recognition of their new West African possessions: in papal bulls of 1455 and 1481, previous popes had recognized Portugal's exclusive rights along the African Atlantic coast from a point level with the Canary Islands right down to the Cape of Good Hope and then eastward across the Indian Ocean. The papal recognition meant, of course, that the whole area was forbidden for anyone but the Portuguese. The Portuguese had gone southward; for Spain the only hope was to sail west.

On Friday, 3 August 1492, Columbus's three ships weighed anchor at Palos de la Frontera in south-western Spain and dropped down the river on the ebb tide to get to the open sea in Cadiz Bay, bound first for the Canaries and then west towards the setting sun in search of many places – the land of the Great Khan, the fountain of Eternal Youth, the gilded king, El Dorado, who bathed in a sacred lake, and the legendary island of Antilea. Columbus expected to find them all on the voyage which, he anticipated, would take him to India and China.

The Old World that he left behind was gradually changing as medieval Europe emerged into the Renaissance and unknowingly stood poised for a series of discoveries which, in the next fifty years, would reveal most of the world. Within weeks Renaissance Europe would meet the New World; within six years Vasco Da Gama would sail round the Cape of Good Hope to reach India; within thirty Magellan would sail right round the world.

However, on the day that Columbus sailed, Europe knew little more about the rest of the world than did the Phoenicians several centuries earlier. It was for once a period of comparative calm in Europe. William Caxton, who was to introduce printing to England, was sixteen years old. The future Henry VIII would not be born for another seventeen years and St James's in London was still a leper colony – the royal palace to which foreign kings, courtiers and ambassadors would deliver threats, pleas and routine messages would not be built in its place for another forty years. In Spain, the Moorish King Abu Abdullah had surrendered Granada to Ferdinand just seven months to the day before Columbus sailed, so the last Arab stronghold fell after an occupation lasting eight hundred years and left as its memorial the Alhambra, the golden palace.

The known world that Columbus left behind was effectively bounded by a line that went round Britain and over the North Sea to include Scandinavia, across western Russia and south down the Volga to the Black Sea, east as far as Tashkent and Samarkand (with the knowledge that China was to the east), down to Baghdad, over to Egypt and along the North African coast to the Strait of Gibraltar, out westward to include the Azores, Madeira, Canaries and Cape Verdes, and finally (thanks to the recent series of Portuguese voyages) south to the Cape of Good Hope.

Beyond these limited horizons there was only myth and conjecture, legends and travellers' doubtful tales of a distant and shadowy world as insubstantial as a politician's talk of the future. Just how limited was the horizon of the Old World is shown by the fact that beyond it, unsuspected by the most hopeful or glib adventurer except as a word here and there mentioned by Marco Polo and other early travellers, lay three-quarters of the world's surface – including North and South America, the Caribbean Islands, the Pacific and its islands, Australia and New Zealand, the whole of the Pacific coast of Asia, which included China and Japan, and the countries bordering the Indian Ocean, ranging from Indonesia to India itself and Africa.

The men who sailed with Columbus never for a moment considered that if they wanted gold from the lands they discovered they might have to dig for it. Columbus sailed with an attitude that was a mixture of ambassador and businessman visiting another country to negotiate a treaty of trade. His companions on the voyage, except for the seamen, were young gentlemen who offered their swordsmanship, should the hosts turn hostile, in return for a chance of a share in the riches. He had neither the knowledge nor tools to find the gold or silver or gems in the earth.

Whether they were kings or cardinals, sea captains or eager young hidalgos, the thought of new land discoveries meant all things to all men in Spain. To the Catholic Church it meant more heretics to be converted and thus a vastly extended field for its priests with many new dioceses, churches and monasteries; for the adventurer there was the thrill of sighting new shores and the prospect of fame and riches; to a monarch it meant primarily new sources of bullion to refill his treasury without trying to squeeze extra taxes out of reluctant subjects. To the merchant in Seville there was the hope of new markets for his goods and new sources, with dreams of the monopoly of silks from Cathay and the choice spices of the east.

One March morning seven months later the *Nina* sailed into the Tagus from the westward and Columbus (risking an unpleasant reception from the King of Portugal and possible accusations of treachery from Ferdinand and Isabella for first having gone to Lisbon) anchored off Belém. His story was of both success and failure: he had not found the Great Khan or El Dorado, Cathay or Antilea, but nevertheless on 12 October the previous year he had sighted the New World – an island which gratefully he named San Salvador.

On the sandy beaches of this small island, in effect an eastern bastion of the Bahamas chain, the representatives of Renaissance Europe met people little removed from the Stone Age: the Taino Indians went almost completely naked, used wooden spears to catch fish and dugout canoes to visit other islands. Apart from fishing they lived on maize and sweet potatoes, neither of which had ever been seen before by Europeans. But what fascinated Columbus was that several had small gold pendants hanging from their noses.

His search for the source of the gold took him south to Cuba and then east, beating against the full strength of the Trade winds, to what he named 'The Spanish Isle', La Isla Espaniola (Hispaniola, the Haiti and Dominican Republic of today). He traded with local chiefs and obtained gold jewellery – the proof that even if he had not discovered Japan he had found rich islands off the China coast; islands which he proved contained gold for the Spanish treasury and which were inhabited by amiable savages decorated with gold and ripe for conversion to Catholicism. He took several of them back to Spain (and the women among them were later blamed for introducing syphilis to Europe).

In the meantime an envoy from Spain was sent to Rome to see the Pope, Alexander VI, a Borgia heavily indebted to Ferdinand and Isabella for help in furthering his own personal aims in Italy. He was told of Columbus's discoveries and, on 3 May 1493, issued the first of a series of bulls, *Inter Caetera*, which, 'by the authority of Almighty God' gave to the Catholic King of Spain and his heirs all the lands in the New World discovered or to be discovered 'together with other dominions, cities, camps, places and villages, and all rights, jurisdictions and appurtenances of the same'. The Pope strictly forbade 'all persons, no matter what rank, estate, degree, order or condition to dare, without your special permission ... to go for the sake of trade or any other reason whatever, to the said islands and countries after they have been discovered and found by your envoys or persons sent out for that purpose'.

The Portuguese envoy in the Holy See promptly protested that this conflicted with earlier bulls referring to Portuguese discoveries and next day the Pope issued another bull, *Inter Caetera II*, which protected Portugal's Atlantic islands by giving Spain the exclusive right to land and trade in all the lands one hundred leagues west of any of the Azores or Cape Verde Islands. Since the Cape Verdes are farther east, this meant that Alexander VI had drawn 'the Line' north and south through a point three hundred miles west of the Azores.

Although the Line was to become the most famous (or infamous, as far as the Protestant nations were concerned) ever drawn on a chart, for the time being it mattered only to Spain and Portugal, and the two papal bulls did little more than confirm in the northern capitals what was already known by gossip and ambassadors' dispatches, that land had been found thousands of miles to the westward.

Columbus's other voyages concern us only to introduce the Caribbean. The first had taken him to the western end, touching the two big islands, Cuba and Hispaniola, which with Puerto Rico form the Greater Antilles. On the second he arrived at the extreme eastern end of what were later called the Lesser Antilles, sighting land one Sunday and naming it Dominica in honour of the occasion.

The next island was named Marie Galante, after the nickname of his flagship. Turning north, he sighted another which he named Santa Maria de Guadalupe (now Guadeloupe) and then one whose vertical cliffs reminded him – as it still does many other voyagers – of the monastery near Barcelona built on a low, square-topped mountain. Accordingly he named it Santa Maria de Montserrate (now Montserrat). Another island in sight to the north-east, which he naturally claimed for Spain but did not visit, was named Santa Maria la Antigua.

The naming of islands became an almost daily occupation; one of them he named St Cristobal after his own patron saint (it was later called St Christopher's, now St Kitt's). He then turned boldly westward well inside the Caribbean, reaching a large island called Boriquen by its natives and which Columbus called San Juan (for St John the Baptist). Much later the town built on the north side round a great natural anchorage was called San Juan de Puerto Rico and subsequently, by a curious juxtaposition, the island was called Puerto Rico (Rich Port) and the town, now the capital city, San Juan.

Convinced that Cuba was in fact China, Columbus made his landfall at Martinique on his fourth voyage, carried on to Hispaniola and then went to Jamaica and over to Honduras, in Central America. He turned eastward against the Trade winds, a ship-killing beat that took him down the coasts of Nicaragua and Costa Rica, where natives wore gold ornaments.

Meanwhile the first Spanish settlers, in Hispaniola, were at first bitterly disappointed and dissatisfied, whether hidalgos from Spain looking for adventure and gold or farmers from the Canary Islands. Instead of living in the rich cities or farming fine lands given them by the Great Khan of Tartary, they found themselves first building and then maintaining log and reed huts for shelter from the tropical heat and often torrential rain. Medicines ran out as men died of diseases the doctors had never before seen; food became short, but the grain they brought with them was slow to grow. Far from trading with emissaries of the Great Khan or ransoming captives, the only gold they could get came from gold washings in the streams: repeated expeditions into the mountainous interior failed to find any mines. And always there was the scorching heat of the tropical sun.

By 1502 a new governor was trying to save the colony. The horses, pigs and cattle brought over from Spain and the Canaries flourished although sheep could not adapt to the heat. Plants brought from the Canaries and Spain grew well and the new governor was determined that for the time being at least they should concentrate on agriculture, to make themselves independent of food from Spain. He found three hundred quarrelling and starving emigrants when he arrived; four years later there were twelve thousand men and women busy on the plantations. All the local Taino Indians were enslaved and forced to work on plantations and gold washing; but the settlers were still short of labour. By 1503 Negro slaves were being brought in from Spain, having been shipped there by the Portuguese trading along the West African coast.

In the meantime the farmers in Hispaniola continued experimenting. Grape vines from Spain would not flourish, nor would the slow-growing olive trees, so the two Spanish staples of oil and wine still had to come from Spain. Nor did they have any luck with wheat or barley, so flour had to be shipped across the Atlantic. But unexpectedly the rice they had brought with them flourished, and so did the oranges, lemons and figs, brought from southern Spain, all of which soon began growing wild. It was discovered that the native corn was excellent to eat, particularly if cultivated more carefully, and it proved such a good substitute for wheat that some was shipped back to Spain, thus introducing maize to Europe. Sugar cane brought over from Spain flourished beyond the farmers' wildest hopes, and the first sugar mill in the New World was working by 1508. Bananas were shipped over from the Canaries a few years later and they too grew success-fully so that, with the exception of cotton, all the major crops for which the West Indies were to become famous had now been introduced – from the Old World.

Yet the New World seemed reluctant to give the Spaniards gold in exchange, and expeditions sent as far afield as the Gulf of Darien in Central America found nothing. Jamaica was occupied and found excellent for raising cattle, and by 1514 the results of a survey of Cuba showed that not only was the land richer for farming but more gold could be found, so people began leaving Hispaniola for the promise of Cuba. They had to leave behind many of their cattle and pigs; already a number had escaped into the mountains and valleys and grown wild, multiplying rapidly because they had no natural enemies, and now these were reinforced by the quantities let loose as their owners left the island.

This chance factor was to be of major importance in the rise of the buccaneers among the islands of the Greater Antilles, providing food in quantity – at first for outcasts, then for the cow killers, and eventually for the buccaneers.

By 1518 the history of the Caribbean was about to take another sharp turn; one that was completely unexpected but which began the real history of the riches of the Indies and laid the foundations for the story of the buccaneers.

The shortage of slaves in both Cuba and Hispaniola had become so great that ships left from time to time on expeditions looking for more Indians. The Bahamas had already been stripped, but occasionally other Indians were found along the Central American coast, particularly near Yucatán. One such expedition was left stranded there among hostile Indians and the governor of Cuba sent out two ships to find it. The ships returned to report that they could not find the expedition, but they had been able to get 20,000 pesos worth of gold in loot from the local Indians; gold which had been worked into sophisticated designs....

Soon after that a squadron left Santiago de Cuba under the command of Hernán Cortés to explore the coast, looking for both gold and slaves. He reached Yucatán and rounded the peninsula to sail well into the Bay of Campeche, the southern end of the Gulf of Mexico. On Good Friday, 1519, the squadron anchored and Cortés landed his men and then founded the city of Villa Rica de la Vera Cruz (the Vera Cruz of today). And 'Rich City' was an appropriate name, for Cortés had stumbled on the riches of Mexico.

He had been met by Mayans bearing gifts of gold which, to them, was simply an easily-worked and beautiful metal. The riches he found were probably greater than dreamed of by the most rapacious of Spaniards, for he had come upon a highly-developed civilization, not a few tribes using small nuggets as lucky charms. Not only was Mexico rich in gold, silver and gem stones, but its people had over the centuries developed a complex religion; their architecture had a Byzantine splendour and an Egyptian scale. The gold production was immense and their gold and silversmiths had little to learn from the craftsmen of Europe.

Although many of the beautiful gold objects that came into the hands of Cortés were melted down, the gifts received included 'shields, helmets, cuirasses embossed with plates and ornaments of pure gold; collars, bracelets of the same metal ... imitations of birds and animals in wrought and cast gold and silver ... two circular plates of gold and silver as large as carriage wheels'. One of them, representing the sun, was 'richly carved with plants and animals', and weighed 200 pounds.

When Cortés eventually took prisoner his former host and benefactor, Montezuma, and seized his kingdom, 'the gold alone was sufficient to make three great heaps'. Goldsmiths then took out 'the larger and coarser ornaments' and spent the next three days melting them down into ingots. From tax records it has been estimated that between 1500 and 2000 lb were melted down and sent to Spain while as much again was shipped back intact.

When news reached Cuba and Hispaniola that Cortés had found – so near, too – a land where temples had sheets of beaten gold on the walls and the priests wore masks of gold while the idols of gold and silver were encrusted with precious stones, all the colonists that could promptly left for New Spain, as Mexico was now called. Then, as if to emphasize that the role of Hispaniola and Cuba was now completed, both islands were subsequently hit by pestilence and hurricanes and most of the remaining Indian slaves died in an epidemic of measles and smallpox.

The Distant Treasury

Spain had found the riches of the world, an apparently inexhaustible source of gold and silver which would pay for a great army and a great navy and make her the most powerful of all nations. However her new treasury was not only on the other side of the Atlantic but at the far end of the Caribbean. Her ships had to bring the bullion back safely to Seville before Spain could benefit from it and all along their route, like Nature's highwaymen, there was the risk of storms and coral reefs, headwinds and unpredictable hurricanes, unexpected currents and the weakness of ships.

Nature and seamanship were the only problems at first because Spain and Portugal were by far the strongest seafaring nations, but Spain was soon at war with France. French privateers sailing out of Dieppe began capturing Spanish ships from the West Indies but for the time being they did not bother to cross the Line to hunt for more prizes in the Caribbean: it was far easier to capture the ships as they closed the Spanish coast, even though heavily-armed caravels were sent out to escort them.

The first recorded breach of *Inter Caetera* occurred in 1527, eight years after Cortés had looted Mexico and at a time when the Spaniards were busy seeking the rest of the gold in the country. On 25 November a three-masted ship arrived off the port of Santo Domingo, the capital of Hispaniola, and hove-to. No fleet was expected from Spain and the ship was much too large to be a coasting vessel. Then her ensign was seen – the flag of England.

The rest of the Spanish side of the story is told in depositions sworn before two judges and the secretary of the royal *audiencia*, the hearing held on the King's behalf: 'Her master with ten or twelve seamen came on shore in a boat and told them [the harbour authorities] that the ship belonged to the King of England; and the ship, together with another cleared perhaps nine months ago from England on order from their King, to make a certain exploration towards the north, between Labrador and Newfoundland, in the belief that in that region there was a strait through which to pass to Tartary.'

Some of the ship's company died from the cold, one of the ships was lost, and the pilot – so called in the deposition, but probably the mate – died, 'for which reasons they came to this land to take in water and subsistence and other things they needed'.

The ship was the *Mary Guilford* (an important fact the depositions omitted to mention), which had been sent out by Henry VIII with the *Samson*. Unknown to the judges they had heard only part of the reason why the *Mary Guilford* was some 2000 miles off course. Henry VIII had recently changed sides in the great struggle between the Habsburgs of Spain and the Valois of France, and he was anxious to know more about the source of Spain's new wealth in the West Indies, which was making itself felt in Europe in the form of money for Spain's armies.

The King of Spain was under no illusion about the significance of this first recorded occasion when a foreign ship had the impudence not only to defy *Inter Caetera*, cross the Line and sail into the New World, but visit one of his harbourmasters as well and tell a cock and bull story. Although the *Mary Guilford* appeared openly and quietly and then went peacefully on her way, the Spanish King's fears for the future were well founded: within a year he was receiving reports that a French ship had arrived off the western end of Puerto Rico and raided San German, burning it down. (This little town, built inland on the side of rolling hills, was rebuilt and raided three times more by the French in the next five years.)

By 1536, nine years after the *Mary Guilford*'s visit and seventeen years after Cortés went to Mexico, French corsairs were successfully attacking Spanish ships in the Greater Antilles, using the Lucaya (Bahama) islands as a base, while four years later an English privateer seized a Spanish ship off Santo Domingo.

The Portuguese finally ignored *Inter Caetera* and began making peaceful (although from the Spanish point of view completely illegal) voyages into the West Indies, bringing slaves direct from Africa and selling them like contraband to Spanish plantation owners desperate for labour. This was a profitable transaction because Negro slaves shipped through Spain were very expensive by the time they reached the West Indies, their prices almost doubling at every stage of their journey, while the Portuguese, shipping them direct from West Africa, could double their normal prices and still find an eager market.

The visits of the privateers and the Portuguese led to the Spanish King trying to stop by decree what he could not prevent in any other way and in June 1540 he ordered that no foreign ships were to be allowed to trade in the Caribbean. The decree showed that he knew only too well that the two bulls of Pope Alexander VI, proclaimed fifty years earlier 'by the authority of Almighty God', were being completely ignored.

He realized that his best chance of stopping the trade was to terrorize his own officials in the islands (ranging from governors to port officials in remote areas) so that they would halt it, if only because they were too frightened to continue participating. By this time the arbitrary arrest of royal officials for actual or alleged misdemeanours was a commonplace. But by now the other European nations were becoming both bold and strong enough to make sure that if the King of Spain would not let them trade, then there would be 'No peace beyond the Line', a phrase used by merchants and seamen as both a slogan and a threat.

Cortés' discovery of the gold of Mexico had woken the rest of Europe to the extent of Spain's wealth in the New World but only a few more years passed before even wilder reports began to circulate in the courts of Europe of greater discoveries. First, Spanish explorers crossed the Isthmus, the comparatively narrow neck of land joining the two Americas, and discovered a great ocean they named the South Sea, to distinguish it from the Caribbean, which became the North Sea. Then, as they searched to the south, along the ridge of the Andes forming the backbone of South America, Francisco Pizarro and his two hundred men found the gold of the Incas; the vast collection which was the result of a nation's two-thousand-year-old culture. He captured the city of the Sun God at Cuzco; he ransomed Atahualpa for 13,000 pounds of gold. He found the world's richest source of gold, silver and minerals. And, more important in the long term, the rich mines whence it came, the great mines of Potosí.

The most blatant huckster and the shrillest politician would be hard put to describe what Pizarro had found, so the effect of the news on a Renaissance Europe – where alchemists were still peering into crystal balls in their search for the secret of how to change base metals into gold – is not hard to imagine.

When Spain had first moved into the West Indies she did so without interference from the rest of Europe. Her navy was powerful and Portugal obeyed *Inter Caetera*. She came, she saw and she took what she wanted, thousands of square miles of new lands. However Spain put herself in a very weak strategic and tactical position because she rested her defences on the wording of *Inter Caetera* rather than on the efficacy of having the weather gage.

The rule in sea warfare until the arrival of steam propulsion was simple but basic: it is vital to secure and keep the weather gage. By being up to windward in a sailing ship you have the absolute choice: you can run down before the wind to attack the enemy or you can refuse to fight by staying up to windward as he tries to beat up towards you. Being to windward gives you the choice of flight or fight.

In the West Indies the phrases 'to windward' and 'to leeward' also have a special geographical significance that few Europeans understand, and it is a significance Spain did not grasp until it was too late. The wind in the Caribbean blows all the year round from the eastern quadrant towards the west – the Trade winds – and the sea current follows it.

That is a generalization covering a sea which is almost the same size as the Mediterranean (971,400 square miles compared with the Mediterranean's 969,100) and there are minor local modifications, but with the wind from between south-east and north-east the harbours and anchorages are all planned accordingly.

A sailing ship crossing the Atlantic by running before the North-east Trades (which in fact blow from between south-east and north-east) arrives off the islands of the Lesser Antilles – extending from Antigua to Trinidad and running north-south – and can then pass through them to continue sailing the length of the Caribbean to reach Cuba and Mexico.

With the Lesser Antilles placed well to windward of the Greater Antilles and the Spanish Main (and in fact acting like a row of fortresses separating the Atlantic from the Caribbean) it follows that any nation holding them is well-placed to send its ships to leeward to make surprise attacks on ships or ports in the Greater Antilles or along the Main or Central American coast.

At the same time the Lesser Antilles are relatively safe from attacks by sailing ships having to beat up from the Greater Antilles, a long hard sail that can take as many weeks as it needs days to go in the other direction – five or six days from Martinique to Cuba, five or six weeks to return.

The Lesser Antilles, then, could also be likened to fortresses on the top of a hill overlooking a long valley: whoever held the islands could control the valley of the Caribbean stretching away to leeward. But the Lesser Antilles were a chain of small islands which had no riches for Spain. Compared with Cuba (44,000 square miles), Hispaniola (29,000) and Puerto Rico (3400) they were tiny, had no gold or silver, and were not worth farming: Barbados, the one with the richest soil, is only 166 square miles, Antigua comprises 171, Dominica 290, Martinique 425 and Guadeloupe 687. In addition, some of the islands were inhabited not by the peaceful Tainos and Arawaks but by the murderous Caribs.

So, not wanting them for settlement and apparently not realizing that they were needed for defence, Spain ignored the Lesser Antilles and put her trust in the efficacy of *Inter Caetera* and her King's decrees. While the nations of northern Europe were weak this trust was justified. Spain went on organizing her trade with her New World possessions, creating a remarkable and complex central bureaucracy which in itself was a guarantee that everything – the construction, ownership and sailing of the ships, the transporting of cargoes, passengers and bullion – would be done in the most inefficient and expensive manner that could be devised by sycophantic men, ranging from those filling in ledgers to their ministers reporting to the King. But for Britain, France and the Netherlands the fact was that the islands of the Lesser Antilles were large enough to colonize and small enough to defend.

* * *

As far as the successive kings of Spain were concerned, the nation's sole interest in the Indies was collecting the gold, silver and gems and transferring them as safely as possible to the Treasury in Spain. The settling of people in the Greater Antilles, New Spain and the Main was of far less concern; a necessary nuisance which had to be tightly controlled.

The vast bureaucracy that controlled ships, bullion and people was in turn governed with an iron hand. A bureaucrat making a wrong decision was promptly arrested and sent back to Spain to face a trial – a system which usually ensured that no one in the New World used any initiative and nothing of any consequence was done without first getting permission from Spain, a procedure which often took more than a year.

The resulting inertia combined with the Spanish predilection for postponing action until *mañana* was not only the easiest way of dealing with affairs in the Indies but by far the safest, and soon approached official policy. In Madrid, though, a distant official's wrongdoings were regarded with brooding suspicion; mistakes were often viewed as treason.

Gold from Mexico (which we shall call New Spain, its contemporary name) was assembled for shipment at Vera Cruz. The second source of gold and silver was the mines of what are now Ecuador, Peru, Bolivia and Chile. This was brought up the Pacific coast in merchant ships and unloaded in Panama, a port built for the purpose on the South Sea (Pacific) side of the Isthmus. There the bullion was loaded on to mules and horses and carried across the jungles and mountains to the 'North Sea', the Caribbean, for shipment to Spain.

At first it was taken to Nombre de Dios, but later Chagres was used when it was found that the Chagres River allowed half the journey to be made by boat during the rainy season. Eventually a third port was established, Portobelo, a well-sheltered but shallow harbour which was easy to fortify. (The Panama Canal was built three centuries later along the Chagres–Panama route.)

Nombre de Dios, Chagres and Portobelo, successively the North Sea terminals for the bullion, were all shallow – the drawback of the Central American coast – and the great defensive harbour for the Spanish Main was built at Cartagena, 250 miles to the north-east, in what is now Colombia. Comprising two great bays sheltered by mountains, it needed only castles and batteries to make it impregnable, and these were soon built. Cartagena then became the main port for the deep-drafted galleons which brought out cargoes and took back bullion, but it was too far from Panama for shipments to be carried there through jungles and over mountains, so the galleons either risked going to Portobelo to load, or the bullion was brought to them by smaller vessels. The procedure frequently changed and usually depended on the size of galleons being used.

This coast (the whole of what is now Panama, Colombia and Venezuela) was called *Tierra Firme* by the Spanish and is better known as the Spanish Main. The plate ships of New Spain sailing from Vera Cruz, and those of the Main from Cartagena, had to meet in Havana, the great port of Cuba, and then sail for Spain in convoy.

By the time the bullion arrived in Spain it had travelled far. After being dug in mines established by the Incas it had travelled by ship almost the length of the Pacific coast of South America to Panama, then in panniers on the backs of horses and mules across mountains and jungles of the Isthmus to Portobelo, by ship to Cartagena, by galleon to Havana and then across the Atlantic to Spain. The Mexican, or New Spanish, bullion had a less venturesome journey, being carried by horse or mule to Vera Cruz and then by sea to Havana. But no one need be a pirate or a strategist to realize how vulnerable was the bullion on every stage of its journey.

Philip II was King of Spain during the most critical years when the pattern of mining and shipping the bullion was finally fashioned – a pattern never properly modified in the light of experience as the countries of northern Europe began to make a vigorous challenge at sea. A brooding, suspicious and introverted man, Philip was concerned with keeping power in his own hands; every inch of the New World was his puppet show, responding as he twitched the strings. But such a show could only respond; it could not initiate policy or ideas – and it dare not criticize. By the time he died Philip had seen the armada he sent against England scattered like chaff, and he had turned Spain into a land power just when the future of the West Indies – and ultimately of the supply of bullion – could be decided only on the sea.

From the time that Columbus first landed on San Salvador and met a Taino Indian with a tiny nugget of gold slung round his neck until the day of the buccaneers, whoever sat on the throne of Spain had one basic problem: the gold found in South and Central America was useless until it reached Spain. Only there could it be transmuted into payments of interest to merchant bankers, pay for armies, or money to sustain the ever-expanding bureaucracy.

While still in the mines of the New World, stored at Panama or even on board the ships at anchor in Cartagena, Vera Cruz or Havana, the gold was not worth a penny to the Spanish Crown. Quite soon no banker outside Spain would discuss even a moratorium on interest already owed, let alone a new loan, if the only security offered was bullion waiting in the New World. Rocks and shoals, hurricanes and privateers, could make nonsense of any royal promise of delivery.

Spain's vast colonial empire and its enormous bureaucracy were devoted to trying to solve New World problems with Old World solutions which were so unwieldy and impractical, so unsuited to a situation where the very survival of Spain could depend on a plate fleet, that the determined efforts

of men like Henry Morgan could throw it into disarray. The failure of a
single plate fleet to arrive in Spain could, and sometimes did, mean that
a Spanish army shivered and starved through a Netherlands winter, unpaid
and unprovisioned; it could and did mean that the King had to agree to
even greater interest rates to get more loans.

Until Spain found the wealth of the Indies, a nation had to depend on
its trade and taxation to put gold into the treasury, with the result that
a wealthy nation was one with a healthy trade. Spain's discovery of gold
had changed all that for her; merely mining the gold and silver brought
her undreamed-of wealth, and trade and industry was neglected, so that
it withered. The long-term effect was that soon Spain could exist only from
the gold shipments because she had no prospering industry to fall back on
if the gold ever failed to arrive. She had become dependent, like a drug
addict.

The privateers who attacked New Spain and the Spanish Main like sharks
savaging a crippled whale were for many years a far greater threat to Spain
than the fleets of France and Britain. Spain could (and did) lose a large
fleet in battle and still afford to build a new one within three years; but
for a couple of centuries the nation would probably have toppled if the plate
fleets had been kept in the New World for three successive years. For this
reason Spain was single-minded in her attitude towards privateers and
pirates. She made no distinction between them. If she captured them they
were hanged, put to hard labour or jailed for the rest of their lives.

Yet there was a great distinction between a privateersman and a pirate,
one that every other nation acknowledged. In time of war few countries
ever had enough fighting ships: it cost a great deal of money to maintain
a navy in peacetime. However, there were usually enough merchant ships
and it was customary in wartime to give any merchant ship master who
requested it a letter of marque, or commission, which allowed him to wage
war against the enemy (at his own risk and expense) as though his vessel
was a ship of war. It was in effect a licence which should ensure that the
ship named in it and her crew were not treated as pirates if they were
captured. Such a ship was called a privateer (from 'private man of war');
the men on board were called privateersmen.

In the decades following Columbus's voyages the Spanish Crown had drawn
up regulations covering every aspect of the New World colonies and voyages.
It entailed the control of every ship and every man, woman and child that
sailed in her, every pound of cargo, and every gun, every ounce of powder
and round of shot. No one could sail without an individual licence; no captain
of a particular merchant ship or captain-general of a whole *flota* could leave
Spain without putting up a cash bond (to be forfeited for any breach of
the rules).

All cargo to be exported was treated in the same way. Stores for the ships, the times they sailed, the charter rates and even the cost of building the ships – all was regulated by the treasurer, comptroller and agent appointed by the King. And only a certain number of ships could sail to the Indies each year.

A Council of the Indies was formed to deal with the New World's political and judicial affairs and answerable only to the King. Very early on a *Casa de Contratación* (House of Trade) was set up, based on Seville, which is sixty miles up the River Guadalquivir. Not only was the excellent and enormous harbour and anchorage of Cadiz a few miles to the south totally ignored, but for years ships returning from the Indies were forbidden to go there. The Indies were to be the monopoly of Seville, and thus of Castille, which was the richest province of Spain.

Ships at first had to go right up to Seville to load their cargoes, and this meant first crossing the shallow bar at Sanlúcar de Borromeo at the entrance and then getting sixty miles up the river. After several ships had been wrecked on the bar, and with heavily-laden ships arriving from the West Indies often having to unload much of their cargo into barges in order to get up to Seville to have the inspectors come on board, the King finally agreed that they could use Cadiz or Sanlúcar when outward bound, but homeward-bound ships, particularly those carrying treasure, still had to use Seville. The regulations were later changed several times, but the general rule was that returning ships had to use Sanlúcar, where a closer watch could be kept on the treasure.

Two separate fleets were used to bring home the plate, and they had different names. The one that went to New Spain was called the *flota* and it usually called at ports in the Greater Antilles before arriving at Vera Cruz. The other, going to the Main, was generally referred to simply as the galleons. The dates that the galleons and the *flota* sailed to and from the Indies and the number of ships forming the convoys were governed by royal ordinances, but if the King ordained one thing, frequently Nature in the shape of the weather and the ingrained tardiness of the Spanish people ordained something else. The *flota* was supposed to sail from Spain for the West Indies in May (at first it was April) and the galleons left in August, which was well into the hurricane season.

The galleons took one of two routes. At first, before privateers and corsairs became a great problem, they left Sanlúcar and made for the Canaries; then they went down to 16° North and sailed along that latitude until they reached the Caribbean, which they entered by either dropping south between Grenada and Trinidad (which was not popular among the pilots because it was possible to sail through the gap without sighting either) or passing Dominica, one of the few islands which had plenty of water for any ships which had run short.

The *flota* took a different route after leaving the Canaries, crossing the Atlantic by sailing along the latitude of 18° North and keeping north of Antigua and the Virgin Islands until it reached Puerto Rico, usually its first port of call. Santo Domingo, in Hispaniola, was the next, and then ports in Cuba. After that the *flota* crossed the Gulf of Mexico to Vera Cruz.

In both cases they usually made good times, the *flota* taking an average of four weeks from the Canaries to Dominica, and needing another three weeks to reach Vera Cruz after various calls in the Greater Antilles. The galleons also took about four weeks to cross the Atlantic, and then needed another one or two weeks to reach Cartagena.

The galleons wintered at Cartagena and the *flota* at Vera Cruz. According to a royal *ordinanza* the galleons were due to leave Cartagena for Havana in January. By then the smaller ships would have brought the bullion from Portobelo, as well as collected cargoes of hides, cochineal and so forth which had been waiting at various places along the coasts, and transferred them all to the galleons, whose crews would have spent the winter repairing sails, checking over the standing and running rigging – and watching the hulls becoming foul. By the time the galleons and the ships of the *flota* were ready to sail the hulls were heavily encrusted with barnacles, with weed and grass three or four inches thick, so that their speed – particularly in light winds – was decreased considerably.

An imaginative man lying in his bunk or hammock close to the ship's side could almost hear the teredo worms munching their way unseen, tunnelling up and down the Spanish oak of the hull planking. Aloft, mildew grew at an alarming rate in furled sails because of the heat and the heavy rainfall – Cartagena and Portobelo have more than a hundred inches of rain a year, much of it falling in heavy thunderstorms. Sails sent down from the yards and stowed below decks hardly fared any better because of the high humidity and hungry rats. Leaving them on the yards meant that on dry and comparatively windless days they could be let fall to air. But then the harsh sunlight began to bleach the strength out of the cloth. The sunlight and rain was also hard on the rope rigging, however much it was tarred.

No one, from the captain-general of the convoy of galleons to the greenest *grummete*, or apprentice, viewed the voyage home from Cartagena with anything but apprehension: most of the first thousand miles of the voyage, as far as the western tip of Cuba, was to leeward, but the ease of sailing was offset by the fact that for almost the entire way they had a coast to leeward that was strewn with large off-lying reefs and small cays. Westerly currents flowing at unpredictable speeds set into great bights, pushing the ship in towards the often low-lying and hazy coast, and the agonized cry of 'Breakers!' at night usually meant disaster because the reef or rocks on which they were breaking would be to leeward, giving a lumbering galleon little chance of bracing up her yards in time to claw off to safety.

Having reached and rounded the western tip of Cuba, they then had a short two-hundred-mile beat to windward to reach Havana, where the galleons would go in to anchor and wait. The *flota* had an even worse voyage to join them. Vera Cruz was a thousand miles to leeward of Havana and few ships and men could short-tack to windward that far against bad weather without heavy damage to the sails, masts and rigging of the ships and the health of the men. The *flota* had by ordinance to sail in February, steering northwards into the Gulf of Mexico as close to the wind as possible until well north of the Tropic of Cancer, and then tacking down to Havana from the north-west.

Both the galleons and *flota* prayed they would not meet a 'norther'. Although well out of the hurricane season, January and February are notoriously bad months for the 'northers', which are usually three-day blows of gale and often storm force winds from the north, and against which the ships could make no progress. Apart from damage, such weather played havoc with navigation, with the ever-present danger that it would drive the ships south and hurl them up on the six hundred miles of shallow coast running from Vera Cruz eastwards and forming the north coast of Mexico. If they were lucky the ships of the *flota* reached Havana in three weeks and found the galleons waiting for them.

After refitting, victualling, watering and taking on cargo, the *flota* and galleons then sailed for Spain, passing north or south of Bermuda, depending on the winds, and making for the Azores, where there was usually a ship waiting to give them the latest news and instructions concerning any enemy privateers lurking along the route from the Azores to Spain. This part of the voyage could often take more than fifty days, with the ever-present prospect of westerly gales making the whole of the Spanish peninsula a lee shore.

The major losses over a thirty-seven-year period show the variety of dangers. Four ships were wrecked off the coast of Florida in 1554, and the following year a *flota* caught in a norther off Puerto Rico was scattered, the flagship finally sinking in a gale off the Spanish coast. A year later three ships were sent to Puerto Rico to collect bullion, and two were wrecked on the Portuguese coast when they returned.

Seven ships of the galleon fleet were driven ashore and wrecked when a hurricane hit Nombre de Dios in 1563; five ships of the *flota* caught by a norther in the same year were wrecked along the Campeche coast, east of Vera Cruz. Two galleons were lost in a hurricane the next year, while 'several' outward-bound galleons were lost on the island of Dominica a year later, 1565. Fifteen of the *flota* were wrecked on the Tabasco coast between 1563 and 1571.

For the next nine years there were few losses, but in 1581 one of the galleon fleet sank in the Caribbean and two on the way back to Spain. The worst disaster until then occurred in 1590 when the *flota* was hit by a norther while at anchor in Vera Cruz: fifteen ships sank and more than three hundred men were drowned. Disaster hit the *flota* again the following year, 1591, when it ran into a storm off the Azores. The flagship sank and sixteen other ships were driven ashore on Terceira, the northernmost of the islands.

The cold facts of that thirty-seven-year period, 1554–91, show that almost as many Indies ships were sunk at sea by royal stubbornness as fell victim to the Gulf of Mexico northers or Caribbean hurricanes. Northers sank a total of fourteen *flota* ships at sea, but the royal ordinance that the *flota* and the galleons had to return to Sanlúcar (instead of using the all-weather harbour of Cadiz) led to the loss of ten ships. In 1579 as the *flota* sailed the flagship and two other ships hit the sandbar and capsized; one was sunk there the next year and in 1587 six galleons were lost as they tried to get in during bad weather. But in the Indies, northers were still more of a danger to the *flota* than hurricanes: in 1601 fourteen ships were lost when a norther caught them as they entered Vera Cruz.

Other than noting the predominantly easterly nature of the wind, the early Spanish navigators knew little of Caribbean seasons or weather systems, though they learned to recognize certain danger signals. The royal ordinances setting out sailing dates not only ignored the northers of the Caribbean winter but completely ignored the hurricane season, which for practical purposes covers the twelve weeks from August to October. The hurricanes tend to start in one of two separate areas – as tropical depressions out in the Atlantic about five hundred miles east of Martinique, and also a thousand miles to the westward, in the Yucatán Channel and Gulf of Mexico. The Cuban ports and the Campeche coast along to Vera Cruz (New Spain in other words) are particularly vulnerable, but the Spanish Main (the actual coasts of Venezuela, Colombia and Panama) is generally reckoned to be out of the hurricane area. Nevertheless galleons leaving Spain at the ordained time in August had to sail right through the hurricane breeding ground east of Martinique at the beginning of September to get there, and the later they sailed the worse the danger.

The bulk of the cargo for the West Indies was carried in the galleons, not the ships of the *flota*, because very soon the majority of Spaniards in the New World were living in towns supplied through Cartagena and Portobelo. The word galleon conjures up a picture of a great ship of the Spanish Armada, but in fact a galleon could be a large merchant ship (usually with two decks) or a ship of war with three decks.

They were cumbersome vessels by later standards, with a length often only three times the beam. More important, though, they were large enough to carry the bullion and were reckoned to have enough men and guns to defend it. The other types of ships used in the convoys going to both Cartagena and Vera Cruz were the *urca*, a tubby and flat-bottomed storeship, and the *petacha*, the small and fast vessel often used for carrying dispatches or mail.

The Crown was concerned with how ships were built and a series of royal ordinances laid down the specifications, whether for the King or private owners. These specifications were rarely if ever modified or modernized, so the effect was to paralyse development in a notoriously traditional industry.

Until the middle of the sixteenth century, merchant ships making the long transatlantic voyage to the Indies were rarely larger than 200 tons and frequently less than 100. The old tonnage measurements (which varied from country to country and often from one decade to the next) gave little idea of actual size of the ships. The Castillian ton at this time was twenty-six quintals (hundredweight), but it was customary to measure ships by their cubic capacity (like a pint mug, or a quart bottle), so that a ton or tun was for Spanish ships about fifty-six cubic feet (compared with a ton of 100 cubic feet used today).

A 100-ton vessel would thus be able to carry 5600 cubic feet of cargo, providing it was not a particularly heavy substance. A ship intended for the Indies trade was therefore subject to royal ordinances from the time the shipwrights first put adze to wood. More ordinances covered her from the moment she was launched until she was rigged, manned, armed and laden with cargo and licences at Seville.

From the very early days the ships sailed in convoy and were escorted by ships of the Navy. However, the cost of providing these escorts was not paid for by the Crown: a duty (*avería*) was charged on all exports and imports to cover the expense of these *armadas*. The warships escorting the galleons and *flota* to and from the West Indies formed in effect a small navy which was entirely supported by the *avería*.

Long before a ship made its way carefully down the shallows of the River Guadalquivir to cross the bar at Sanlúcar and head for the Indies, the officials of the House of Trade were ready with inspectors and forms. Every item of cargo had to be entered in the House registers and once the entries were complete the hatches were battened down and sealed: nothing more could be taken on board without special permission and, just to make certain, the captain had to put up a bond. All this was done to ensure that the cargo a ship delivered to 'the Treasury officials in the Indies corresponded with the entries in her register.

The whole system was based on the assumption that every officer, seaman and passenger in the ships, and the officials of the customs and excise, House of Trade and Treasury in Spain and the Indies was actually or potentially dishonest, intent on defrauding the Crown. Informers were encouraged and rewarded. The amount varied from time to time, but, based on the value of the cargo, was usually between a third and a fifth. (At one point the judge before whom the informer made the denunciation also shared in the reward.)

Human beings travelling privately to and from the Indies were subject to much the same paperwork as cargo but were viewed by the House of Trade with more suspicion. To begin with, no one, whether hidalgo or seaman, emigrant or merchant, could go to the Indies without a licence from the Crown. In addition every detail about the person had to be entered in the register of the ship – particularly the reason for the journey. Nor were the licence and the register entries matters to be shrugged off lightly: until 1570, crossing the Atlantic without a licence or shipping articles without registration meant a fine of 100,000 maravedis and ten years' banishment for those of 'gentle birth', while those of 'meaner condition' received one hundred lashes and ten years' banishment. By 1604 the one hundred lashes had been changed to four years in the galleys; by 1622 to eight years. The banishment for those of 'gentle birth' was to be served in the penal colony at Oran, in North Africa. Eventually the onus was put on the captains of the ships: each had to put up a bond of 100 ducats and, if caught carrying an illegal passenger, served the same sentence.

The ration for the crew of a merchant ship at the time of the buccaneers was comparatively generous. Each man had 1½ lb of bread (a hard substance more like tough biscuit) daily, with ½ lb of salt pork or beef on three days a week and ½ lb of salt fish (or fresh if it could be caught) on the remaining four. The peas and beans so beloved by Spaniards were served more frugally, 2 oz being issued on four days and 1½ oz of rice on the other three. Cheese was issued once a week while each man received a *cuartillo* of wine daily. (This was a comparatively weak wine, the equivalent of the English small beer.)

Having registered cargo, passengers and crew, each ship then joined the convoy, either the galleons or the *flota*, depending on her destination. Each convoy had two commanders: the senior one, called the captain-general, was rarely if ever a sailor and might just as well have been referred to as the governor; the junior was the admiral.

The captain-general was appointed by the King (usually for a single voyage) and he had to pay the Crown a substantial amount of money for the privilege. He made his profit by appointing many of the people serving in the ships. Quite apart from naming the chaplains, doctor, and barber-surgeons and collecting a fee from each of them, his patronage extended down to carpenters and caulkers.

The captain-general was in effect the head of a small government which ran the convoy. He had with him a *veedor*, a lawyer appointed by the King, whose task was to make sure no laws or ordinances were broken (and who was one of the few men in a convoy immune from arrest). Each ship carried a 'constable' whose duties can only be compared to the mayor of a small Spanish town; a captain of artillery; 'master of the plate' in those ships carrying bullion and gems; and a notary or commissioner of oaths for attesting the ships' innumerable documents, including bills of lading. The captain-general travelled in considerable style – apart from a large retinue of servants he was allowed eight gentlemen-in-waiting and four trumpeters.

Although the King ordained that the *flota* should leave in May and the galleons in August, there was in fact no guarantee that two fleets a year went to the West Indies. Sometimes the *flota* did not sail, or the galleons left in January, returning to Spain with the bullion in August or September. The sudden early departure of the galleons and their equally hurried return in the same year was invariably a signal that the King was short of money.

Smuggler's Joy

The whole Spanish approach to the Indies – the administration, emigration and trade – was arranged in a medieval fashion, right down to the actual marketing of the goods sent out: they were sold at fairs of the type which had been familiar in Europe and the Near East at the time of the Crusades. The fair at Portobelo, the largest, was typical of smaller ones held at Panama and Vera Cruz, and a description of it shows the workings of the whole Spanish system in the Indies.

The captain-general of the galleons was under orders to give as much notice as possible to the viceroy of Panama (which had become a province as well as a port) and before reaching the Windward Islands he sent a *petacha* ahead giving news and the approximate date of his arrival. This was usually the viceroy's first warning that the galleons had left Spain, and he told the local merchants, who immediately began packing saddle bags for their annual visit to Portobelo. They also began sending their wares by mule because they would be selling local produce for export as well as buying goods that had come from Spain.

The most important task in the preceding months had been to get the bullion sent up the Pacific coast to Panama. The viceroy of Panama sent word to the viceroy of Peru, 1600 miles down the coast at Lima. He in turn warned the mines that the bullion must be brought down to the coast. The silver ingots from the Potosí mines, for instance, took at least two weeks to reach the coast. The mules had to make their way through the Andes in the shadow of mountains 20,000 feet high to reach La Paz, skirt Lake Titicaca and pass through the mountains again before reaching Arica, the port on the Pacific.

By the time the Pacific ships reached Panama with their gold and silver (usually at least six weeks after the viceroy received word from Portobelo) the Atlantic galleons had arrived. Then soon after the Cartagena ships sailed between the forts into the almost landlocked harbour of Portobelo, the fair erupted: the guns of the fort fired salutes answered by the ships; landlords rubbed their hands, tenants bemoaned the crowding and the high rents, and sewage began to cause sickness that, augmented by the heat and humidity, always killed a large number of people before the fair was over.

Portobelo was almost deserted for more than ten months in the year; apart from being a port at the end of the track across the Isthmus from Panama it had no other reason for existing. There was little or no coasting trade to occupy it during those ten months; the rains just fell – it is in one of the wettest parts of South America – and the mosquitoes and flies multiplied. But for the six or eight weeks in the year that the fair lasted, Portobelo was so crowded that the proudest merchants were glad to take the meanest rooms at the highest rents.

Once the ships arrived from Cartagena, the royal officials went on board and inspected the registers. Customs duty and local taxes were computed, and the cargoes were brought on shore to the warehouses. Bargains were then struck, with a seller trying to ensure that a buyer took delivery in Portobelo: that left him with the task of carrying the merchandise to Panama, a six-day journey on the back of a mule, a lot of it through tropical rain forests where four inches of rain in a day was quite normal.

An English Catholic priest, Thomas Gage, was in Portobelo in 1637 and saw what happened when too many people crowded into a small town where the sanitation was non-existent: five hundred people, traders from Panama and seamen from the ships, died within fifteen days of the fair opening. He described how the mule convoys arrived daily from Panama with the gold and silver bullion, coming along the single track which was alternately dusty and thick with mud. There was a slave to each mule and soldiers guarded the whole convoy, which made for the market place where the panniers on the mules' backs were emptied and gold and silver ingots left 'lying around like stones' before being carried on board the ships.

With the bullion finally loaded on board the ships and the merchants folding their tents and settling their rents, the fair came to an end. The merchants returned to their wives and businesses in Panama; the ships returned to Cartagena where the galleons prepared for the January voyage to Havana and the rendezvous with the *flota*. Although the fair lasted from six to eight weeks in the early days, as Spain found it more and more difficult to obtain the goods or find the ships in which to send them, the fair was shortened until it lasted little more than two weeks.

The rest of the riches of the Indies were brought to the galleons and merchant ships while they waited at Cartagena. From Isla de Margarita, off the coast of Venezuela, came pearls brought in by a *petacha* which the captain-general had sent there. Emeralds came from New Granada (the Colombia of today) while more mundane but profitable cargoes included tobacco, indigo and cocoa from what is now Venezuela.

In the meantime the merchants had returned to Panama and begun the complicated series of business deals that would see their goods travelling as far down the Pacific coast of South America as Callao and Arica. Each year their complaint was predictable and justified – Spain was sending fewer goods and charging even more outrageous prices. These prices were of course further inflated by the export and import duties. The export duty charged at Seville and other ports before goods left the country was usually two and a half per cent of the value of an item, plus four per cent *avería*. The import duty when it arrived in the Indies was rarely less than ten per cent, and based not on the item's value in Spain but its vastly increased value in the New World.

The people who suffered worst from the inflation of prices lived along the Pacific coast, in Peru, Chile and Ecuador, because all their goods were charged extra duty. On top of the first import duty at Portobelo there was another of at least five per cent and based on the increased value between the Caribbean and Pacific ports. In addition all goods except vegetables, wheat and flour had to pay yet another duty when shipped from one colony to another in the Indies.

At Potosí, which with its rich mines was the wealthiest city in the New World, prices were four to six times those in Panama, which in turn were often double those at Portobelo. The buyer in Potosí was usually paying twenty to fifty times the original cost in Europe. The whole scale of values became absurd: in Chile a *fanega* of wheat (1.6 bushels) cost two pesos – the same price as a cow. A packet of paper (at 100 pesos) was worth fifty cows, while a sword was three hundred cows and a cloak five hundred.

The customers having to pay these high prices were, of course, the immigrants: almost everything they used had to be imported – ranging from cooking oil to cutlery, wine to woven material, kitchen pots to a hunter's powder and shot. Although there was a continual and ever-increasing demand in the Indies for these goods, the quantities ordered from Spain fell each year as the prices increased.

The reason was simple for the Treasury officials in the New World to describe in their reports to the Spanish Crown but it was almost impossible to prevent: Dutch, French and English smugglers were providing many of the items needed and at a very much lower cost. By 1600 the King was being warned by the archbishop of Seville (the man responsible for the spiritual welfare of all those who navigated from the Guadalquivir) that the Indies trade was 'so weak and failing' that it would vanish in a few years unless the King did something. Three years later there was not enough freight to justify sending merchant ships to the Main, and by 1612 the president of the Council of the Indies was forced to admit that 'the decay of the trade' was the only reason for reducing the number of ships.

The Spanish Crown, the Council of the Indies and the House of Trade, all sworn enemies of foreign smugglers, were in fact the *contrabandistas'* best allies. Without them the market would certainly have existed (thanks to the exorbitant profit margins charged by the merchants in the Indies) but would have been far less attractive. The smugglers could often supply the goods needed at a price which was not only reasonable but very low, and the reason for this was not hard to find – frequently an item exported through Spain had been manufactured in France, Holland or England in the first place.

Although Spain forbade foreign countries to trade direct with the Indies and her own industry had collapsed, her merchants in Spain were quite free to buy goods from abroad, bring them into Spain and then ship them out again to the Indies, paying both import and export duties. Indeed foreign merchants were at times allowed to set up business in Spain. But by the time the goods reached the Indies through Spain many middle men had taken a profit and the Crown had charged many duties. Obviously English, Dutch or French shipowners with cargoes from Bristol, Honfleur or Antwerp bought at local prices could afford to sell the goods direct in the Indies at as little as twenty-five per cent extra and still make a good profit (especially as they could then buy hides, cochineal and even contraband bullion to sell when they returned to Europe). So the Spanish in the Indies had little choice; in spite of harsh penalties, they bought from the smugglers whenever possible. Treasury officials were not above conniving at the smuggling and there was an accepted ritual, which will be described later.

The total amount of gold, silver and gems that Spain shipped home from the Indies from the conquest until she lost them will never be known, but thanks to the Council of the Indies' meticulous book-keeping there are enough figures to be able to draw certain conclusions. From New Spain (Mexico and the Greater Antilles) the yearly totals slowly increased from 52,700 pesos in 1522, when Cortés began looting Mexico, to 811,400 in 1570, and 1,500,000 by 1600.

The silver from the Potosí mines began to flow to Spain in quantities from 1556, and a glance at the royalties paid to the King shows how Spain could finance her wars. The amount registered in 1556 was 1,339,900 pesos, with 278,700 paid to the Crown in royalties, 3,535,700 (735,400 in royalties) by 1580 and 4,149,300 (879,600) ten years later, two years after Philip II sent the Armada against England. It is important to remember that these are the figures for silver only; the total amount going to the King each year was about four times the silver royalty.

Putting a modern cash value on the bullion means very little because the rapid inflation of the twentieth century defies any comparison with the slow inflation which faced Spain centuries before economics became a political hobby, but there are other ways of describing the actual quantity. In the hundred years after Columbus reached the Indies, Spain found, looted or mined three times the total amount of gold and silver which had been in circulation in Europe on the day that Columbus began his voyage. It has been estimated that the gold weighed 750,000 lb, of which at least a tenth went to the Treasury. While Charles V was on the throne of Spain, the yearly average was reckoned at six to seven thousand pounds a year – the same amount as the Queen of Sheba gave to Solomon.

At the risk of oversimplifying, the Spanish King was getting from his royalties on the gold and silver mines of the New World far more wealth than all other countries could levy, be it by direct taxation, customs or excise. The French, Dutch and English governments could prosper only if their merchants prospered; there was no El Dorado for them to find, no Potosí to mine.

Yet Spain always knew that a lost plate fleet could cause a grave financial crisis: campaigns had to be put back or cancelled, ships' companies paid off and the ships laid up. Nature or privateers became a factor in foreign policy. Like an alcoholic, the King of Spain found that the more he had the more he wanted, yet the country stayed in an almost continual state of bankruptcy ... instead of being the gateway through which the gold and silver of the Indies flowed into the Spanish treasury, Seville became in effect the funnel through which the gold ran as interest or repayments into the coffers of the great bankers of Europe, the Fuggers of Augsburg and the Welsers, and the Strozzi of Florence ...

Any monarch who seriously thought the countries of northern Europe would accept a papal prohibition on crossing the Line into the New World was an unrealistic optimist. As long as Spain was strong at sea and the other nations weak then only isolated ships commanded by adventurers dared go to the West Indies, but it took the Spanish Crown and the Council of the Indies many years to understand that passing laws never kept a burglar out of the house and the moment Spain weakened at sea those same nations would declare open season on the plate fleets, reducing *Inter Caetera* to a pious hope.

French privateers soon crossed the Atlantic in their hunt for the plate fleets, finding one in 1556 as it worked its way through the Bahamas. A few months later Jean d'Argo, the leader of the Dieppe privateers, attacked the galleons, capturing nine of them. In the same year French privateers attacked Spanish coastal towns in Cuba, Hispaniola and Puerto Rico; in 1553 ten ships under François le Clerc attacked towns in Hispaniola and Puerto Rico and then went on to attack Santiago in Cuba while his second-in-command seized Havana, held it for three weeks and then burned it down when no ransom was paid.

Finally in 1559 a peace treaty ended the sixty-year-old quarrel between France and Spain and – so the Spanish thought – brought peace and quiet to the West Indies. The signatures were hardly dry on the treaty when Philip II ordered work to begin on the defences of Havana, a city which Le Clerc's ships had left a flattened and blackened ruin. Over the next two decades the engineers and masons, as well as thousands of slaves, were kept busy building fortresses to defend other Spanish ports in the West Indies.

With those built to cover Spanish possessions in the Mediterranean, they remain today as perhaps Philip's most durable monuments.

England continued to regard the New World as part of a 'general domain'. Bishop Alvaro de la Quadra, who was Spanish ambassador to England, wrote to Madrid on 27 November 1561 a dispatch which expressed the English attitude succinctly: 'Cecil simply said that the Pope had no authority to divide the world,' and the bishop was reminded 'that his compatriots enjoyed freedom to trade in her Majesty's dominions'.

The first real attempts by the English to trade 'beyond the Line' were the three voyages of John Hawkins between 1562 and 1568, but the English were not the only 'intruders': the French and Dutch were soon feeling their way, the shipowners of Scheveningen and Havre de Grace, Delfzil and Honfleur venturing small expeditions to sell contraband and buy goods. And the Sea Beggars arrived for the first time in the Caribbean, a very real symbol of the religious aspect of the fight of the Dutch against the Spanish and one which was to be repeated by the buccaneers a few decades later.

Before launching the Armada against England, Philip II was facing difficulties in the Spanish Netherlands because the Inquisition and a ruthless army had not succeeded in subduing the Dutch people or converting them to Catholicism. Those putting up a fight became well organized under the Seigneur de Dolhain with a squadron of privateers committed to sink, burn or capture Spanish ships wherever they found them. Called the Sea Beggars, they became a rallying point for many other Protestant seamen who had suffered under or were threatened by the Inquisition. The Flemings and Dutch soon found themselves joined by French Huguenots and gradually they began operating farther afield. From the Chops of the Channel they raided across the Bay of Biscay and down to the Spanish coast and then west to the Azores, seeking the Spanish plate fleets returning from the Indies. They headed south-west for the Canaries and soon ventured across the Atlantic to the Caribbean, where they were joined by more sturdy men from Rochelle, Protestants fighting the Huguenot cause against the French King.

About this time the Spanish made a significant change in the method of shipping bullion across the Atlantic. Up to the 1560s it had gone in the galleons, slow ships which, by the time they had their quota of passengers (who would get in the way if the ship went into action) and cargo were floating low on their marks, making them easy prey for privateers if they became separated from the convoy. The Council of the Indies decided that in future *gallizabras* would be used to carry bullion. Smaller, much faster and more manoeuvrable than the galleons, and better able to get to windward and elude privateers, they would not carry passengers.

At this time the West Indies could only reflect the situation in Europe, and the growing tension between Elizabeth of England and Philip II saw an increase in the activities of Englishmen in the Caribbean. Francis Drake made several voyages, waging what was in effect a private war against the Spanish. In 1592 he left yet again for the Caribbean to set up the first English trading post ever established there, at a secret bay not far from Nombre de Dios. His famous attack on Nombre de Dios followed, an attack made before Portobelo became the terminal on the Caribbean shore and which led to him discovering piles of gold and silver ingots stacked in the royal warehouses awaiting shipment – a sight which led Drake to tell his men: 'I have brought you to the treasure house of the world.' On the same expedition Drake crossed the Isthmus, with the help of the Indians, to become the first English-man to see the South Sea and then the port of Panama, with the treasure ships anchored in the roadstead.

In 1586 Drake looted Santo Domingo and then sailed south across the Caribbean to do the same to Cartagena before sailing home in triumph. Two years later Philip sent the Armada against England. In January 1596, some twenty-eight years after he took his first ship 'beyond the Line' to the West Indies, Francis Drake died and his body was buried at sea off Portobelo. As *El Draco* he had become a name used by the Spaniards to frighten themselves, and to the English he became a symbol of all that was brave and honourable.

4

The Road to the Isles

By 1600 the Elizabethan age as measured by the calendar was coming to an end but the last few years of the old century were as crowded with significant events as the first few of the new. Edmund Spenser died in 1589 after having coined the phrase 'Divine tobacco' and three years later came Shakespeare's first play. One of Elizabeth's leading advisers, Lord Burghley, died in 1598 and a year later Oliver Cromwell, the man whose vision did more than anything else to smash Spain's influence in the West Indies, was born on a Huntingdon farm.

In 1603 Queen Elizabeth I died. James VI of Scotland now became James I of England and there was a brief peace with Spain. James not only ended a twenty-year war with Spain but, he hoped, began a new period of friendship because he wanted his son to marry the Spanish Infanta. Spain promptly brought up the question of the West Indies and James's answer was one which brought out into the open the attitude of northern Europe to Spain's claims. He said he was prepared to forbid his own people from going anywhere in the West Indies where the Spanish already 'were planted', and instruct them 'only to seek their traffic by their own discoveries in other places whereof there are so infinite dimensions of vast and great territories' in which the Spanish 'have no interest'. In other words, the Spanish could monopolize what they actually held; all the rest was open to anyone who discovered or developed it.

Philip III's negotiators would have none of it; they recognized the thin end of a wedge sliding across the conference table. The English, they said, should be excluded from every part of the Indies, or the King should tell them – in writing, too – that they went there at their own peril.

The Protestant Dutch, fighting alone, had been successful in the East Indies: there they had in defiance of papal bulls carved into the old Portuguese monopoly, establishing the powerful Dutch East India Company. Now, in 1604, they proposed a West India Company. The man behind the scheme, which lacked neither money nor boldness, was William Usselincz: he planned Dutch colonies as well as Dutch trade in the New World. The idea was so alarming for Philip III that in 1607 Spain began negotiations with the Dutch, with whom they had been at war for many years. Spain took a firm line – the Dutch should quit not only the West Indies but the East Indies as well. The negotiations dragged on, so there was in fact a truce lasting nine years rather than a peace treaty.

In the West Indies it meant only that the clock was stopped; the effect on the British, Dutch and French ships which had been operating as privateers was that legally they were now pirates. In practice it made little difference: as privateers in time of war they were hanged or sold into slavery if they were caught by the Spanish because they were 'beyond the Line'. If they were caught in peacetime and charged with piracy, the penalties were still the same, so there was no incentive for the successful wartime privateer to change his habits in times of peace.

In a sense Spain was now frozen in time, a medieval monster preserved in a glacier, having learned nothing, never changing anything, and incapable of reacting swiftly. Although her colonial empire in the Indies was run in an antiquated fashion, the nations challenging her in the New World were young and vigorous and, more to the point, often the challenge was in fact being made by merchants or individual young sea captains, brave and competent men driven by ambition or dreams of wealth and whose activities and decisions were not bogged down in the nervous bureaucracy that, busily evading responsibility at every level, tried to control and defend the vast Spanish territories in the Indies.

For the next fifty years, until the century reached the halfway mark, the lively governments of northern Europe could do little more than argue with Madrid that only effective occupation of territory could establish legal ownership; that it was absurd for Spain to claim that she owned every scrap of land sighted in the distance and named by Columbus because much of it had never been trodden by Spanish feet, let alone occupied: whole islands had seen a Spanish flag only as it went past on board a distant ship. As the nations argued – in the case of England while the King's son was supposed to be wooing the Spanish Infanta – their sturdy traders continued to sail their ships into quiet creeks and mangrove-lined bays to visit settlements and towns and discreetly sell their contraband goods and buy what the Spaniards had to offer.

In her prolonged negotiations with Spain, France had consistently refused to exclude her ships from any but the main ports of the Indies. The best that the Spanish diplomats could get was an oral agreement that French 'corsairs' sailed in the Indies at their own risk and that if the Spanish authorities captured and hanged them whenever possible, this use of the gibbet would not damage Spain's official relations with France. This proved to be a very important agreement, even if never graced with ink, paper, signatures and seals, because it established the important point that the West Indies was an area where the rules for normal relations between nations did not apply.

Thus French and English privateers could fight the Spanish in the Indies without causing tempers to rise unduly in Paris, London or Madrid, although there would be a flurry of diplomatic notes.

As the story of the buccaneers unfolds it will show that this had an enormous effect for the whole of the century and leads to one of history's more interesting 'ifs': what would have happened if Spain had agreed to let foreign ships trade in the Indies? It is absurd to seek answers fitting preconceived notions that such nations had vast, devious and long-term plans for the conduct of foreign policy because then, as now, foreign policy was always a quirkish, short-term affair and always subject to the whims of individuals, whether sovereigns or ministers. In Britain, for instance, a pro-Spanish faction had the King's ear while James I tried to arrange the marriage with the Infanta, yet only a few years earlier the Spanish Armada had sailed up the Channel.

The only continuity of policy for France, Holland and England came from the merchants: whatever the official policy of their respective governments, they wanted to trade with the West Indies. Although this concern can be attributed to various high-sounding motives the reason was prosaic enough – they wanted to make a profit. All three nations had to trade to exist; unlike Spain they had no well of gold and silver into which they could dip to pay their bills. This meant that they *forced* a trade over the years: although in time of war they tried to capture the bullion fleets their main aim in war or peace was commerce. The answer to the 'if', then, is that as they carried on trade even though Spain forbade it, there is no reason to suppose they would have done anything except trade had Spain permitted it to be done openly and, making a good profit from trade, they would have tried to make sure their sovereigns pursued peaceful policies towards Spain – all of which would have also have helped to safeguard the plate fleets.

The main Dutch interest in the West Indies was not gold or silver, tobacco or pearls, but a far more prosaic substance – salt. Holland's smacks sailing out into the North Sea in all weathers ensured that the fishing industry flourished but vast quantities of salt were needed to preserve the catches. Earlier this salt came from the Portuguese coast (in Spanish hands between 1580 and 1640), but disputes with Spain forced the Dutch to find other sources. By then the salt mines on the Spanish Main were operating with slave labour along the coast of what is now Venezuela, and very soon Dutch ships were carrying on an illicit salt business which developed into shipping goods from Holland to West Africa, slaves from there across the Atlantic to the Spanish Main and salt back to the Netherlands.

Salt to preserve their herrings was not the only contraband of interest to the Dutch; many Spanish planters along the Venezuela coast grew excellent tobacco, but all the various Spanish duties added to the profits demanded in Seville meant that the price was far too high for European countries, and demand had dropped disastrously. At this point the Dutch began to buy it illicitly and ship it home, building up a very profitable industry for which the country is still famous.

Slowly, as the world moved into the new century, the situation in the West Indies changed, although Spain, like a Canute in the Tropics, tried to hold back the tide. More ships came out from Holland, Britain and France and the contraband trade and privateering increased. There was such a demand in Europe for the products of the West Indies that a small Spanish ship laden with logwood from Campeche, for instance, fetched a high price when captured and sailed to Europe. The logwood was much sought after for dyeing and Campeche, on the coast of New Spain, was one of the few available sources. Equally profitable, and just as likely to be found sailing from one port to another in New Spain or on the Main, were ships carrying mixed cargoes of hides, cochineal and indigo. The clothmakers of Europe would always pay well for dyes.

The privateers taking these prizes all faced one major difficulty: every captured ship needed a prize crew to sail her to Europe, where both ship and cargo could be sold, and a man to command her who could be trusted. Like their fellow countrymen who were busy with the contraband trade, they lacked bases in the West Indies; they were all having to operate from home ports more than four thousand miles away on the other side of the Atlantic. Every fathom of new rope for the rigging and yard of sail canvas, every roundshot and ounce of powder, paint for the woodwork and pitch for the seams, more men to replace those killed in action or who died from disease – all had to come across the Atlantic.

By contrast the Spanish had large and well-defended bases. Whether galleons or small coasting vessels, Spanish ships could refit at Cartagena or Havana, Santo Domingo or Vera Cruz, Portobelo or San Juan; they could take on provisions or water, find more men or bring shipwrights on board to make repairs.

The way the Spanish had colonized the Greater Antilles but ignored the smaller islands of the Lesser Antilles at the eastern end has already been described. Still uninhabited except for the wild Caribs (who, although brave and fierce, were eventually at the mercy of patient men with muskets), the islands stretched from Trinidad in the south to Antigua and St Martins in the north, with Barbados well out to the eastward of them all, like a sentry box to windward in the Atlantic. (The prevailing easterly wind has more south than north in it, so it is easier to sail through them from south to north, and for this reason the southern group were soon called the Windward Islands and the northern ones the Leeward Islands.)

Each treaty that Spain had signed with France, Britain and Holland appeared to repeat her determination to stop anyone going 'beyond the

Line' but she was doing little more than whistling in the dark. By 1607 the first permanent English colony had been founded in Virginia, and Samuel Champlain was establishing a French colony on the St Lawrence River. Three years earlier Captain Charles Leigh had started a tiny colony in Guiana, on the north-east coast of South America, hoping to find gold as well as plant tobacco, sugar and cotton. French adventurers tried to settle in Cayenne; Dutch groups began small settlements nearby, interested in tobacco and the salt from Venezuela to the north. These were all small and privately financed, often poorly planned and with little knowledge of the problems to be faced, whether Carib attacks, sickness or starvation when crops did not grow and ships failed to arrive with supplies.

While the British, French and Dutch nibbled at the north-east corner of South America the truce between Spain and Holland was running out and by 1620 Spain was in a chaotic state. When Philip III died in 1621 and his dissolute young son Philip IV came to the throne, power went to his favourite, Gaspar de Guzman, count of Olivares. The new King was a curious mixture; a frivolous youth who was a religious bigot and loved bull-fighting and music, the theatre and wenching. Olivares behaved more like a father than a favourite minister, a man obsessed with power but erratic in the way he used it. This improbable pair were determined that the foreigners would be forced out of the Caribbean. To begin with, they decided, the truce with the Dutch would not be extended, and as far as Olivares was concerned there was little to stop the Spanish armies sweeping through the United Provinces. A glance at Europe at that time shows why Olivares reached that conclusion. Although England was always sensitive about who controlled the River Scheldt, she would make no trouble because James I was still hoping his son would marry the Infanta; France was having her own troubles, once again facing civil war; in Germany the Thirty Years War had begun.

Olivares had, however, underestimated the Dutch, who were now a rich people. They had finally founded the West India Company and were planning an attack not on the West Indies (that would be left to the privateers already there) but on San Salvador, then the capital of the Portuguese colony in Brazil and the Bahia of today. A fleet of twenty-seven ships with 1700 soldiers on board sailed under Jacob Willekens and Pieter Pieterszoon Hein (better known as Piet Hein) and by May 1624 the rich colony had been captured and looted. The effect on Olivares was predictable: this was the first time that a Spanish or Portuguese colony in the New World had been captured and held. He took every available Spanish and Portuguese ship of war and manned them with trained seamen stripped from both the galleons and the *flota*. After assembling the largest possible fleet and putting Don Fadrique de Toledo in command, he gave him orders to destroy the Dutch at Salvador.

This Don Fadrique did – but his great fleet was almost completely destroyed on the way back to Spain by bad weather and Dutch ships; a terrible blow to Spain's maritime strength because she lost not just ships but highly-trained seamen from the plate ships. There had been times in Spain's history when weakness at sea did not matter because possible enemies were even weaker; but those days were past; within a few years the West Indian empires of Britain, France and Holland were founded.

It began in a quiet fashion. Thomas Warner was an Englishman who had gone to Guiana, but he had seen how James I had, under pressure from Spain, revoked a patent granted to plant tobacco in Guiana. Deciding to try his luck elsewhere, Warner sailed northward in the *Hopewell* to the Lesser Antilles.

The first of the islands he came to was Grenada, which he found beautiful, with good rainfall and a fine natural harbour but too mountainous for tobacco. He carried on to St Vincent which, although less mountainous, was still not right for tobacco and probably had too much rain. St Lucia had the same drawbacks. He thought Martinique was possible, but it had so many Caribs that a small army was needed to keep them off. Dominica, a great block of mountains covered with dense rain forests and often shrouded in thick cloud, was quite unsuitable, although Guadeloupe, the next to the north, was comparatively flat but probably too dry. The next island he considered was Nevis, which had no natural harbour and only a very exposed anchorage. However, just to the north, so close that from certain directions it appeared to be joined, was St Christopher's, a larger version of Nevis, which seemed to Warner to have just the right amount of rain and a natural but open anchorage.

So Warner stayed there and planted tobacco, knowing that the only way of finding out if St Christopher's (today's St Kitts) was his ideal island was to plant, harvest and dry a season's crop and then smoke some of it. The taste, and hence the value, depended so much on soil and climate that 'growing and smoking' was the only test. With rich and aromatic leaves as a sample, he could then return to England and find people who would back him financially until he had a plantation flourishing, and then take his tobacco crop each year and sell it for him. (This, incidentally, later became the regular pattern for planting and marketing.)

His first crop of tobacco proved so good that he found plenty of backers to start a permanent colony. Thus Warner had, quietly and unobtrusively, finally broken the Spanish monopoly: his settlement in St Kitts, founded on his return from London in January 1624, was the first set up by foreigners in the Caribbean 'beyond the Line' and showed that the Lesser Antilles were islands of promise for men who had efficient farming in their eyes, not the glitter of gold.

From then on the rush began: Captain John Powell, sailing back to England from Brazil, landed at Barbados in the same year that the *Hopewell* left St Kitts with the first harvest, and took possession of the island in the name of James I. Within months the first eighty settlers had landed there, and some Frenchmen, seeking shelter at St Kitts to repair their damaged ship, arrived in time to help Warner and his people fight off an attack by the Caribs. The French stayed and agreed with Warner to divide the twenty-three-mile-long island between them.

The fact that defiant foreigners had now settled in Barbados and St Kitts was, for the time being, a mere pinprick for Spain because all her calculations about the balances of power had gone completely adrift. Spain's assumption that England would not interfere in the West Indies because of James I's anxiety that his son should marry the Infanta did not allow for the proposed romance to collapse, with Prince Charles and his friend the duke of Buckingham returning to London sufficiently outraged, piqued and rash to change Britain's policy towards Spain. James I died a few months later and Charles came to the throne in 1625. As Charles I, he and Buckingham managed to rally the country round them and their new policy by conjuring up visions of another Elizabethan age in which gentlemen would, in the style of Drake, wage a profitable sea war against the Dons in the Indies.

The Spanish assumptions about France had also proved completely wrong: instead of the country tearing itself to pieces with internal squabbling, Richelieu had come to power and was proving a shrewd and strong-minded statesman determined to unify the country. Thus in one year Philip IV and Olivares found that not only had they lost an ardent suitor across the English Channel and a complacent friend across the Pyrenees, but in their places they had a combative England where the name of Drake was being used to rouse the people and a France under the influence of a man who saw that only Spain stood in the way of France's greatness. Their third assumption, about how easily the Spanish army would sweep through the United Provinces, had been blown to shreds by the wind that took the Dutch fleet to Salvador.

The colonizing of Barbados and St Kitts caused much excitement in Britain and France and, small as the settlements were, neither country lacked for venturesome spirits. Within two years of Captain Powell taking possession of Barbados two thousand settlers had gone out there and more went on to St Kitts and nearby Nevis. Spain made an attempt to dislodge the settlers from St Kitts, but it was like a reflex action by a badly hurt boxer: a few ships burned homes and plantations at St Kitts, sending their prisoners to England with a warning that next time they would put to death any foreigners found in any land belonging to Spain. It was an empty threat, because by now her ships were spread so thinly that Spain's main concern had to be the safety of the plate fleets.

The real danger came from the Dutch, not the British and French, because the Dutch were equipping and sailing fleet after fleet to harry the Spanish in the Indies. The Dutch admirals, captains and seamen dreamed of capturing a plate fleet, as all sailors had dreamed since the French privateersman Jean Fleury had captured two galleons off the Azores a hundred years earlier. Sometimes the dreams came true. In 1628 Piet Hein left Holland with thirty-one ships and orders which were as simply written as they were complex to carry out: he was to capture the galleons with the riches of Peru and the *flota* with the riches from Mexico. He succeeded in taking the galleons, and when boarding parties reported to him on the booty it was almost unbelievable, even for men who had dreamed of such a capture: nearly 100 tons of silver (177,350 lb), 135 lb of gold, pearls from Isla de Margarita and emeralds from Columbia.

The effect on Spain was disastrous: in a few hours she had lost a year's income. Bankers in Genoa, Milan, Naples, Florence and Venice were waiting to be paid their interest; some were owed principal as well. A Spanish army in the Netherlands needed cash for pay and provisions; there was a bigger army in Germany needing even more money. Overnight Spain was almost bankrupt. Her armies went unpaid and she had to default on her loans – something for which the international bankers never forgave her. They saw their security, the apparently bottomless gold and silver mines of the Indies, only as safe as the Spanish ships that carried it. From now on the interest rates soared upwards as banking took on an element of the risks that usually faced marine insurance underwriters.

Piet Hein's fleet had been the third to range the Indies and Brazil in a year and was followed by a fourth. More Dutch privateers followed in their wake like gulls, attacking settlements and seizing Spanish coastal vessels carrying local products to the main ports for collection. By 1630 Spain's colonies along the Main, New Spain and the three big islands of the Great Antilles were reduced to isolated, almost besieged settlements. Bales of hides rotted in warehouses or were sold to the smugglers because no one dare ship them to the main ports; logwood stayed where it had been felled, a happy hunting ground for termites. Spices remained unharvested and all of Spain's hopes and efforts were concentrated on getting the galleons and *flota* home with the plate.

Thus by 1630 the Spanish government had lost its grip in the West Indies; the Dutch had swept the seas and left them open for the traders. Whatever Spanish laws said and ordinances decreed, the majority of Spanish settlers were now concerned with the problem of sheer survival. They had to get money for their hides and their cochineal, their sugar, indigo and cocoa, or they starved. To live in the Indies they had to buy cloth, thread and needles, wood and nails, and hammers to drive them; pots and pans, cutlery and bottles – all the items manufactured in Europe and needed daily by the settlers. And the Dutch trading vessels were always close, ready to buy and sell.

5

The Planter's Apprentice

In England the favourites at Court busily manoeuvred with the King to get themselves royal patents granting rights to various islands in the West Indies. By 1630 there were more than three thousand settlers in Barbados and James Hay, earl of Carlisle, had been granted a royal patent to be 'Lord Proprietor of the English Caribbee Islands' – a description which included Barbados, St Kitts and Nevis.

These early days in Barbados were bad. Almost every foot of soil had to be cleared of thick undergrowth and trees before tobacco (for which the island seemed ideally suited) could be planted, and the planters wanted cheap labour. For this the merchants, most of whom held mortgages on the land, sent out white servants, using a system of indenturing which sounded better for the servants in theory than it proved in practice. Young men signed indentures in England binding them to masters in Barbados for a period of years, usually between four and seven. At the end of their time they were paid a sum of money, five or ten pounds, which they had been told in England would allow them to start on their own as settlers.

Usually recruited from the poorest classes – the indenture system seemed an excellent opportunity for large families to get rid of surplus sons – these apprentices went out with considerable enthusiasm because Barbados had the same romantic association as El Dorado and the Spanish Main. So first the tobacco and then the sugar estates came into being, and one of the products of refining sugar was rum. In an island chronically short of water, rum was cheap and easily available, and it was an age where people of all classes drank heavily.

The Tropics have a curious effect on many Europeans: all too often the sun magnifies and exaggerates a man's shortcomings, latent or otherwise. A man who enjoyed a couple of drinks of an evening in Europe was likely to become an alcoholic in the Tropics. A lawyer or accountant who passed for honest in England for lack of temptation found it in the Tropics and often succumbed. Standards of moral behaviour often collapsed; standards of physical behaviour often slipped because of crude and difficult living conditions.

However, the sun and the rum were not entirely to blame because there were men who could and did resist the ravages of both. There were two other factors. First Barbados was thousands of miles away from the established codes of behaviour, be they those of the Inns of Court, the merchants of Basinghall Street, or those found among thieves, pimps, panders and foot-pads. Second, the type of people that went to Barbados varied enormously, from thieves sentenced to transportation for ten years to debtors who saw flight to Barbados as the safest way of avoiding a cell in the debtors' jail; from shady lawyers who saw a future in the litigation bound to arise as planters quarrelled to men hoping to move up from horse coping. Superimposed on this motley group were those men who went out with plenty of capital and the firm intention of making a new life outside Europe. They would be followed in time by men who left England for political or religious reasons.

The earliest records of life in Barbados are almost unanimous in saying that although the island itself was delightful, the early settlers left much to be desired. One contemporary visitor's description of the planters is illuminating:

> For the merry planter, or freeman to give him a Character, I can call him no otherwise than a German for his drinking, and a Welshman for his welcome, he is never idle; if it rains he topes securely under his roof, if fair he plants and works in the field; he takes it ill if you pass by his door and not taste of Liquor ... It's the Custom for a Christian servant to serve four years, and then enjoy his freedom; and (which he hath dearly earned) £10 or the value of it in goods if his Master be so honest as to pay it. The Negroes ... are Slaves to their owners to perpetuity. The ordinary price a Negro is bought for, is 10 or 11 hundred pound of sugar.

The best picture of a wealthy man going out from England to the West Indies to buy a plantation is given by Sir Henry Colt, who sailed out four years before Henry Morgan was born. He describes in his journal and letters the life at sea just before buccaneers appear on the scene and the island conditions that were to have a lot to do with their appearance. Life in Barbados in 1631 was very similar to life in Jamaica twenty and thirty years later.

Sir Henry Colt lived in London and had a large family. His two sons were grown up and he was very fond of them, though he had little affection for his wife and made no secret of the fact, writing to one of the sons: 'I love her nott.' He was careful to buy all he and his servants and workmen would need for the voyage which would take him a sixth of the way round the world to the new English colony 'beyond the Line', and also for the first year in Barbados. He visited various merchants, and among those supplying stores was Mr Wicks in Blackfriars just beyond the Playhouse, from whom he bought a supply of 'hott waters' (spirits) for seven shillings a gallon and aquavit at four shillings a gallon.

He arranged for a passage to Barbados in 'Ye ship called Ye *Alexander* whereof William Burch was Captayne and Robert Shapton Master, accompanied wth Diuers captaynes and gentlemen of note'. He probably owned the ship and his description of the voyage is vivid, losing nothing in the spelling, for this was an age when the only standard for tutors and printers was the newly-published Authorized Version of the Bible, and 'ye' was the written and printed convention for 'the', with U interchangeable for V and I for Y.

On Sunday morning, 22 May 1631, Sir Henry 'arrived by poast' at Weymouth after a tedious journey from London. He was met by Captain Burch and other passengers and after dinner (the main meal of the day and taken at about two o'clock in the afternoon) they 'immediately quitted ye towne & went to our shipp then riding in Portland road. Now we are all mett, our Joy not to be expressed.

'Neyther doe we loose time,' he continued, 'for we presently weigh Anchor, hoyse upp our sayles, puttinge ourselues to sea, takinge our Course South South West, alongst our English Channel. The first care of Captayne Burch is ye fitting of his ordinance, appoyntinge to these particular men ye charge thereof.'

The *Alexander* was well armed with sixteen guns but Sir Henry knew well enough that the voyage was risky: the English, French and Dutch privateers that harried the Spanish were often rather doubtful that a ship was flying the correct ensign and tended to open fire before they asked questions. For the captain, whether of a merchant ship like the *Alexander* or a privateer, all sail on the horizon belonged to potential enemies; none could be treated as a friend.

He then went on to describe the rest of the preparations (punctuation has been inserted and spelling modernized for clarity):

The ordnance thus assigned and placed, his [Captain Burch's] next care is the defence of the decks with all the other parts of the ship. He repairs to us alleging that, we having so many good men aboard and so many able commanders, we should endeavour to make our men fit to fight, that every man might know his place and quarter, that no occasion might breed confusion. Whereupon thus we concluded that 60 musketeers of the ablest men should presently be chosen forth, and these to be divided into 4 small squadrons ...

Our next care is the sparing of our victuals, that we might speed with discretion ... Captain Burch having already been well acquainted with the cross blows and checks of fortune ... presently puts us to the allowance of every mess, making no difference between the highest and the lowest in the ship's provisions. Every man hath enough without waste.

However, Captain Burch was not the only one watching the rationing:

'Mr Beningfield, my chief overseer in all my affairs, seeing we began our wine at too high a pitch for our store, makes a daily allowance both for our wine and hot water [spirits] for our cabin in such abundance as I am sure to be thus far a true prophet, that no any man will be drunk all this journey, except it be with cold water.'

Sir Henry then describes an incident while the ship crossed the Bay of Biscay:

> Early this morning we discover a small barque just ahead of us. We bear up to know what they are, the wind blows strong at north-northeast. We soon approach and hail them we do; but there is no reply nor man appears. But drawing more nearer we make a greater noise, and which the French awake. For French they are, but all asleep; a notable security, and a negligence in that nation that in a sea so dangerous, in winds so contrary to them, and in such a season, their destiny should bring them in a way so spacious, well nigh unkindly to jostle with us for sea room. But yet they gave us thanks for our courtesy.

The sleepiness of the French barque was not repeated by other ships, which kept as sharp a lookout as the *Alexander*. On Whit Monday, their eighth day at sea, 'two ships appear, the one in the morning, and other towards night, but they seeing us altered their course and move towards the north, and we tended ours south-west by west'.

Sir Henry was proud to note at the end of the second week at sea that 'unto this hour not any man is sick, but it happened otherwise to our four-footed companions, for our water dog, a hog, a sheep and a lamb, being the most part of our living provisions die upon the way . . . Our water by reason of the easy motion of our ship doth now stink, having no time to work. This was the greatest discommodity we find in all this journey'.

Like many sailing ships before and since, the *Alexander* had trouble finding the Trade winds, not going far enough south before heading west. Finally on 17 June Sir Henry wrote: 'Here begins the first entrance into a long reach, with a Trade wind . . . Here do we meet with our first Tropic birds, in colour, wings [and] flying not unlike our English swallows but 4 times bigger, and some are white.'

At the end of their fourth week at sea Sir Henry gave it as his opinion that 'our ship grows too light. I would have had our empty casks filled with sea water, but they would not do it for spoiling their vessels [i.e. casks]'.

By 23 June the *Alexander* was still steering west-south-west to reach the latitude of Barbados and then sail along it until they reached the island, the regular way of making an ocean passage. 'In all this time,' Sir Henry wrote, 'we run so directly before the wind that our mainsail only draws, the foresail and spritsail affords us little help. This made our ship roll the more because the seas drive continually upon her stern.'

Five days later he was able to report that the *Alexander* had reached a position 'which brings us into the height of all our journey ... now we equal the Barbados, bearing just west of us. But the longitude is now harder to find'. He added that 'last year's example of how many ships that missed it do well declare the difficulty thereof. The Barbados may well admit of this simile, to be like a sixpence thrown down upon Newmarket Heath, and you should command [someone] to go and find it out, for it lies due west from such a place 13 miles'.

The *Alexander* was lucky because there was a moon, but both Captain Burch and the Master were worried about their position. With no land in sight all that day, Tuesday, the ship spent the night sailing westward for six hours and then west by south for another six, 'yet nothing is discovered but the heavens'. Nor did Wednesday bring any sight of Barbados, the noon sight showing they were much too far north.

Thursday brought nothing; then on Friday, which was also the first day of July, 'between two and three o'clock in the morning the master's boy from out of the forecastle of the ship calls out "Land!" The moon shines bright – for [many] nights they had played at cards and tables upon the deck with no other light. But now I could discover nothing else but a dark cloud, and the worst of all is that within this half hour the moon will hide herself and leave us to darkness when we had most need of light. But resolved they are it is land, but what land they know not'.

Now they had to look around them, he commented, 'more longing for daylight than the woman with child for her good hour. Upon the break of day the first thing I could discover is that, within less than a mile of us, lies a great ridge of white sands intermixed with rocks, upon which the sea doth break ...' Beyond that was low land which rose and revealed woodland. 'By this time it was apparently known to be the Barbados.'

He wrote proudly that they had arrived 'in five weeks and five days since our setting forth from Weymouth', with no sickness among any of the many people on board. 'We were so gently led along, so favoured with winds and seas, that a London wherry without danger might have born us company. I have seen greater seas between Gravesend and London than between London and the Barbados.'

Sir Henry and the *Alexander* planned to stay only thirteen days in Barbados, but his Journal showed the worthy knight to be a sharp-eyed man who missed very little. He began by saying that it was his habit to observe and write something each day, and he wrote the truth 'but with favour'. Nevertheless he wrote with a refreshing frankness:

You are all young men, and of good desert if you would but bridle the excess of drinking, together with the quarrelsome condition of your fiery spirits. You are devourers up of hot waters and such good distillers thereof that I am persuaded a ship of good burthen laded therewith could not return from you but instead of hot water you would have [loaded] it with cold. I, in imitation of this bad example of yours and for your society, was brought from 2 drams of hot water a meal to 30, and in a few days, if I had continued this acquaintance, I do believe I should have been brought to the increase of 60.

But the worst of all was your manifold quarrels. Your young and hot bloods should not have oil added to increase the flame but rather cold water to quench it. As your quarrels have slight beginnings, so they are without much difficulty soon ended, but only to the trouble of your Governor. In a few days you corrupted me, who has seen more and lived many more years to be more wise and temperate.

He was very critical of the state of the plantations. The conditions under which many of the indentured servants lived was appalling, and he noted that in the thirteen days he was in Barbados forty of them 'stole away in a Dutch pinnace, although they can live in no place so well'. As we shall see later, these were the type of young men who became the first buccaneers.

Sir Henry was looking for a plantation to buy, and having found it he made notes of his requirements. The *Alexander* would return to England for supplies and Captain Burch would also buy a small pinnace – he thought one of thirty or forty tons, armed with six guns, would be sufficient – and bring it out to Barbados, because Sir Henry had some other bold plans afoot. He then wrote a long frank letter to his son George in London in case he should 'prove a seaman and undertake such voyages' – in fact it was a fairly unsubtle attempt to get him out to the West Indies – and which gave 'some rules for your diet and health' while in the Tropics. It also gave an excellent picture of daily life of what was to become the West Indies of the buccaneers.

Your stomach is ever to kept warm, either with a cotton or woollen stomacher, and never go unbuttoned after sweating, for the wind is cold and your stomach must be kept warm. For digestion and to avoid the flux in which consists the chiefest danger, use pepper in all your broths ... Eat not much flesh, fruit or saltmeats. Oatmeal, pease, rice, wheat flour, butter and Holland cheese [are] your best diet of all. A hen stewed with pepper and biscuit is good meat.

There were other matters concerning a voyage: 'Carry no sick man out with you lest they die and infect others. Your best hot waters to carry with you are rosemary water, Angelica water, aniseed water, and for your men aquavita. Wine will not last long ... Cases of glasses are the best but they are more subject to be broken.' He was recommended to go to Mr Wicks in

Blackfriars for his spirits and reminded that he should have everything well marked with his own name.

He was told what had to be done straight away and given an indication of Sir Henry's anger against the Spaniards for forbidding trade:

> At the return of the ship I would have two stout nags and two mares sent of £5 apiece. I care not for their paces, they are worth here £30, and also two cows. The ways [lanes] begin here to be good for riding and it is too laborious to travel on foot ... I must have two pack saddles, and the rest saddles and bridles, little and light.
>
> I want at least 40 men more. I have a great plantation ... This of the Spaniards I would have printed or else published to all, that the Spaniards might take notice thereof, that I be not blamed hereafter if I seek my own compensation, for next year I shall offend them.

He told George that the *Alexander* had already taken on a hundred tons of salt and about 50 tons of fustick (a wood used for yellow dye), and was going to St Martins for more salt and also a large quantity of tobacco 'which by reason of the Customs [duty] of 12d a pound in England we must put off in Holland'. In fact the ship would not go on to England because Captain Burch would also buy the pinnace in Holland.

Sir Henry then revealed the reason for the pinnace, the forty men and his warning that next year he would 'offend them': he had heard of the high profits to be made dealing in contraband and 'I mean to trade unto the Main ...'

While Sir Henry Colt built up and extended his interests in Barbados, many other islands of the Lesser Antilles were settled. To the north the Dutch were settling in St Eustatius (Statia) and St Martins, and to the south, after various brushes with Spain, settled in Curaçao close to the coast of Venezuela with a good natural harbour. They soon garrisoned the nearby islands of Buen Ayre (Bonaire) and Oruba (Aruba), which had in plenty the salt ponds they needed. By securing these three islands Holland had assured herself of an effective base close to the Spanish Main and a steady supply of salt, which had been rising enormously in price.

One of the most remarkable English settlements in the Caribbean was more than fifteen hundred miles west of the Lesser Antilles. A group of people had settled on an island close to the Isthmus and just off the coast of Nicaragua, athwart the course of the Spanish galleons sailing from Cartagena up to Havana.

Ironically these people were not interested in attacking the plate fleet: they were devout men, women and children, members of a company of Puritans headed by the earl of Warwick and with John Pym as treasurer which arrived in 1629 at the island of Old Providence. Nominally owned by

Spain, which called it Providencia, it was named Old Providence to distinguish it from New Providence, in the Bahamas. The island was three-quarters of the way from Jamaica to the Main and subsequently one of the favourite haunts of Morgan and the Brethren of the Coast.

The Cow Killers

The twenty-four years between Sir Henry Colt's landfall at Barbados and the arrival of a British expedition that captured Jamaica almost by accident were turbulent both in Europe and the West Indies.

In Barbados, where the planters of the 1630s had concentrated on tobacco, there was early disappointment: the tobacco was 'so earthy and worthless as it would give them little or no return', while the rival tobacco from Virginia was proving excellent and setting a very high standard. However, as Sir Henry Colt noted, one of Barbados's most enterprising planters, Colonel Holdip, had begun growing sugar and as soon as fellow planters saw his success they were quick to follow, while others planted cotton. By 1650 the year's sugar crop in Barbados was valued at £3 million.

The rise of the buccaneers has often been attributed to the strategic designs of kings and ministers, but the real reason was much more mundane and begins with the earthy taste of tobacco that led to the planters changing their crops. The story of the conflicting influences which would lift up Henry Morgan and then throw him down like waves tossing jetsam on a beach therefore starts with the planters being reinforced from time to time by men fleeing from a Britain first on the brink of and then rent by Civil War. Some of them were wealthy and others impoverished, but with the collapse of the Royalist cause many more fled to a Barbados which was rapidly changing in character.

Until 1640 most of the plantations had been small (the average was only a few acres), growing tobacco, indigo and ginger. With the collapse of the tobacco crop many of the small planters gave up, selling out to wealthier neighbours so that the average size of plantations increased as sugar, which needed much more land, became a successful crop.

Until then the planters had been using white indentured servants for the tobacco harvest, but sugar required many more men to work every acre. The planters solved this problem by importing slaves from West Africa. Bought cheaply at first, more than five thousand had been brought in within five years and worked far more effectively in the tropical heat than the indentured whites. The result was that many of the planters simply tore up the indentures of whites not needed to work in the fields, saving themselves the cost of feeding men who were comparatively useless compared with the slaves and also avoiding paying the lump sum due at the end of an apprenticeship.

It was ruthless behaviour but at times was perhaps justified. In 1645, when six thousand of the 18,300 white men on the island were indentured servants, they were described by one of Captain's Warner's backers at Nevis, Charles Jeafferson, in these terms: '... If Newgate [the criminal prison] and Bridewell [debtors' prison] should spew out their spawn into these islands, it would meet with no less encouragement; for no gaol bird can be so incorrigible but there is hope for his conformity here, as well as his preferment...'

Sir Josiah Child, who published his book *New Discourse of Trade* in 1668, was even more scathing:

Virginia and Barbados were first peopled by a sort of loose vagrant people, vicious and destitute of means to live at home (being either unfit for labour or such as could find none to employ themselves about, or had so misbehaved themselves by whoring, thieving, or other debauchery, that none would set them on work, which merchants and masters of ships by their agents (or spirits, as they were called) gathered up about the streets of London, and other places, clothed and transported to be employed upon plantations; and these, I say, were such as, had there been no English foreign plantations in the world, could probably never have lived at home to do service to their country, but must have come to be hanged, or starved, or died untimely of some miserable disease, that proceed from want or vice; or else have sold themselves for soldiers, to be knocked on the head or starved, in the quarrels of our neighbours ...

In addition to the servants sent out by the 'spirits' with indentures signed, there were those sentenced by the courts to transportation, which usually meant ten years and was often an alternative to being hanged (which was punishment for several score crimes, many quite minor). At the time of the Civil War, transportation was a useful way of disposing of prisoners of war and others whose politics did not fit the new Commonwealth. (Descendants of these prisoners still live on some of the islands today, closely-knit groups, their complexions red from the sun and known generally as 'Red legs'.)

Tearing up their indentures was in many case regarded by the servants as unexpectedly getting their freedom and their first thought was usually to escape from Barbados before something else should bind them in servitude. Yet not all of them were scoundrels: some were youths who had first been adventurous enough to go to the Tropics and now were toughened by hard work and immune from various vile tropical diseases. Many signed on Dutch or English ships, deserting the moment they arrived at a promising

looking island. Yet Antigua, Nevis, St Kitts and St Martins, often the first ports
of call, had little need of such youths: their own apprentices were having
the same problems. But all these young men – and older ones on the run
from the law or discontented with their lot – had heard of the cow killers
living along the coasts of Hispaniola and Cuba, and many of them made
their way westward to join them.

Not all the cow killers were white: some were Negro former slaves
(*cimarron*) who had fled their Spanish masters, to live in the bush or jungle
along the coasts of the islands of the Great Antilles, feeding on the wild cattle
and hogs left by the early settlers. These men were usually known as
'maroons' and they and their white comrades were often joined by Dutch,
British and French seamen who, proving mutinous or lazy, had been put on
shore by their captains to live as best they could among the cow killers
and maroons, a process soon called 'being marooned'.

Within a very few years the cow killers became a cosmopolitan collection
of men scattered in small groups along most of the coasts. Their way of life
will be described later; at this point it is only necessary to mention how they
were suddenly reinforced by the former indentured servants displaced by the
introduction of African slaves.

The settlers had tried to keep out of the problems in Britain, but as the
Civil War progressed it became increasingly obvious they could not stay
neutral. The majority of planters were Royalist, and although depending
on supplies from England they were able to remain uncommitted until the
end of 1643, when the Roundheads set up a Committee for the Colonies
which included Cromwell, the earl of Warwick and John Pym, the former
treasurer of the Old Providence island colony (which had since been re-
captured by the Spanish).

The King was executed in 1649 but two years earlier a young Devon man,
Thomas Modyford, arrived in Barbados. Although not one of them himself, he was to have a great influence on the Age of the Buccaneers, and he
became a staunch friend of Henry Morgan, a relationship which at one time
led to him being imprisoned in the Tower of London. Born the first of the
five sons of a former mayor of Exeter, Modyford was a cousin of George
Monck, Cromwell's general. A barrister by training, a Royalist and described as 'a restless spirit', he left an England whose Puritan grimness was little
to his liking and travelled to Barbados with a few thousand pounds in his
pocket.

He eventually paid Major Hilliard £7000 for half an estate, so that
Modyford's first stake in the Caribbean comprised about five hundred
acres. (This purchase gives a good indication how land prices were soaring:
seven years earlier Hilliard had bought the entire plantation of one thousand
acres for £400.) Two hundred acres were growing sugar while the rest was

divided into tobacco, ginger and cotton. Within twenty years of that purchase his 'restless spirit' was able to take advantage of being part of the web of influence slowly being woven round George Monck to become one of the most powerful influences in the Caribbean, a man hated by Spain and, if any single person after Cromwell deserved the title, the architect of Britain's golden age in the Caribbean.

The details of the quarrels between Cavalier and Roundhead in Barbados for the next few years need not concern us. Cromwell sent out a squadron under Sir George Ayscue and forced it to surrender, but under reasonable terms. Several months later the lookouts on the island's east coast raised the alarm that ships were approaching.

They were in fact a squadron belonging to the King's cousin, Prince Rupert, who had sailed from Europe knowing only that Barbados had been Royalist and declared for the King, who was of course living in exile in France. When he found that the island had already surrendered, Prince Rupert sailed on, trying unsuccessfully to obtain provisions from the other British and Dutch islands. He managed to get a few things from the French islands and continued cruising with his brother Prince Maurice, who commanded another ship in the squadron. Finally, after being caught in a hurricane in the autumn of 1652, during which Prince Maurice's ship vanished, he took his squadron back to Europe.

Because his ship was not actually seen to sink, Prince Maurice's fate is to this day a mystery, a rich source of romantic stories. Henry Morgan later tried to solve it; for several years British officials sent depositions to England giving any information reported by British and foreign seamen. One modern authority on Puerto Rican history wrote that Prince Maurice 'was shipwrecked on the eastern coast of Puerto Rico. The prince was captured by the Spanish authorities and put in a dungeon at Morro Castle, where he apparently languished for many years. The story of his capture and confinement passed from mouth to mouth until it spread through the islands'.

Spain still had not grasped the strategic significance of the islands to windward being colonized by the British, Dutch and French, and the King and his ministers were concerned only with the immediate situation. The Dutch, for instance, had captured more than five hundred ships in the thirteen years up to 1636, an average of nearly one a week.

The Spanish living in the West Indies did the best they could to protect themselves with the resources at their disposal. Some French had seized the island of Santa Cruz (south-east of Puerto Rico and now called St Croix, one of the US Virgin Islands) and an expedition left San Juan in 1635 to drive them out. The French fled to St Kitts but were soon back and the Spanish had to attack them again in 1637 and 1641. An expedition from Puerto Rico against St Kitts in 1629 showed the Spanish the difficulties of attacking an island two hundred miles dead to windward: sails blew out, hulls leaked as the planking worked, soldiers were violently sick. By 1644 the fishermen of Puerto Rico were fearful of going to sea because of the risk of being captured by Dutch corsairs, a subject about which the bishop of Puerto Rico wrote to Madrid.

However, not all the news reaching Spain from the West Indies was bad: bullion from New Spain alone was worth 132,000 pesos in 1640, compared with 20,000 pesos ten years earlier. Within five years, though, Madrid was becoming very worried not just by the ships being lost to corsairs but for the very safety of the three big islands of the Greater Antilles. The Spanish ambassadors in various European countries were sending back pessimistic dispatches. The minister in Münster reported in December 1645 that if they lost Brazil, the Dutch West India Company intended to capture Hispaniola or Puerto Rico. The news from London also continued to be bad: the Puritans, having executed their King in 1649, were busy destroying every trace of Catholicism, real or imagined, that they could find. Even the most optimistic of the Spanish Court could see that once Cromwell had put the country back on its feet he would be looking towards the West Indies.

In the meantime the trespassers in the Lesser Antilles were becoming stronger, not by the actions of individual governments but because of individual men who had emigrated, eager to start plantations, trade or smuggling. While Puerto Rico tried to stop the French living in Santa Cruz, more Frenchmen settled in a tiny island off the north-western corner of Hispaniola which had been named Tortuga by the Spanish because it looked something like a turtle. Tortuga had been deserted until a group of French and English settled there but these soon began quarrelling among themselves. In 1640 the governor of the French part of St Kitts, de Poincy, decided to seize Tortuga as a place to which he could send troublesome French Protestants. The Huguenots were causing him many problems in St Kitts and here was a perfect opportunity of both using them and getting them out of his way.

The task was made easier because the cleverest and most troublesome Huguenot in St Kitts was a man called Jean Le Vasseur, a military engineer whose training had been rounded off by his experience in the siege of La Rochelle, the last Huguenot stronghold to fall in France. Le Vasseur soon had the new settlers building fortifications which, not only capable of defending Tortuga against Spanish attacks, were also intended to cover the sheltered anchorage which gave the island its importance.

This strengthening of Tortuga, right in the centre of the Great Antilles, coincided with the westward migration of outcasts and refugees from the British, French and Dutch islands who were intent on joining the cow killers; the men who within a score of years would make Tortuga the centre of piracy and buccaneering in the Caribbean.

However Le Vasseur, having built the powerful citadel on the top of Tortuga, spent the next nine years going mad, tyrannizing the motley band of outcasts, rogues, vagabonds, thieves and genuine Protestant refugees who made up his colony. He then decided that Tortuga should be an independent nation with himself as its king, but at that point his 'subjects' murdered him.

For the time being the Spanish could do little, but once a force could be collected in Santo Domingo, the capital of Hispaniola, it sailed against Tortuga and in January 1654 captured it after a ten-day siege. Yet this attack and the various expeditions against Santa Cruz were more the actions of a sick man slapping at mosquitoes than the stirrings of a powerful nation, because Spain was by then almost bankrupt. The Thirty Years War, ending in the winter of 1648, had left Spain exhausted. There was no money in the Treasury and she had no credit; her industry had withered almost to nothing in a process which had begun with the arrival of the first of the plate fleets in Seville.

For several years the merchants at Seville and Vera Cruz had been requesting the Council of the Indies to cut down the number of merchant ships – and thus the quantity of cargo – sent to New Spain. The warehouses of Vera Cruz were still piled high with goods sent out in previous years and which people did not buy because of the high prices demanded – and because they could get them cheaply from the foreign smugglers. By 1651 the requirements of New Spain did not merit an annual *flota*: ships came only for the bullion.

Spain now found that although nominally she held four thousand miles of Caribbean coastline and the three big islands of the Greater Antilles, she was being challenged by foreigners based on islands so small that, by comparison, they barely showed on the charts. With her vast and complicated bureaucracy radiating out like a spider's web from every port and city, with a complex society which strove to reproduce in each Spanish town in the tropical Indies the society of an old Spanish city, it had previously seemed quite impossible that there could be any threat from tiny islands settled by foreigners living in a state of quarrelsome anarchy, their actions governed more by their own whims than the dictates of governments in Europe. Finally it became clear to Madrid that a threat existed, but by then the Spanish government could see no way of destroying it. There were neither ships nor men to evict the foreigners from the islands, and even if they had been available the foreigners would return within a few weeks.

The problem was mainly inertia. For scores of years the successive Spanish kings had insisted on keeping all the power in their own hands, and now it meant that no man in the Indies, be he the viceroy of a province or the customs collector in a small settlement, dare make a decision.

*　　*　　*

While Spain faced a growing crisis both at home and in the Indies, in Britain Parliament was becoming alarmed at the amount of goods carried in Dutch ships to British colonies in the West Indies and North America and, in the same month that Ayscue's squadron arrived off Barbados, passed the Navigation Act.

This flatly prohibited goods being imported into Britain from the continent of Europe except in British ships or those belonging to the country of origin. Dutch ships could bring in Dutch goods and French ships French goods, but Dutch ships could not carry French goods, nor French ships Dutch goods. Cargoes carried to and from the rest of the world – which meant primarily the colonies – had to be carried in British or colonial ships which in turn had to be manned by a majority of British subjects, although exports could be carried by the manufacturing country's ships.

The Dutch, who had watched their once friendly relations with England start to deteriorate with James I's pro-Spanish policy, now saw Cromwell acting to smash the Netherlands as the carriers of world trade. A year later the first of the three Anglo-Dutch wars began. Lasting two years, it was a series of naval actions when for the most part Robert Blake was pitted against van Tromp and de Ruyter, and ended in favour of the British in 1654.

At this point, with Britain and Holland enjoying a brief period of peace and with Barbados firmly under Commonwealth rule, we can see how the various nations stood in the West Indies. Apart from Spain, only three nations were concerned – England, France and Holland.

England owned Barbados, Antigua, St Kitts (sharing it with the French), Nevis and Montserrat (as well as Bermuda, which stands well north of the Caribbean). Not one square inch of any of this territory had been won by military conquest; all had been acquired by private individuals arriving and settling, and none of it had been seriously settled by Spain. France had or was about to settle in Martinique, Guadeloupe, St Lucie (now St Lucia), Grenade (Grenada), part of St Kitts, Désirade and Marie Galante. She too had acquired these territories without military conquest, but most of the islands were inhabited by the warlike Caribs, so that at this time they had few settlers. The Dutch held Curaçao (capturing it from Spanish cattle breeders), Bonaire and Aruba off the Main, and Saba and St Eustatius (Statia) in the Leewards.

Spain claimed the coast from Trinidad to Vera Cruz but in fact held Puerto Rico, most of Hispaniola (stretches of the coast at the western end were effectively held by the French and groups of 'cow killers'), Cuba and Jamaica. Along the Spanish Main she held fifteen hundred miles of the coast from Trinidad along what is now Venezuela and Colombia to just west of Cartagena. The Gulf of Darien was left to Indians. The Spanish held another stretch of coast covering Portobelo and Nombre de Dios, but had left the Mosquito Coast to the north (what is now Honduras) to the Indians.

In New Spain the Yucatán peninsula and north-eastern Mexico were occupied, but a long stretch of the coast either side of Campeche had to be left to the Indians, while Spain held the coast each side of Vera Cruz. From there north and east round the Gulf of Mexico to Florida was no-man's-land.

Kings and princes could claim all the land they liked (Spain 'owned' four thousand miles of coastline on the Main and New Spain alone) and try to protect it with papal bulls and threats, but the real owners of some of it, the people who effectively controlled certain areas, were often of quite a different nationality. Apart from isolated towns, large sections of the coasts of south and central America were still controlled by the original Indians, who had a bitter hatred for the Spanish. Besides stretches of Colombia, they held the Gulf of Darien, the San Blas islands, much of the mountain and jungle in Panama, and the Mosquito Coast (the Caribbean side of Nicaragua).

In the three big islands of the Greater Antilles, long stretches of the coast were controlled by the cow killers, most of whom were the forerunners of the buccaneers and who were about to change the history of the West Indies. Originally they were a mixture of cheated apprentices, religious refugees, social outcasts and criminals, but it is important to understand that to begin with they were not vicious men. Many were Protestant refugees – Dutchmen who fled the Spanish invasion of the Netherlands because they feared or had suffered from the Inquisition, and Huguenots who had left France to escape harsh treatment by their Catholic fellow countrymen. Many of these had earlier landed in the French islands of the West Indies only to find they were not popular there either: the regular Catholic governors and priests looked askance at the arrival of any staunch Calvinists.

The British provided the most cosmopolitan groups. There were Royalists who had fled the early days of the Civil War, and many of them were High Church, even if not actual Catholics. There were Scots who escaped as Cromwell's army under George Monck and Henry Morgan's uncle Thomas Morgan subjugated the country. There were Irishmen who fled their country before Cromwell's army finished its work in 1649. And there were men from all four countries, England, Wales, Scotland and Ireland, who had been sentenced to transportation for periods ranging from ten years to life after being found guilty by Cromwell's courts of anything from treason to sheep stealing.

The newest arrivals were former prisoners-of-war who had escaped after being shipped out to the islands by Cromwell, who regarded the West Indies as a convenient dumping ground for the prisoners still in his hands at the end of the war. All these men of various nationalities and backgrounds joined the original cow killers, Negro slaves who had escaped from their Spanish, English, French or Dutch masters, and the foreign seamen who had been marooned by their captains.

Whatever their reasons for going to the West Indies, once they had joined the cow killers their nationalities rarely mattered because they were united in their hatred of the Spaniards and in the desperate business of surviving. If any of them were caught by the Spanish, their crime was that they were in the West Indies beyond the Line, and they were usually treated as heretics, with torture waiting at the hands of the Inquisition. If they survived that, a life sentence had to be served in the salt pans of Cuba, Venezuela or Colombia, or in the quarries preparing stone for the fortifications at Havana or Cartagena, Portobelo or Vera Cruz.

At first the cow killers lived in small groups of five or six men scattered along the coasts of Hispaniola and Cuba: coastlines alternately girt by high cliffs or banked by low mangroves; indented by deep bays strewn with rocks or shallow bays laced with coral reefs and sandbanks. Inshore there were mountains and rain forests or rolling hills, jungle and flat plains. The cow killers always chose places where cattle and hogs ran wild in large numbers, the animals left behind by those early Spanish settlers as they moved from Hispaniola to Cuba and then on to Mexico. By the time the first cow killers arrived, the islands of the Greater Antilles were enormous natural ranches.

The cow killers' wants were few: they had – or soon obtained – matchlock muskets with which to shoot the cattle and hogs, so their most usual requirements were powder and shot. These they obtained from passing ships, trading the hides from the cattle. They had simple canoes (usually made from tree trunks) holding three or four men and which they used to row out to the ships, so the places they chose for their bases usually had good beaches or landing places sheltered by reefs.

Meat and bones were tossed aside where they lived, so that flies swarmed, but worse for the men were the sandflies and mosquitoes. Stinging all day long, they were particularly bad an hour before sunset until after dark, and at dawn, and it was not uncommon for a man to be almost demented with fifty or a hundred stings at a time. However, the tropical heat was usually bearable and the temperature varied little more than ten degrees, with a water temperature rarely dropping much below eighty degrees.

A governor of Tortuga wrote to the great French minister Colbert about the French cow killers in Hispaniola and described them in shocked tones because he regarded it as his duty to bring them under French control:

Seven or eight hundred Frenchmen are living along the shores of this Spanish island in inaccessible places surrounded by mountains, or huge rocks, or the sea and go abroad everywhere in little canoes.

They live three or four or six or ten together, more or less separated one group from the other by distances of two or three or six or eight leagues wherever they find suitable places, and live like savages without recognizing any authority, with a leader of their own, and they commit a thousand robberies.

They have stolen several Dutch and English ships, which have caused as much trouble; they live on the meat of wild boars and cattle, and grow a little tobacco which they trade for arms, munitions and supplies.

Thus it will be necessary for His Majesty to give an order which will compel these men to leave the Spanish island. They should be ordered under pain of death to settle in Tortuga...

Another Frenchman, the Abbé du Tertre, writing several years earlier, described them as:

...an unorganized rabble of men from all countries, rendered expert and active by the necessity of their exercise, which was to go in chase of cattle to obtain their hides, and from being chased themselves by the Spaniards who never gave them any quarter.

As they would never suffer any chiefs, they passed for undisciplined men who for the greater part had sought refuges in these places and were reduced to this way of life to avoid the punishment due for the crimes which could be proved against many of them [in Europe].

In general they were without any habitation or fixed abode, but only rendezvoused where the cattle were to be found, and some sheds covered with leaves to keep off the rain and to store the hides of the beasts they had killed until some vessel should pass to barter for them with wine, brandy, line, arms, powder, bullets and cooking vessels which they needed and which were the only moveables of the buccaneers...

They were dressed in a pair of drawers and a shirt at the most, shod with the skin of a hog's leg fastened on the top and behind the foot, with strips of the same skin girded round the middle of their body with a sack which served them to sleep in as a defence against the innumerable insects which bit and sucked the blood from all parts of their bodies which were left uncovered...

(The Abbé forgot to mention that they also smeared their bodies with lard to protect themselves against the bites of sandflies and mosquitoes.)

When they returned from the chase to the *boucan*, you would say that these are the butcher's vilest servants who had been eight days in the slaughterhouse without washing themselves ... I have seen some of these who had lived this miserable life for twenty years without seeing a priest or eating bread.

The worthy Abbé failed to point out that many of the men had little choice: religious refugees faced persecution in their own countries, while those transported from Britain by Cromwell faced death if they returned before their sentences expired.

The original name for these men, cow killers, was an obvious one, and it did not change into 'buccaneers' for many years. The word buccaneer conjures up a picture of a bold and reckless man with glittering eyes and flashing teeth, curling black beard and gleaming sword, a diamond-hilted dagger and a pistol tucked into the belt, but the original meaning could hardly be more mundane.

The Indians living in the Caribbean islands had a method of curing meat which the cow killers copied. The problem for the Indians was that, having no knowledge originally of salting meat, they saw a whole carcase go bad within twelve hours in the tropical heat unless something was done to preserve it. The solution was a simple one. First they dug a shallow pit in which a good fire would burn. Then they cut four long stakes, making a V at the top, and drove one into each corner of the pit to act as supports for a grating which would go over the top of the fire. The grating, shaped like a farm hurdle, was made from branches of a hardwood like lignum vitae, which grows in all the islands of the Greater Antilles, or green wood. This grating, placed on the four supports, was called a *barbecu* by the Indians and a *grille de bois* by the French.

The fire was lit and stoked up to produce a slow heat. The meat was boned and cut into long strips, put on top of the *barbecu* and left to cure from the heat of the fire and the smoke. When cured the meat was called *boucan* by the Indians. The whole 'kitchen' – the pit and the grating – was also called a *boucan*.

The cow killers did not use salt while preparing *boucan* from beef, unless they intended to keep it for a long period, but pork was usually salted first. Sometimes, wrote an historian of the area, to give

a particular relish to the meat the skin of the animal was cast into the fire under it. The meat thus cured was of a fine red colour, and of excellent flavour; but in six months after it was *boucanned* it had little taste left, except of salt. The *boucanned* hog's flesh continued good a much longer time than the flesh of beeves, if kept in dry places.

From adopting the *boucan* of the Caribbees, the hunters in Hispaniola, the Spaniards excepted, came to be called *boucaniers*, but afterwards, in a pronunciation more in favour with the English, buccaneers.

The writer adds: 'Many of the French hunters were natives of Normandy; whence it became proverbial in some of the seaports of Normandy to say of a smoky house, "*c'est un vrai boucan*".'

There were other words used instead of buccaneer – a much older English word, freebooter, and the Dutch *Vrijbuiter*, one who plundered freely. It has often been said that both freebooter and the French *flibustier* derived from flyboat, the English translation of the Dutch *fluyt*, and that in turn flyboats were used to chase the Spanish. In fact it would not have occurred to anyone to use a *fluyt* or flyboat, to chase another ship: despite its fast-sounding name, a *fluyt* was a slow vessel.

One of the buccaneers, a Dutchman, wrote in an account of his adventures that after the French gained control of Tortuga the men were described as follows: those who lived entirely by hunting cattle and hogs were called *boucaniers*; those that went cruising were *flibustiers*; those who tilled the soil, planting crops, called themselves *habitans*. However, the *boucanier* occasionally went cruising, thus becoming a *flibustier*, so after a few years the two words came to mean the same thing.

The Spaniards outside the main towns did not live very differently from the cow killers. A buccaneer who knew Hispaniola well later described the people of San Juan de Goave, west of the city of Santo Domingo, as mostly hunters and butchers who flayed the beasts that were killed. They were 'for the most part a mongrel sort of people of several bloods; some are born of white European people and Negroes, and these are called *mulattos*. Others are born of Indians and white people, and such are termed *mestizos*'. The village exported yearly 'vast quantities of tallow and hides, they exercising no other traffic nor toil'.

Up to 1654 the cow killers were rough, tough men for the most part living peacefully as long as they could keep out of the hands of Spanish troops. The governor of Tortuga referred to them capturing Dutch and English ships, but this was probably to strengthen his case: the cow killers depended on just those ships for bartering their hides for powder and shot, and obviously no ship would come near their canoes if she risked capture. Spanish ships, however, knew better than to venture near the coast in a light wind...

Young Harry

Sir Henry Colt had sailed out to Barbados in 1631. The following year
Christopher Wren was born, one of the greatest of all architects, whose work
is still represented by some of London's most stately buildings. Samuel
Pepys, who has been called the architect of the Navy, was born the following
year and two years after that came the birth of Henry Morgan.

Where, when and to whom? The questions are simple and, despite lively
speculations and fabrications, so is the answer to them: we are far from sure.
We can identify his uncles, his first cousins and his second cousins, and the
lineage of his wife, but we know the year Henry was born only because
in a deposition sworn on 21 November 1671 he gave his age as thirty-six.

He swept the Caribbean like a hurricane, apparently coming from
nowhere and then disappearing almost without a trace, leaving no children
and no objects that can be identified as his. Even his grave vanished. Like
many men who left their mark on the world, he appears first as a grown
man, but almost from his first recorded appearance he was able to impose
his will on events.

He was born either in the village of Penkarne (Monmouth) or at
Llanrhymny (Glamorgan) – there is no documentary proof either way. The
only clue that Morgan gives us – and it seems a strong one – is that he
later named his favourite estate in Jamaica not Penkarne but Llanrhymny
(the Welsh village is called Rhymney today and is two miles from Tredegar),
but to confuse the issue he called a smaller one Penkarne. In the only
reference to Wales in his will be writes of 'my ever-honest cozen, Mr Thomas
Morgan of Tredegar'.

There is no doubt that he was related to the Morgans of Tredegar, and
his father was probably Robert Morgan, a member of the cadet branch
of the family. We know he had two uncles, his father's brothers, called
Edward and Thomas, both of whom were army officers fighting on opposite
sides in the Civil War. One of them became Henry Morgan's father-in-law
posthumously.

They in turn were probably the nephews of Sir Thomas Morgan, who
takes the story back four decades to when Elizabeth was on the throne and
she was helping the Dutch in their fight against the Spanish. One of the
southernmost fortresses of the United Netherlands was Bergen-op-Zoom,

close to the mouth of the Scheldt. As in Nelson's day and Hitler's, so in the sixteenth century, England has always been concerned that the mouth of the Scheldt should be controlled by a friendly nation: the broad Scheldt estuary provides a perfect anchorage and departure for any enemy fleet intending to invade England. In 1594 the garrison at Bergen-op-Zoom was an English regiment later known as The Buffs (the Queen's Own Royal East Kent Regiment), commanded by Colonel Thomas Morgan. He and his men fought off the Spanish attempt to capture the town and its fortress, and Morgan eventually received a knighthood. It seems highly likely that his example led his nephews Edward and Thomas to make the Army their career, so that the Morgan of Bergen-op-Zoom began a tradition of army service that would last three generations.

While the young Henry Morgan passed the first years of his childhood in Wales, his two uncles served as soldiers of fortune on the Continent. At that time being a mercenary was an honourable occupation: a man deciding to follow a military career could find neither advancement nor training if his own country was at peace, so he sought employment in the army of a country at war. There was rarely a question of divided loyalty: if his own country went to war then the man usually returned to serve under his own flag, a very welcome officer because he would have experience in the latest methods of warfare at a time when gunnery, for example, was a comparatively new science, particularly as applied to siege warfare, a subject in which the younger Thomas Morgan was specializing.

Thomas fought in the Low Countries and then Germany. At one time he was employed by the French; at another he was an officer with a high reputation in the army of the young duke of Saxe Weimar, who, four years before Henry was born, had won his spurs by seizing Mannheim, which had been held by Spanish troops for two years.

Edward also served in the Low Countries (where he was mentioned in Dutch records as Heer van Lanrumnij, which establishes that he, at least, came from the village near Tredegar) and fought over countryside familiar to Sir Thomas, of Bergen-op-Zoom fame. His service in Holland gave him a military reputation which made him welcome in most armies. He left to serve in Germany, and while in Westphalia he met the von Pöllnitz family. The head of the family was Johan Ernst, Freiherr von Pöllnitz, who was governor of Lippstadt. In something approaching a fairy-tale romance, the young Welsh soldier of fortune fell in love with the governor's daughter, Anna Petronilla, and married her. The marriage was to provide several daughters who would later find husbands in Jamaica (as yet an island where a few Spaniards bred cattle), one of them marrying Henry Morgan.

While his two uncles fought in the Thirty Years War as soldiers of fortune, Henry grew up in a Britain gradually sliding towards a civil war which broke out in 1642, when he was seven years old. Galileo died that same year and Isaac Newton was born. We do not know what happened to Henry during this time, but as the fighting between King and Commonwealth became widespread his two uncles came home, Edward to join the King's army, Thomas to serve in the Commonwealth forces.

Thomas had a wider experience of warfare, particularly of artillery and siege warfare, and a man with this kind of knowledge was extremely valuable. He soon came to the notice of George Monck, who was to become Cromwell's greatest general and, in the curious way that so many people were to interlock like bricks in a wall to make up the life of Henry Morgan, ensured Thomas's promotion. After the battle of Dunbar in 1650, when Cromwell left Monck to subjugate Scotland, his second-in-command was Major-General Thomas Morgan.

In the year before Dunbar, Thomas's brother Edward was made captain-general of the King's forces in South Wales, under the earl of Carberry. He had left his wife Anna Petronilla staying with her brother on the von Pöllnitz family estate at Aschbach, near Bamberg. His young nephew Henry was fourteen years old and there can be little doubt that the boy saw his Uncle Edward frequently in Wales and absorbed some of the Cavalier's love of soldiering. When the Royalist cause collapsed and Charles I was executed, Colonel Edward Morgan managed to escape from the new republic and joined his wife at Aschbach, beginning a new life as an exile and a guest of his brother-in-law.

The Parliamentary victory gave his brother, Major-General Thomas Morgan, yet another opportunity of using his military skill, because Cromwell made him second-in-command of the expedition to Flanders, when the Welshman was described as 'a little, shrill-voiced choleric man'. Wounded in one battle, he recovered in time to be wounded at another, and all the time his reputation was growing in a republic which prided itself on the professionalism of its new army.

While the boy Henry grew into youth, we can only assume that his father had managed to avoid becoming committed to either the Royalist or the Roundhead cause. Having one brother who had fought for the King in South Wales was perhaps later balanced by having another brother who was 'next to the General'. When the third and last of the civil wars ended in September 1651 with Prince Charles escaping by sea to France, Henry Morgan was sixteen years old. For the last nine years battles had been fought the length and breadth of the country, men had been denounced to the authorities of one side or another, property had been seized by Roundheads and Royalists, and treason had been a word with two meanings. The Morgans were a good example of the many families where brother found himself fighting brother.

With such uncles and in such surroundings, and from what we know of his personality in adulthood, Henry Morgan spent these years thinking of very little else except war and soldiering. He never wrote of these days or spoke of them to anyone who recorded his thoughts except for one sentence. When he was forty-five years of age he wrote from Jamaica to the Lords of Trade and Plantations in London, commenting to Their Lordships: 'The office of Judge Admiral was not given me for my understanding of the business better than others, nor for the profitableness thereof, for I left school to young to be a great proficient in that or other laws, and have been more used to the pike than the book.'

In 1654 Henry Morgan was nineteen years old, and all we know about his life during the Civil War and the years immediately following is that he survived. Yet one thing is certain: all the influence on his life up to the age of nineteen had been military, not naval. From the time he was seventeen the first Dutch war had been fought, with Blake and the Navy fighting many actions up and down the Channel. Had a young Henry Morgan shown any enthusiasm for a naval life, his uncle Thomas Morgan had more than enough influence through George Monck to get him a berth with a good captain, but significantly the youth stayed at home.

When Cromwell was deciding on his policy for the West Indies in 1654 it revolved round how best to make Spain recognize the new English colonies and allow England to trade freely with Spain's Caribbean and New World possessions. Would it be by negotiation or war?

Cromwell had earlier made a proposal to the Dutch which was breathtaking in its scope: the two countries should sign a perpetual alliance against their common enemies, sharing the world beyond Europe between them, the Dutch having the Far East and England getting America. The Dutch, already hard hit by Cromwell's Navigation Acts, rejected it, so with France and Spain at war, Cromwell negotiated with France to see what help she would give him in return for an alliance against Spain and with Spain to see what Philip IV had to offer for an alliance against France. Neither country was even lukewarm.

In August, a few weeks after Cromwell decided to carry out his Western Design but before he had drawn up the instructions, he sent for the Spanish ambassador and told him bluntly that England's friendship for Spain now depended upon two things: complete freedom of worship for all Englishmen in the Spanish colonies, and freedom for the English to trade in the West Indies. The ambassador's answer was explicit: it was impossible, he said, for it was to demand of the King of Spain his two eyes.

It may seem strange that Cromwell should dream and plan on such a scale for the West Indies, but apart from his own leanings he had advisers who knew the area well, although this did not ensure that their advice was correct. Among these advisers were Thomas Modyford, the Barbados planter and island leader, the earl of Warwick and John Pym from the ill-fated Old Providence colony, and Thomas Gage, who had spent several years in Central America as a Dominican priest and who described the Portobelo fair.

Gage was the most vociferous of the advisers. He had quit the Catholic Church and turned his zeal to the Puritan cause, publishing a book on Spain's rôle in Central America, *A New Survey of the West Indies*. When it came out in 1648 it was the first written in English to give such details. With all the energy and prejudice of a true convert, Gage advocated a wholesale attack on Central America (which, even omitting Mexico, totalled 205,000 square miles, almost the size of France), saying that it could be captured within two years – startling advice from a man who knew some of the area well, because much of it comprises mountain ranges, impenetrable jungles and rain forests, and yellow fever, malaria and dysentery were as common as the cold of northern climates.

The whole of Gage's plan for capturing Central America was based on first capturing Cuba or Hispaniola. Thomas Modyford did not agree with the plan. Understanding both the tactical and strategic advantages of keeping up to windward, he proposed first an attack on Trinidad, thus securing a good base from which to attack Cartagena more than a thousand miles to leeward.

Neither Gage nor Modyford succeeded in persuading Cromwell of the merits of their respective plans and he then drew up orders which could only result in a complete failure. Nevertheless, his decision to go ahead signalled what was to be one of the turning points in British history because, for the first time, the government was acting overseas to found an empire, sending a fleet and troops instead of leaving settlers and merchant adventurers to find places to trade and land to plant.

Unfortunately Cromwell's skill in equipping the expedition did not match his vision. He allocated a sea regiment and instructed his brother-in-law, Major-General Desborough, to recruit five land regiments. Desborough told all the regiments in England to send volunteers, giving commanding officers a golden opportunity to get rid of their bad characters. Because they did not total 2500 men Desborough then began recruiting through the streets of London and other cities 'by beat of drum', so that the little army was reinforced by what one of them described as 'hectors, and knights of the blade, with common cheats, thieves, cutpurses and suchlike lewd persons, who had for a long time lived by sleight of hand and dexterity of wit, and were now making a fair progress unto Newgate, whence they were to proceed towards Tyburn [gallows]...' When the expedition reached Barbados it was hoped that many men there would be persuaded to join. They might not be fully-trained soldiers but they should be an improvement on those provided by the streets of London.

The troops were put under the command of General Robert Venables, an experienced soldier who had spent the last five years in Ireland and was so inspired by the Western Design that he decided to take his wife with him, in case they should decide to settle in the West Indies. Although the officers included a young ensign named Henry Morgan and among the captains were several men who would be Morgan's close friends for the rest of his life, the majority of them did not inspire Venables, who later commented that they 'had a large portion of pride but not of wit, valour or activity'.

Having failed to provide the proper men, Desborough then went to work to provision the expedition with the same skill. The storeships were in the Thames, so the provisions, powder, shot, guns for the artillery and horses for the cavalry were loaded in London. However, General Venables' troops were on board ships at Portsmouth, and it was an essential part of the plan that the storeships should arrive at Portsmouth in time for the whole squadron to sail together.

The naval commander was Vice-Admiral William Penn, and soon everything was far from well on board his ships at Portsmouth. The crews and the men of the Sea Regiment were well-trained and the ships themselves well-found but when the troops were brought on board they were in many cases separated from their officers. Rumours swept through the five regiments and one affecting the 4th Regiment, which said that the troops had been sold to a foreign country, led to the men forcing their way on shore at the Isle of Wight.

The squadron sailed from Portsmouth in December without the storeships which, thanks to Desborough, were still in the Thames. Judging from the way he later organized his own operations, the young Henry Morgan had learned two valuable lessons before the expedition was clear of the English Channel: that timing and concentration of forces were vital, and if you wanted your men to be loyal and cheerful, they must be told what was going on.

Henry Morgan's first sight of a West Indian island was the expedition's arrival at Barbados on 29 January 1655. General Venables immediately set about finding more recruits and two ships were sent off to beat the drum among the northern islands. They were lucky in finding 1200 men 'of fair quality' at St Kitts, Montserrat and Nevis, but the 3500 recruited in Barbados were of a different type – the planters took the opportunity of getting rid of their worst men. They were 'not to be commanded as soldiers', Venables wrote later with understandable bitterness, 'nor be kept in any civil order, being the most profane, debauched persons that we ever saw ... and so cowardly as not to be made to fight; so that, had we known what they would have proved, we should rather have chosen to have gone ourselves [i.e. alone].'

The planters had little sympathy with Venables; instead of consulting them he sent out recruiting sergeants offering indentured servants their freedom if they would volunteer. Many did, and they were joined by men so in debt that their horizon was obscured by creditors. In the Tropics the expedition's worst enemy was disease, not the Spaniards. Yellow fever and dysentery could – and soon would – decimate a battalion more thoroughly than three squadrons of cavalry, so although the five thousand recruited in the islands included a high proportion of craven scoundrels they were healthy and acclimatized. The cynic might say they were fit enough to flee from a battle.

The Navy's view of Barbados did not vary much from the Army's. The master of Vice-Admiral Penn's flagship, Henry Whistler, kept a diary in which he expressed his opinions forcefully and with a spelling entirely his own (rubbish became rubidg; rogue became rodge) but without ambiguity: 'This illand is the Dunghill whereone England doth cast forth its rubidg. Rodgs and hors and suchlike peopel are those which are generally broght heare. A rodge in England will hardly make a cheater heare. A Baud brought over [here] puts on a demuor comportment, a whore if hansume makes a wife for sume rich planter.'

Penn and Venables waited through February and March for the storeships to arrive in Barbados. In addition they had to decide where to attack. Cromwell had put the expedition under the command of five commissioners – Penn, Venables and three others, one of whom was a former governor of New Plymouth who had sailed to America in the *Mayflower* and then returned to England. The instructions he gave were deliberately vague ('We shall not tie you up to a method of any particular instructions'), written in broad terms and well-larded with sarcastic references to the Spanish. The commissioners had two main choices. In the first they could attack Puerto Rico or Hispaniola and, having secured one or the other, go on to capture either Cartagena on the Main or Havana in Cuba, a total of six permutations. The second choice was to land anywhere on the Spanish Main between the mouth of the River Orinoco and Portobelo (a distance of some 1500 miles).

The commissioners had Thomas Gage to give them advice – the former Catholic priest was now General Venables' chaplain. They rejected a landing on the Main because Venables apparently understood that there were no plantations or water 'east of Cartagena' to maintain his army. This information probably came from Thomas Gage and was only partly correct. The commissioners finally decided to attack Santo Domingo, the capital of Hispaniola and the first city established by the Spanish in the New World. It was also conveniently located to leeward of Barbados.

Venables then called a council of war because the storeships had not arrived. Apart from food his army, now a few short of seven thousand, lacked two thousand muskets and eight hundred pikes. Penn was asked to help out but could do little more than supply some pike heads which were used as patterns from which blacksmiths in the island made 2500 more, while carpenters cut and shaped hafts for them. The planters and Penn supplied 1500 muskets and, because the horses were in the storeships, Venables took from Barbados enough for a troop.

The fleet sailed at the end of March on an expedition unworthy of Cromwell's New Model Army, being badly recruited, badly equipped, badly supplied and, with very few exceptions, badly led at all levels. Yet on the face of it Cromwell had chosen two experienced leaders. Venables, a man of very strong religious views, had fought through the Civil War, while Vice-Admiral Penn, whose eldest son was to become a Quaker and found Pennsylvania, had fought in several actions during the Dutch war and commanded his own squadron in the Mediterranean. He had been made a general of the Fleet the year before the Dutch war ended, yet at heart he was a Royalist. As soon as Cromwell appointed him to the command of the 'Western Design' squadron, Penn had written secretly to the King in exile, offering to sail the expedition wherever Charles wanted. However, there is no hint that he failed to do his best for Cromwell; the squadron was carrying the largest army the West Indies had ever seen, although it was beyond the present ability of government, navy or army to organize it.

The attack on Hispaniola is of importance to this narrative because it provides a standard against which the later buccaneer attacks by Henry Morgan on towns and cities like Portobelo, Panama and Maracaibo can be measured and shows just what comparatively small groups of apparently untrained, undisciplined and untrustworthy men of various nationalities could achieve by comparison with the best of Cromwell's army and navy.

Admiral Penn had read accounts of Sir Francis Drake's attack on Santo Domingo nearly seventy years earlier and, with Venables, decided to copy 'El Draco's' tactics. Penn wanted to avoid a direct attack because this would involve sailing his ships right into the large and well-fortified harbour, and the first and last time that Santo Domingo had been captured from the Spanish was in 1586, when Drake made a diversion and then landed his men in open country to the west of the city. They decided to follow suit: Penn and some of his ships would make the diversion, landing one and a half regiments a few miles to the east of the city, while Venables sailed past with the main force, landed a few miles to the west, where the River Jaino met the sea, and marched back to capture the place.

The squadron split up as it approached Santo Domingo on 14 April, with Venables on board the *Paragon* with Penn's second-in-command, Vice-Admiral Goodson. Venables then watched Penn's ships heading for the shore to make the diversion while beyond, in the distance, he could see the city. Soon the *Paragon* had passed Santo Domingo; then Venables saw they were off the Jaino, but Goodson refused to close the coast. The landing place was unsuitable, he said, and they would risk putting all the ships aground. Finally Goodson anchored thirty miles west of Santo Domingo...

After a landing more suited to a comic opera Venables marched his troops eastward towards the city and, three days later, arrived at the west bank of the Jaino, where they should have landed in the first place. They had just discovered that the river was too deep to ford when a flag was seen on the far bank and a man ordered to swim over came back with the news that the flag belonged to part of the diversionary force that Admiral Penn should have landed several miles on the other side of Santo Domingo. In fact Penn, like Goodson but unlike Drake, had also lost his nerve: having failed to find anywhere to land to the east of the city he had ended up running west and putting his diversionary force on shore at the mouth of the Jaino.

This farce continued for a few days before tragedy rang down the curtain. Venables marched on Santo Domingo but sporadic shooting on the outskirts of the city started a retreat which did not end until the whole force was back at the River Jaino. A chastened Venables spent the next three or four days on board Penn's flagship in the company of his wife. In the meantime more than seven thousand of his men were living on shore without tents but with a formidable enemy approaching.

The enemy was not the Spanish (although reinforcements were being brought in) but the bacillus of dysentery. As men began collapsing by the score, the Spanish launched attacks using cow killers. These were not the cosmopolitan bands described earlier but men regularly employed by the Spanish to hunt and kill the wild cattle and bring in the meat and hides. Accustomed to moving silently through the countryside and using long lances, they were an enemy of a type the British had never before seen. They came in small groups which suddenly erupted out of clumps of brushwood or from behind hills, attacked and escaped before the British had time to defend themselves.

On 24 April General Venables began his second attempt to capture Santo Domingo and it was even more disastrous than the first. His leading troops had once again reached the outskirts of the city and passed Fort Jeronimo when they were ambushed by Spanish cavalry and cow killers and routed. Just four days after they had left it, the British were back on the banks of the Jaino. The only men who had fought bravely were fifty-five extra officers who had volunteered to make up a *reformado* company. Only eighteen of them survived. Following this second débâcle there was an immediate need for scapegoats, and they were not hard to find. The most senior was the adjutant-general of the expedition, who was court-martialled for cowardice, found guilty and sentenced to be cashiered, his sword being broken over his head.

The next few days must have led them to think the world was coming to an end. While Venables tried to reorganize his troops more and more of them collapsed from dysentery, yellow fever and malaria. Then it began to rain heavily and the soldiers struggled to make shelters – their tents were stowed on board the storeships, which still had not arrived – as the ground flooded and tracks turned into canals of mud. Sodden clothes and leather mildewed and rotted; gunpowder caked and the slow match used in the muskets became useless.

Venables and his officers were by now blaming Penn for landing them in the wrong places and in turn Penn and his officers blamed Venables for incompetence in the field. Amid the mutual recrimination all of them saw with an awful clarity that back in England an unsuspecting Cromwell was waiting confidently for the first news of the success of his Western Design.

The senior Navy and Army officers met in a council of war to decide the next step and, as do most such councils, it ended up giving its members a chance of recording excuses and face-saving formulae. Both Penn and Venables knew that the desperate need was for an easy but spectacular success elsewhere if they were to avoid disgrace (if nothing worse) at Cromwell's hands.

The exploits of three men and one island came to mind. In 1598 Sir Anthony Shirley had attacked the Spanish island of Jamaica and captured the island's capital, St Jago de la Vega, holding it to ransom. When the Spanish would or could not pay, he burned it down. His attack inspired a privateer captain, Christopher Newport, eight years later. Newport called for volunteers in Barbados and in 1603 landed at Caguaya (later to become Port Royal). His attempt to capture the whole island was beaten not by the Spanish (there were only a few hundred) but by a bonded warehouse: when his men broke into it they found enough wine and spirits to bring the attack to an abrupt and drunken finale.

Forty years later another privateer captain, William Jackson, had landed at Caguaya with five hundred men and after bitter fighting drove out the Spanish defending it – he estimated they numbered two thousand – and then looted the place. His attack was a complete success.

Jamaica is only a sixth of the size of Hispaniola but with an area of 4400 square miles it is larger than Puerto Rico, one of the alternative targets mentioned in Cromwell's orders. Although Venables and Penn did not realize it and Cromwell did not mention it in his orders, Jamaica was strategically one of the most important islands in the Caribbean, and was to remain so for the next three centuries.

It has an enormous natural harbour which is almost completely enclosed and can shelter a large fleet. The island is very fertile although mountainous in places, and at that time had plenty of wild cattle and hogs. Its significance then was that as a naval base it was perfectly placed to harry the Spanish Main: the galleons carrying the gold and silver from Cartagena sailed most of their voyage to Havana within a 300-mile radius.

None of this was fully understood or appreciated by Venables and Penn, for whom the successful capture of the island would mean only that the expedition was not a complete failure. Their own explanation of the attempt makes it clear that no strategic considerations were involved – they 'resolved to attempt Jamaica' because the troops were 'so cowardly and not to be trusted or confided in, except raised in their spirits by some smaller successes'.

After sending word to Cromwell and seeing nearly two thousand of his men buried on Hispaniola soil, most of them killed by sickness, Venables embarked the survivors of his little army and on 4 May the squadron sailed for Jamaica, which was fortunately well placed to leeward.

8

The Letters of War

Early on 8 May the lookouts in Admiral Penn's squadron sighted land to the west so far off that it was just a tiny cloud of blue haze low on the distant horizon. The island of Jamaica, fifty miles away, was going to make radical changes in the lives of all the men watching it, but to none more than Henry Morgan, who was a few months short of his twenty-first birthday.

The wind was light and the ships slow and it took two more days for them to sail into what is now Kingston Harbour. Within twenty-four hours the island's inland capital, St Jago de la Vega, was in English hands, the governor having fled into the hills. By the 16th the governor had returned to St Jago and signed a surrender which allowed the Spanish to be taken to a port on the Main or in New Spain. There was also a clause which showed that Captain Jackson's attack of a dozen years earlier had not been forgotten; nothing in the surrender terms should 'be taken to include those subjects of the English nation which some time ago coming to this island under the command of Captain William Jackson fled from their ensign and colours and joined the Spanish enemy'.

Henry Morgan's rôle in these early days of the British capture of Jamaica is not known, so they must be dealt with only briefly. A week after the landing two storeships arrived from England, having called at Barbados and heard of the new destination. They came into the harbour at a time when the troops were almost starving. St Jago provided some food because the island had for years supplied homeward-bound Spanish ships, but in the excitement of the first attack the troops had driven off the herds of cattle normally kept near the city.

With the army on shore starving and the crews of the ships having their daily rations heavily cut, the rainy season started. Within a week the ground which had been parched for months was wet and then sodden; shrubs started sprouting and their colours freshened. (The flamboyant trees with their red flowers that make the whole tree look like a great bonfire had not yet been brought to the West Indies; many of the beautiful shrubs and flowering trees that are a familiar sight in the Caribbean today were completely unknown in Henry Morgan's day.)

The worst part of the rainy season (which is, of course, also the hurricane season) is the increase in temperature and humidity. Disease spreads more rapidly in the heat and the damp; men are quickly exhausted doing a task that during the cooler months of the year, between December and the end of February, would leave them mildly tired. Mosquitoes and sandflies multiplied so rapidly that in many places, particularly the Cayman Islands and certain low-lying parts of Jamaica, they swarmed in whining black clouds and knowing men slept in hammocks with bonfires burning to windward, the smoke from green leaves keeping the insects at bay.

Venables' men knew nothing of these tricks and anyway there were not enough hammocks available. Mosquitoes were treated as a violently irritating nuisance, but no one knew that they were the carriers of the malaria that had a man shivering with cold one moment and tossing with a raging fever the next. Nothing was known of hygiene, and men drank contaminated water, so typhoid waited in ponds and wells and dysentery was in almost every field kitchen.

At first lacking tents in which to sleep and facing starvation, it was hardly surprising that within two weeks of landing three thousand of Venables' army were sick. Discipline hardly existed – Venables had lost the stiffening of the well-disciplined Sea Regiment because it was serving in the ships once again. Then Penn announced that he was taking his fleet back to England, and he sailed at the end of June, leaving behind his second-in-command, Goodson, with a dozen frigates. Venables followed five days later, pleading bad health but obviously worried what Penn might report to Cromwell. In fact when Penn arrived in England and Cromwell heard his story he was promptly arrested, charged with deserting his post and sent to the Tower of London. When Venables arrived he too went to the Tower. (Both were freed a few weeks later.)

Cromwell, although furious at the failure of the Santo Domingo expedition, had already sent 850 men and another commissioner to reinforce Jamaica and acted quickly and firmly to establish the new colony. To encourage settlers, 'all planters and adventurers to that island' would be exempt from excise or customs duty for the next seven years and products from the island would be imported into England free of tax or duty for ten years. Within a few months Cromwell and his Council of State voted that a thousand girls and a thousand young men 'should be listed' in Ireland and sent to Jamaica; a few weeks later he ordered that 'all known idle, masterless robbers and vagabonds, male and female' in Scotland were to be taken up and sent out as well. A messenger was sent across the Atlantic to New England to encourage some of the settlers there to move down to Jamaica.

Spain and England were still at peace, but news of the English capture of Jamaica was received in Spain within a few weeks of the landing. By the end of July 1655 the Spanish ambassador was trying to persuade

Cromwell to return the island. The diplomatic exchange went on for three months before the ambassador left England and the two countries were at war. A few weeks later Cromwell spelled out the nation's position in a Parliamentary speech: 'The truth is that no peace is possible with any popish state. Sign what you will with one of them, that peace is but to be kept so long as the Pope says "Amen" to it ... The Papists in England have been accounted Spanielized ever since I was born...'

Making an enemy of Spain enabled Cromwell at long last to conclude an agreement with France which meant in effect that joint English and French action against Spain would be confined to Europe.

The seven years between the capture of Jamaica and the first mention of Henry Morgan in the island's history in 1662 was a turbulent time in the West Indies, beginning with Vice-Admiral Goodson using his motley collection of frigates to attack the Spanish Main.

Leaving a few ships behind to defend Jamaica, he sailed 450 miles to the nearest point of the Main, the Guajira Peninsula, the most northerly part of South America. After taking Santa Marta, expecting to catch the Spanish unawares, he found that the capture of Jamaica had so alarmed the Spanish that they had carried all their valuables inland and hidden them. He then sailed eastward along the coast to Riohacha, but the story was the same. Making full use of Jamaica's strategic position, Goodson took his ships up to the western entrance of the Florida Strait the following summer, intending to capture the galleons from Cartagena as they made their way into Havana. Unfortunately he arrived late – the convoy had not only reached Havana but sailed again for Spain. Goodson then settled down to wait for the *flota* from Vera Cruz with the bullion of Mexico, but his luck was out: a warning reached New Spain, so the *flota* spent the winter at Vera Cruz.

Meanwhile the galleons, little knowing how close to capture they had been off Havana, arrived off Cadiz to run into Admiral Blake's blockading squadron which captured the Spanish flagship carrying bullion worth two million pesos.

This was a far more serious loss to Spain than the amount of money indicated because within a year of losing Jamaica and finding herself at war with both Britain and France she had lost the bullion needed to pay the interest on her enormous loans from the merchant bankers of Europe. Yet the loss of the galleon was only the beginning: the *flota* which Goodson had frightened into staying in Vera Cruz finally made a dash for Spain in early 1657 and, reaching the Canaries in February, was warned that Blake waited off Cadiz.

The bullion, worth 10,500,000 pesos, was immediately unloaded in Tenerife and carried up into the hills which rise up to the volcano of Teide in the centre of the island. The ships themselves anchored close in to the shore, covered by the fort, and there the *flota* waited. It did not have to wait long. Blake arrived and sailed boldly into the Tenerife anchorage to sink every one of the ships.

Judged simply as a naval action it was brilliant, but it also had far-reaching effects. The almost-bankrupt Spanish government now had more than ten million pesos worth of bullion up in the hills of Tenerife and no ships to carry it to Spain, even if it dared take the risk. However, Blake's bold attack had another effect because even before it happened Spain was so short of ships that she was having great difficulty in preparing a fleet for the recapture of Jamaica, and his destruction of the *flota* ensured the island's safety. There was no chance of reinforcing the Spanish garrisons in Cuba and Hispaniola, even though both islands were now in danger from Jamaica. The governors were sent a warning from Madrid telling them that their safety now depended entirely on their own resources.

While Goodson was roaming the West Indies with his ships other Englishmen from Jamaica were busy laying the foundations of what was to become part of the buccaneering empire. Elias Ward (Abbé du Tertre rendered his name as Elyazoüard) sailed from Jamaica with his family and a dozen colonists intending to see if the Spanish had reoccupied Tortuga, which was 260 miles to the north-east, close in to the north-western corner of Hispaniola and perfectly placed to cover the Windward Passage, across which lay Cuba. Finding it deserted and, with its citadel, ideal for his purpose, he hurried back to Jamaica, received a commission as Tortuga's new governor and sailed after embarking another 160 colonists.

The Caribbean's newest colony prospered over the next three years. English and French privateers found it an excellent rendezvous with a sheltered anchorage, and Governor Ward was not a man to ask too many questions. Bands of cow killers and *boucaniers* who had been living round the coast of Hispaniola soon made their way to the island, either rowing round in their canoes or marching overland to the coast opposite.

All were welcomed by Ward, particularly if they brought their own muskets and pikes. The cow killers soon became *boucaniers* and provided a pool of men upon whom the privateers could rely when extra were needed to make up a crew. They were ideal men, too: they had long forgotten about sleeping under a roof and cared nothing about getting wet, whether from rain or a breaking sea; they were crack shots, having that accuracy with their matchlock muskets which only comes when supplies of powder and shot are limited and the next meal depends entirely on a clear eye and steady aim.

The relationship between Jamaica and Tortuga was excellent as far as the privateer captains were concerned, whatever their nationality. As traders and merchants of every type, tavern keepers and whores, importers and builders, chandlers and gunsmiths – and all the rest of the people catering to every need and whim of a ship's captain and his seamen – arrived in Jamaica and set up their businesses in Cagway, as the Spanish Caguaya was now called, the privateers found it a perfect main base.

Ships from Europe intending to enter the contraband trade often decided to apply to Jamaica's chief commissioner for commissions allowing them to sail as privateers. This did not prevent them from trading; it meant, for example, that if a ship carrying a general cargo from Barbados to Jamaica had a commission, she could attack and capture any enemy ships she might meet without being accused of piracy and, more important, dispose of a capture legally.

A letter of marque, or commission, issued in wartime by a government was in fact permission for the vessel to operate as a 'private ship of war' (hence the name 'privateer') against the enemy's ships. All the risk and expense was borne by the owner of the ship: if the enemy's gunfire brought a mast crashing by the board, stove in a dozen planks or knocked off a few heads, that was too bad; they were the risks of privateering. The letter of marque, more usually called a commission, was simply a letter, suitably embossed with a seal, identifying the named ship as a privateer; it did not mean a government took any responsibility for the ship's activities.

A privateer had certain responsibilities and the main one facing an English captain was that the enemy ship he claimed as a prize had to be taken to a British port where an Admiralty Court would condemn her and her cargo as lawful prize. Once this was done the privateer could take his profit from the sale of both ship and cargo, although he had to pay a percentage to the government (to the King and also the duke of York after the Restoration).

The British government gained all round from privateers with Jamaica commissions. These ships tended to base themselves on Port Royal (then still called Cagway) or Tortuga, so that in case of a Spanish attack at least a dozen armed ships were usually in the area. This was as good as having three or four sixth-rate ships of war in the anchorage. The privateers also bought supplies in Port Royal, ensuring a profit for the tradesmen.

The moment peace was signed, all commissions had to be withdrawn, with the privateers supposed to go back to more peaceful ways of earning their living. However, a government rarely insisted that a ship given a commission flew its flag: for example if England was at peace with France and Spain, but France was at war with Spain, English privateers often sailed with French commissions. Thus any privateer in the West Indies could operate quite legally providing the French, Dutch or English were at war with Spain. Dutch ships based at Curaçao sometimes fought with French commissions issued in St Kitts; an English privateer from Jamaica might have a Dutch commission issued in Curaçao.

As a general rule privateer captains played their dangerous game by the accepted rules. Nevertheless the West Indies had more than its share of pirates, men of many nations who preferred to dispose of their prize ships and booty in secrecy rather than through prize courts, regarding the sea as an adequate guardian of prisoners who would otherwise need feeding and might later talk too freely. Happily selling their prizes and booty illicitly to the highest bidder the pirates ranged the seas in peace or war in the same way that highwaymen lurked near crossroads. Privateersmen had little time for them and rarely let them join an expedition for a very practical reason – they could not be trusted.

Although the privateers based in Jamaica soon settled down to harass the Spanish, the Army in the island's early days found that it was its own worst enemy. Each commissioner, acting as the governor, was facing and failing to solve the problem of how to make the soldiers plant the crops without whose yield they would probably starve.

The soldiers were not unwilling to put down their pikes and take up hoes but many of the officers, terrified of illness and convinced there would be no more fighting, wanted to go home to England before they ended up in one or other of the cemeteries that were becoming a common sight round St Jago de la Vega. They wrote letters home to anyone with influence, urging that the island be abandoned; they were less than wholehearted in giving orders to their troops to plant because they saw every turn of a spade as digging their own graves.

When all this failed to get them home they began conspiring. In response to a proclamation urging the soldiers to plant and promising each of them a plot of land, many of the officers drew up a petition asking to be sent back to England so they could serve the Parliamentary cause elsewhere. The petition was rejected, and the Army split into two factions: one group of officers wanted to stay in Jamaica and become planters; the other viewed the island as a pestilential death trap where yellow fever, dysentery and malaria, under other names, waited patiently but inexorably. The second group knew that the weakest part of their case for returning to England was the presence of the first and they decided to get them out of the way by bringing false charges against them.

One of the first victims was Colonel Holdip, a former governor of Surinam who commanded the Liguana Regiment (by this time the regiments had been named after areas in Jamaica) and was one of the most enthusiastic planters. His second-in-command, Lieutenant-Colonel Samuel Barry, accused him of embezzling regimental funds. The plotters had done their job carefully and Holdip was court-martialled, found guilty, cashiered and sent back to England. Professionally it did him no harm because Cromwell, well aware what was going on and angered by it, reinstated him. (By a piece of irony Barry, who engineered the ruin of his 'planter' commanding officer, remained in Jamaica and within five years had become the chief justice.)

The next officer chosen by the plotters was Henry Archbold, a friend (and later brother-in-law) of Henry Morgan who had been a major in the Liguana Regiment but had just been promoted to lieutenant-colonel and transferred to another regiment. Once again Samuel Barry was involved, but he had changed his tactics: Archbold was accused of speaking against Cromwell and saying that the Army and Navy should leave Jamaica 'and join the Venetians' – a reference alleged to mean joining the exiled King. After a court of inquiry cleared Archbold, the dissident officers, slowly realizing they would never succeed, began planting.

While the Army faced the problem of dissident officers it also had to dispose of the Spanish guerrillas who had become powerful in the hills and along the north coast, where they could be supplied from Cuba. They were led by Don Cristobal Arnoldo y Sassi, a member of one of the oldest families in Jamaica. His father was a former governor while one brother was the lieutenant-general of Havana and another the head of the Church in Puerto Rico.

They ensured that more than five hundred men had been landed by the spring of 1658, and Arnoldo used them to establish a strong point on the north coast. Three Spanish ships landing cannon there were sighted by a small squadron under Commodore Christopher Mings, who had replaced Vice-Admiral Goodson, and as a result six hundred troops arrived by sea and most of the guerrillas were wiped out. The recently landed cannon were hoisted on board the British ships and taken to Cagway, where they were installed in emplacements with plenty of Spanish roundshot.

Colonel Samuel Barry, one of the former dissident officers, had been in the expedition and he was chosen to return to England with the dispatch informing Cromwell of the destruction of Arnoldo's force. Barry arrived to find that Cromwell had just died.

Although all resistance in Jamaica ended in April 1660, the Spanish government was far from accepting the loss of the island and hoped to gain by diplomacy what it could not achieve by force. As part of this concern to see the King restored to the English throne the Spaniards signed a secret treaty with Charles II which promised that Dunkirk and Jamaica would be restored to Spain. This meant, in the Spanish view, that time was on their side and as soon as the Commonwealth collapsed – they were sure it would – Jamaica would be returned without any cost to the Treasury or strain on the military and naval forces.

The only drawback to this waiting policy was that Commodore Mings was busy with his ships: every few weeks his squadron sailed out past the new fort just built on Cagway and bound for the Spanish Main, to return

with flags flying, drums beating and trumpets blowing, laden with plunder
from Spanish towns. On one raid he sacked the town of Tolu; on another
he captured three large ships bound to Cartagena from Portobelo. He
brought them back to Jamaica, where they were sold as prizes.

These three ships soon became the island's most famous and profitable
privateers. Their captains, with Henry Morgan, became the leaders of the
buccaneers. The largest of the ships, 60 tons and armed with eight guns,
was bought by Captain Robert Searle and renamed *Cagway*; the 50-ton,
4-gun ship bought by Captain Lawrence Prince was renamed the *Pearl* while
the third, later owned by Captain John Morris, was called the *Dolphin*.

Mings soon became famous for his luck and skill in plundering the Main,
and as the news spread dozens of privateers either joined his expeditions
or followed his example. Arnoldo had an efficient intelligence service in
Jamaica and reported that in the harbour 'there were generally fifteen or
twenty vessels, some entering, some leaving, with a reserve of eight ships
of war'. By early 1660 it was recorded that there were about thirty 'stout
vessels' working as privateers based on Cagway, and that they were manned
by about three thousand men.

There was little excuse or need for piracy at this time because every
encouragement was given to privateers to base themselves at Cagway. The
Army had finally built fortifications on the spit of land covering the entrance
to the harbour and emplacements had been dug for the guns which Goodson
and Mings always made a point of bringing back from their raids. The spit
of land which the Spanish had called Caguaya (a name which also included
the whole harbour) and which the English turned into Cagway, and would
later call Port Royal, was flat and more convenient for tradesmen wanting
to do business with ships than the Passage Fort area on the west side of
the anchorage.

The harbour soon became the busiest in the Caribbean. At Cartagena,
Portobelo, Vera Cruz, Havana, Santo Domingo and San Juan the Spanish
lived in daily fear of attack by Mings or privateers, and the quays at the
Main ports were empty. By contrast at Cagway privateers were sailing for
the Main or returning with flags flying and often a small prize in company,
their shouts and cheers warning the merchants that more business was
coming their way.

The population of Jamaica was recorded at this time as 4500 whites and
1400 Negro slaves. Ships arrived frequently from England with supplies,
immigrants wanting allocations of land, merchants with money enough to
set up business and adventurers with stars in their eyes. Other ships came in
from New England laden with settlers wanting to look at Jamaica before
deciding whether or not they would uproot themselves and start all over again
in the Tropics. These New England ships brought salt fish to sell in the islands
– they had for a long time been trading with the islands of the Lesser

Antilles, particularly Barbados – and had ready money to buy whatever the island merchants had to sell.

Gradually Cagway became a cosmopolitan market where buccaneers, for the word was now becoming widely used, could buy everything from powder and shot to liquor and women, and sell whatever they had plundered from the Main, be it a handful of jewellery or a religious relic snatched from the altar of a Catholic church, a bundle of fine clothes, a well-tempered sword from Toledo, or a bale of hides.

The privateers were therefore a blessing to the new colony. In exchange for commissions and a warm welcome, the island's safety did not depend entirely upon Mings' squadron, so that the bluff, brave and bluntly-spoken little captain could range far afield.

The news of Cromwell's death brought dismay to Jamaica, and with it the unease of knowing that the news was weeks old; even now the whole country might again be torn by a new war, or a new government be making laws or announcing decrees which would change the way of life of everyone on the island. Although the Protector had been succeeded by his son Richard, who was thirty-two, it was known that Richard had neither liking nor aptitude for the task. The Army had a liking for him – he was an amiable young man – but no respect. And always at the back of everyone's mind was the thought of Charles II waiting across the Channel, four years younger and, from all accounts they had heard, a lively personality.

Most of the senior Army officers in Jamaica were outwardly staunch Parliamentarians who had served Cromwell since the organization fourteen years earlier of the New Model Army and the cavalry which became famous as the 'Ironsides'. In Europe, British forces under General Monck and Henry Morgan's uncle, General Thomas Morgan, had captured Dunkirk after a bitter battle against the Spanish and had begun an occupation which was to last four years. Morgan had particularly distinguished himself and Richard Cromwell, within two months of succeeding his father, was knighting the man 'esteemed in the Army next to the General [Monck], a person of the best conduct then in arms in the three nations, having been [a soldier for] nearly forty years and present in the greatest battles and sieges of Christendom for a great part of that time'.

In the West Indies Commodore Mings had even more success in 1659 than the previous year. Guessing that the Spanish were once again hiding their valuables inland, he decided to attack the ports and towns at the windward end of the Main hundreds of miles farther east than he or Goodson had ever previously operated. There, he hoped, the Spanish would be so certain of their safety that he would be able to achieve complete surprise, seizing and looting towns before the startled populations could hide their valuables.

Sailing in the *Marston Moor* and taking only two other ships with him, Mings left Jamaica and started off on the most punishing sail in the West Indies. His first target, Cumaná, was only six hundred miles away to the south-east of Jamaica, but Mings and his little squadron, constantly tacking, had to cover well over a thousand miles before sweeping in to the Venezuelan coast between the pearl island, Margarita, and yet another island named Tortuga.

Cumaná is the capital and port of the province of Sucre, and Mings' squadron was at anchor and the landing parties in their boats and pulling for the shore before the Spanish realized that the ships in the roads were the enemy. With Cumaná sacked and providing good plunder Mings hurriedly weighed anchor and ran westward before the easterly wind, knowing that the chance of success against his next target, Puerto Cabello, depended entirely upon him reaching there with his ships before horsemen from Cumaná could gallop along the coast and raise the alarm.

Puerto Cabello, the port of the province of Carabobo, was fringed with coral reefs and islets and the coast backed by palm trees. Mings again achieved complete surprise, pillaged the port and then sailed again before the alarm could be raised along the coast. So far, with two ports taken, the amount of treasure found was barely satisfactory and with the *Marston Moor* once again leading the way westward Mings hoped for more success at Coro, the capital of the province of Falcón, and almost abreast the Dutch island of Bonaire.

Mings anchored his ships off the port of Vela de Coro and his men had then to march the seven miles to Coro itself. Despite the time this took, his arrival had been so unexpected that they soon found twenty-two chests of silver, each weighing 400 pounds and valued at 1,500,000 pieces of eight and thus worth £375,000 at the ruling rates.

While Mings had been raiding the Main, there had been a curious change in the affairs of Tortuga. One of the original group of Frenchmen was Jérémie Deschamps de Moussac et de Rausset. Knowing of Elias Ward's success as governor he applied to the French government for a commission as governor and received it. With that he went to London, where he persuaded the British government, in a move of almost baffling illogicality, to give him an order to the governor of Jamaica authorizing him to recognize de Rausset as the lawful ruler of Tortuga. Elias Ward, having heard about all this in advance and determined not to live under a French governor, left for New England with his family. In the meantime France and Spain ended their war with a treaty which did not mention the West Indies.

9

Tea for Mr Pepys

On 15 August 1660 the *Convertine* ship of war arrived in the Cagway anchorage from England with news that would affect the lives of every man, woman and child in Jamaica. At that time Henry Morgan was twenty-five years old and with his fellow officers had been active in the earlier forays into the mountains hunting down Arnoldo's guerrillas.

By now Morgan was well acclimatized; he had survived at Santo Domingo; he had survived when newcomers to Jamaica had perished from yellow fever and dysentery. He had learned guerrilla warfare over mountains, through jungles and across savannah, when the only water to drink under a scorching sun was what he carried, along with food, powder, shot and bedding. He and his friends had fought and beaten guerrillas who were men born in Jamaica and trained as soldiers.

By the time the *Convertine* arrived the officers who had come out with Venables had formed friendships and made enmities which were to last for the rest of their lives and play a vital part in Jamaica's early political history. Apart from Morgan they included Henry Archbold, Samuel Barry and Samuel Long. Most of these men had spent their adult life under the Commonwealth. A few, like Henry Morgan, came from divided families where some supported Parliament while others were Royalists. Many like Barry and Long were Old Standers and firm supporters of Parliament. Samuel Long, for example, had used a family relationship with Venables to become an ensign at the age of sixteen in Venables' regiment. When Venables, promoted major-general, was sent off to carry out Cromwell's Western Design, Long had come out with the regiment.

The news that the *Convertine* brought them was that Charles II was now on the throne of England. General Monck, seeing that most of the country wanted a change, had stepped in with his army and invited the King to return. Thus Charles was back in London and the Restoration had been achieved without bloodshed.

The news hit Jamaica like the tremors of an earthquake: the Old Standers did not know at this point that General Monck, the most powerful man in the country (Cromwell's great general had shown that he could be a kingmaker as well), had advised the King to be generous, to grant pardons rather than harbour grudges and make use of the best men for the important posts without paying too much attention to past political loyalties.

As a reward for his rôle Monck was created duke of Albemarle and given a generous pension, as well as becoming the most influential man in the new kingdom. His influence, like the ripples from a stone thrown into a pond, spread out to affect those round him and people like General Sir Thomas Morgan were not discarded now the country was once again a monarchy. Having been a mercenary for most of his life it is doubtful if Sir Thomas had any strong Puritan or Royalist feelings. His Royalist brother Edward, though, who had been in exile for several years, was now able to return to England with his wife Anna Petronilla and his many children and look for some reward for the loyalty which had taken him into a long exile and near poverty.

So, while Samuel Pepys tasted tea for the first time (it came from Holland), the new duke of Albemarle and the King set about putting the country in order again. The war with Spain came to an end and, since France and Spain had already concluded their treaty, the West Indies were officially at peace.

The new Spanish ambassador extraordinary, the Prince de Ligne, arrived in London with a splendid retinue and at his first audience with the King demanded the return of Jamaica and Dunkirk under the terms of the secret treaty signed when Charles was in exile. However, Charles had returned to London to find that he was out of touch with certain attitudes, one of them being that of the London merchants towards the West Indies: they were vociferous in their demands that Britain should keep Jamaica.

Already they had a lot of money invested in the West Indian islands and although the trade with Jamaica was as yet small, they could see how it was going to grow. The King listened to the merchants and then consulted the Privy Council, who agreed. The Prince de Ligne was told that Charles did not find himself bound to give up either Jamaica or Dunkirk, and Parliament agreed. The British possessions abroad were now sufficiently extensive to need a proper organization to run them, and the Privy Council set up a permanent committee to deal with 'Foreign Plantations'.

After hearing of the Restoration in August, the people of Jamaica had to wait many anxious months for more official news about their future. In the meantime the Army officers who had been granted land under the Commonwealth but had not received documents confirming it waited to see if the King would stand by the grants; others waited to see which of them would be recalled to England under arrest, brought to account for their activities under the Commonwealth.

While Jamaica waited to see what the Restoration meant for them, Spain thought she could look forward to receiving her bullion from the Indies without fear of it being captured by the British or French and, with the nation tottering on the verge of bankruptcy, the arrival of the plate fleets was greeted like the lifting of a siege.

Although she had signed peace treaties with France and England, Spain's policy had not changed: no country could trade with her possessions in the West Indies and all British, Dutch and French now living on the islands there were trespassers. There was still 'no peace beyond the Line', however much envoys and ministers in Europe exchanged polite bows.

Spain had by now become a hollow shell. For more than 150 years she had brought home gold, silver and gems on a scale the world had never before seen or even dreamed of, yet the most powerful country in the world under Philip II had begun to slip under Philip III, and under Philip IV the decline became rapid, with the ever-present worry now that the heir to the throne was a cretin.

At the very time of the Restoration in England, when that nation looked forward to advances in all fields of activity, ranging from art to industry, Spain had become like a withered old man, his family existing on limited withdrawals from a limitless bank account in the New World. Industry in Spain was almost completely dead and inflation had sent the prices of everything rising month after month and year after year. There was little to show – apart from the ruined industry and the massive inflation – for all the gold and silver that had been brought across the Atlantic for the past 150 years: no great theatres and plazas, no flourishing merchant class and no powerful fleets to protect Spain's interests in the Atlantic and the Mediterranean.

The reason was not hard to find: the bullion did not stay in Spain. It was always needed urgently to pay off interest and principal owing to foreign bankers, to pay and provision Spanish armies which for so many years had been fighting in foreign lands in wars that owed more to prejudice than reasoned policy, to build and repair ships. Perhaps its only memorials were the massive forts that guarded ports in the Mediterranean and the Indies.

The colonies in the New World were in fact bedraggled and almost medieval outposts representing the mentality of Old World Spain; they had become solely the centres for mining while the ports were simply depots for shipping the bullion back to Spain. Much of the local trade in the colonies was contraband organized by the English, French and Dutch. Although Jamaica waited for a new constitution, the whole of Spain's administration in the West Indies was not only completely outdated but by this time hardly functioning: it still clung to the annual fairs which were originally timed to start after the galleons or *flota* arrived from Spain, but now there were few ships and sometimes none and the system of fairs had long since become a relic, utterly unsuited to the time, place or requirements.

In contrast the foreign colonies in the West Indies, islands like Barbados and Curaçao, Jamaica and St Kitts, had no gold and silver to mine; their prosperity was related to what their planters could get from their crops and the prices the merchants and traders could get for their goods. They were busy islands where planters were clearing more land and merchants constantly ordering more goods from Europe. In their hunt for the trade along the Main the Dutch traders from Statia and Curaçao competed against French from St Kitts and Martinique and English from Barbados and Jamaica, and those quoting the lowest prices sold their contraband goods. There was no House of Trade or Council of the Indies to inhibit or protect them.

The Dutch, French and British governments thus encouraged new settlers because they meant more demand and more skills available, and experience so far had clearly shown how this led to prosperity. For Spain the reverse was true: because the government was concerned only with the gold, silver and gems, anyone who did not contribute directly to the mining and transportation of bullion or its defence was simply another mouth to feed and therefore not to be encouraged.

However, try as she might Spain could not stop the contraband trade: within a few years of her signing the peace treaties with France and England, the governors of Santo Domingo, Cartagena and Buenos Aires were to be sacked for allowing foreign ships to land goods. Yet no galleons arrived at Cartagena or Portobelo in the two years after Charles II returned to England, and when they did finally come they found that no one wanted the cargoes they carried: the goods were far too expensive. The people's needs were supplied by the contraband market.

Père Labat, a French missionary who later wrote an account of this period, describes how the contraband trade was carried on. The foreign ship arriving off a Spanish port would send a note on shore to the governor saying that the ship had sprung a leak (or had run out of water or provisions), and with it would be 'a considerable gift'. A leak was the best excuse, and usually the governor gave permission for the ship to enter 'for repairs'.

The cargo would have to be landed so that shipwrights could get at the leak, and Spanish laws were carefully observed: the cargo was stored in a warehouse and the door was officially sealed. However, there was always a second less obvious door through which the cargo was removed during the night by the local merchants, who substituted bars of gold or silver, sacks of coin, hides, or cocoa to the value already agreed with the master of the ship. With the repairs completed, the seal on the warehouse door was officially broken, the 'cargo' reloaded, and the ship sailed. Officially the laws had been observed.

That was the routine with comparatively large ports and cargoes, but along the coasts of the Main and New Spain there were scores of small settlements and villages, often built along the banks of rivers or round the edge of sheltered bays. For trading with these settlements, each merchant ship usually had one or two small shallow-drafted sloops which acted like floating shops.

The merchant ship would anchor out of sight of the village and send a message to tell the inhabitants they should be ready to trade that night. The sloops laden with goods would leave the merchantman after dark and anchor close to the village, waiting for the Spaniards to come out by canoe. If the sloop was alone armed guards usually limited the number of Spaniards on board at any one time, for fear of being outnumbered and seized.

In the long term, quite apart from bleeding them in taxation and stifling them with bureaucracy, Spain treated her colonies like backward children: they were not encouraged to become in the slightest bit independent. Land had long ago been given to the Church and to families of the early conquerors. The colonies were thus ruled by privileged nobility and a powerful Church which, as one writer commented, 'while it did some splendid service in converting the Indians, engrossed much of the land in mortmain, and filled the New World with thousands of parasitic and often licentious friars.'

The Privy Council's committee in London soon produced a constitution for Jamaica which allowed for a governor (Colonel D'Oyley, in command of the troops) who would be advised by a council of twelve men elected locally. Among those chosen were two of Henry Morgan's close friends, Thomas Ballard and Henry Archbold, as well as the man who had engineered Archbold's court martial, Samuel Barry. The new governor was instructed to withdraw all commissions granted to privateers and order all the captains to return to Jamaica.

The crier, preceded by an energetic drummer, read a proclamation to this effect at various vantage points, and at Cagway the merchants were quick to show their wrath because the privateers were responsible for most of their business. The governor and the new council were in a quandary: there was still 'no peace beyond the Line' despite the treaty signed with Spain; the ships could not trade and Spain called every foreigner a trespasser. Equally important, England was now impoverished and it was doubtful if the duke of York – the new Lord High Admiral and the King's brother – would have many ships to spare to defend Jamaica.

Jamaica's fear of a surprise attack by Spain is the key to the island's whole attitude towards its privateers over the next thirty years. The sheer physical distance from England meant that it would take at least six weeks, and more likely two months, to warn London that Jamaica had been attacked, with at least another eight weeks (depending on the season) needed for effective help to reach Jamaica, quite apart from the time it would take for the ships to get ready.

The governor charged by the Privy Council with the defence of the island had nothing with which to defend it. In the event of an attack – which could come direct from Spain, Havana, Vera Cruz or Cartagena – he had to assume that they could not possibly get help from England in less than four months, but more likely in five or six. This meant that the privateers were Jamaica's only certain defence. They needed Jamaica as a base and market for their goods just as much as the island needed them for its defence, and this joint need was something that was always neglected and rarely understood in London.

It is also the key to the story of Henry Morgan and the buccaneers. By doing nothing to drive them away and being ready in time of war to issue them with commissions, a wise governor could assure himself that Jamaica had its own private navy, small but effective and not costing the island a penny to maintain or send into battle. The ships were always seaworthy and the crews well-trained for warfare, even if they lacked skill in wielding a paintbrush or a polishing rag. The captains were men who knew the waters over which they had to fight with the certain knowledge that comes when ignorance puts a ship on a reef. And it would be an up-to-date knowledge of virtually uncharted waters, because in peacetime the ships were smuggling to the very places that in wartime they might have to attack.

Colonel D'Oyley, finding himself unpopular with the Army, settlers and privateers, soon asked to be replaced, and the Committee for Foreign Plantations recommended Lord Windsor, the seventh baron and later earl of Plymouth, as the new governor.

A few months earlier the Privy Council had recommended that everyone granted land in Jamaica should pay no rent for seven years. New settlers would be granted land providing they were Protestants 'and will be obedient to the government and laws of England'. Three weeks later the Lord Mayor of London was told that everyone in Newgate Prison 'under condemnation, and not for murder or burglary', along with everyone convicted of being 'incorrigible rogues or vagabonds' should be transported to Jamaica. He was assured that the merchants (who would pay to have them shipped out as labourers) had undertaken 'to keep them from returning for ten years at least'.

Lord Windsor sailed for Jamaica in the *Centurion* and with him was the forthright Commodore Christopher Mings. After leaving Barbados on the last leg of the voyage to Jamaica, Windsor sent the *Griffin* frigate ahead to call at San Juan and Santo Domingo with letters for the governors asking a simple but significant question: would they admit English ships to trade? Had the question been asked in London of the Spanish ambassador, he would have been quick to realize that its very simplicity showed that matters between the two countries were taking a complicated turn, but the two governors were administrators not diplomats, and eventually they gave equally simple answers.

When Windsor arrived in Jamaica one of the first things he did was to read to the Council the instructions he had received from the Privy Council. The most important of these concerned Jamaican trade and Spanish possessions, and explained why the *Griffin* was visiting the two island capitals. 'You shall,' the Privy Council told him, 'endeavour ... to obtain and preserve a good correspondence and free commerce with the plantations and territories belonging to the King of Spain' for all English subjects who traded there 'with security to their persons, and goods.'

The Jamaica Council must have been hard put to believe their own ears as His Lordship continued reading. 'But if the Governor of the King of Spain shall refuse to admit our subjects to trade with them, you shall in such case endeavour to procure and settle a trade with his subjects in those parts by force, and by doing any such acts upon and against them as you and the Council shall judge most proper to oblige them to admit you to a free trade with them...'

This was a complete and utter change in British policy, and although it depended upon the replies the *Griffin* brought back there was no doubt about what Lord Windsor was to do if the answer was no. In case of a refusal or an emergency, he was 'to grant such commissions [to privateers] as to you seem requisite for the subduing of all our enemies by sea and by land, within and upon the coast of America'. In other words, England was prepared to take a firm line but trouble should be confined to the West Indies; beyond the Line, in fact.

While waiting for the *Griffin*, Lord Windsor, a man of considerable energy, carried on with his other tasks. He had to disband the Army in Jamaica itself, thus saving the shipping needed to take them home and providing Jamaica with many new settlers. A force of 400 infantry and 150 cavalry was to be kept for 'as long as shall be thought fit for the preservation of the island with two ships of war constantly plying upon the coast' – the two ships were the *Centurion* and the *Griffin*. He had £12,274 to share out between 1523 soldiers, this being the pay they had not received and also a gratuity. The fort on Cagway was to be completed and His Lordship had already decided to name it Fort Charles in honour of the King. More important, Cagway, the whole spit of land forming the eastern entrance to the harbour, was renamed Port Royal, with a battery to be built beside Fort Charles to help defend it.

Windsor then formed a militia of all the able-bodied men on the island. This comprised five regiments, each of which was named after a particular area. One of them was the Port Royal Regiment and among its officers was Captain Henry Morgan, then aged twenty-seven and starting an association with the new regiment which was to last for most of his life.

With military affairs out of the way, Windsor then published a proclamation that the King had declared 'that thirty acres of improvable land shall be granted to every person, male or female, being twelve years old or upwards' then living in Jamaica or arriving within the next two years. Windsor was to call an assembly to make laws which would be in force for two years 'and no longer' unless approved by the Crown.

The buccaneers were interested in a recent decision taken in England which extended the maritime authority of the Lord High Admiral, the duke of York, to the colonies. The Lord High Admiral was the head of the Navy and now gave commissions to all governors appointing them vice-admirals and instructing each of them to set up an Admiralty Court and appoint a judge. An Admiralty Court heard cases which involved disputes concerning ships and the sea. In wartime it had to decide whether or not a ship was a lawful prize to her captors and, if so, condemn her, although before the captors saw their money the court made sure that a fifteenth of the value was paid to the King and a tenth to the Lord High Admiral. This was the extension of an existing situation where the King and Lord High Admiral shared in the prize money earned by the Royal Navy.

While they waited for the *Griffin* to return, the members of the Council did their best to convince Lord Windsor of the danger threatening from Cuba, describing how for five years Arnoldo and his guerrillas had been supplied and reinforced from there. Bearing in mind that the Army had just been disbanded and the northern coastline of Jamaica is more than four hundred miles long, with Cuba almost encircling it, and that the second biggest port, Santiago, is only a hundred and fifty miles distant, it is not hard to accept their fears as being those of honest men.

In London that autumn the King, despite his new policy in the West Indies, appointed Sir Henry Bennet (later Lord Arlington) to be secretary of State. This was not a popular move in Paris or Jamaica. Bennet had spent several years in Spain; when Charles was still in exile he had negotiated the secret treaty restoring Jamaica and Dunkirk to the Spanish and since the Restoration had been trying to get the King to honour it. The French ambassador to Charles's Court regularly referred to him in his dispatches as 'The Spaniard'.

The Privateers Sail

The *Griffin* sailed into Port Royal and delivered the Spanish governors' answers to Lord Windsor's question. Both were polite but firm, obviously thinking they were doing no more than giving a standard answer to a standard question. Windsor now called the Council, which resolved unanimously 'that the letters from the governors of Puerto Rico and Santo Domingo are an absolute denial of trade, and according to His Majesty's instructions to Lord Windsor, a trade by force or otherwise [is to] be endeavoured'.

The English were not the only ones seeking a peaceful trade among the Greater Antilles: a few months later the French at St Kitts sent a Dominican friar to Puerto Rico as an emissary to propose an annual exchange, St Kitts sending five hundred slaves a year in return for cattle 'and products of the land'. The governor of Puerto Rico was unimpressed by the physical appearance of the emissary and put him in jail, commenting that 'he looked more like a soldier than a friar'.

Two Capuchin friars arrived in San Juan a few weeks later, announcing that they represented the governor of Tortola, one of the group of Virgin Islands only seventy miles to windward of Puerto Rico and held at the time by the Dutch. They offered salt and cassava in exchange for cattle, and although he did not question their vocation the governor turned them down.

The Jamaica Council was not at a loss to know what to do next: the 'most proper' act to force the Spanish to allow a free trade would be to attack Cuba, and the target should be Santiago, the nearest port and the second largest in the island. Such an attack would serve two purposes: it would tell Madrid that Jamaica (and thus England) was absolutely serious about the demand for free trade, and at the same time remove any threat of invasion from that direction. No time was lost in converting the Council's decision into action and by now Lord Windsor, who had been in the island only five weeks, was proving a popular and effective leader.

Just as the Council reacted favourably to Lord Windsor's confident and decisive manner, so the islanders made no secret of their approval of the way the Council was not only passing resolutions that would put the Dons in their place but voting for them unanimously. Nowhere were the praises of both governor and Council sung more loudly than in the taverns and gin shops

of Port Royal: shipowners, captains and seamen who had seen their commissions withdrawn by D'Oyley not so many months before, and had shaken
their heads when they heard of the new King's disastrous mistake over the
secret treaty with Spain, now had proof that the King really meant business.

Ten of their ships were out in the anchorage along with the 46-gun *Centurion*
and the *Griffin*. The fiery little Commodore Mings was back in Port Royal
and the recently disbanded soldiers were still cheerful enough, flush with
the back-pay and gratuities in their pockets.

While the details of the attack on Santiago were being drawn up, a rousing
call was made for volunteers to form a regiment. The response was immediate
as criers went through the streets of St Jago, Port Royal and other centres
announcing the proclamation. Many of the discharged soldiers saw an opportunity of enriching themselves by plundering Spaniards, and within three
days 1300 volunteers were being mustered and officers appointed. At the
same time commissions were issued to the ten merchant ships, which meant
that at the stroke of a pen Commodore Mings had a squadron of twelve
ships – the *Centurion* and *Griffin* and ten privateers – with the hope of more
joining later. Fast boats and messengers on horseback were sent round to
various bays to offer commissions to other ships and warn them to get to
Port Royal as quickly as possible.

One of the first of the ten ships issued with a commission signed by Lord
Windsor was commanded by Captain Henry Morgan. It is not certain that
he owned the small ship outright; more probably he had partners, who are
likely to have included his friends Lieutenant-Colonel Archbold and Colonel
Thomas Ballard. Among the other ships commissioned was the *Cagway*,
owned by Robert Searle.

The captains set their men to work rowing to the shore with empty water
casks and filling them. More casks of salt beef and salt pork were also taken
on board along with slabs of *barbecu*, which kept well in the ships although
care had to be taken to keep the rats away from them. Fresh fruit and vegetables were bought in the shops of Port Royal, along with great cheeses,
casks of small beer and jars of tobacco shipped in from the Dutch island
of Curaçao.

With the ships provisioned and watered, the volunteer troops were sent
on board with their bedding, weapons (ranging from matchlock muskets
to pikes and cumbersome pistols to swords) and a varied collection of light
armour. On 21 September 1661 the squadron, led by Commodore Mings
in the *Centurion*, sailed out past Port Royal with flags flying and men cheering
as they waved to wives and sweethearts standing on the Point. The circular
tower of Fort Charles was now nearly completed and by the time they
returned it would probably be finished.

The weather was typical for the hurricane season, cloudy with the wind
light and from the east. The two King's ships and the privateers ran down

to Point Negril, at the western end of Jamaica and then bore up to reach across to Santiago, 150 miles away to the north. The wind stayed light with the ships hard put to make three knots. Mings intended to make a landfall well to the east of Santiago. The current flows to the south-west but the rate can vary between half and two and a half knots, and with the light wind Mings had to be careful the squadron was not swept to the west of the port, wasting time and losing his most valuable weapon, surprise.

He was close in to the Cuban coast with the wind still light when he sighted a ship anchored in the lee of a cay. This turned out to be commanded by Sir Thomas Whetstone who, although a nephew of Oliver Cromwell, was a Royalist. He had been living well beyond his means in the heady days immediately after the Restoration and found himself clapped in the Marshalsea Prison for debt. Because he could be released only by paying his debts he eventually petitioned the King and received £100 to settle with his creditors and get to Jamaica. Once there he went in for privateering although when Mings met him he seems to have become a pirate, because he was now at sea acting against the Spanish without a commission.

Mings also anchored his ships in the lee of the cay and saw that Whetstone's vessel was manned mostly by Indians; men who hated the Spanish and now seized every opportunity of fighting the people who had driven them from their own lands. There were now thirteen ships at anchor. Whetstone told Mings that he had been on this coast for some time and, the Commodore reported to Lord Windsor, 'assured us of no additional forces in St Jago upon Cuba [sic: Santiago de Cuba], and likewise rectified our former advice, being most by English prisoners, whose restraints [i.e. imprisonment] there gave them not the advantage of full discovery'.

Mings then called all the captains together on board the *Centurion* to decide how they would attack. The meeting had to take the form of a council of war because, although they had accepted commissions, the privateer captains had certainly not submitted themselves to naval discipline. They would follow Mings only so long as they trusted him to lead the raid successfully.

The entrance to the port of Santiago is little more than a long slot cut into the cliffs and leading into a big bay beyond, which is completely sheltered by high hills and cliffs. The slot is only sixty yards wide in places and with the wind fluky, bouncing off one side or the other and eddying round hills, is very difficult for a sailing ship because of the risk of her sails being caught aback so that she drifts on to the rocks.

Defending the entrance of the city was the Castillo del Morro, built on top of the cliffs at the east side of the entrance, a powerful fortress with thick walls. Below it, almost at sea level, was a battery on Punta Estrella. The Spanish authorities considered that the fluky winds in the slot and the guns above providing plunging fire made Santiago impregnable.

The Army officers attending the council had bitter memories of the abortive landings at Hispaniola many miles to leeward of the chosen places and the terrible marches to Santo Domingo, so they favoured a direct attack. Commodore Mings ('a very stout man, and a man of great parts, and a most excellent tongue among ordinary men', according to Samuel Pepys) had already shown that his own penchant for bold approaches brought the most success. The council, he reported to Lord Windsor, judged that a direct attack was feasible 'and upon debate resolved the manner of attempting it, which was to land in the harbour, the mouth of which was very strongly fortified'.

Having decided what they would do, they all had to wait patiently: the light winds were punctuated with long periods of flat calm when the ships seemed suspended in the clear blue water rather than riding to anchors, heading this way and that and leaving captains worrying in case their cables dragging on the bottom had caught round sharp coral heads which would chafe through the rope in a few hours.

Finally a breeze came in from the east and the squadron weighed, but within a few hours it became fitful again, with puffs that came from nowhere, and went nowhere, dying as soon as the men in the ships had finished trimming sheets and braces. For two or three days progress towards Santiago was due to the current setting to the west, but the delay was fortunate because seven more privateers from Port Royal managed to catch up, bringing Mings' squadron to twenty.

Soon after daylight on 5 October they sighted the Castillo del Morro perched high on the cliffs in the distance, but the breeze was weak and variable, blowing from the east for a few minutes before switching round to the west as ships struggled to avoid collisions, the lookouts watching anxiously for the pewtering that would reveal the direction of the next puff.

By noon they could just make out the entrance to the harbour but it was late afternoon before they were close enough for telescopes to show the swell waves crashing in white breakers across the reefs and rocks on each side, and the fitful wind was dying altogether. They all knew only too well what would happen next – as soon as the sun was low a land breeze would come up, a gentle wind blowing straight out through the narrow entrance. A ship needed a commanding wind to get in or out of Santiago; there was no question of trying to beat in against a head wind.

Mings knew that the brief land breeze would be all he would get until the next day, by which time the squadron would have drifted past, so he promptly changed his plans to take advantage of the land breeze when it came: he told his captains that they would use it to reach the shore off the small village of Aguadores at the mouth of the San Juan river and only two miles short of Santiago.

In the city itself the squadron had long ago been sighted and the governor,

Don Pedro de Morales, had sent drummers through the streets calling out the militia while the garrison at the Castillo stood to arms. The Spanish officers were watching Mings' motley squadron with great care and saw that unless it suddenly blew half a gale – which was impossible – there was not the slightest chance of the English reaching the harbour entrance until long after nightfall, and they would never dare risk trying to get in during darkness.

Then, just as the Spanish decided they were safe for the night and the land breeze set in, they saw the English squadron head for the shore. Two hours later breathless riders from the village arrived in the city to report that the English were anchored off Aguadores and hundreds of heavily-armed men were landing from boats ...

The whole operation was proving a perfect lesson for Captain Henry Morgan: he had seen how Mings had embarked the troops in Port Royal and sailed without wasting time, how he had taken advantage of every puff of wind and the west-going current to get to Santiago and now at the last moment had snatched at a foul wind and turned it to his advantage. Finally he saw how Mings put 1300 men on shore with their powder dry.

'Before our whole party was on shore it was night, the place rocky and narrow,' Mings wrote. 'We were forced to advance the van in the wood to make way [for] the rear to land, the path so narrow that but one man could march at a time, the way so difficult and the night so dark that we were forced to make stand and [light] fires, and our guides with brands in their hands to beat the path.'

The governor of Santiago hastily changed his plans, too. He put the militia under the command of Arnoldo, the former leader of the Jamaica guerrillas, and ordered a barricade to be built across the main street, blocking the route the English would have to take from Aguadores and covering it with two guns. Don Pedro then took more than one hundred and fifty regular soldiers from the garrison of the fortress and used them to defend the barricade while Arnoldo stood by with a reserve of five hundred men, many of whom had fought with him in Jamaica.

The English had marched through the night and arrived at Santiago soon after daylight, attacking the barricade with wild yells. 'With themselves and the help of Don Christopher [Arnoldo] who fairly ran away, we routed the rest,' Mings told Lord Windsor, 'pursuing them divers ways through the town ... Some six small vessels were swum to and possessed by our soldiers, their men through fear deserted them.'

The next five days completed Henry Morgan's education in the science of buccaneering. That was the time it took for Mings' men to plunder the city, carrying the loot down to their ships now anchored in the harbour. Barrels of gunpowder from the fortress's magazine were used to blow up various buildings in the city while more were put on board the ships for Port

Royal's own magazines, along with some bronze guns. Finally, Mings wrote, '700 barrels was spent in blowing up the main castle . . . and truly it was so demolished as the greater part lies level with the foundations.'

The squadron then sailed for home with its six prize vessels, arriving at Port Royal on 22 October with guns booming and flags flying, having captured and sacked the second largest city of the largest Spanish island in the Caribbean. Apart from the stories they had to tell, the privateersmen soon had their plunder on display at Port Royal. It included silver plate, many bronze cannon, sacks of sugar and bales of hide, church bells and barrels of wine. The six prize ships were an ideal size for trading round the coast of Jamaica itself. The price to the British of this demonstration was six men killed in the fighting and twenty dead from illness, out of 1300 soldiers and the crews of twenty ships.

The success of the Santiago raid set the pattern for the next twenty years. More important, eighty per cent of the men in the Santiago attack were former soldiers who volunteered, not sailors, and with losses so light and profits so high they saw there was money to be made with the privateers. The privateer captains suddenly found they had a great reserve of trained fighting men living in Jamaica, ready and willing to volunteer the moment they heard the drums beating: men who did not want the security of a grant of thirty acres of land, but a chance to find sudden riches (or death) on the Main.

Lord Windsor did not stay long in Jamaica. Having disbanded the army, set up the militia, organized the new government of the island and a judicial system, unsuccessfully tried for trade with the Spanish and sent out the privateers, he pleaded ill health and went back to England, leaving the lieutenant-governor, Sir Charles Lyttelton, in charge. Samuel Pepys noted in his diary: 'Lord Windsor being come home from Jamaica unlooked for, makes us think these young Lords are not fit to do any service abroad.' It was an unfair comment because few colonial governors before or since ever displayed a half of Windsor's energy, achieved a quarter as much or so inspired the people he ruled.

In the meantime both the Council and the lieutenant-governor had to carry out one remaining part of the King's instructions to Lord Windsor. This was the reduction of Tortuga, and it resulted from a report Colonel D'Oyley had made to London many months earlier when he received the order to withdraw commissions from the privateers. He had warned that Jamaica privateers would use Tortuga as a base and 'take French and Portugal [sic] comissions or none at all, and will hinder all trade to and from Jamaica'.

Lord Windsor had been told to use his 'utmost endeavours' to reduce the island and its French inhabitants to obedience, but the problem was to avoid provoking the King of France. Finally Captain Robert Blunden of the privateer *Charles* sailed to take Colonel Samuel Barry and Captain Abraham Langford to Tortuga to demand its surrender. Nothing was heard for several months, until Barry returned to report complete failure – he had not even sighted Tortuga. He said that when Captain Blunden had heard that the French might resist he had flatly refused to go on; instead he made for the south side of western Hispaniola and joined a group of buccaneers living there. Colonel Barry then saw an unusual sight: the buccaneers elected Blunden their chief, and he hoisted the English flag – the first time it had been hoisted in Hispaniola, apart from its brief appearance with the Venables expedition.

Christopher Mings was soon trying hard to persuade Lyttelton and the Council that the time had come for the *Centurion* and *Griffin* and as many privateers as possible to raid New Spain, but the governor had to wait in case there was some conciliatory gesture from the Spanish after the Santiago attack.

Surprisingly enough there was already a small English settlement on the coast of New Spain made up of logwood cutters. The northern coast of Mexico, stretching eastward for 750 miles from Vera Cruz and ending at the tip of the Yucatán peninsula, is mostly a sandy plain, arid and laced with salt marshes, which forms the provinces of Tabasco, Campeche and Yucatán. The part of the Campeche coast where the logwood grew was almost deserted and inaccessible except from seaward. The water is shallow with many off-lying cays and reefs often merging almost imperceptibly with the land in miles of mangrove swamps.

The logwood cutters were men from many nations living and working at the eastern end of the province in an area where the heat and humidity is intense, with much of the land marshy and swarming with mosquitoes. The temperature from March to October reaches 90° or more; July's rain usually averages more than eight inches. However, the men had little choice because they had to work where the logwood grew and it also had to be somewhere that the Spanish soldiers could not reach by land. The cutters were tough, but comparatively law-abiding; they wanted to be left in peace by the Spanish and asked only that English, French or Dutch ships called regularly to buy their logwood and sell them food and rum. The logwood trade had been going on for years; small British coasting vessels brought it to Jamaica, where it was transhipped for Europe, although the Dutch and French, having no convenient port, usually took their cargoes direct to Europe.

Just before Christmas 1662, the indomitable Christopher Mings finally persuaded Lyttelton and the Council that it was time for the attack, his strongest argument being that there had been no approach by the Spanish and the King's instructions to Lord Windsor had told him to 'force a trade'.

He chose San Francisco de Campeche, a town originally founded by the Mayas and which gave the province its name. Built at the eastern end of a small bay, it was a reasonably large town and had never been attacked before, so it should be unprepared. Apart from anything else, he said, an attack on Campeche would help the logwood cutters.

After the success at Santiago there was no shortage of volunteers; nor did the privateer captains delay in telling Mings they would sail with him. They included one of the youngest, Henry Morgan, and one of the oldest, Edward Mansfield, a man who had for several years successfully combined trading with piracy and within a short time was to become the elected leader of the buccaneers. Sir Thomas Whetstone was happy to join Mings again and so was Captain Abraham Blauvelt, a Dutchman who gave his name to a settlement on the Mosquito Coast of Nicaragua which is today a town called Bluefields. Captain John Morris, who was a great friend of Henry Morgan and later became his second-in-command, also joined Mings' squadron along with Captain Jackman.

Very soon more than a dozen ships normally based at Port Royal were ready with 740 men, then four more arrived from Tortuga with 250 men, most of them French. Three smaller privateers sailing under the leadership of a Dutch captain then came in with a hundred men and were issued with commissions. On 12 January 1663, Mings took the *Centurion* out past Fort Charles followed by a squadron of more than eighteen English, French and Dutch privateers. Apart from his own ship's company he had more than 1100 privateersmen, buccaneers and volunteers.

Running to the north-west, the squadron had gone a thousand miles and rounded the Yucatán peninsula before turning south to reach Campeche, in itself a good piece of seamanship on Mings' part because charts were almost non-existent and men navigated by log, lead line, memory and hearsay, with perhaps a few lines drawn on a sheet of paper.

Shallow banks and shoals extend up to 150 miles off the coast inside the Bay of Campeche, and often a seaman's first warning of a dangerous shoal is a discoloration of the water, with currents unpredictable. Campeche is typical of a town along that coast: it is surrounded by a small amphitheatre of low hills and summer haze often means the town can be sighted from seaward only if the sun is reflecting on white roofs or the cupolas of the church of San José.

As soon as the *Centurion* anchored a boat was hoisted out and Mings sent it on shore with a flag of truce demanding that the governor surrender. San Francisco de Campeche had a garrison of regular soldiers and was defended by two fortresses, the Castillo San Miguel standing on a low hill two miles to the south-east, and Castillo San José the same distance to the north-eastward, where one end of the amphitheatre meets the sea, as well as three batteries along the shore between them. The governor looked to his defences with confidence and made no reply.

Mings decided to attack. Boats were lowered and filled by men armed with muskets, pikes and swords and, led by Mings with the *Centurion*'s boats, they pulled for the shore. Roundshot from the batteries threw up plumes of water but soon each of the privateer captains was rallying his men as the boats grounded and leading them to attack the batteries, all three of which were captured in the first wild dash. Within a few minutes all the buccaneers were rushing for the town, shouting wild threats in several languages but rapidly slowing down amid a hail of musket balls as they found that many of the flat-roofed houses were strongly built of stone, so that each became a little castle.

Although regular troops formed Campeche's garrison they were no match for the swarm of buccaneers, many of whom were sharpshooters and all of whom had their courage strengthened by greed. After a day of bitter fighting Mings was in command of Campeche, and by nightfall the town was being systematically plundered by the buccaneers. Fourteen Spanish ships lying at anchor and used for transport between Vera Cruz and Havana were captured.

With the plunder taken on board and stowed, the squadron then weighed with the prizes in company and headed for Port Royal, more than seven hundred miles dead to windward. At this point Mings' usual good luck deserted him and the ships had to beat against strong head winds and current for the whole voyage, taking so long that rumour after rumour swept Port Royal that the expedition had met with disaster.

Then, for the second time in five months, Mings led his squadron and fourteen prizes into Port Royal with the *Centurion*'s guns booming out in salute as she passed Fort Charles. That night the buccaneers, whether they were former soldiers not yet over seasickness or privateersmen who had been at sea for years, hurried to the streets of Port Royal for a celebration that lasted for days.

Morgan's Raiders

The Campeche expedition revived happy memories for the privateersmen: few could forget the heady days of Commodore Mings' earlier attacks on the Main which had yielded all the chests of silver. Five of the younger captains from Port Royal now decided to fit out an expedition of their own for a long cruise – John Morris, Henry Morgan, Freeman, Jackman and David Marteen, a Dutchman. Their ships could carry at least two hundred men, and providing they were hand-picked that would be enough. Mings had already revealed the secret of success – surprise.

One had to choose a place which had never been attacked before or had been left in peace for many years; then one could be sure that the garrison would be slack and sentries more in the habit of going home at night to wives or mistresses than standing guard and being eaten alive by mosquitoes and sandflies. Rain and humidity made a fort's roundshot rust; months and perhaps years without sight of an enemy meant that the gunners neglected to see if each shot would pass through a shot gauge, a circular metal disc with a hole the same diameter as the bore of the gun. Sometimes they simply painted over the rust with coat after coat of paint, never checking the ever-increasing diameter of the shot so that when the time came for action the shot would be much too fat for the gun, swollen by the paint that was intended to protect it. Apart from the rusting of shot, gunpowder could be ruined by damp and slow match became unreliable. Gun carriages rotted, heavy rains washed the earth away from emplacements. Time was always on the side of the buccaneers.

Mings had shown at Campeche how a garrison with two castles and three batteries could be less effective than determined men with muskets firing from the roofs of private houses. He had also shown that people who had not been frightened did not hide away their treasures. At Coro they had neglected to conceal twenty-two chests of silver; at Campeche silver plate was still in the houses. The privateers themselves had also found that there was plenty of other profit to be made – bales of hides, casks of Spanish wines, small vessels left at anchor: all could be taken back to Port Royal and sold for good prices.

When Morgan and his companions considered where to cruise they ruled out the areas which had been attacked in the past year or so. Every town and village along the thousand miles of coast from Cartagena eastward to Trinidad would be on the alert after the Cumaná, Puerto Cabello and Coro raids; the eastern end of Cuba would be nervous after Santiago; no doubt Campeche now expected raiders every night.

That left two areas, three hundred miles of coastline east of Vera Cruz in the Bay of Campeche, and twelve hundred miles of coast from Portobelo to the northern end of the gulf of Honduras (better known as the Mosquito Coast, and covering Panama, Costa Rica, Nicaragua, Honduras and Guatemala). Much of this coast is littered with scores of small cays and reefs, and all of it is shallow and swept by currents which can be circular and certainly unpredictable.

After selecting their crews and provisioning, the five privateer captains slipped out of Port Royal in November 1663, heading for New Spain. They still had their original commissions signed by Lord Windsor and for the next year and a half few people except the Spanish had news of them.

In the five months between the Santiago and Campeche raids much had been happening in the political life of Jamaica, where there was now a definite split between the Old Standers of Cromwell's original Western Design and the Royalists, many of whom had come to Jamaica after the Restoration. Lord Windsor's arrival had emphasized that the power had gone to the Royalists, and the Old Standers who had been in the island since the first day of Venables' arrival saw themselves losing control of island affairs just as trade and the plantations were becoming profitable.

In Spain the British ambassador in Madrid, Sir Richard Fanshaw, received a letter from Henry Rumbold, the under-secretary of State, soon after the Santiago raid telling him that the Spanish King had sent to England 'To know if the King will own Lord Windsor's action in Cuba but it will probably be easily answered' because experience shows 'that the Spaniard is most pliable when well beaten'.

In fact, Spain once again demanded the restoration of Jamaica and this predictable request arrived in London just as the Privy Council was considering whom to appoint as the next governor of the island. Telling Fanshaw that the new governor had not yet been chosen, Rumbold noted that reports from Cadiz said the Spanish 'are much dejected there at hearing from the West Indies of our hostile carriage towards them, which has wholly ruined their trade'. Then, almost as an afterthought, he added that the King had sent orders to Lyttelton in Jamaica telling him 'to desist those hostilities upon the Spaniards and other neighbours, as much disturbing the settlement of that plantation'.

This startling new change of policy towards Spain was easy to explain, although the causes were complex: war with the Dutch was becoming inevitable and it was almost certain that France would be on the Dutch side because under the terms of an earlier treaty the French agreed to help the Dutch in any war in which they were not the aggressor.

Commodore Mings and his two ships had already been recalled to England, leaving the islands without warships, when the actual order to Lyttelton 'to desist those hostilities' arrived at Port Royal on board the aptly-named *Friendship* on 4 August 1663. Very soon criers were reading the King's proclamation at Port Royal, St Jago and Passage Fort.

Following Mings' recall, its contents were almost as frightening to many of the islanders as the threat of Spain, because the proclamation showed a complete lack of understanding of how Jamaica could defend herself against what might well be a triple threat – from the Dutch and French as well as the Spanish. And, as the island had always feared, all the Royal Navy ships had been recalled to England at the first sign of crisis.

Lyttelton, pleading ill health, finally received permission to return to England, leaving the Council with authority to govern. An Old Stander, Colonel Thomas Lynch, had been elected its president so Lyttelton gave him a commission putting him in command of all the naval and military forces. Sir Charles had no choice, and it was an unfortunate coincidence that the president of the council was also violently against the privateers because they stood between his dream of selling slaves by the hundreds to the Spanish and the reality that the Spanish refused to do business.

Lynch had become a powerful man in the island. He had secured a large plantation and although he commanded one of the regiments of the militia he was one of the strongest advocates of trade with Spain. He had also become the unofficial leader of the Old Standers group, bitterly opposed to those regarded as Royalists.

In London a new governor was finally chosen. The chairman of the Privy Council's Committee for Foreign Plantations was the duke of Albemarle, who had been careful to follow his own advice to the King, that the best man available should be given a particular job regardless of his past politics. When various people considered as governor of Jamaica had been rejected he proposed his cousin, Sir Thomas Modyford. This was not nepotism, because Modyford had much to recommend him. He had been a very successful planter in Barbados for the past sixteen years and was at present speaker of the Barbados Assembly.

The King agreed to the duke's choice and Modyford's commission as governor was drawn up and dated 15 February 1664. The King then approved of Albemarle's nomination for lieutenant-governor – Colonel Edward Morgan, the Royalist brother of Major-General Sir Thomas Morgan, Albemarle's former second-in-command (who was governor of Jersey, one of the Channel Islands), and uncle to Henry Morgan, now away on a buccaneering expedition.

Colonel Edward Morgan's appointment was perhaps more significant of the British government's forthcoming policy towards Holland than an example of Albemarle or the King rewarding a faithful Royalist who had spent years in exile. Colonel Morgan spoke excellent Dutch and, with the drift towards war, the Dutch working from their bases at Curaçao and St Eustatius (Statia) would be far tougher opponents in the West Indies than the Spanish. The lieutenant-governor's job was likely to be a fighting one.

Colonel Morgan's long years of exile and unemployment had left him a poor man. He had a large family – two sons and four daughters – and by the time he reached London he was hard put to raise the money to buy a house. This purchase had hardly been arranged before his wife Anna Petronilla died. As soon as he received his new appointment, at a time when he was almost impoverished, he decided to take his children with him to Jamaica. Getting passages for them was not difficult because a ship was being provided and, like Sir Thomas Modyford, who was also being given extra ships, he was instructed to take as many settlers as possible.

Before leaving London Modyford was given the draft of a letter by Sir Henry Bennet, the secretary of State, which he was to write to the governor of Hispaniola saying that he had orders from the King to restrain the people of Jamaica from molesting Spanish ships or territory. The English ambassador in Madrid was working to produce a lasting friendship, he said, and meanwhile 'let us not only forbear all acts of hostility, but allow each other the free use of our respective harbours and the civility of food, water and provisions for money'.

Colonel Morgan went ahead with two ships, calling in at Santo Domingo on the way so that Modyford's messenger, Colonel Theodore Cary, could deliver the note and receive the Spanish governor's reply. He arrived at Port Royal on 21 May, followed by Modyford on 4 June in the *Westergate* with the *Marmaduke* and *Swallow* in company, all three ships carrying a large number of settlers.

Modyford found the governor of Hispaniola's reply polite but evasive, making up in graciousness what it lacked in substance. Thomas Lynch, who had been in complete sympathy with the pro-Spanish Sir Henry Bennet's motives in sending the note, had to admit in a letter to the secretary of State that as far as the Spanish reply was concerned 'it is improbable Jamaica will be advantaged by it, for it is not in the power of the [Spanish] governor to have or suffer a commerce'.

He added: 'When the King was restored the Spaniards thought the manners of the English changed too, and adventured two or three vessels to Jamaica for blacks, but the surprises and iruptions of C. Mings ... made the Spaniards double their vigilance, and nothing but an order from Spain can gain us admittance or trade.' Lynch wrote with strong feelings about slaves because he had become a factor for the Royal African Company (a trading monopoly whose members included several of the royal family) and was therefore a leading supplier of slaves in Jamaica.

Calling in the privateers, he told Bennet, 'will be but a remote and hazardous expedient and can never be effectually done without five or six men of war ... Naked orders to restrain or call them in will teach them only to keep out of this port and force them (it may be) to prey on us as well as the Spaniards. What compliance can be expected from men so desperate and numerous, that have no other element but the sea, nor trade but privateering?

'There may be above 1500 in about twelve vessels, who if they want [i.e. lack] English commissions can have French or Portugal papers [instead].' If they captured Spanish ships they could be sure of a good reception at Tortuga or Curaçao. For this, Lynch added, 'we shall be hated and cursed, for the Spaniards call all the rogues in these seas, of what nation soever, English'.

The Morgans at War

The arrival of the Morgan family in Port Royal on 21 May 1664 should have been a happy occasion: while still in London the girls had conjectured about meeting their cousin Henry for the first time and the newly-widowed colonel, faced with creating a fresh future for his two sons and four daughters, had decided to settle in Jamaica.

He had very little capital – before leaving London he had mortgaged his house for £200 because he needed ready money – and apart from his pay of £600 a year as lieutenant-governor his only income was a pension of £300 a year. Once in Jamaica, though, he would be given a grant of land enabling him to become a planter.

When the Morgans arrived at Port Royal their cousin Henry was not there to meet them and they were all wearing mourning – dark clothes which had been hastily prepared in the ship, because the colonel's eldest daughter had died on the voyage. She was, Sir Thomas Modyford wrote to the secretary of State, 'a lady of great beauty and virtue', and had died of 'a malign distemper by reason of the nastiness of the passengers'.

The colonel had arrived at Port Royal to discover that his nephew Henry not only commanded a privateer but had sailed for New Spain six months earlier, since which time no one had news of him.

The grant of land was soon arranged and the colonel left the day to day running of the new plantation – which meant clearing the land – to his eldest son, Charles. Fortunately, although Henry Morgan was away at sea his friends were quick to make the colonel and his family welcome, and they had not been installed in a house at Port Royal for long before two of these friends were paying regular calls. One of them was Colonel Henry Archbold, who probably had a share in Henry Morgan's ship and who soon began to woo the colonel's third surviving daughter, Johanna Wilhelmina. Another friend was Major Robert Byndloss, a young soldier who now had a large estate and who soon fell in love with Anna Petronilla, the colonel's second daughter. Their eldest sister, Mary Elizabeth, seemed to be waiting for her cousin Henry to return.

The new lieutenant-governor was not the only one to lose a member of his family as a result of coming to Jamaica: Sir Thomas Modyford's wife was in England and a month after arriving he sent his eldest son Jack to fetch her in the *Griffin*. He never saw Jack again and nearly three years were to pass before he heard rumours that the *Griffin* had been sunk by a Spanish ship of war.

In the meantime Sir Thomas settled down to carry out his orders, writing to the secretary of State that he was delighted with his lieutenant-governor, whose skill as an administrator had obviously been underrated. 'I find the character of Colonel Morgan short of his worth and am infinitely obliged to his Majesty for sending so worthy a person to assist me, whom I really cherish as my brother.'

One of Sir Thomas's first actions was to move the governor's residence from The Point (the local name for Port Royal and referring to the fact it was on the end of a long, sandy peninsula) to St Jago. Then he settled down to persuade the planters of Jamaica of the advantage of growing sugar, which was a flourishing crop in Barbados. It was far from being a new suggestion, but at last the planters could get first-hand advice from a man who had considerable experience in its cultivation and whose crops in Barbados had made him wealthy.

By now the King had received a full report from Mings on the Campeche raid and the protest from Spain had been delivered by her ambassador. A letter to Modyford told him that 'His Majesty cannot sufficiently express his dissatisfaction at the daily complaints of violence and depredation' against the Spanish by the ships of Jamaica and Modyford was 'again strictly commanded not only to forbid the prosecution of such violence for the future, but to inflict condign punishment upon offenders, and to have the entire restitution and satisfaction made to the sufferers'.

That letter, signed in London eleven days after Modyford landed at Port Royal at the beginning of June, did not arrive until early September and caused something of a sensation because at that moment there were two Spanish ships from Cuba at anchor in Port Royal. Both were heavily guarded and prizes to Captain Robert Searle, a privateersman now owning the 10-gun *Pearl* and who had already landed the boxes and bags of Spanish coin so that the King's fifteenth share and the duke of York's tenth could be calculated.

Modyford promptly called the Council and showed them the letter. The members, obviously very alarmed and taking particular notice of the last paragraph, decided that the governor of Cuba should be told at once that the ships and money were being returned. They also resolved that 'all persons making further attempts of violence upon the Spaniards be looked upon as pirates and rebels, and that Captain Searle's commission be taken from him and his rudder and sails taken ashore for security'.

A few weeks later the Council showed that its reference to 'pirates and rebels' was not an empty threat. A certain Captain Munro had been sailing with a commission but when he heard that it had been withdrawn he decided to become a pirate. The first Modyford knew of this was when English ships arrived in Port Royal protesting that Munro had plundered them. Luckily Modyford still had the *Swallow* ketch and she went off and captured Munro. Several gibbets had long since been built just inside The Point (the site was later known as Gallows Point) and there Munro and his men were publicly hanged in sight of all the ships in the anchorage. To make sure that the spectacle would not be lost for several months the bodies were bound in chains as they swung from the gibbets.

It was, however, becoming increasingly clear that skeletons hanging in rusty chains were not going to intimidate pirates, and there were still buccaneers like Henry Morgan and his four companions at sea in distant waters who had what they thought were perfectly valid commissions. The Privy Council in London finally accepted suggestions by Modyford which were put forward obliquely in a letter from his brother-in-law, Thomas Kendall, who was on a visit to London.

He wrote that the privateers must be allowed to dispose of their prizes when they came in to surrender their commissions, 'otherwise they will be alarmed and go to the French at Tortuga, and his Majesty will lose 1000 or 1500 stout men' who would continue attacking the Spanish and then start capturing ships bound for Jamaica, 'for they are desperate people, the greater part having been [private] men-of-war for twenty years'. He added that it would be 'much to the advantage of the Spaniards that the Governor has orders to permit them to sell their prizes and set them a'planting; and if his Majesty shall think fit to have Tortuga or Curaçao taken, none will be fitter for that work than they'.

The bait of Curaçao offered by Kendall and Modyford was taken in London and the Committee for Foreign Plantations suggested that the Caribbean privateers should stop all hostilities against the Spanish but be allowed to take Curaçao and the other Dutch islands. The actual excuse to act against Curaçao soon came: the Dutch, driven out of several of their West African forts and trading centres two years earlier, were worried at the prospect of losing their monopoly of the slave trade. In January 1665 Admiral de Ruyter arrived off the West African coast with a fleet, drove the English out of the forts and trading posts in Guinea, and then sailed across the Atlantic to the West Indies. He arrived off Barbados in April but, failing to capture the ships in the harbour or anchored off, sailed up to Martinique. There he repaired damage with the help of the French and then sailed off to attack Virginia and New England.

In the meantime Sir Thomas Modyford had acted on the instructions from London and given Colonel Edward Morgan his orders: he was to prepare an expedition to attack all the main Dutch islands – Statia and Saba in the Leewards and Curaçao and Bonaire off the coast of Venezuela. The word was passed that privateers were needed and by the time de

Ruyter eventually arrived off Barbados to make his abortive raid Sir Thomas was reporting to Lord Arlington (Bennet was by now a peer) that 'the privateers come in a-pace and cheerfully offer life and fortune to his Majesty's service'.

Colonel Morgan was soon ready to sail with his expedition. He had assembled nine ships – including Captain Searle's *Pearl*, with sails and rudder restored – and drummed up five hundred soldiers. His second-in-command was Colonel Theodore Cary, who had sailed out with him from England.

Morgan, with forty years' active service, was a realist, and with his circumstances once again radically changed he drew up a new will. He left his plantation, at present little more than uncleared acreage, to his two sons, while the mortgaged London house and his claim on an estate in Wales (which he called his 'pretence upon Llanrumney') were left to his eldest surviving daughter, Mary Elizabeth. The rest of his possessions were to be divided among his other two daughters. His will, written as a memorandum to the governor, said his two sons should use their money 'to the increase of the said plantation, and they both having brought it to perfection shall not only maintain their sisters according to their qualities but also add to their portions when they marry'.

Morgan sailed in the 18-gun *Speaker*, owned by Captain Maurice Williams, on 16 April bound first for a rendezvous he had arranged with more privateers. His force ranged from the *Speaker*, which was the largest, to John Bamfield's *Mayflower* armed with one gun and Nathaniel Cobham's *Susannah*, which had two. Sir Thomas was very satisfied and told Lord Arlington a few days later:

> They are chiefly reformed privateers, scarce a planter amongst them, being resolute fellows, and are well armed with fusees and pistols. Their design is to fall upon the Dutch fleet trading [to] St Christopher's, capture St Eustatius, Saba and Curaçao, and on their homeward voyage visit the French and English buccaneers at Hispaniola and Tortugas. All this is prepared by the honest privateer, at the rate of 'no purchase, no pay', and it will cost the King nothing considerable, some powder and mortar pieces.

'Purchase' was the word used by pirates and buccaneers to describe booty or plunder. The method they used for sharing and their pay scale will be described later but the sense of 'no purchase, no pay' survives today when 'no cure, no pay' is an accepted term in marine insurance, referring to salvage attempts, and means just what it says: there is no pay, or reward, unless the operation is successful.

*   *   *

In August, four months after Colonel Edward Morgan's expedition had sailed against the Dutch islands eight hundred miles to windward but before any reports about it arrived back in Jamaica, a privateer came into Port Royal with the startling news that the expedition in which Henry Morgan had sailed twenty-two months earlier had ranged far inland across Central America, sacked and plundered three great towns, lost all their ships and captured more ... Morgan, John Morris, Jackman and Freeman would be arriving soon, he said, and sailed again before anyone thought to detain him, for he was David Marteen, the Dutch member of the expedition, who had just discovered that England and Holland were at war.

Colonel William Beeston, who kept a detailed diary of events in the island, made a mistake in the Captain's name but noted on 20 August: 'Captain Freeman and others arrived from the taking of the towns of Tobascoe and Villa de Moos in the bay of Mexico, and although there had been peace with the Spaniards not long since proclaimed, yet the privateers went out and in, as if there had been an actual war ...'

This was the first news the Morgan family had of Henry since before they left London, when it seems likely that Mary Elizabeth kept up a correspondence with the cousin she had never met. Both Henry Archbold and Robert Byndloss had kept the Morgan girls and their brothers informed of the stories circulating in Port Royal and St Jago, and Sir Thomas Modyford took care to keep himself abreast of the trends because the political power structure in the island was becoming complex, with Henry Morgan's return likely to become an important issue.

In London the pro-Spanish group was of course led by Lord Arlington, the secretary of State who, as Sir Henry Bennet, had shared the King's exile. In Jamaica the leader was Thomas Lynch, the Old Stander who although a devout Protestant regarding Catholicism as only slightly removed from witchcraft was determined to sell slaves to the Spanish. Modyford's strength at Court came from his ties with his cousin, the duke of Albemarle. Modyford sent his official dispatches to Arlington and his private opinions to Albemarle, so the information the King received from Jamaica passed through various filters. In the island, then, Lynch as the factor of the Royal African Company came to represent the merchants (though not the traders at Port Royal) while Modyford reflected the interests of the planters, who had no particular wish for trade with Spain (for one thing it would put up the price of slaves).

The first stories of the raids established Henry Morgan and his fellow captains as heroes among the majority of people in Jamaica. The King might decree friendship with Spain but the Dons were the traditional enemies: Drake had been dead for only seventy years; the Armada had been driven up the English Channel to its destruction only seventy-seven years earlier. This basic hatred for the Spanish, an inheritance from the recent Elizabethan age, must never be forgotten; it was the tide against which Thomas Lynch had always to swim. The Morgan girls had an even stronger reason for detesting Spain; with their close ties to Holland they knew what Spain had done in the Netherlands.

Finally the four ships arrived at Port Royal, and strange looking vessels they were to British eyes, obviously Spanish-built. As soon as they had anchored their captains were hurried to the governor's residence, where Sir Thomas listened to their story, the like of which had not been heard for a hundred years, since Sir Francis Drake's famous march across the Isthmus to the South Sea.

Several things were glaringly obvious to the governor. First, the captains were now rich men – providing they were not forced, like the unfortunate Searle, to return their plunder to the Spaniards. Second, they had left Port Royal two months short of two years ago equipped with valid commissions, issued by Lord Windsor, to wage war on the Spanish. They all claimed that they had not heard that all commissions had since been withdrawn. Because they had been operating more than 750 miles from Jamaica, and mostly well inland, it was unlikely that they were lying and anyway impossible to prove.

After hearing the story Modyford showed considerable shrewdness: the account of their twenty-two month expedition was set down in the form of a report to the duke of Albemarle, not the secretary of State. It described all the places they went to in detail, along with the products and the size of garrisons, and ended with Modyford noting that he was convinced that 'if ever the reasons of state at home require any attempt on the Spanish Indies, this is the properest place and the most probable to lay a foundation for the conquest of the whole'.

Despite many fanciful accounts of this raid, Modyford's report to the duke is the only contemporary record in existence, and while it is certain that the buccaneer leader Edward Mansfield did not go on it, it is also unlikely that Henry Morgan started off as its leader because Morris, Jackman and Marteen were among the most experienced privateer captains in the West Indies (a year later Modyford described Marteen as 'the best man of Tortuga').

This was far from being a normal privateering raid, however: it is probable that Morgan soon became the leader because he was the most experienced soldier among them – and a soldier was needed, not a sailor. He had service going back to Venables' disastrous attack on Santo Domingo and, more important, had helped drive Arnoldo and his Spanish guerrillas from the highlands of Jamaica, gaining unusual and valuable experience. Most significant of all, this privateering expedition is typical of the pattern later established by Morgan when he was the undisputed leader of the buccaneers, able to raise hundreds of men and march them the width of the Isthmus.

The five ships left Port Royal in December 1663, crossed the 125-mile-wide Yucatán Channel and rounded the north-eastern corner of Mexico. Here the current was stronger, the Caribbean funnelling to its narrowest as it forked west to pour into the Gulf of Mexico and east to the Strait of Florida. From now on, because of the season, the great danger facing them was not the Spaniards but the risk of a norther hurling them up on the flat coasts of Yucatán, Campeche or Tabasco. Staying well out to make sure they had a good offing brought even more dangers: dozens of small, low cays litter the Campeche Bank seaward for more than a hundred miles while reefs, many only a few inches below the surface, await the unwary mariner.

They ran westward for three hundred miles until they were abreast of Campeche, then sailed on for another 150 miles, watching the land closely, looking for signs of two rivers – the discoloured water can often be seen twenty miles out to sea. The first was sighted and passed, and then a second was seen running into the sea – the Grijalva. They were off Punta Frontera and almost exactly halfway between Campeche astern and Vera Cruz ahead. Their target was the town of Villahermosa, fifty miles up the Grijalva and capital of the province of Tabasco.

The mouth of the Grijalva River was enough to daunt most seamen: the coastline, low and lined with dense woods (and in summer hard to see if there is the slightest haze), had no distinguishing features, and the approach to the river mouth, off which the ships intended to anchor, could only be made after sounding from boats. Their first target was the village of Frontera, three miles up the river (and now a small city, Puerto Alvaro Obregón). The ships anchored and the five captains landed 107 men, leaving only a few on board, and marched on Frontera, finding that the local Indians living there not only hated the Spaniards but were willing to act as guides.

At the same time the buccaneers found that their fifty-mile journey to Villahermosa was going to be considerably longer and more difficult than they expected: the land stretching out twenty miles on each side of the river was impassable swamp criss-crossed by muddy streams and laced with small lakes. The usual approach to Villahermosa from the coast was by boat up the river, but that was ruled out for the buccaneers, whose main hope of finding plunder was by making a surprise attack.

The Indians finally provided the answer, leading Morgan and the rest of the party on a three hundred mile march right round the outside of the swamps, avoiding all villages and settlements until they reached Villahermosa as it went about its daily business and which, Modyford told the duke of Albemarle, 'they took and plundered, capturing 300 prisoners...'

Modyford's account – based on the report given him by Morgan and his fellow captains – does not say what happened to the prisoners, but when the buccaneers went back to the mouth of the river with their booty, this time using boats captured in the city, they found that their five ships had been captured by Spaniards who had apparently arrived by chance from Vera Cruz and 'who soon attacked them with ships and 300 men. They gave a short account of this fight in which the Spanish were beaten off without the loss of a man [i.e. buccaneer]'.

Even allowing for the frequency that the figure three hundred comes into Modyford's report, the raid on Villahermosa, fifty miles inland and protected from seaward by a forty-mile-wide band of swamp, surpassed Drake's march across the Isthmus – the buccaneers travelled at least three times as far over equally difficult terrain – even if it now left Morgan and his ship-mates marooned on the Tabasco coast, many hundreds of miles from Port Royal and with all their food, water and ammunition in Spanish hands.

The buccaneers' luck soon changed: two unsuspecting Spanish barques and four canoes arriving off the river entrance were captured. This type of canoe, used for coastal traffic and carrying goods up the Grijalva, was often forty feet long and generally propelled by paddle, although it usually had a single mast and rudimentary sail but no ballast other than its cargo.

The buccaneers loaded their cargo on board and paddled and sailed their way back eastward to the Yucatán Channel, five hundred miles against a foul current usually running at more than a knot and giving them an extra twenty-four miles or more to make up every day. They had to stop frequently to get water and forage for food and on one occasion attacked a coastal town which cannot now be identified.

Finally they rounded the Yucatán Peninsula, passing southward towards Honduras outside the great barrier reef which is the longest in the Western hemisphere. They then crossed the Gulf of Honduras and anchored off 'the isle of Rattan' (Roatán, one of the Bay Islands). Their target this time was Trujillo, thirty miles away on the mainland at the foot of Pico Colentura, which rises 3200 feet to begin a mountain chain.

Trujillo was protected by a small fort, but the buccaneers sailed over from Roatán, sacked the town, captured a ship at anchor in the lee of Punta Castilla and, the moment they had their latest plunder stowed on board her, sailed for a place near Bluefields, 450 miles farther south.

By now Morgan and his fellow captains had sailed and paddled more than 2600 miles since leaving Port Royal (the distance from the North Cape of Norway to Gibraltar, or from the Canary Islands to Barbados), and more than half of it in canoes off the most dangerous coasts in the Caribbean and Gulf of Mexico. The voyage – and it was by no means over – was epic by anyone's standards, and the most remarkable so far undertaken in the Caribbean.

They had chosen their next anchorage, Monkey Point, south of Bluefields, with great care. The neck of land joining North and South America is only two hundred miles wide in this latitude and after crossing seventy-five miles of mountain range the traveller going westward meets a great lake which is fifty miles wide and a hundred miles long and with its far shore often less than twenty-five miles from the Pacific.

There are islands in the Lago de Nicaragua and at its northern end was a city the buccaneers knew of only as Gran Granada, and about which they heard stories of great wealth. They were stories that may have grown in the telling, but Granada was like Villahermosa, a city so far inland that threats of *corsaros* were used only to frighten children. Adults slept soundly in their beds at night, secure in the knowledge that the South Sea, only 30 miles away, contained no enemies, while the North Sea was more than 150 miles across the Cordillera Chontaleña, with peaks more than 2000 feet high. The Spanish had built their life round the lake: it provided fish for their meals while the flat land between it and the mountains was farmed.

Morgan and his fellow captains knew that the wealth of the Aztecs had first been found only a few hundred miles to the north, and although relying on rumours to know what Granada had to offer they were better informed on how to reach it. Although the lake is on the western side of the isthmus, its flood water runs eastward down the San Juan River and after more than ninety miles pours into the Caribbean, after dividing into two main branches, the northern one meeting the sea at San Juan del Norte, known to the buccaneers as Monkey Bay, and the other at Colorado.

At Monkey Point (which can be identified from well out to sea) the motley collection of seven ships anchored and some of the buccaneer leaders went on shore to find guides from among the local Indians who, Modyford noted, were 'hostile to the Spaniards, and nine of them willingly came with them'. With the guides on board the ships they then dropped down the coast to Monkey Bay, where the buccaneers began preparing for their raid.

Swords were sharpened, lead was heated to cast more shot, barbecued meat was stowed in bags, casks, jars and bottles were filled with water. At this point the canoes in which they had paddled all the way from the Grijalva River came into their own: they were ideal for the passage to the Lake of Nicaragua.

Paddling up the river by night and hiding by day, the buccaneers reckoned they had covered thirty-seven leagues, or 111 miles, before they reached 'the entrance to a fair laguna, or lake ... of sweet [fresh] water, full of excellent fish, with its banks full of brave pastures and savannahs, covered with horses and cattle, where they had as good beef and mutton as any in England'.

They estimated the size of the lake fairly accurately ('fifty leagues by thirty') and 'hiding by day under cays and islands and rowing all night, by the advice of their Indian guides, they landed near the city of Grand Granada'.

Modyford wrote: 'This town is bigger than Portsmouth with seven churches and a very fair cathedral, besides divers colleges and monasteries, all built of free stone, as also most of their houses. They have six companies of horse and foot besides Indians and slaves in abundance.'

The buccaneers kept to their habit of surprising the enemy: they marched into the centre of the city in broad daylight, 'fired a volley, overturned eighteen great guns in the Parada Place, took the serjeant-major's house [i.e. the town hall] wherein were all their arms and ammunition, secured in the Great Church 300 of the best men prisoners, abundance of which were churchmen, plundered for sixteen hours, discharged the prisoners, sunk all the boats and so came away...' More than a thousand of the Indians 'joined the privateers in plundering, and would have killed the prisoners, especially the churchmen, imagining the English would keep the place, but finding they would return home requested them to come again, and in the meantime secured themselves in the mountains. A few of them came away and are now in Maryin's [sic: Marteen's] vessel ...'

Modyford's narrative was cleverly written, avoiding any difficulty arising from Henry Morgan's relationship to his uncles, making a few digs at the Spanish 'churchmen' which would strike a chord in the heart of a good Protestant, and turning the whole buccaneering expedition into a useful reconnaissance for a possible English attempt on Central America – a subject dear to Modyford's heart.

The Buccaneer Takes a Wife

The great raid on Granada was celebrated for days in Jamaica and the seamen who had served in the privateers and rowed canoes the length of the Mosquito Coast were the heroes of the taverns and stews, only too glad to tell their stories yet again for anyone willing to put up the price of a gill of rum. Marteen missed the celebrations because, as Modyford told the duke, 'being a Dutchman and fearing his entertainment at Jamaica, [he] has put into Tortugas'. With Britain and Holland now at war, Tortuga was a safer place for him to sort out his share of the plunder and decide what to do with the Indians from Granada who had decided to leave with the buccaneers and sailed in his ship.

The other captains, Henry Morgan, Morris, Freeman and Jackman, heroes alike of the drawing rooms of St Jago and the bars of Port Royal, were men who worked together as buccaneers but had their own circles of friends when they were on shore. At the age of thirty, Henry Morgan was wide-shouldered, slim and powerfully built, with a sallow complexion partly hidden by a pointed black beard worn in the style of Drake and Ralegh. Deeply tanned, he appeared the typical swashbuckling adventurer and his return to Port Royal had been an exciting time for the Morgan girls. They had been waiting patiently for the first sight of their cousin, about whom they had heard many stories told by Robert Byndloss and Henry Archbold. He had come back wearing strange clothes bleached by sun and saltwater -- with his original ship captured by the Spanish off Frontera he had been relying on finding Spanish breeches and jerkins, shirts and stockings that fitted him to replenish his wardrobe.

Once he had recovered from his surprise at finding his Morgan cousins in Port Royal, with Charles and a younger brother already clearing a plantation and his uncle away at the head of an expedition against the Dutch, Henry was obviously delighted with the girls, who were very different from any of the young women he had previously met.

To begin with they were more sophisticated. They had been infants when they had to flee into exile with their father to live on their uncle's estate in Prussia, and there they had absorbed the way of life led by a nobleman in northern Europe. More recently they had returned to the sophisticated glitter and bustle of Restoration London. By comparison with the planters' daughters who had spent most if not all their lives in Jamaica they must have seemed vivacious, gracious and cosmopolitan, more than able to put a man at ease in a drawing room, whether he was a buccaneer like cousin Henry (who for the past two years had eaten most meals without much help from cutlery) or planter and former soldier like Henry Archbold and Robert Byndloss. Their brother Charles, now twenty, was acting as head of the family during his father's absence, and receiving much help and advice from Archbold and Byndloss.

Henry Morgan came back to Port Royal to find that his old friend Byndloss, busy with a plantation of 2000 acres as well as his duties as an officer in the militia and commandant of Fort Charles, had been made a member of the island's Council. Yet he had found time to woo Henry's cousin Anna Petronilla, the old colonel's second daughter. The couple were waiting for the colonel to return from the expedition against the Dutch islands so that Byndloss could formally ask for Anna Petronilla's hand.

The raid on Granada may well have made Henry Morgan a wealthy man – that would depend on the governments. Previously he seems to have been able to accumulate just enough to buy a share in a privateer; but soon he should be able to obtain a good plantation – and take himself a wife. The fact that he was still a bachelor at the age of thirty could mean anything. That he had not found an eligible young woman in Jamaica is quite likely: neither Byndloss nor Archbold wasted any time in wooing the Morgan girls. That Henry was not a ladies' man and had spent his spare time drinking and carousing in taverns is likely as well. In view of what was about to happen, however, he may have been waiting.

Jamaica at this time was not a good place for a young man to find a suitable wife: the more promising daughters of the planters were often sent back to England to find titled husbands in need of good dowries. Neither Jamaica nor Barbados had yet become places to which mothers in England sent out unmarried daughters in the hope that the less discriminating planters would discover charms that were not so apparent to eligible young men in England.

For the time being, though, Henry was in a financial limbo. His plunder had certainly made him rich but would he and his fellow captains be allowed to keep it? He had heard how Captain Robert Searle of the *Pearl* had brought in two Spanish prizes and was unloading sacks of gold and silver coins when he was ordered to send everything back to Cuba. The bitter fact was that the British government's policy was so unpredictable that Henry and the other three captains would be unwise to spend any of the money until Modyford had received a reply from the duke...

Any doubts that Henry and the girls might have had about each other were resolved when he and the eldest of them, Mary Elizabeth, fell in love. It was indeed the kind of genuine romance to gladden the hearts of aunts and uncles and bring satisfied smiles to the face of grandparents because obviously Henry was not marrying Mary Elizabeth for her money – she had none, and her father had less than some of his young lieutenants.

So Robert Byndloss and his Anna Petronilla and Henry and Mary Elizabeth waited for Colonel Edward Morgan to return from Curaçao with his expedition, so that they could have his permission. The third sister, Johanna Wilhelmina, was too young to marry, but the man who had fallen in love with her, Henry Archbold, was prepared to wait.

Then in November, some six weeks after Henry Morgan and the other buccaneers reached Port Royal, a ship came in at last from the Dutch island of Statia with a dispatch from Colonel Cary, who had been Colonel Morgan's second-in-command. The island had been captured, Sir Thomas was told, but Colonel Morgan had died in the attack. 'The Lieutenant-general [Morgan] died not with any wound, but being ancient and corpulent, by hard marching and extraordinary heat fell and died,' Cary wrote, 'and I took command of the party by the desire of all.'

Despite Modyford's high hopes and the colonel's careful planning, the expedition had been beaten by bad weather and a poor 'purchase'. To begin with, very few extra privateers had joined at the rendezvous. April can bring strong east to south-east winds in the Caribbean and this year was no exception, so the expedition had a beat of hundreds of miles against head-winds of twenty-five knots and more and a steady foul current. Two privateers lost the squadron in bad weather one night; a third, with most of her sails torn to shreds, limped back to Jamaica. The squadron made such slow progress that off Hispaniola the colonel put into Santo Domingo harbour and asked permission to buy provisions and take on water and firewood, but the Spanish refused.

From a distance the southern end of Statia, an extinct volcano with three distinct peaks, one nearly 2000 feet high, looks like a vast anthill sloping down to flat plantations in the middle and rising again at the northern end to rounded hills. When Colonel Morgan arrived in the *Speaker* and anchored his squadron of ten ships in Oranje Bay he had only 350 men available for the landing. The town of Oranjestad, built on top of a low cliff behind a long, sandy beach, had no harbour, all goods being loaded into open boats. A fort built into the edge of the cliff guarded the bay, which is simply a slight curve in the coastline.

Sir Thomas Modyford's report told the rest of the story: 'The good old Colonel, leaping out of the boat and being a corpulent man, got a strain, and his spirit being great he pursued over earnestly the enemy on a hot day, so that he surfeited and suddenly died, to almost of the loss of the whole design.'

Although Colonel Cary took command by popular consent, he was not the man to control the buccaneers. Nevertheless the island was secured and they searched the long row of red brick warehouses built just below the cliffs at the back of the beach, carrying anything they considered of value down to the waiting boats. The houses in the town at the top of the cliff were plundered; the twenty cannon in the fort were dragged out through the gate and some of the nine hundred slaves they had captured were used to haul them down the steep road to the beach, where they were taken out to the ships. The main magazine on the cliffs at the outskirts of the town was emptied of powder and the battery and small magazine at the northern end of the beach were destroyed.

After three weeks Colonel Cary managed to persuade some of the buccaneers to attack the almost circular island of Saba, also owned by the Dutch and lying a few miles to the north-west, looking like a squat tooth nearly 3000 feet high. After that the buccaneers, bitterly disappointed at their 'purchases', refused to go on to attack Curaçao, 450 miles away. All they wanted now was to go to the Windward Islands or run back to Jamaica, an easy sail with the easterly wind, and try to make up for their losses in raids against Cuba. They were not the slightest bit interested in defending Statia and Saba against counter-attacks by the Dutch. Their 'purchase' included 942 slaves, twenty cannon, sugar coppers and stills, and a few horses and sheep; not enough to pay wages and expenses, let alone allow them a profit.

Modyford was later to tell the duke 'how poor the fleets returning from Statia were, so that vessels were broken up and the men disposed of for the coast of Cuba to get a livelihood, and so be wholly lost from us. Many stayed at the Windward Islands, having not enough to pay their engagements, [i.e. crews the wages] and at Tortuga among the French buccaneers'.

By this time the governor had, in yet another change of policy in London, received permission to grant commissions against the Spanish, but Modyford said that he was trying to avoid this with the former Statia privateers, 'hoping that their hardships and great hazards would reclaim them from that course of life'.

Apart from the Statia expedition, Modyford told Arlington, little had changed in Jamaica in recent weeks. 'The Spanish prizes [from the Villahermosa and Granada raids] had been inventoried and sold, but the privateers plunder them and hide the goods in holes and creeks, so that the present orders little avail the Spaniards but much prejudice his Majesty and his Royal Highness [the duke of York] in the tenths and fifteenths.'

Modyford concluded that the King could save the charges of a new deputy governor – 'I shall never again meet with one so useful, so complacent and loving as Colonel Morgan was; he died very poor, his great family having little to support them...' However, Arlington already knew about the late colonel's financial situation. As though Edward Morgan had a presentiment that he would not survive the expedition he had written to Arlington four days before sailing. Serving the King had left him poor, he told the secretary of State: instead of being worth more than £7000 he would be hard put to leave his children £2000 – and that depended upon him being paid back money he had spent on the King's service, although he did not doubt he would receive it 'considering how generously I have spent life and fortune in the [King's] service'.

Modyford's own letter could not be sent until the next convoy left for England in the following March, by which time he was able to add (making a mistake in the girl) that the old colonel's 'eldest daughter is since married to Bindlosse of good estate'. Anna was, of course, the second surviving daughter, not the eldest, but the governor's reference to the marriage places it between November 1665 and March 1666, and it is probable that she and Byndloss were married at Port Royal – as befitted the commandant of Fort Charles – after three months' mourning. Unfortunately all the registers of births, deaths and marriages for the parish were subsequently lost.

For this reason we also do not know the date on which Henry and Mary Elizabeth were married, but it was probably soon after and, because lifelong friendships were involved, it is likely that Morgan and Byndloss stood as best man for each other. Morgan stayed in Jamaica for many more months; for the time being he retired from buccaneering and helped his cousin, and now brother-in-law, Charles Morgan, to get the plantation on its feet.

By the spring of 1665 Henry Morgan had, without realizing it, reached a crossroads in his life. He had taken a leading part in the most daring buccaneering expedition ever mounted in the West Indies and it had made him rich. His reputation with the governor stood high – the report to the duke of Albemarle made that clear – and his prestige with the buccaneers was such that they would always flock to follow him on another expedition. He had fallen in love with his cousin Mary Elizabeth and married her. He was about to buy a plantation for himself and in the meantime rented a house in Port Royal. At that point he could have left the sea after his brief encounter with it and his name would have been as little known to history as his four fellow captains on the Granada expedition; he could have settled into the comfortable life of a prosperous Jamaica planter – and few people lived more luxuriously.

It was a way of life that did not seem to appeal to him. He was already a heavy drinker, well known in Port Royal, where he would tipple in a tavern in Cannon Street or seek company at another in Thames Street, but whether he was drinking in Lime Street, Broad Street or Tower Street (the names in Port Royal were mostly taken from the City of London) he could always be sure of finding lively companions.

Morgan's friends always called him Harry, not Henry, and for the moment he was still the accepted leader of the small group of buccaneers who raided Granada. Before the raid many names had stood higher than Harry Morgan's in the aristocracy of the buccaneers, whose uncrowned king was Edward Mansfield, the most experienced of them all and who had been Commodore Mings' second-in-command at Campeche. Mansfield was so reticent about his past that most people were far from sure whether or not he was originally Dutch, with the surname Manfeldt or Mansvelt. He had a consuming hatred for the Spanish and Catholicism, which seemed to indicate that he or his family had suffered under the Spanish – the background of so many Dutch buccaneers.

Yet the Captain Henry Morgan of the Port Royal Militia who sailed away on the Granada expedition was a vastly different person in the buccaneers' eyes from the Harry Morgan who came back two years later. Although he had been a Johnny-Come-Lately as far as veterans like John Morris and David Marteen were concerned, he had led them so well they were now quite prepared to accept him as Mansfield's crown prince.

The buccaneers had by now become widely known as the Brethren of the Coast, and they had long ago elected Mansfield their admiral. Yet it seemed that Harry Morgan, newly married, on shore once again after two years' buccaneering, was not interested in becoming the second-in-command.

14

The Old Admiral Dies

Despite the arguments of men like Thomas Lynch, there was certainly no
change in the attitude of the majority of the people of Jamaica towards
Spain, particularly because Commodore Mings and his ships of war had
been recalled to England with a cynical disregard for the island's safety.
Their situation was now far worse because they had to worry about possible
attacks from three different nations, not just the Spanish. A Dutch squadron
sent to reoccupy Statia and Saba might well sail on to seize Jamaica; the
French had not only Martinique and other Windward Islands but owned
Tortuga nearby and were busy trying to lure over the Jamaica privateers
and, according to Modyford, were offering them Portuguese commissions.

Modyford knew only too well that Jamaica was in a desperately weak
state. First, many privateers had gone elsewhere after their commissions were
withdrawn. Some had sailed to the Windward Islands whence they could
raid the Venezuelan coast of the Main; others were attacking the coast
of Cuba, operating from among the hundreds of cays along its south coast.
In other words they were all doing their best to make a living, bitter because
the tradesmen in Port Royal had stopped their credit the moment their
commissions were withdrawn.

Second, the volunteer militia in Jamaica had become so run down that
many people were grumbling that the government in England cared so little
about the island that not content with saving money by sacking the Army
garrison, getting rid of 1500 men who could have been relied on to defend
the island, it had recalled every ship of the Navy.

Modyford was well aware of the plight of the privateers, knowing better
than most that Jamaica was at present far from prepared for a trial of
strength with the Spanish. The moment he heard of a group of privateers
gathering off the Cuban coast to attack Sancti Spíritus he sent off Colonel
Beeston with three ships and orders 'to find them out before they fell on
the town, and to divert them'. For this, Beeston wrote in his journal, he
also had 'a proclamation from the King to keep peace with the Spaniards',
but he searched for six weeks without finding a responsible person to whom
he could read it and then returned to Jamaica, an unfortunate piece of
timing for Sancti Spíritus because 'in the meantime they took the town and
plundered it'.

Beeston added: 'The proclamation from the King was that since there was peace with the Spaniards none of his subjects should sail under other [i.e. foreign] commissions against them.' He said that Modyford was trying to get them to attack Curaçao, 'but these parcel of privateers and ships were commanded by Mansell [Mansfield], and he cared for dealing with no enemy but the Spaniards, nor would go against Curaçao, neither were any of them taken any notice of for continually plundering the Spaniards, it being what was desired by the generality...'

Modyford must have realized that he was almost trying too hard to avoid provoking the Spanish because in fact he had already received permission from the King to issue or recall commissions 'as should seem most to the advantage of the King's service and benefit of the island'. This letter, signed by the duke of Albemarle, was written on 1 June 1665, soon after Colonel Edward Morgan's Curaçao expedition had sailed, but Modyford had done his best to avoid having to issue commissions against the Spanish by directing the privateers against the Dutch. As Mansfield's attitude shows only too well, the privateers did not have their hearts in operations against the Dutch who were like themselves in religion and attitude.

Finally, in February 1666, the island's resentment against the Spanish came to a head. Modyford discovered that Jamaica's former pride, the Port Royal Militia, of which Henry Morgan had been one of the first officers and which had been six hundred strong a year earlier, now numbered fewer than 150. This was an alarming indication of the island's lack of defences – for the forts were also in disrepair – and he called a Council meeting on 22 February to arrange for reinforcements of militia to be brought in from elsewhere on the island. Eight of the twelve Council members attended and, he told Albemarle, when he raised the question of the militia, they said that 'the only way to fill Port Royal with men was to grant commissions against the Spaniards, which they were very pressing in'.

It is highly likely that the meeting had been carefully arranged, because Modyford then told them formally that if they passed a resolution in favour of granting commissions, they should also give all their reasons so that they could be recorded in the Council minutes (copies of which were regularly sent to London for the minister to read). The entry says: 'Resolved that it is in the interest of the island to have letters of marque granted against the Spanish.'

It then went on to give a round dozen reasons:

Because it furnishes the island with many necessary commodities at easy rates. It replenishes the island with coin, bullion, cocoa ... and many other commodities, whereby the men of New England are invited to bring their provisions and many merchants to reside at Port Royal.

It helps the poorer planters by selling provisions to the [private] men-of-war. It hath and will enable many to buy slaves and settle plantations ... It draws down yearly from the Windward Islands many an hundred of English, French, and Dutch, many of whom turn planters.

It is the only means to keep the buccaneers on Hispaniola, Tortuga, and the South and North Cays of Cuba from being their enemies and infesting their plantations. It is a great security to the island [of Jamaica] that the [private] men-of-war often intercept Spanish advices and give intelligence to the Governor...

The said men-of-war bring no small benefit to his Majesty and his Royal Highness by the 15ths and 10ths [shares in prize money]. They keep many able artificers at work in Port Royal and elsewhere at extraordinary wages. Whatsoever they get the soberer part bestow in strengthening their old ships, which in time will grow formidable. They are of great reputation to this island and of terror to the Spaniards, and keep up a high and military spirit in all the inhabitants.

The last of the reasons in fact sets out the Council's views (and almost certainly Modyford's) on the whole question of present relations with Spain, saying:

It seems to be the only means to force the Spaniards in time to a free trade, all ways of kindness producing nothing of good neighbourhood, for though all old commissions have been called in and no new ones granted, and many of their [Spanish] ships restored, yet they continue all acts of hostility, taking our ships and murdering our people, making them work at their fortifications ... For which reasons it was unanimously concluded that the granting of said commissions did extraordinarily conduce to the strengthening, preservation, enriching and advancing the settlement of this island.

Modyford told Albemarle that 'looking on their weak condition, the chief merchants gone from Port Royal, no credit given to privateers for victualling &c., and rumours of a war with the French often repeated', he agreed to the resolution. Nor is it likely he was very reluctant, because the very next day the criers went through the streets of Port Royal, St Jago and Passage Fort and as soon as the drummers finished their ruffles the proclamation was read aloud.

The town criers had hardly finished their work before Colonel Cary arrived back in Port Royal to report. Modyford had sent him off after Beeston's return to try once again to persuade the buccaneers off the South Cays of Cuba to change their minds and attack Curaçao. Cary told Sir Thomas that he had been completely successful: not only had the buccaneers agreed but they had promptly elected Mansfield their 'admiral' and sailed after drawing up a letter which, Modyford said, professed 'much zeal in his Majesty's service and a firm intention to attack Curaçao. They are much wasted in numbers, many being gone to the French, where Portugal commissions are in force against the Spaniard'.

Beeston's earlier reference to the privateers attacking Sancti Spíritus 'in the meantime' was something of an understatement because, as Sir Thomas wrote frankly to the duke of Albemarle a few days after the Council meeting, two or three hundred privateers, 'being denied provisions for money', took and fired the town of 'Santo Spirito', 'routed a body of 200 horses, carried their prisoners to their ships, and for their ransom had 300 fat beeves sent down ...'

All this had been done without orders from Jamaica, Modyford said, and 'under colour of Portugal commissions'. The privateersmen, he warned, would 'in time be totally alienated from this place, which we must prevent or perish', and the only way of keeping the men loyal to Jamaica was to issue commissions.

Since he had been told he could issue commissions and was in fact already doing so, Modyford was not pleading a case but describing the situation as he saw it. He knew that Madrid would never grant the Royal African Company an *asiento*, but men like the pro-Spanish secretary of State, Arlington, and Thomas Lynch, the Company's factor in Jamaica, let imaginary ledger entries blot out logical thought; the dreams of profits from slave sales justified the opinion that after one and a half centuries of 'No peace beyond the Line' the Spanish would miraculously change overnight, tossing away pride and hatred of heretics along with their claim to Jamaica.

In Spain the constant complaints of provincial governors in the West Indies that they could not fight off buccaneer raids were reminding the Council of the Indies of six small ships of war and a caravel that had been allocated for the *armada de barlovento*, the windward fleet, four years earlier but taken over by the Navy before they could cross the Western Ocean to defend the Caribbean. The Council began the lengthy process of applying for them to the Queen-Regent.

There had been considerable agitation over letters of marque. Several Spanish merchants in Seville and shipowners along the Biscay coast wanted commissions so that they could operate as privateers against the country's enemies in the West Indies, but the strongest influences against the idea were the Council of the Indies and other Seville merchants. Their reason was short-sighted to the point of absurdity: they were afraid the Spanish privateers would break Seville's monopoly of trade.

Edward Mansfield and his fleet of buccaneers in the meantime had sailed for their promised attack on Curaçao, a voyage of a thousand miles, all to windward, and Modyford heard nothing more for a couple of months. Then Mansfield arrived in Port Royal on 12 June to report that instead of taking the Dutch island of Curaçao he had captured the Spanish island of Old Providence, as well as raiding the city of Cartago, more than half-way across the province of Costa Rica.

'Mansfield complains that the disobedience of several officers and soldiers was the cause of their not proceeding on the design of Curaçao,' Modyford told the duke. 'In the meantime, the old fellow was resolved (as he tells me) never to see my face again unless he had done some service to his Majesty, and therefore with 200 men, which were all that were left him and about eighty of them French, he resolved to attempt the island of Providence, which was formerly English...'

Modyford wrote that to avoid driving the privateers away he had only reproved Mansfield for taking Old Providence without the King's express orders. 'Neither could I without manifest imprudence but accept the tender of it in his Majesty's behalf, and considering its good situation for favouring any design on the rich Main ... I hold it my duty to reinforce the garrison and send some able person to command it.

'Meantime we are increasing apace in ships and men, privateers daily coming in and submitting to the strictness of the commissions and instructions I put on them for his Majesty's service.'

The Cartago raid and capture of Old Providence is the last privateer operation where there is any doubt about the rôle of Harry Morgan. Did he sail to Curaçao and then on to Costa Rica with Mansfield, or did he stay in Jamaica with Mary Elizabeth until Mansfield arrived with the news he had captured Old Providence and needed a garrison? At this stage there is no way of being sure. One account, written by a buccaneer, says he was second-in-command of the expedition, but makes no mention of Curaçao; another says much the same but gets the year wrong; a third, written nearly three hundred years later, says flatly that Morgan was still in Jamaica, resting after the Granada raid.

For reasons which will soon be apparent, all three accounts are probably partly true. Morgan is likely to have stayed behind in Port Royal when Mansfield went off to Curaçao because, better than most, he could organize the militia. The shortage of soldiers was worrying the Council, and merely calling for volunteers was not sufficient: officers and non-commissioned officers had to be selected and the volunteers formed into companies and issued with arms.

By the time Mansfield arrived with the news that he had captured Old Providence, the whole position had changed in Port Royal: Modyford was now much more cheerful and confident at the way the privateers were coming in, and anxious to send off reinforcements to Old Providence. It seems very probable that Morgan, having organized the militia, then sailed for Providence.

In the meantime Mansfield had left for Tortuga but he was far from being the contented admiral of the Brethren of the Coast that Modyford would have the duke believe. The Jamaica commissions being granted were far too limited in scope for him: they restricted privateer attacks to Spanish ships; no Spanish towns or villages were to be touched, a prohibition he had ignored in taking Old Providence.

Mansfield's last raid had been daring but yielded little or no purchase. Even before his fleet of privateers reached the first of the Dutch islands the soldiers on board his own ship were muttering against the proposed attack on Curaçao, 'averring that there was more profit with less hazard to be gotten against the Spaniard, which was their only interest'.

Mansfield was obviously concerned with placating Modyford and making sure his Brethren would again be welcome in Port Royal, instead of having their credit stopped and those unwise enough to linger finding themselves clapped in Port Royal's Bridewell for debt. But while everyone was having doubts about Curaçao, a prisoner from a Spanish prize talked of Cartago, which was then the capital of the province of Costa Rica, between Panama and Nicaragua. It was a rich city, he said, undefended and never yet attacked. He claimed he could guide them there from Almirante Bay, where the ships could be left safely anchored...

It was a tempting proposition, with memories of Henry Morgan's success against Granada, and most of the captains knew Almirante Bay well enough: it was almost enclosed, its entrance channels easy to find, and once inside there were islands and cays giving good protection, the names of many of them showing how often they were used by English buccaneers and pirates – Sister Cays, Shepherd Harbour, Middle Channel Hill, John Crow Point, Sail Rock, Lime Point, Careening Cay ... What the buccaneers had never realized in the past as they rode at anchor inside the great bay and listened to the sea which almost always breaks up to a mile offshore was that the provincial capital of Cartago was so near.

So Mansfield and his fleet turned away from Curaçao and steered westward for a run of eight hundred miles to Almirante Bay, where Mansfield landed about six hundred of his men and began the march at once, determined to take Cartago by surprise. The first seventy-five miles were comparatively easy, with small towns and villages to raid for food. Then they had to turn west and cross the mountains, an 11,000-foot peak on their left and a 12,500-foot peak to their right, with the only pass to Cartago rising more than 2000 feet in front of them. Food became short and quarrels began among the different nationalities, which included English, French, Dutch, Portuguese and Negroes. Then a local Indian raised the alarm, rousing out the Spanish militia. The buccaneers had started off from Almirante Bay on 8 April; the governor of the province had received the alarm on 14 April; by 20 April the buccaneers were defeated, back on board their ships and heading out of Almirante Bay with not a penn'orth of purchase between them.

It was at that point that Mansfield decided to take Old Providence, which had of course been settled in Cromwell's time by a group of Puritans who were later driven out by the Spanish. Almost halfway between Jamaica and Portobelo, Old Providence is a rocky, rugged island almost completely surrounded by barrier reefs with good anchorages inside and a smaller island, Santa Catalina, separated to the westward only by a narrow boat channel. The names known to the buccaneers are still used – Jones Point, Split Hill (aptly named with a sixty-foot-wide chasm dividing it), The Brothers, Crab Cay, Iron Wood Hill, Boat Rock. At the western end of Santa Catalina is a large black rock, forty feet high and shaped like the profile of a human face. At the time of Mansfield's attack it had no name; now, although the island is owned by Colombia, its official name is 'Morgan's Head'.

Mansfield's idea of making the island a permanent base for the Brethren was a good one. It was much closer to the Main and cut down considerably the distances the Jamaica and Tortuga privateers had to cover. Jamaica is 450 miles north of Old Providence while Almirante Bay is only three hundred miles south and Portobelo three hundred miles south-east, compared with 625 miles from Port Royal to Portobelo. A radius of two hundred miles covers almost anywhere on the Mosquito Coast, including Monkey Bay. The island has plenty of fresh water and there are enough reefs and shoals round it to make it a dangerous approach for ships that do not know the area.

By the evening of 2 May, when he had first sighted the three peaks forming the centre of the island, Mansfield had only half a dozen ships with him; the other eight, disappointed with the Cartago purchase or short of supplies, had left. Modyford described the actual attack on the island in his report to Albemarle. Mansfield had set sail from Almirante Bay,

and being an excellent coaster [i.e. navigator], which is his chief, if not his only virtue, in the night he came within half a mile of [Old Providence] by an unusual passage among rocks, and in the early morning landed, marched four leagues, surprised the Governor, Don Esteban del Campo, who was taken prisoner. The [Spanish] soldiers got into the fort, being about 200, but on conditions to be landed on the Main they yielded.

Twenty-six pieces of ordnance, 100 double jars of powder, shot and all things necessary were found, and the fort very strongly built, they acknowledge very little plunder, only 150 negroes; they brought off 100, and left Captain Hattsell, keeper of the magazine, and so have rendered it to me for his Majesty's account; they say that many of the guns have Queen Elizabeth's arms engraven on them.

Mansfield left a Frenchman in command of Old Providence while he went to Jamaica to report to Modyford and get reinforcements. The Frenchman was known as Le Sieur Simon, the captain of a Tortuga privateer, and he set his small garrison to work on the island's defences while he waited for Mansfield to return.

A disappointed Mansfield, dissatisfied with the limits put on the Jamaica commissions, left Governor Modyford and went to Tortuga to recruit more men. He was an old man by now, and tired, and in the words of the buccaneer John Esquemeling, who described many raids, 'death suddenly surprised him and put a period to his wicked life'.

Sir Thomas hurriedly arranged a garrison to be sent to Old Providence. He could not draw on the newly-organized militia, which was intended for the defence of Port Royal itself, so he called for volunteers and among the first was the gallant Sir Thomas Whetstone, who had been the speaker of the House of Assembly for the past two years. As an experienced privateer captain he was never a man to miss some excitement, and he now offered his ship to carry the garrison. The most experienced Army officer to come forward was Major Samuel Smith, and he was put in command of the rest of the volunteers – a Captain Stanley and thirty-two soldiers.

The expedition sailed early in July and Modyford was very careful in wording his orders to Major Smith, making it clear that, far from engaging in some privateering expedition, he was to govern the island 'for his Majesty'. That placed the whole operation on a more elevated plane; the seizure of Old Providence was now an official act, not just a whimsy for the late admiral of the Brethren. Modyford certainly regarded it as recovering what had originally been an English possession – it had never been settled by the Spanish and their ill-treatment of the original British settlers was still remembered by some of the survivors living in Jamaica.

Harry Morgan in Jamaica did what he could to reinforce the island, and the buccaneer Esquemeling, referring to it as St Catharine (from the Spanish name of the smaller island, Santa Catalina), wrote that since Mansfield was now dead, Morgan 'endeavoured as much as he could ... to preserve and keep in perpetual possession the isle of St Catharine ... His principal intent was to consecrate it as a refuge and sanctuary unto the pirates of those parts, putting it in a sufficient condition of being a convenient receptacle or storehouse of their preys and robberies ... writing for the same purpose unto several merchants that lived in Virginia and New England, and persuading them to send him provisions and other necessary things' towards strengthening the island's defences.

Esquemeling's account, one of the most interesting written by a buccaneer, shows that although he admired Morgan – this is clear from later accounts – he did not like him, and he erodes his own credibility by saying that

Morgan was preparing Old Providence as a refuge for pirates. Quite apart from Modyford's orders, Morgan's great strength was that whatever he did he always had a genuine commission signed by the governor of Jamaica to cover it, so that legally he was never guilty of piracy. In peace or war the Spanish, hardly likely to appreciate commissions issued against them, always referred to Morgan or any privateer captain of whatever nationality as a pirate, or corsair, and on the strength of 'No peace beyond the Line' treated them as such, but that was clinging to the original papal bulls. Furthermore, while Esquemeling's original narrative was in Dutch the subsequent English editions were taken from the Spanish, and the Spanish translator was careful to use as many pejorative terms as possible.

After reporting that Whetstone and Smith had sailed, Modyford told the duke:

> Your Lordship cannot imagine what a change there is on the face of the men and things, ships repairing, great resort of workmen and labourers to Port Royal, many returning, many debtors released out of prison, and the ships of Curaçao voyage [previously] not daring to come in for fear of creditors, brought in and fitted out again, so that the regimental forces at Port Royal are near 400. Had it not been for that seasonable action [i.e. granting commissions] I could not have kept this place against French buccaneers, who would have ruined all the seaside plantations, whereas I now draw from them mainly, and lately David Marteen, the best man of Tortuga, that has two frigates at sea, had promised to bring in both.

When Major Smith arrived at Old Providence at the end of July, he found fewer men than he expected – only fifty-one to defend the two islands. However, no word from him arrived at Port Royal during August, but this did not cause concern and a small ship sailed to join him, taking another fourteen men and the wife and daughter of one of them. By 1 September – the day the Great Fire of London began – this ship was only a few miles south of Jamaica, making a slow passage in a very light easterly wind.

By the end of September, when Sir Thomas Whetstone did not return with his ship after landing the garrison, there was some anxiety at Port Royal. Had Whetstone's ship foundered? What of the second ship? How was Major Smith's garrison? Did he need more men and supplies?

Almost exactly two years were to pass before Sir Thomas Modyford had the full details of what had happened at Old Providence. In August 1668 two men arrived in Port Royal, prisoners freed by the Spanish in Havana. They were little more than skeletons, their arms and legs heavily scarred and covered with sores, the result of having been kept in irons in Spanish dungeons for more than twenty of the previous twenty-three months. One

was Major Samuel Smith, the other was Captain Henry Wasey, the former
master of the *Concord* merchant ship. Two months later three more men
reached Port Royal with an even more horrifying story to tell, and with
their arrival the only four known survivors of the Old Providence garrison
(for Captain Wasey was not there) were accounted for. The rest ended their
days as Spanish slaves.

The official Spanish account of their capture of Old Providence is detailed
and, combined with depositions sworn by Major Smith, Captain Wasey and
the other three survivors, shows that there was little to choose between
the way the Spanish treated their enemies and the way the pirates of the
Caribbean handled their victims.

The viceroy of the Province of Panama, Don Juan Perez de Guzman,
had for some weeks been worrying about fourteen 'English vessels' off the
coast of the Main and had warned his garrisons (one of the reasons why
the governor of Cartago had been on the alert against Mansfield). Then
a British ship flying a flag of truce arrived at Portobelo with the governor
of Old Providence, Don Esteban del Campo and his garrison of 270, who
had surrendered to Mansfield 'on conditions to be landed on the Main'.
Mansfield had kept his word and the first the viceroy of Panama knew of
the fate of Old Providence was Don Esteban's arrival.

Perez promptly called a council of war (a prudent move by the viceroy
which made sure the responsibility for wrong decisions would be shared)
and declared that 'it was absolutely necessary to send some forces unto
[Old Providence], sufficient to retake it from the pirates, the honour and
interest of his Majesty of Spain being very narrowly concerned herein'.
Several members of the council disagreed, saying the pirates would 'not be
able to subsist in the said island'.

As the council was meeting at Panama, in sight and sound of the South
Sea where the chances of attack were apparently so remote as to be
negligible, this 'let them starve themselves' approach was reasonable, but
Perez, 'as one who was an expert and valiant soldier', ordered that the
militia in Portobelo should sail to retake the island, and according to the
Spanish account, 'neither to be idle nor negligent in his master's affairs,
he transported himself thither, with no small danger of his life'.

Quite what that danger was, except perhaps from a bolting horse, it is
hard to guess, but he found two ships in Portobelo which were suitable for
carrying troops to Old Providence. One was the British merchant ship
Concord of 185 tons. She was lying with Spanish sentries guarding her because,
although one of the few foreign ships granted a Spanish licence allowing
her to trade and now in Portobelo unloading a cargo consigned to Spanish
merchants, the mayor, José Sanchez Ximenez, had ordered the arrest of
the *Concord*'s master, Henry Wasey, on 25 May, the moment he heard about
Old Providence. Wasey was taken to the city jail in irons and locked in

its dungeon. The immediate effect of course was that the local merchants did not have to pay their bills; in the long term the ship was available for the governor when he arrived in Portobelo on 7 July.

Perez acted vigorously the moment he arrived: Sanchez was put in charge of the expedition and the 270 Old Providence soldiers recently landed from Mansfield's flag of truce ship were mobilized along with men from the garrisons of Portobelo and Cartagena. The force sailed for Old Providence on 2 August and comprised, by the Spanish account, 517 fighting men.

Major Smith, Captain Stanley and Sir Thomas Whetstone had a force of fifty-one effective men (out of a total of seventy-two) to defend Old Providence and Santa Catalina, and although the details of the attack need not concern us – there could be only one ending – the Spanish found it far from easy. After losing one of his ships on a reef and exchanging fire with one of the forts, according to the Spanish account, Sanchez 'sent on shore unto the pirates one of his officers, to require them ... to surrender the island ... The pirates made the answer, "That [the] island had once before belonged unto the Government and Dominions of the King of England; and that instead of surrendering it, they preferred to lose their lives."'

Sanchez discovered that there were only seventy-two men on the island so he landed five hundred troops and began a siege. Two days later the Spanish were puzzled by the sound that shot from the cannons of one fort made as they ricocheted from the rocks they were using for shelter, and later discovered that the British, running out of proper ammunition, had sawn organ pipes from the church into short lengths and were firing them – 'discharging in every shot three score pipes at a time', according to the Spanish account. Finally, with the Spanish attacking from three directions at once, 'the pirates, seeing many of their men already killed and that they could in no manner subsist any longer ... surrendered themselves and likewise the whole island into our hands'.

A few days later the British ship which had earlier sailed from Port Royal was sighted and Sanchez 'gave order unto Le Sieur Simon, who was a Frenchman, to go and visit the said ship, and tell them ... the island belonged still unto the English. He performed the commands and found in the said ship only fourteen men, one woman and her daughter, who were all instantly made prisoners'.

In the light of Major Samuel Smith's deposition two years later the final few lines of the Spanish account are of particular interest: 'The English pirates were all transported to Portobelo, excepting only three, who by order of the Governor [Perez] were carried to Panama, there to work on the castle of San Geronimo.' Those three men were Sir Thomas Whetstone, speaker of the Jamaica House of Assembly, Major Samuel Smith, appointed governor of the island by Sir Thomas Modyford, and Captain Stanley, Smith's second-in-command.

On 18 August 1668, some twenty-three months later, Major Smith gave a sworn statement to Modyford that he finally agreed to surrender 'upon articles of good quarter, which the Spanish did not in the least perform, for the English, about forty, were immediately made prisoners, and all except Sir Thomas Whetstone, myself and Captain Stanley, who were the commanders, were forced to work in irons and chains at the Spaniard's forts, with many stripes [i.e. lashes], and many are since dead through want and ill-usage'.

Whetstone, Stanley and himself 'were sent to Panama, where they were cast into a dungeon and bound in irons for seventeen months'. There they were joined by Henry Wasey. Eventually he and Wasey were sent to Cuba and put in jail there. Whetstone's eventual fate is not known.

Major Smith's account of the surrender terms was borne out by the joint deposition of the three Britons who had escaped to Port Royal from Portobelo – that they would all be allowed to go back to Jamaica in a barque. This would have been similar to the terms allowed the Spanish by Mansfield, who sent the Spanish garrison back to Portobelo. But, the deposition said,

> when they laid down their arms the Spaniards refused them the barque and carried them as slaves to Portobelo, where they were chained to the ground in a dungeon ten feet by twelve, in which were thirty-three prisoners.
>
> They were forced to work in the water from five in the morning till seven at night [i.e. the hours of daylight in that latitude], and at such a rate that the Spaniards confessed they made one of them do more work than three negroes, yet when weak with want of victuals and sleep, they were knocked down and beaten with cudgels, and four or five died.
>
> Having no clothes, their backs were blistered in the sun, their necks, shoulders and hands raw with carrying stones and mortar, their feet chopped, and their legs bruised and battered with the irons, and their corpses noisome to one another. The daily abuse of their religion and King, and the continual trouble they had with priests would be tedious to mention...

Major Smith had some further news for Modyford who, soon after arriving in Jamaica, had sent his eldest son Jack in the *Griffin* frigate to fetch Lady Modyford (see page 106). The frigate was never seen again, and four years later Major Smith had to tell him that he had heard that the *Griffin* had been sunk by a Spanish galleon.

The Buccaneers Attack

Mansfield's capture of Old Providence coincided with yet another change in the British policy towards Spain. The ambassador in Madrid, Sir Richard Fanshaw, had died in June 1666, and despite Britain's impatience the negotiations came to a halt.

The Privy Council not only approved Modyford's acceptance of Old Providence when the news reached London in September 1666, but appointed his brother Sir James as its lieutenant-governor. The slow communications meant, however, that Sir James's commission was dated just two months after Major Smith had been forced to surrender.

Although he did not hear the details for two years, Sir Thomas Modyford knew by Christmas that Old Providence had been lost, but by that time he was worrying more about the French than the Spanish. For many months they had been trying to lure the Port Royal privateers to Tortuga, as though intent on undermining the British in Jamaica, and with 1667 approaching it seemed likely that France would declare war.

If that happened Modyford knew (and had already commented on it in letters to London) that Jamaica faced a formidable threat from both Dutch and French privateers. Nor would he rely on the privateers in Port Royal; they had shown that they had no heart in fighting the Dutch. 'I had no money to pay them,' Modyford later grumbled to Arlington, 'nor frigates to force them; the former they could not get from our declared enemies, nothing could they expect but blows from them, and (as they have often repeated to me) "Will that pay for sail and rigging?"' Had he been sent the frigates he had so often requested he would have compelled the buccaneers to put up with 'their wants and necessities' until they had 'accomplished his Majesty's intentions' of attacking the Dutch.

The French finally declared war on Britain in January 1667 but the fighting in the West Indies was mostly among the islands of the Lesser Antilles, while in Jamaica the privateers, with their cosmopolitan crews, continued spasmodic attacks against the Spanish.

Within a few months the whole situation changed once again in Europe. The treaty of Madrid was signed on 23 May between Spain and Britain but made no mention of Jamaica, a tribute to the tenacity of the Spanish in claiming it back and Britain in refusing. The only article that even

obliquely referred to the West Indies was the second, which guaranteed the
safety of subjects of each country by land and sea 'through the territories,
dominions, possessions, cities, towns, villages ... their havens and ports,
where they have been previously accustomed to deal and trade'.

Were the British 'accustomed to trade' in Portobelo or Cartagena, the
ports of Cuba or the towns of New Spain? The article could (and would)
mean whatever each government later decided, particularly because Spain
had granted licences to certain foreign ships – like the *Concord* – when it
suited her. As far as Jamaica was concerned, the treaty of Madrid had
changed nothing.

Almost exactly two months later the British, French and Dutch signed
a peace treaty at Breda. Britain kept the Dutch settlement of New Amsterdam (which would become the colonies of New York and New Jersey) while
in the West Indies the British ownership of Antigua and Montserrat and
part of St Kitts was confirmed. France was left in possession of St Lucia
and her part of St Kitts.

News of both treaties reached Jamaica before Christmas and of the two
only the one signed at Breda had any significance so far as Sir Thomas
Modyford was concerned. By now he had a regular group of men round
him who acted as both friends and advisers. They were not people to whom
he turned for advice on specific subjects but rather planters, men with similar
attitudes to his own who could be trusted to give honest opinions.

The merchants were not part of Modyford's circle and they were bitterly
disappointed at the terms of the treaty with Spain; there was not a word
of encouragement for traders, no *asiento*, not a hint that would help guide
Thomas Lynch, the factor of the Royal African Company. Not even the
logwood cutters of Campeche were satisfied: the treaty had made their
position no safer. Although they had been cutting logs there for more than
a quarter of a century the Spanish had never admitted it and would not
now accept any right of 'safe passage'.

Modyford's first charge as governor was still the defence of the island and
there was nothing in the treaty of Madrid which guaranteed that a Spanish
fleet would not suddenly attack the island they claimed as their own. Yet
the island's only defence, apart from the militia, was still the privateer
fleet...

A few weeks earlier in answer to a letter from Arlington about privateers
Modyford had said: 'I will, suitable to your Lordship's directions, as far
as I am able, restrain them from further acts of violence towards the
Spaniards, unless provoked by new insolences.' But he was not afraid of
pointing out the absurd contradiction of the British government calling for
peaceful trade in the West Indies but providing neither the frigates for defence
nor the diplomatic pressure on Spain which could bring about the trade.
'Truly it must be very important to run the hazard of [losing Jamaica] for

obtaining a correspondence which could not but by orders from Madrid be had,' he told Arlington.

'The Spaniards look upon us as intruders wheresoever they find us in the Indies, and use us accordingly; and were it in their power ... would soon turn us out of our plantations; and is it reasonable that we should quietly let them grow upon us until they are able to do it? It must be force alone that can cut in sunder that unneighbourly maxim of their government to deny all access to strangers.'

While he and the rest of Jamaica were still considering the treaty of Madrid, Modyford had several reports from Cuba that the Spanish, apparently emboldened by their recapture of Old Providence (and perhaps with new orders from Madrid), were preparing troops and a squadron of ships for an attack on Jamaica. Coming on top of the Old Providence attack, Modyford was more than prepared to believe there was some truth in the reports, so he called a meeting of the Council.

The Council had no doubts and decided that as big a force of privateers as possible should be assembled at Port Royal and sent off to Cuba to find out what was going on. Who should they put in command? There was little choice because one man stood head and shoulders above all others, Colonel Henry Morgan, now commanding the Port Royal Volunteers.

Harry Morgan had become wealthy and powerful in a way perfectly acceptable to the Jamaican society that was slowly emerging – by his own bravery and skill with sword, pike and musket. He had a strong and forceful personality and quick intelligence at a time and place when they, and known bravery, were the main elements of leadership. Someone might bluster and shout and fool a few people for a short while, but a man then less than thirty years of age who could lead several score desperadoes of various nationalities for hundreds of miles across marshes and arid pampas, along dangerous coasts in canoes and then up strange rivers, and at the end have those men boast about it all as 'Harry Morgan's Way', had that indefinable and very rare magnetism which in any age will make him famous.

There was no question of patronage; no suggestion that Sir Thomas Modyford was looking after the nephew of his late lieutenant-governor, of whom he had become so fond. Modyford recognized in Morgan the kind of young man upon whose shoulders the very safety of Jamaica might one day depend. So, from the time of his return from Villahermosa and Granada, Henry Morgan became a frequent visitor to Modyford's official residence, the King's House. Having bought his own plantation, he mixed with other plantation owners on level terms, discussing the problems facing them all: sugar yields and costs, slave prices and cane cutting, land clearance and house building.

He had helped his two Morgan cousins start their plantation and with

Charles not yet twenty-one it was clear that if the plantation failed, all of them were going to be a charge on Harry Morgan and his brother-in-law, Robert Byndloss. Uncle Edward's legacy to his nephew had been a moral obligation which showed every sign of being a financial one too.

When the Jamaica Council held its famous meeting of February 1666 and Sir Thomas Modyford wanted the Port Royal Militia restored to a reasonable strength and the fortifications repaired and improved, Harry Morgan had been chosen for the job. Before sailing on the Granada expedition he had been a captain in the Militia; now he was made colonel, put in command of the regiment and given the responsibility of restoring the port's fortifications. This was the first time that he was concerned with fortifications and it seems to have started an interest that, along with siege operations, would last the rest of his life.

Men obviously wanted to follow him and very soon he was able to report to the governor that the Port Royal Volunteers, as they were now called, were four times as strong as before. Fort Charles was completed to the satisfaction of his brother-in-law, Major Byndloss, who commanded it (and was now outranked by Henry). Various batteries were established on the Point to cover the harbour and the nearby magazines were soon well stocked with powder. Morgan had then done his best to raise a garrison for Old Providence, trying to get help from New England and Virginia.

He was a man of some influence in the island, whose advice was sought. He and Mary Elizabeth were frequent visitors to the King's House. Those who eyed Mrs Morgan to see if she was pregnant were disappointed, but there was time enough for a family – or so it seemed. This was the thirty-three-year-old man now chosen to investigate the Cuba reports. He was given a commission signed by Modyford ordering him to collect the privateers and sail to 'take prisoners of the Spanish nation, whereby you may gain information of that enemy to attack Jamaica, of which I have had frequent and strong advice'.

Morgan was described in the commission as 'Admiral', while about this time Colonel Beeston referred to him in his Journal as 'General' Morgan. The governor had the authority to appoint a commander-in-chief, and the appointment of admiral or general was made as appropriate. The rank was absolutely legal but, of course, referred only to the forces of Jamaica.

Rounding up privateers and privateersmen was easier than it might have been because the French were now not only at peace with England but at war with Spain, the war of Devolution having begun the previous May, to the delight of the French privateer leaders in Tortuga. One of the first to volunteer was Morgan's old friend John Morris, a man now in middle age who had been in the Granada expedition. Another was Morris's son, also John, who now had his own ship. Captain Edward Collier agreed to sail, and soon Morgan's flotilla comprised more than half a dozen ships of various sizes and some five hundred men. Other privateers at sea would probably join later, as well as the French at Tortuga, so Morgan arranged a rendezvous among the hundreds of tiny islands on the south side of Cuba, the so-called South Cays.

Although Colonel Henry Morgan now held a commission from the governor appointing him admiral commanding this expedition to Cuba, whatever was written in the commission did not affect the fact that 'Harry Morgan' was leading the buccaneers on a raid which should yield a useful purchase.

More important, the Brethren of the Coast now accepted Morgan as their leader in place of Mansfield. Henry Morgan was the admiral of Jamaica's privateer fleet by virtue of Modyford's commission; he was the admiral of the Brethren because that motley band of privateersmen and pirates had now chosen him.

The buccaneers had a regular method of preparing for an expedition and John Esquemeling, who was then one of their number, describes it, referring (as became a reformed character) to his erstwhile shipmates as 'pirates'.

'Before the pirates go to sea,' he wrote, 'they give notice unto everyone that goes upon the voyage, of the day on which they ought precisely to embark.' Each man was told to bring 'so many pounds of powder and bullets as they think necessary for that expedition'.

As soon as they met on board the ship they held a council meeting to decide where they should first raid to get provisions 'especially of flesh, seeing they scarce eat anything else. And of this the most common sort among them is pork. The next good is tortoises [sic: turtles] which they use to salt a little. Sometimes they resolve to rob such or such hog-yards, wherein the Spaniards often have a thousand head of swine together'.

Having collected enough meat for the voyage they returned to the ship. 'Here their allowance, twice a day to everyone, is as much as he can eat, without either weight or measure. Neither does the steward of the vessel give any greater proportion of flesh, or anything else, unto the Captain than unto the meanest mariner.'

They then called another council to decide on their target, and also 'they agree upon certain articles, which are put in writing, by way of bond or obligation, which everyone is bound to observe, and all of them, or the chiefest, do set their hands unto'. These articles set out very clearly the wages for each man – although of course everything had to come from the purchase and 'it is the same law among these people as with other pirates: no prey, no pay'.

The captain's pay was decided first and then 'the salary of the carpenter or shipwright who careened, mended and rigged the vessel. This commonly amounts unto 100 or 150 pieces of eight [worth five shillings in 1668], being, according to the agreement, more or less.' The surgeon was also voted a salary – usually 200 or 250 pieces of eight, and this included 'his chast of medicaments'.

Finally they agreed in writing 'what recompense or reward each one ought to have that is either wounded or maimed in his body, suffering the loss of any limb, by that voyage'. This scale was very fair and comparable to modern insurance practice, and Esquemeling wrote: 'Thus they order for the loss of a right arm 600 pieces of eight, or six slaves; for the loss of a left arm 500 pieces of eight, or 5 slaves; for a right leg 500 pieces of eight or five slaves; for the left leg 400 pieces of eight, or four slaves; for an eye 100 pieces of eight or one slave; for a finger of the hand the same reward as for an eye.'

These sums were taken first from whatever money the ship earned. After that 'a very exact and equal dividend is made of the remainder' but the proportions were agreed. The captain received five or six shares, the master's mate two 'and other officers proportionable to their employment', a seaman receiving one and a boy a half. The boys were included 'by reason that, when they happen to take a better vessel than their own, it is the duty of the boys to set fire unto the ship or boat wherein they are, and then retire unto the prize which they have taken'. Esquemeling continues:

> All the men observe among themselves very good orders. For in the prizes they take, it is severely prohibited unto every one to usurp anything in particular unto themselves. Hence all they take is equally divided, according to what has been said before. Yea, they make a solemn oath to each other not to abscond or conceal the least thing they find amongst the prey. If afterwards anyone is found unfaithful and has contravened the said oath, immediately he is separated and turned out of the society.
>
> Among themselves they are very civil and charitable to each other. Insomuch that, if any wants what another has, with great liberality they give it one to another...

The reports reaching Modyford from Cuba that the Spanish were assembling a fleet were quite true, although it was fortunate for his peace of mind that he had heard only a garbled version. The Council of the Indies had at last managed to get their ships away from the Navy and the *armada de barlovento* had arrived in the West Indies, six ships of war whose upkeep was to be charged to the various provinces.

Two went to Vera Cruz to guard the base of the *flota*, two to Cartagena to protect the galleons, and two operated from Havana, keeping the western end of Cuba clear of any privateers tempted to attack the plate fleet. They came out complete with an admiral, Alonso del Campo y Espinosa, but although in Spain they had seemed just the sort of vessel to drive off the privateers, the viceroy of Mexico was the first to complain about them.

The ships were much too expensive for the provinces to maintain, he said, and anyway they were too large: they drew so much water they could not chase the small and nimble privateers among the shallow channels between the cays or seek them out among the scores of bays.

Morgan had arranged his rendezvous at a particular group of the South Cays: they provided a good lee for vessels to anchor, the reefs and islands to seaward keeping out the swell waves whose sudden snatch at an anchor cable was more likely to part it than the steady strain of a strong wind. Another danger for an anchored ship was, curiously enough, no wind. In many tropical bays and anchorages an otherwise good sandy bottom has a scattering of coral heads which rear up like large cauliflowers, often six feet high and many feet across. The danger for a ship is that when the wind drops her cable, having no strain on it, gets caught round a coral head. This is not always obvious at the time and a breeze coming up puts a strain on the rope, which soon gets sawn through and the ship finds herself adrift.

After arriving at the rendezvous with his Port Royal ships, Morgan waited patiently. The moment a ship was sighted the buccaneers would prepare for action, but almost always someone recognized her as a privateer coming to the rendezvous, where she received a commission from Morgan.

By the appointed date at the end of March 1668, he had a dozen vessels ranging in size 'between ships and great boats' and carrying some seven hundred men, a mixture of British and French. The fact that Henry Morgan had been appointed admiral by the governor, and that the group of vessels was often referred to as a fleet, gives a wrong impression of the size of the usual privateer. One of the larger ships in this expedition was John Morris's *Dolphin*. She had been built in Spain to carry four guns and was of fifty tons, one of three ships captured from the Spanish by Commodore Mings in 1659 and brought back to Port Royal as prizes. The *Dolphin* was now armed with eight guns, instead of four, and she could carry sixty men for a reasonably lengthy cruise. Her dimensions are not known, but she is unlikely to have been more than fifty feet long on deck, with a beam of about sixteen feet – the size of a large fishing smack or shrimper. Many of the privateers were much smaller, simply large open boats decked over forward to provide shelter for the crews and a comparatively dry place to store provisions. Fitted with a single mast, they could be rowed in calms or to manoeuvre among cays.

When possible, the men anchored close to a beach and slept the night on shore, and the distance they could sail was often governed by the amount of liquid they could carry for drinking and how long the men could stand being soaking wet – as they were bound to be in a stiff breeze – and short of sleep. Frequently such boats were not armed, or at most carried a gun in the bow. The people manning them were often not seamen in the normal sense of the word; they rarely attacked ships, preferring to land near some village or small town and attack overland. Like Henry Morgan, many of these people were former soldiers; they thought more in terms of out-flanking a town's defences than getting to windward of a Spanish ship. They preferred to march twenty miles to assault a town than sail a hundred, because they could collect food and drink as they went.

While Morgan's ships and boats waited at anchor, men rigged awnings of canvas and fished over the side, hoping to lure a big grouper or snapper to the hook. Others gambled, often using playing cards made from the leaves of the signature tree, which could be carved and dried until they were like thin and durable pieces of leather. The sun was scorching in the middle of the day and at night it was warm enough for them to sleep on deck with a blanket or, more usually, a cow hide that acted like a small tent if there was one of the frequent showers that come before dawn. The advantage of anchoring well away from the land and in the lee of the cays was that the men avoided the mosquitoes which otherwise swarmed over them and made their lives a misery.

Finally it was 28 March, the last day of the rendezvous, and Morgan had to decide where they would first attack. 'They called a council,' wrote Esquemeling, 'and some were of opinion 'twere convenient to assault the city of Havana under the obscurity of the night,' an enterprise which would be made easier 'if they could but take any few of the ecclesiastics and make them prisoners.' He described Havana at this time as 'one of the renownedest and strongest places of all the West Indies'.

The council of buccaneers must have been a bizarre sight, ranging in types from Henry Morgan, tall and well built, wearing a beard at a time when men of his class usually had only a flowing moustache, to muscular Negroes, escaped slaves who spoke English with a Spanish accent. There were Frenchmen who were well educated, privateersmen only because their religion had forced them to flee France, and there were others of all nationalities who had fled a life of crime to avoid the executioner. All were united by a desperate desire to get rich and a consuming hatred of the Spanish and the Catholic Church.

So the buccaneer leaders discussed Havana in voices which had many accents: the Welsh lilt of Morgan himself, the English accent of Morris, the French accents of various captains and mates, the heavy tones of the few Dutchmen. However sinister the subject they discussed, the surroundings were beautiful: a sea of an almost gaudy blue, the ships and boats anchored all round painted in bright colours, the frequent splash as pelicans dived in, wriggled and surfaced, gobbling the fish in their beaks like old and toothless men sucking gruel.

Several of the buccaneers at the council and at least one of Morgan's captains had been imprisoned at Havana, and they reckoned that 1500 men would be needed – representing at least another dozen privateer ships. When

Morgan declared there was no chance of getting them, Havana was finally ruled out.

Where should they attack, then? Once again the discussion started with no shortage of suggestions. There was Santiago – they could all remember how successful Commodore Mings' attack had been – or Trinidad, Sancti Spíritus (where the early Spanish settlers had found placer gold), Bayamo and San Cristobal on the south side of the island, while Baracoa and Santa Cruz waited on the north shore. Each had its drawbacks, as man after man explained in detail. Santiago had been strengthened since Mings' attack; Trinidad was so close to the South Cays its inhabitants kept their money hidden and a sharp lookout; Santa Cruz was so near Havana that the capital's troops would be there ready by the time the buccaneers could reach it.

At last, wrote Esquemeling, one man spoke up 'and propounded they should go and assault the town of El Puerto del Principe', saying he knew it well and, being at a distance from the sea, 'it never was sacked by any pirates, whereby the inhabitants were rich, as exercising their trade for ready money with those of Havana, who kept here an established commerce which consisted chiefly in hides'.

Morgan and 'the chiefest of his companions' agreed and the order was given for the privateers to get under way. Despite its name of 'Puerto', the city was by no means a port and was now forty-five miles inland, although it had started off a century and a half earlier as a port on the north coast, one of seven towns set up as administrative centres of the island. Later it had been moved inland, to the centre of the province of Camaguey, but still kept its old name (although now called Camaguey after the province). The buccaneers went to the Gulf of Ana Maria, found a sheltered bay and anchored, intending to land next morning.

There was a Spanish prisoner on board Morgan's ship, a man they thought could not speak English, so they had not bothered to send him to another ship while the council meeting was held at the South Cays. Unfortunately for the buccaneers the prisoner could understand English and that night he escaped, jumped over the side, swam ashore, 'and came unto the town of Puerto del Principe, giving account to the inhabitants of the design the pirates had against them'.

The Spaniards, said Esquemeling, 'as soon as they received this fortunate advice, began instantly to hide their riches, and carry away what movables they could. The Governor also immediately raised all the people of the town, both freemen and slaves; and with part of them took a post by which of necessity the pirates were to pass'. He also set some ambushes 'with some pieces of cannon, to play upon them on their march. He gathered in all about 800 men'.

Morgan led his men, about 650 altogether, in a march to the north-east, and appears to have learned several important lessons by this stage in his career. First, a buccaneer leader had to assume that there would be treachery in the course of an expedition: it was all too easy for a man to become a renegade the moment he knew what town was to be attacked and go to the Spanish with a warning, knowing he would be well rewarded.

Second, Morgan never made the mistake of assuming his enemy was stupid, inexperienced or unprepared. In fact the governor of the province who was organizing the defence of Puerto del Principe was an experienced old soldier who had made valuable use of every moment. The third lesson that Morgan had learned was always to achieve surprise. In the case of the attack on Puerto Principe, the wily young Welshman made three assumptions – the town had been warned, the governor had gathered a large defence force, and ambushes had been prepared.

He led his men off the road, climbing over the rolling hills that stood between the plain and the coast. Patrols sent out ahead made sure that any Spanish settlers, cow catchers or herdsmen were seized before they could bolt for the city, and where possible they were forced to act as guides.

The rest of the story is best told by Esquemeling, who describes how 'at last they came into the plain ... called by the Spaniards La Savana, or The Sheet. The Governor, seeing them come, made a detachment of a troop of horse, which he sent to charge them in the front, thinking to disperse them, and by putting them to flight pursue them with his main body'.

This failed because 'the pirates marched in very good rank and file, at the sound of their drums and with flying colours. When they came nigh unto the horse they drew into the form of a semi-circle, and thus advanced towards the Spaniards, who charged them like valiant and courageous soldiers for some while. But, seeing that the pirates were very dextrous at their arms and their Governor with many of their companions killed, they began to retreat towards the forest...'

There was now little left to stop Morgan's men: within an hour they reached the city and captured it. 'They enclosed all the Spaniards, both men, women and children, and slaves, in several churches and gathered all the goods they could find by way of pillage.'

Finally, according to Esquemeling, the prisoners were told they must pay a ransom for themselves or be transported to Jamaica, and also a ransom for the town, otherwise the buccaneers 'would turn every house into ashes'. Four prisoners were released to fetch the ransom – which was to be paid by all the inhabitants who had earlier fled to the woods. The four came back after a few days saying they could not find their people and asking for more time, promising the ransoms would be paid within fifteen days. 'Captain Morgan,' noted Esquemeling, 'was contented ... to grant them this petition.'

A few hours later several buccaneers reported to Morgan that out in the woods and fields they had found 'considerable booty', and that they had taken prisoner a Negro carrying letters. Morgan read them and found they were from the governor of Santiago, capital of the next province and 160 miles to the eastward, and written to some of the prisoners, telling them 'not make too much haste to pay any ransom'. On the contrary, he said, they should 'put off the pirates as well as they could with excuses and delays, expecting to be relieved by him within a short time, when he would certainly come to their aid'.

Morgan's feelings as he translated the governor's letter can be imagined. He was sitting in the third or fourth largest city in Cuba, one which he had captured with little more than a handful of men, all of them subject only to the discipline which he could enforce by his own personality. He had been appointed 'admiral' by Sir Thomas Modyford, but it was simply a word; he was just the leader of seven hundred privateersmen who would follow him across the ocean and over mountains as long as they trusted him; they would fight against odds and in their cups boast that it was 'Harry Morgan's Way' – as long as he was successful. With men of so many nationalities, personalities, skills, habits and perversions, only success ensured loyalty.

So far Morgan had made no mistakes and, reading between the lines of Esquemeling's account, it is clear that he was being patient with his Spanish captives. There had been no threat that he would hold a few of the city's leading residents over a barbecue pit. Now he discovered that they had deceived him; the fifteen days' grace they had asked from him and received was not to find their friends in the forests; it was to give the governor of Santiago time to gather his troops and cover the distance to Puerto del Principe and rescue them. Henry Morgan was having his first lesson in holding a city to ransom, and it was one he learned thoroughly.

Morgan called his captains, explained how the Spanish had deceived them, and gave orders that all the booty collected so far should be carried over the hills to the ships. 'And withal,' wrote Esquemeling, 'he intimated to the Spaniards that the very next day they should pay their ransoms for as much as he would not wait one moment longer but reduce the whole town to ashes in case they failed to perform the sum demanded.'

He did not reveal to them that his men had intercepted the letters although he knew that the prevarication would be prolonged until the troops arrived. He decided there was no point in staying any longer, so he demanded a thousand cattle, he told Modyford, and sufficient salt to preserve the meat. There was one condition – the Spanish should carry them on board his ships – and they agreed. He formed up his men and, taking six of the leading citizens 'as pledges of what he intended', marched off back to the coast, warning the Spaniards against any delay in delivering the cattle.

Two days later the Spanish arrived at the beaches nearest the anchored ships, driving the cattle and carrying the salt. The cattle were killed and salted 'in great haste', the casks were stowed in the ships, and then Morgan 'set at liberty the prisoners he had kept as hostages of his demand'.

While the cattle were being killed there was one of those sudden episodes which test the leadership of a man leading a combined force, and Esquemeling, who was there, describes it:

> A certain Frenchman being employed in killing and salting one of the beeves, an English pirate came to him and took away the marrow-bones which he had taken out of the ox, which sort of meat these people esteem very much. Hereupon they challenged one another. Being come unto the place of the duel, the Englishman drew his sword treacherously against the Frenchman, wounding him in the back before he had put himself into a just posture of defence, whereby he suddenly fell dead upon the place.
>
> The other Frenchmen, desirous to revenge this base action, made an insurrection against the English, but Captain Morgan soon extinguished this flame by commanding the criminal to be bound in chains and thus carried to Jamaica, promising to them all that he would see justice done upon him.

The ships then sailed back to the South Cays, 'where Captain Morgan intended to make a dividend of what they had purchased in that voyage'. The cash was counted and objects valued, and the total was reported to Morgan – only 50,000 pieces of eight in money and goods. 'The sum being known,' commented Esquemeling, 'it caused a general resentment and grief to see such a small purchase, which was not sufficient to pay their debts at Jamaica.'

New Coins for Old

Morgan's stay in Puerto Principe had not been entirely concerned with ransom: he had extracted some valuable information from prisoners and he reported it to Sir Thomas Modyford with characteristic brevity:

> We were driven to the South Cays of Cuba where, being like to starve and finding the French in like condition, we put our men ashore, and finding all the cattle driven up country and the inhabitants fled, we marched twenty leagues to Porto Principe on the north of the island, and with little resistance possessed ourselves of the same.
>
> There we found that seventy men had been pressed to go against Jamaica; that the like levy had been made in all [the towns of] the island, and considerable forces were expected from Vera Cruz and Campeachy, to rendezvous at the Havannah and from Porto Bello and Cartagena to rendezvous at St Jago of Cuba [Santiago], of which I immediately gave notice to Governor Modyford. On the Spaniards' entreaty we forebore to fire the town, or bring away prisoners, but on delivery of 1,000 beeves, released them all.

Although the buccaneers were bitterly disappointed with their purchase, if Modyford had intended that Morgan's attack should so frighten the Spanish that they would lose any enthusiasm for the proposed attempt on Jamaica, then he was successful.

The governor of Santiago was Don Bayona Villanueva, who wrote a lengthy and revealing report to Madrid in which he told the Queen Regent that he was far from satisfied with the way the commander of the garrison and the mayor of Puerto Principe had behaved before and during Morgan's attack. He may have been covering himself against the often arbitrary punishment handed out from Madrid, or perhaps he really considered they had failed, but he told the Queen Regent that he had 'already charged them with misconduct, and will hear their excuse for the loss of that town...' Having followed the usual system of assuming treachery, Don Bayona wisely made no comment on his own relief attempt; instead he told the Queen Regent that if the evidence warranted a conviction, they should be punished as a warning to other towns which might surrender to 'any insignificant number of the enemy' rather than risk their lives 'in the defence of their country and their Sovereign'.

The raid's small purchase decided most of the Frenchmen to try their luck with L'Ollonais, the leading privateer of Tortuga whose cruelty was, like his bravery, a legend, so they weighed anchor and sailed. This left Morgan in the South Cays with a tiny force, but according to Esquemeling who, since he disliked the Welshman, was hardly biased in Morgan's favour: 'Captain Morgan, who always communicated vigour with his words, infused such spirits into his men as were able to put every one of them instantly upon new designs, they being all persuaded by his reasons that the sole execution of his orders would be a certain means of obtaining great riches. This persuasion had such influence upon their minds that with inimitable courage they all resolved to follow him.'

A little earlier 'a certain pirate of Campeche' whom Esquemeling does not name arrived with some ships and, having heard Morgan's speech to the buccaneers, decided to join the Welshman 'to seek new fortunes under his conduct...' The Campeche men brought Morgan's force up to 460 men in nine ships, and in May they sailed south from Cuba and not a man among them, except Morgan, knew where they were going and what town they would attack. It is a tribute to Morgan's leadership (and fluent tongue) that he did not need to dangle the names of towns in front of the buccaneers; it is also an indication that he knew that few men were above treachery, and the longer he could keep the destination secret the better for the expedition.

Land was sighted ahead after a few days: flat land with a single, isolated mountain rearing up, a flattened sugar loaf. Many of the buccaneers recognized it as the Pilon de Miguel de la Borda, nearly 1700 feet high and close to the mouth of the Chagres River. Morgan then bore up for Naos Bay (now the northern end of the Panama Canal), finally sailing into an inlet formed by some small islands and signalling his ships to anchor close to Isla Largo Remo, whose name was recorded at the time as 'longa de Mos'.

He then called a council of war at which, according to one account, he 'imparted his design of attacking Puerto Velo to his whole company'. Known variously as Puerto Velo, Puerto Bello and Portobelo, it was a formidable harbour defended by three castles which covered the entrance and anchorage with more than sixty cannon. It was the third most strongly defended port in the Indies (after Havana and Cartagena) and its castles had regular garrisons. The governor was the same Don José Sanchez Ximenez who had recaptured Old Providence and dishonoured the surrender terms.

Not all the buccaneers were overjoyed at Morgan's proposal. 'Several objected against the attempt because they had not a sufficient number to think of success against such a city.' To this Morgan is reported to have answered: 'If our numbers are small our hearts are great, and the fewer we are the better shares we shall have in the spoils.' This seems to have had a magic effect, according to Esquemeling, and the buccaneers 'being stimulated with the ambition of those vast riches they promised themselves from their good success, they unanimously concluded to venture upon that design'.

Although Portobelo was many miles to the eastward, Morgan had no intention of trying to fight his nine ships into the harbour against the concentrated fire of the three forts: that would be suicide. Again Morgan thought and planned as a soldier: viewing it as a soldier assaulting a town, not a sailor seizing a port, he saw how Portobelo could be attacked with such a small force, and the problem now was to land his men at the right place without raising the alarm – which would certainly be the case if ships were seen tacking up the coast. The privateers had been towing astern or carrying hoisted on deck a large number of canoes which they used for going among cays and along narrow and shallow channels. Now Morgan intended using them to carry his men to Portobelo.

While still at anchor he was joined by more men who had heard of his arrival and who brought remarkable intelligence – startling enough for Morgan to be able to use it in his report as a justification for attacking Portobelo: levies were being made on towns in the province of Panama for an expedition against Jamaica, in addition to the levies in Cuba which he had already reported to Modyford. The levies in Panama were confirmed by Englishmen 'who had made their escape from Providence' but, far more important, they told him 'that Prince Maurice and divers Englishmen were kept in irons in the dungeon of the castle [of Portobelo]'. After having heard all that, Morgan wrote: 'We thought it our duty to attempt that place.'

Certainly it would be hard for the King or government to criticize Morgan if Prince Maurice was in irons in the dungeon of the castle of San Gerónimo: nothing had been heard of him since his ship vanished near Puerto Rico five years earlier.

On 26 June, Morgan wrote, 'we took our canoes, twenty-three in number, and rowing along the coast, landed at three o'clock in the morning and made our way into the town, and seeing that we could not refresh ourselves in quiet we were enforced to assault the castle...' His quaint excuse for attacking San Gerónimo was no doubt intended to cover an important point: his own commission was to discover Spanish intentions against Jamaica, but the commissions issued to the privateers allowed them to attack only Spanish ships, not towns or villages.

One of the men in Morgan's party had once been a prisoner in Portobelo's dungeon and worked on various buildings and fortifications. Now the knowledge gained at such a price paid a dividend because he acted as a guide.

A sentry at an outpost on the road leading into the city was captured and taken to Morgan, 'who asked him "How things went in the city, and what forces they had?"...' While the sentry was being questioned ('they made him a thousand menaces to kill him, in case he declared not the truth') the rest of the buccaneers remained hidden on either side of the road. They were armed with a variety of weapons but the favourites were swords or pikes. Muskets were not popular: whether matchlock or wheel-lock, they were heavy, cumbersome and slow to load, and the wheel-lock mechanisms were unreliable: the spring of the lock sometimes gave trouble – especially if the gun was left cocked overnight – and often the pyrites did not spark. The humid atmosphere and the rainfall (which was always heavy along this part of the Main) meant that powder became damp. Worst of all, if a musket misfired the enemy was usually so close that the buccaneer was in great danger. Pistols were the usual firearm: more convenient to carry, whether in open boats or through tropical jungle, they were light enough that a man could carry a sword or pike as well.

A young Scottish barber–surgeon, Lionel Wafer, who was serving in another expedition, wrote that Portobelo was,

> a very fair, large and commodious harbour, affording good anchoring and good shelter for ships, having a narrow mouth and spreading wider within. The galleons from Spain find good riding here during the time of their business in Portobel; for from hence they take in such of the treasures of Peru as are brought thither overland from Panama.
>
> The entrance of this harbour is secured by a fort [San Felipe de Todo Fierro, the Iron Fort] upon the left hand going in; it is a very strong one ... At the bottom of the harbour lies the town, bending along the shore like a half moon, in the middle of which upon the sea is another small low fort [Triana], environed with houses ... And at the west end ... upon a gentle rising, lies another fort [Castillo de San Gerónimo], pretty large and very strong, yet overlooked by a neighbouring hill...

It was, Wafer wrote, an unhealthy place; the sea at low water 'leaves the shore within the harbour bare a great way from the houses, which having a black filthy mud, it stinks very much and breeds noisome vapours, through the heat of the climate'.

The captured sentry, gagged and with his hands tied, was made to lead the buccaneers along the road towards San Gerónimo, at the outskirts of the city. This was the road over which the mules and horses brought the gold and silver from Panama, and at that time of night they saw no one. Finally they reached the castle without the alarm being raised and surrounded it.

Silently muskets and pistols were loaded, slow matches were laboriously lit and care was taken that the faint glow could not be seen from the castle walls. As soon as all the buccaneers were in position, 'Captain Morgan commanded the sentry whom they had taken prisoner to speak unto those that were within, charging them to surrender and deliver themselves up to his discretion – otherwise they should be all cut to pieces, without giving quarter to anyone.

'But,' wrote Esquemeling, 'they would hearken to none of these threats, beginning instantly to fire; which gave notice unto the city, and this was suddenly alarmed.'

The garrison had no chance: buccaneers swarmed through the gate and within half an hour every Spaniard inside had surrendered or been killed. The buccaneers gave little quarter. Henry Morgan wrote that San Gerónimo was undermanned, 'being about 130 men, whereof seventy-four were killed, among whom the castillano [commander of the castle] was one'.

The reason why the buccaneers gave so little quarter was not hard to find, and Morgan explained to Sir Thomas Modyford: 'In the dungeon were found eleven English in chains who had been there two years; and we were informed that a great man had been carried thence six months before to Lima of Peru, who was formerly brought from Puerto Rico . . .' The inference was that the 'great man' had been Prince Maurice. The eleven prisoners in chains were the survivors of the buccaneers who had surrendered at Old Providence to the governor of Portobelo. There is little doubt that Sanchez knew he could now expect little mercy.

Much ill-considered nonsense has been written about the cruelty of the buccaneers during this raid on Portobelo, but it should be remembered that until they ran down the dungeon steps all they knew about the events at Old Providence two years earlier was that the Spanish had retaken it a short time after Mansfield captured it. They knew nothing of what Sanchez had done to Major Smith, Sir Thomas Whetstone, the volunteer soldiers, the two women in the second ship or the original buccaneers – many of them their former shipmates – whom Mansfield had left behind as a garrison.

Now, wildly excited after seizing the castle in hand to hand fighting, they went into the dungeon and by the light of burning brands they found eleven men chained to the wall of a cell measuring ten feet by twelve and which was reeking of urine and excrement, the prisoners' arms and legs covered with sores from the chafing of the chains.

Within moments they discovered that the men spoke English. A hurried search among the Spanish prisoners produced keys so the men could be freed, and they were taken to Henry Morgan. The story he heard that night of Sanchez and Old Providence was as dishonourable as any ever told about bad faith by the buccaneers. Morgan was told how Major Smith and Sir Thomas Whetstone had agreed to surrender to Sanchez on condition they were shipped back to Jamaica, but that the Spanish simply put them in jail.

Where were Major Smith and Sir Thomas Whetstone? The prisoners did not know. Were there other prisoners in Portobelo? No, the men said; the rest had died because of maltreatment by their Spanish guards.

The wild stories of the buccaneer behaviour were worsened by Esquemeling, who wrote that the buccaneers had no sooner taken the castle than 'they resolved to be as good as their word in putting the Spaniards to the sword, thereby to strike a terror in the rest of the city. Hereupon, having shut up all the soldiers and officers as prisoners into one room, they instantly set fire to the powder (whereof they found great quantity) and blew up the whole castle in the air, with all the Spaniards that were within'.

It is a splendid story but utterly untrue: the complete castle was there ten years later because Lionel Wafer saw it when Portobelo was again taken by buccaneers and he described it as 'pretty large and very strong'. The walls and lookout towers are still standing today, more than three hundred years later.

What followed is confirmed by Morgan and described by Leslie, an historian writing several years later.

> They next marched to the city, which they entered without any difficulty, for the inhabitants were like so many distressed persons, running about and not knowing which hand to turn to.
>
> The Governor [Sanchez] did his utmost to rally and reduce them to order, but in vain. He therefore, with some of the chief inhabitants, retired to another castle [Fort Triana] which was as yet unassailed by the pirates; thither a great many resorted and carried their riches and best goods.

Fort Triana is right in the town; Lionel Wafer described it as 'environed with houses except only to the sea'. When the buccaneers 'began a miserable havoc' the governor and his men, perched on the battlements of Triana, 'fired incessantly upon them ... yet it had no effect but spur them on to do their business with the greater dispatch. They rifled not only the houses but the churches'.

In the meantime prisoners questioned by Morgan gave more information to alarm Sir Thomas Modyford: 'the Prince of Monte Circa had been there [Portobelo] with orders from the King of Spain to raise 2200 men against us out of the Province of Panama, which [Portobelo] stands in, the certainty whereof was confirmed by all the grandees'.

The buccaneers, wrote Leslie, found they had lost a great many of their companions, and 'being flushed with desires of revenge unanimously resolved to attack the castle which had done them so much mischief and where they knew there was a vast quantity of riches lodged'. A large number of the buccaneers were sharpshooters because of their earlier life: and now they hid on the roofs of the houses round Triana, picking off the Spanish gunners as they reloaded and ran out their cannon. 'Amidst the horror of this assault,' says Leslie, 'both parties behaved with equal courage and the pirates, observing the stout resistance they met with, prepared fire balls with which they designed to fire the gates.' This attempt failed because as the buccaneers approached the wooden gates 'the garrison threw down great stones and flasks of powder [grenades], which killed a great many and compelled the rest to retire'.

Leslie then went on to give a significant picture of Morgan, who saw that Fuerte Triana, although much smaller than the already-captured San Gerónimo, nevertheless covered the harbour: until her guns were silenced along with those of the fort opposite, San Felipe, he could not bring in his ships and load them with the booty already in his hands. 'In this disorder Morgan scarce knew how to behave; he saw it was most impracticable to carry the place; and yet his high spirits would not allow him to give over the assault.'

Morgan was in the position of a man who owned the whole house but could make no use of it unless he unlocked the front door and, as Leslie reported, 'he had certainly been obliged to desist if at that very instant he had not perceived English colours set upon the walls of the other castle [San Felipe], which another body of [his] pirates had successfully stormed. This sight encouraged his fainting troops to renew the attack ...'

Morgan ordered his men to make ten or a dozen scaling ladders, heavy affairs with rungs wide enough for two or three men to climb up side by side. These were dragged close to the walls of Triana but still sheltered from the cannon and musket fire which swept the approaches.

The only authority on what followed is Esquemeling, whose improbable account was copied by Leslie. He says that Morgan passed a message to Sanchez inside the castle saying that unless Fort Triana surrendered he would use monks and nuns to put the scaling ladders into position. The governor's answer was short – he would never surrender himself alive. Sanchez would have made this answer because he must have guessed his fate now that the buccaneers had found and freed the Old Providence survivors. Yet he also knew the fate the Spanish government had in store for officers who surrendered. He was in fact doomed from the moment the attack started.

For all that, Esquemeling wrote:

Morgan was much persuaded that the Governor would not employ his utmost forces, seeing religious women and ecclesiastical persons exposed in front of the soldiers to the greatest dangers. Thus the ladders were put into the hands of religious persons of both sexes; and these were forced at the head of the companies to raise and apply them to the walls.

But Captain Morgan was fully deceived in his judgment of this design, for the Governor, who acted like a brave and courageous soldier, refused not, in the performance of his duty, to use his utmost endeavours to destroy whosoever came near the walls ...

The religious men and women ceased not to cry unto him and beg of him by all the Saints of Heaven he would deliver the castle and thereby save both his and their own lives. But nothing could prevail with the obstinacy and fierceness that had possessed the Governor's mind.

Thus many of the religious men and nuns were killed before they could fix the ladders – which at last being done ... the pirates mounted them in great number and with no less valour, having fireballs in their hands and earthern pots full of powder – all which things, being now at the top of the walls, they kindled and cast in among the Spaniards.

Morgan successfully sued Esquemeling's publishers and they published a denial of this story; nor is it clear why men who would climb the ladders under heavy fire would leave it to the monks and nuns to place them.

The final attack by some two hundred buccaneers, with Henry Morgan among them, was too much for the Spanish:

They all threw down their arms and craved quarter for their lives. Only the Governor of the city would admit or crave no mercy, but rather killed many of the pirates with his own hands, and not a few of his own soldiers because they did not stand to their arms.

And, although the pirates asked him if he would have quarter, yet he constantly answered, 'By no means: I had rather die as a valiant soldier than be hanged as a coward.' They endeavoured as much as they could to take him prisoner, but he defended himself so obstinately that they were forced to kill him ...

The casualty figures reported by Morgan show that nearly a score of buccaneers had been killed and thirty wounded – a ninth of his total force and an eighth of the number of men he had with him in Portobelo, the rest having to stay with the ships. He told Modyford that by the time he had possession of the town and three castles, 'in the former were 900 men that bare [sic] arms'. With their wounded bandaged, the dead buried and the prisoners under guard, the buccaneers 'fell to eating and drinking after their usual manner – that is to say committing in both these things all manner of debauchery and excess', wrote Esquemeling, whose imagination then ran riot.

By now a Spanish horseman who had escaped from the city had managed to cross the Isthmus to reach Panama, where he reported at once to the

Viceroy, Don Juan Perez de Guzman, the man who two years earlier had sent Sanchez to recapture Old Providence. Now, faced with the alarming news that a large force of English buccaneers was besieging the town, Don Juan mobilized three thousand troops and set out immediately for Portobelo.

In the meantime Morgan had told the leading citizens of Portobelo that if they paid him a ransom of 100,000 pieces of eight he would free them and sail away. 'Two of that miserable number were deputed by the rest to go to Panama to raise that sum,' Leslie noted. The next event was described by Morgan, who wrote that 'the fifth day arrived the President of Panama, with about 3000 men ...'

The Spanish had few friends in the jungle; they treated the Indians badly, but over the years various buccaneering expeditions had made friends with groups of them. Now the Indians warned Morgan that an enormous force of Spaniards from Panama was coming over the mountains. Morgan promptly took a hundred men and marched off down the only road – which became little more than a wide track beyond the town – to a narrow pass over the mountains, and through which he knew Don Juan's force had to pass. Here Morgan place his hundred men in ambush. Behind him, in the city, his ships had been sailed round and were now anchored under the guns of the castles and boats were loading the booty on board. Morgan had to wait a day or two before his sentries warned that Don Juan's leading troops were approaching, massing together in the narrow pass but completely unaware of the ambush.

Esquemeling needed only a few words to describe what followed: the hundred buccaneers 'at the first encounter put to flight a good party of those of Panama'. Don Juan's troops fled, and by the time he reorganized them it was quite clear there was no question of using them to drive the buccaneers out of Portobelo. Morgan described to Modyford how Perez's force was beaten off 'with considerable damage, in so much that next day he proffered 100,000 pieces of eight [£25,000] for the delivery of the town and castles in as good condition as we found them'.

Esquemeling records that Perez 'was brought into an extreme admiration, considering that four hundred men had been able to take such a great city with so many strong castles, especially seeing they had no piece of cannon nor other great guns' – so much so that he sent a messenger to Morgan, asking him for 'some small pattern of those arms wherewith he had taken with such violence so great a city'. Morgan is said to have treated the messenger with great civility, giving him a pistol with a few lead bullets for the viceroy and a message to the effect that Morgan 'desired him to accept that slender pattern of the arms wherewith he had taken Portobelo, and keep them for a twelvemonth; after which he would come to Panama and fetch them away'.

It was a flamboyant gesture though perhaps not without justification, and

Perez returned them with a gold ring set with a fine emerald and a message, 'That he desired [Morgan] not to give himself the labour of coming to Panama as he had done to Portobelo for he did certify to him he did not speed so well [to Panama] as he had done there.'

After Morgan's fleet had loaded all the booty it wanted, including the best of the brass guns, the rest of which were spiked, it set sail from Portobelo, passing close to the point where Sir Francis Drake had been buried in a lead coffin just over seventy years earlier.

Morgan rounded off his report to Modyford, which he delivered early in September, by saying he had lost eighteen killed and thirty-two wounded, and that they had held Portobelo for thirty-one days. He added:

> For the better vindication of ourselves against the usual scandals of our enemies, we aver that having several ladies of great quality and other prisoners, they were proffered their liberty to go to the President's [Perez's] camp but they refused, saying they were now prisoners to a person of quality who was more tender to their honours than they doubted to find in the President's camp among his rude Panama soldiers, and so voluntarily continued with us until the surrender [by Morgan] of the town and castles, when with many thanks and good wishes they repaired to their former homes.

When Admiral Morgan and his captains returned to Jamaica they sailed into Port Royal with flags flying and drums beating in the kind of triumphant return last seen at the height of Commodore Mings' operations. There had been no time to total up the purchase in Portobelo and Leslie says that when Morgan arrived at Port Royal he 'found that his purchase amounted to 250,000 pieces of eight, besides all other merchandises'.

Leaving aside the merchandise and counting only the coins, each of the 450 buccaneers shared in the 250,000 pieces of eight, which were from then on used as additional legal currency in Jamaica and valued at five shillings. The number of shares received by each man varied, depending on his rank, but Modyford recorded later that seamen received £60 each while the King's share was £600. (The King fared worst of all because his share was kept to pay for repairs to Port Royal's fortifications.)

The 250,000 pieces of eight equalled £62,500, and because of the changes in value since 1668 the only way of comprehending the enormous amount of money the men shared from the purchase is to compare it with other values or costs. It compares favourably with the value of London's entire export that year to all 'the Plantations' (ranging from Barbados to Jamaica), £107,000. It was three times the customs paid in 1676-7 by Barbados, Nevis, Antigua, Montserrat, St Kitts and Anguilla, £20,700. It was almost exactly a tenth of the year's exports from the Plantations to England, £605,000.

A seaman's share, reported by Modyford to be £60, makes an interesting comparison with salaries paid in Jamaica. If Colonel Edward Morgan had survived, he would have received £600 a year as lieutenant-governor. With a single share of £60 in his pocket, a buccaneer would, as an ordinary citizen of the island, have to pay 3d a gallon duty on a gallon of 'English spirritts', 2d on a pound of tobacco, and 1s or 6d on a gallon of rum, depending on the quality. From these figures it will be seen that there were a lot of long faces among the men in Jamaica who had not gone with Admiral Morgan but, more important, it meant that the admiral would never again lack for men.

Modyford had the difficult task of explaining all this to the King; in fact he decided to address his reports to the duke of Albemarle. In a letter written a month after Morgan's return, Modyford made his first reference to the attacks on Puerto Principe and Portobelo by saying that 'the privateers have had the confidence to take two towns from the Spaniards', and that when he had reproved them because they had commissions only against Spanish ships, they had drawn up a 'declaration' protesting at being blamed for acting against the Spanish whom they had shown to be planning a move against Jamaica.

'It is almost certain that the Spanish had full intention to attempt this island but could not get men,' Modyford told the duke, 'and they still hold the same minds, and therefore I cannot but presume to say that it is very unequal that we should in any measure be restrained while they are at liberty to act as they please upon us ...'

This letter also gave some bitter personal news. He enclosed the deposition of a Spanish captain, Francisco Martin, about Jack Modyford, his eldest son, missing for the previous four years in the *Griffin* frigate. He was 'questionless either murdered or sent into the South Seas by these, our cruel neighbours', Modyford told his cousin. The Spaniard's deposition said that when two English ships had been wrecked on the Florida coast in August, 1664, only five men survived and were captured by the Spanish after living with the Indians. One of the survivors was a young man with a 'very good face and light hair somewhat curling' who told Martin that his name was John and that he was the son of the governor of Jamaica.

For more than two years Sir Thomas Modyford had been trying to persuade the Privy Council to send him ships. Colonel Theodore Cary, on a visit to London, had told the Privy Council: 'Two of his Majesty's nimble fifth-rate frigates would do manifest service in commanding the privateers on all occasions to their obedience, making the discovery of any enemies' actions, and guarding the coast from rovers.'

Finally, in February 1668, when Admiral Morgan and his fleet were in the South Cays for the attack on Puerto Principe, the Privy Council gave orders to the duke of York, as Lord High Admiral, to allocate one of the King's ships 'of the fifth rate for the defence of his Majesty's plantation of Jamaica, and suppressing the insolence of privateers upon that coast ...'

The King was not going to be responsible for the cost of running the ship, though: the governor and planters of Jamaica had undertaken 'to set out and victual the said ship and pay the wages of the seamen, and keep the said ship and furniture in repair'.

The duke of York chose the *Oxford*, a ship built twelve years earlier at Deptford and armed with 26 guns. She was 72 feet long (measured along the keel, but roughly that length on deck) with a beam of 24 feet.

The man who had 'moved his Majesty in Council' to give Jamaica a frigate was of course the duke of Albemarle, and he kept a close watch on the situation, ensuring that the ship was in good condition when she left England (following the peace treaty with the Dutch, there had been heavy cuts in the amount of money allocated to the Navy). He was soon writing to the duke of York to hurry up the work, saying that 'since the government had undertaken to defray the [cost of] sheathing of the ship, it is desired that orders should be given to the Commissioners of the Navy for fitting her with all other repairs'.

Four months later Charles Modyford was petitioning the Privy Council for sails, running rigging and extra anchor cables. A month after that he was reporting that the Commissioners of Ordnance would not supply powder and shot without a written order. The ship did not sail from England until August 1668, eight months after the Privy Council's first order, and by the time she arrived in Port Royal on 14 October the situation had changed radically.

Harry Morgan had arrived back from Portobelo two months earlier and sailed again, and Jamaica was full of confidence. The Brethren were not unduly perturbed by the Jamaica Council's resolution earlier that captains of privateers were to be instructed 'To give fair quarter when demanded; to send all their prisoners hither; to receive into their ships all buccaneers of the Protestant religion ...'

No Heir for the Admiral

For all the honour paid to Harry Morgan and all his wealth, when he saw Mary Elizabeth again after an absence of eight months on the Puerto Principe and Portobelo raids, she was still childless. The fortune he found on his buccaneering expeditions seemed to desert him when it came to producing an heir. As if to rub in their lack of children – and as far as Harry Morgan was concerned it was the lack of a son – Anna and Robert Byndloss already had a son, named Thomas after Anna's uncle.

His brother-in-law Charles Morgan had recently bought a commission in the Port Royal Volunteers and was a captain at Fort Charles, which was commanded by his sister's husband, Robert Byndloss. He was proving impetuous and a drinker; there were already signs that he was unbalanced and unpredictable when excited and drunk. His younger brother and third sister were growing up quickly, their lives supervised by their older sisters, Mary Elizabeth (usually called Elizabeth) and Anna. Now about sixteen years old, it was accepted in the family that Johanna Wilhelmina would soon marry Henry Archbold, who had a fine plantation.

The daily life of a successful planter's wife in the West Indies was an easy one. Often she lived in a two-storey stone house, the ground floor functioning almost as a vast cellar and storeroom with impressive stone steps leading up to the first floor, which was surrounded by balconies. Some houses near the coast, where there was a risk of enemy raids, had no balconies, and heavy shutters were ready to close the windows while gun loops pierced the walls.

The houses looked more elegant than they were, and no value was placed on privacy. Inside they were often divided into rooms only by low wooden walls, little more than partitions which did not reach the ceiling but allowed a cooling breeze to circulate. The wealthier people slept in beds but many others used hammocks – described by the Abbé du Tertre as 'hanging cotton beds in which they sleep like savages; and besides that the custom is very convenient; it is not expensive because no pillows, sheets or quilts are necessary, so that a good cotton bed lasts a man for his life'.

The best description of the needs of a settler in the Tropics was given in Sir Henry Colt's letter to his son George, advising him to buy 'knapkins, tablecloths, a leather bed, a flock bed – your hammocks are naught, they are too cold and you cannot turn yourself in them ... A chamber pot basin, a tankard or pot to drink from, low, coarse glasses of 2d apiece, dishes, spoons, trenchers [wooden plates], a stew pan, wax lights, a candlestick ...'

For clothing a young man Sir Henry suggested, 'three or four suits of fine cloth jerkins and hose ... all suits else are in vain. Two or three fine hats [of] strong grey, and feathers, handkerchieves to wear about your neck ... shirts of 8 shillings apiece, fine ones are not good [and] they must come but to your knees for they be troublesome when they be long. Pockets in the sleeves of your jerkins. They be better than in your hose, and less subject to sweat when the sleeves hang down. All leather pockets or doublets are naught; they are ever moist and will rot'. George was also told to bring two dozen pairs of shoes, 'russett all, black are naught, they mould and grow red'. He would also need buttons, thread, needles, sixpenny ribbons of various colours and extra sleeves for shirts 'because you wear them out with the jerkin'.

Elizabeth Morgan, like every newcomer to the West Indies before or since, took time fully to comprehend the basic problem of living in the Tropics: everything that was manufactured had to be brought across the Atlantic by ship, whether a bolt of cloth or a needle, a reel of thread or a packet of nails, a shoemaker's last or a blacksmith's hammer. Craftsmen had to be brought over in the same way: there was stone in the islands but masons were necessary to work it; carpenters and their tools were needed to shape and fashion the rich mahogany wood coming from the sawyers' pits.

By the time Henry and Elizabeth Morgan were married, Port Royal was as cosmopolitan a place as anywhere in Europe. The meats available were the same as in Europe – beef, pork (2d a pound in Jamaica by 1664) and mutton; there were plenty of turkeys and ducks, although hens tended to be tough. A planter's cellar could hold whatever appealed to his palate – Customs returns gave the separate duties on brandy from France and eight Rhenish wines, gin from England and the Netherlands, wines from France, Spain and Madeira, metheglin (made of fermented honey) from England and mead.

With sugar being produced in most of the islands, rum was as commonplace as water. Originally called rumbullion, it had an early nickname of 'Kill devil' and was described by one visitor to Barbados as 'a hott, hellish and terrible liquor'. Potatoes, which grew well, were used to make another cheap drink called moby. The same visitor described how the potatoes were boiled, then 'beaten to a mash, then strained with water through a bag, and so drunk. It will not last above one day', he warned.

Prices were, at first glance, often quite irrational, but in many of the islands the current price of sugar was the yardstick. In the early days in Barbados the Dutch sold their goods at the rate of a penny for a pound of sugar. Thus a man's hat with a peak or brim cost 120 pounds of sugar (i.e. ten shillings). A pair of men's shoes were 16 pounds, although 'new fashioned' fetched 30 pounds. A yard of good bleached linen cost 6 or 7 pounds and a pound of thread was worth 40 pounds of sugar. An anker of brandy (8⅓ gallons) fetched 300 pounds of sugar while a horse in poor condition was 2400 pounds and a good one fetched 3000.

Sickness remained the major problem. A man bustling and fit one day could be dying of a raging fever the next; another man who had been in the islands for several years might suddenly collapse, wracked by a recurrent bout of malaria. An insignificant cut, a mosquito bite, a minor scratch from a thorn – all could flare up and cause gangrene, which usually resulted in death. The universal cure-all was bleeding; the vapours of the night air were blamed as the cause of many illnesses.

Apart from ever-present sickness there were few natural dangers among the Caribbean islands. A few had poisonous snakes, but never enough to drive people away. Scorpions lived under rocks or in dark corners of houses but they were no larger or more dangerous than those familiar to anyone living in southern Europe. Centipedes gave a vicious bite but were not lethal. The sun was scorching hot in the middle of the day but an intelligent man would soon notice that most of the stories told about its effect were old wives' tales.

One of the difficulties facing the Europeans living in the Tropics was sleeping in the heat and the humidity, but far worse, then as now, were the mosquitoes and sandflies. These varied, depending on recent rain and also the strength of the wind. No rain for a month meant they were less troublesome, but within a day or two of a heavy shower they would be back in strength. The only protection possible in a house was to have a smoky bonfire to windward for the whole night, or to keep tobacco burning in the room.

However much the settler tried to model his life in the West Indies on what he knew in Europe, Nature always made it more of a gamble. In Europe a long and hot summer bringing drought could wreck a harvest but rarely was there such a shortage of water that wells dried up and people died of thirst, or a winter storm so bad that it raged across the countryside tearing down houses and washing away acres of a precious and thin layer of soil in which the crops were planted. In the Tropics these are ever-present threats.

A few weeks after the Abbé du Tertre left the Lesser Antilles a devastating hurricane hit Guadeloupe, smashing down most of the houses on the butterfly-shaped island, sinking every ship at anchor and flattening the plantations which had been cleared and planted with so much effort. Most of the domestic animals perished and after it was all over the settlers shook their heads knowingly: there had been an omen – all the pelicans in the islands to the south had suddenly died.

The life of Jamaica revolved round Port Royal. The capital was St Jago, several miles inland and soon to become known as Spanish Town, but most people preferred the port, which was cooler and bustled with ships constantly arriving or departing. Many of Port Royal's street names were familiar to Londoners – Thames Street ran into Tower Hill, Broad Street was near Aldgate. While the original Tower Hill overlooking the Tower of London was still a place of execution, complete with block, the one in Port Royal was simply a small square, a *plaza* in the style of Spanish towns on the Main, but Gallows Point was only a few hundred yards away, with its rows of gibbets from which some of the West Indies' finest pirates had already been hanged and many more were to follow.

Although small, taking up every available inch on the sandspit, Port Royal was the busiest port in the New World. Several thousand people already lived here, scorning the more roomy inland capital as being staid and lifeless – which indeed it was, because Port Royal boasted more taverns and bordellos than the rest of the New World put together, catering for more vices than the respectable folks of Havana and Cartagena ever dreamed existed, though no more sinful than any large port in Europe.

Many of the inhabitants (who would total eight thousand within a decade) were tradesmen, buying or selling, importing and exporting. They brought in mundane goods from England for use on the island and exported exotic goods to New England and Europe. An average of a ship a week completed loading in Port Royal, battened down its hatches, secured hatch covers and sailed north through the Windward Passage out into the Atlantic, carrying a large range of goods.

Largest in bulk were sugar, cotton and hides. Then there was tortoiseshell which European craftsmen carved and polished to make fine fans and combs, buttons and buckles, and ebony.

There were cinnamon, pimento and ginger to provide spices for European palates jaded by meats and fish which could only be preserved by salting, drying or pickling. There were indigo plants to dye madam's cloth blue, the heart of logwood to dye it red and fustic bark to colour it yellow; there was cocoa and there were sarsaparilla roots, a favourite among apothecaries for their tonic qualities.

The ships arriving from Europe and New England carried less profitable cargoes – butter and cheese (often from Holland), corn, live horses, salt fish (mostly from New England), nails, roofing tiles, cooking utensils and liquor. But the Customs returns showed the dozens of other items that also had to be imported – clay pipes by the dozen gross, grindstones, lace and shoes (although local shoemakers were in business, using leather from the island cattle), tobacco (the Dutch blended the finest) and flints for muskets and pistols.

As befitted such a bustling place, Port Royal had three markets which were open every day, though most stalls closed on Sunday afternoon. The meat market and the combined fruit and herb markets were both in the High Street. Because of the heat, which turned fresh meat bad within twelve hours, the meat market was almost a small slaughterhouse: butchers made sure they had enough customers to dispose of a whole carcase – whether a beeve, hog, goat or one of the island's scrawny sheep – before an animal was slaughtered. The buyers usually cooked the meat that day, unless they intended to salt or *boucan* it. Salt beef and pork could be bought by the piece or by the cask.

The stalls in the fruit and herb market sold just about everything else that could not be bought at the meat market in the High Street or at the fish market down on the wharf, and one traveller, John Taylor, commented a few years later that the only thing lacking was fresh bread – 'they make their bread every day . . . but for want of yeast and by reason of the staleness of the flour 'tis not comparable to our English bread'.

The fish market had the best bargains for the gourmet because it sold everything from fresh snapper and grouper – among the most succulent of the Caribbean fish – to turtle and live lobster. The customer could specify the size of lobster he wanted and take it away alive because there were two lobster crawls beside the wharf, large shallow pens made of wooden stakes some thirty yards long by twenty wide in which live lobsters were kept, awaiting buyers. An order for a six-pound lobster would result in a slave wading through a pen, a long stick in his hand with a well-greased bight of marline at the end, a snare which he slipped over the lobster's tail to lift it out for inspection.

Although there were fresh meat, fish and fruit, Port Royal lacked fresh water: it had to be brought in canoes from Liguanea and Passage Fort, across the harbour, and sold by the gallon in earthenware containers. A high wind kicking up a lop inside the harbour often meant a day without water because it was too rough for the canoes to make the crossing.

Port Royal's people lived in about a thousand houses at this time, many of them substantial buildings as high as four storeys. Half of them were built of red brick (much of which had been brought out in ships from England as ballast) with plastered walls, and the rest of wood. John Taylor noted that the houses 'yield as good rents as those in Cheap Side in London'. Many of the houses belonging to the more prosperous citizens were made comfortable with furniture looted by buccaneers from towns and cities on the Spanish Main and Cuba; substantial items originally constructed from the dark Spanish oak of Galicia and Asturias and shipped out by early Spanish settlers, brass-bound linen chests, carved tables which might well have served as altars in village churches, and richly-embroidered screens.

Ornaments in the houses owed their presence to the buccaneers who disposed of the plunder of New Spain and the Main in Port Royal, where it was then sold from shops and stalls. A pair of silver candlesticks here probably once graced a bishop's dining room, the row of pewter goblets there may have come from a monastery, the complete service of silver plates on that rack no doubt belonged to a hidalgo who fled his home the moment he heard the English were coming. Similar stories could be told of a canteen of silver cutlery or a pair of Brescian wheel-lock pistols in a mahogany case which had found their way from Alpine Italy to tropical Jamaica by way of Spain and a town on the Main . . . These were obvious signs of a town founded on buccaneering.

Less obvious, indeed usually hidden away behind chimney pieces and sections of brick walls, beneath flagstones forming kitchen floors or in innocent-looking pottery jars stored at the back of pantries, were hundreds of Spanish coins, silver pieces of eight and ducats, silver and gold pesos, and a fair share of Portuguese coins too. These hoards were the reserves of tradesmen and the savings of private individuals; they had all lived under the threat of Spain so they knew wealth was what was portable; what could be snatched up and carried into the hills.

During his stay John Taylor saw there were many Negro and Indian slaves, and 'the merchants and gentry live here to the height of splendour, in full ease and plenty, being sumptuously arrayed . . . not wanting anything requisite to satisfy, delight and please their curious appetites'. Their houses were 'stored with strong and delicious viands brought thither from Madeira and England'.

Port Royal also provided adequate accommodation for those who stepped outside its lax laws, having two prisons. These were named after their counterparts in London – the Marshalsea for sailors 'and other unruly elements', and the Bridewell for debtors (although a visitor noted with what was obviously unintentional ambiguity that it was also used as 'a house of correction for lazie strumpet of which there are plenty').

For the relaxation of buccaneers and the officers and seamen from the merchant ships anchored in the harbour, there were 'many taverns and abundance of punch houses, or rather may be fitly called brothel houses', and also 'a bull and a bear, for sport at the Bear Garden, and billiards, cock fighting, shooting at the target, etc.'

The trades in Port Royal included 'all sorts of mechanics and tradesmen, as smiths, carpenters, bricklayers, joiners, turners, cabinetmakers, tanners, curriers, shoemakers, taylors, hatters, upholsterers, ropemakers, glaziers, painters, carvers, armourers and comb makers [using turtle shell from the nearby Cayman Islands], watermen and [all] earning thrice the wages given in England . . . Some honest surgeons . . . an honest apothecary and druggist, one Mr Mathews'.

Even in a century when hard drinking was a commonplace and allowing for the fact that seamen became accustomed to drinking small beer because at sea it was impossible to keep water fresh, the amount of liquor consumed in the taverns of Port Royal beggared the imagination. The verdict of a newly-arrived cleric about this time (and who left by the same ship that brought him) was: 'This town is the Sodom of the New World and since the majority of its population consists of pirates, cut-throats, whores and some of the vilest persons in the whole of the world, I felt my permanence there was of no use and I could better preach the Word of God elsewhere among a better sort of folk.'

However, by and large it was only men of religion who criticized. The buccaneers, wrote Leslie,

> were very welcome guests at Jamaica, the planters and men in power caressed Morgan, while the inferior sort contrived every kind of bait to drain his associates of their money. They were very liberal and in a short time came clamouring to their Captain [Morgan] to put to sea; for they were reduced to a starving condition.
>
> Immediately he set about making preparations for a new expedition, and his fame being now increased to a new high pitch, he saw himself in a short time at the head of a thousand brave resolute fellows.

After Portobelo, Harry Morgan was the second most important man in Jamaica. Sir Thomas Modyford had not wanted a new lieutenant-governor and with his commission as admiral still in force Harry Morgan was effectively second only to the governor, being the commander-in-chief of the island's defences. The two of them had many long discussions about future plans. They had convinced each other that the Spanish were planning an assault on Jamaica, and the obvious way of keeping the enemy off balance was to attack various of their ports. This brought profit to Jamaica, kept the privateers together and under a measure of control, and not least made a profit for Morgan, Modyford, the duke of York and the King. It was a happy association of circumstances for everyone except Thomas Lynch and other merchants.

Morgan and Modyford agreed that towns along the Main were more important targets than those in New Spain or Cuba, and Cartagena was the most important of them all. As the largest port on the Main and the terminal for all the gold and silver of Peru, it was also the obvious port from which a Spanish attack on Jamaica would be launched, and Morgan had already received intelligence that preparations for such an attack were being made there.

However, it is most likely that when he sailed from Port Royal at the beginning of October 1668, with ten ships and eight hundred men (not the thousand described by the enthusiastic Leslie) he had an open mind: the only firm decision was that his force should rendezvous at Île-à-Vache, better known to the buccaneers as Cow Island, off the south-west coast of

Hispaniola. With the Spanish Main spread out to the south, Cow Island was a good starting place for an expedition because a broad reach would take the ships down to most targets and bring them back again.

A few days after Morgan left for Cow Island with his ships the *Oxford* frigate arrived in Port Royal after her long voyage from England. At last, and for the first time, the Jamaica government had its own ship of war. Sir Thomas had long ago discussed the frigate's rôle with Morgan: it had been decided that she would be sailed as a private ship of war. This seems like a scheme to make sure Morgan and his buccaneers could use her to increase their purchase, but Modyford had no choice: the *Oxford* was no longer part of the Royal Navy and her new owner, the government of Jamaica, had neither the money nor the machinery for running its own Navy. It was now responsible for paying the 125 men forming the ship's company and the best way of preventing them becoming a burden to the island's taxpayers was to give them a chance of earning their keep by way of a share in the purchase.

The *Oxford* was a sixth-rate and therefore still had twenty-six guns (certain reports increased the number to thirty-four, which would have made her a fifth-rate, unless small guns mounted on the bulwarks were included). She had been brought to Jamaica by Captain Samuel Hacket, who was ordered by Modyford to refit the ship after her Atlantic crossing and then take on stores for a six-month cruise.

The surgeon of the *Oxford*, Richard Browne, had some influence with Lord Arlington and the Privy Council's secretary, Sir Joseph Williamson, and all the time he served in the West Indies he was careful to write long and detailed reports giving news of events and his views on people. He wrote the first within three weeks of arriving in Port Royal and commented on the main topic of conversation, the Portobelo raid. He found it hard to believe that 'six captains with 500 men' had captured the city and three castles. He told Sir Joseph that all the ships had gone to sea again under 'a Captain Morgan', although he did not know their destination.

The *Oxford*'s captain sailed in November under Modyford's orders 'to face Cartagena'. To begin with he took the frigate eastward to Port Morant, probably to finish off refitting away from the heady atmosphere of Port Royal. Although Port Morant had fewer temptations for the ship's company, it did nothing to cool a long-standing disagreement between Captain Hacket and the *Oxford*'s master. Surgeon Browne told Sir Joseph Williamson that Captain Hacket, 'falling out with the Master, ran him through the body'. Despite Browne's attention the man died and Hacket 'then fled for it'.

This caused more delay for the *Oxford* but Modyford sent Captain Edward Collier to take command. He was an eminently suitable man, being one of the most experienced of the privateer captains and standing high in

Morgan's estimation. Sir Thomas's first orders for Collier were straight-forward: the French privateer *Le Cerf Volant*, registered at La Rochelle and armed with fourteen guns, was a pirate, according to the British master of a ship from Virginia, and Collier was to investigate the complaint and then join Admiral Morgan. Collier guessed that he could carry out both orders at Cow Island because Morgan was there and the French ship had probably joined him.

As the *Oxford* sailed into the Cow Island anchorage and fired a salute to Morgan (who was seeing the frigate for the first time), Collier sighted *Le Cerf Volant* anchored nearby. Admiral Morgan was delighted with the *Oxford*: her twenty-six guns made her the most powerful privateer in the Indies. She was in excellent condition and her bottom, newly sheathed before she left England, was comparatively clean, so she was still fast.

Collier then dealt with *Le Cerf Volant* (an episode completely distorted by Esquemeling). He ordered her captain to come to the *Oxford*. This the Frenchman did – and was startled to see the master of the Virginia ship waiting for him. The Frenchman was arrested and, with his crew, taken to Port Royal under guard in the *Oxford*, which escorted *Le Cerf Volant*. In the Court of Admiralty there the captain was found guilty of piracy and his ship condemned as prize to the *Oxford*. The captain was condemned to death (though later reprieved by Modyford) and the ship, renamed *Satisfaction*, was sent to Cow Island with the *Oxford* to rejoin Morgan.

The *Oxford* and her former prize managed to reach Cow Island before 1 January, the final date for Morgan's rendezvous, and they brought the total number of ships to twelve. Morgan hoisted his flag in the *Oxford* and, as his fleet greeted the year, 1669, passed the word that there would be a council of war on 2 January. Next day the captains came on board to be greeted by Morgan and Collier. Among them were the two Captains John Morris, father and son, Captain Aylet (who commanded the *Lily*, a 10-gun vessel of 50 tons) and Captains Thornbury, Bigford and Whiting. Several had their mates with them and they all settled down to hear what the admiral proposed.

Morgan reported that he had a total of nine hundred men, double the number on the Portobelo expedition, and he intended to attack Cartagena. Surgeon Browne, attending his first buccaneer council of war, heard the captains agree, even though Cartagena was by far the most powerful harbour on the Main, its great bays shaped like clover leaves and defended by several castles, including the enormous San Felipe.

Morgan was his usual cheerful and ebullient self, delighted with the size and comfort of the *Oxford*. As soon as the council agreed to his proposal, he invited everyone to stay on board for dinner, and the drinking started. In the late afternoon they went down to dinner in the great cabin, with Morgan at the centre of one side of the table. The captains sat round the table and, apart from Collier on Morgan's right, chose places at random. The elder John Morris sat down on the same side as Morgan and his son sat opposite, with Aylet of the *Lily*, Thornbury, Whiting and Bigford. Surgeon Browne sat towards the foot of the table on the same side as the admiral.

Elsewhere in the ship the crew were eating and drinking with gusto, combining a successful council of war party with yet another New Year celebration. One of the buccaneers wrote that from the moment it was decided to go to Cartagena, 'they began on board the great ship to feast one another for joy of their new voyage ... In testimony hereof they drank many healths and discharged many guns, as the common sign of mirth among seamen used to be.' There were 125 men from the *Oxford's* original ship's company, upwards of another seventy-five who signed on when she was commissioned as a privateer, and another twenty-five captains and their officers who had come over for the council.

It gets dark suddenly in the Tropics, and candles were lit in lanthorns. On the foredeck the ship's company sang, danced, joked and drank. In the great cabin toasts were made in profusion. Wine and rum were mixed; few of the men were sober.

Suddenly there was a blinding flash and a terrible detonation made Cow Island tremble as the *Oxford's* magazine exploded and blew the ship apart.

A quirk of the blast killed all the captains sitting on the side of the table opposite Morgan – the younger John Morris, Aylet, Thornbury, Whiting and Bigford – and flung Morgan, Collier and Surgeon Browne high into the air. They found themselves swimming in a sea covered with twisted planks, shattered oak beams and frames, splintered masts and yards, and the bodies and torn limbs of men killed by the explosion. Browne, splashing around in the darkness, found a piece of the *Oxford's* mizenmast floating nearby and managed to climb on to it.

Soon the boats of the other ships arrived and were rowed through the great circle of wreckage. Men searched with lanterns and listened for shouts. By dawn they had saved Morgan, Collier, Browne, the elder John Morris, two seamen, and four cabin boys. Everyone else who had been on board the *Oxford*, more than 250, was dead. 'Many more, 'tis thought, might have escaped had they not been so much overtaken with wine,' commented Esquemeling. The *Oxford* had served Jamaica for three months.

Trapped at Maracaibo

Happily unaware that at that very moment Harry Morgan and his fleet were sailing back to Jamaica after sacking Portobelo, the Spanish government in July 1668 sent new instructions to its ambassador in London. He was to protest about a particular ship and also deliver sworn copies of the depositions received from the Indies describing various other outrages against Spanish shipping.

On August 8 the ambassador called on the secretary of State and presented a note protesting at the 'several violences' which had been committed 'in a hostile way . . . on the ships and territories of the King of Spain in America'. Lord Arlington, according to the ambassador later, promised a satisfactory answer.

In fact he set Privy Council clerks to work going through Sir Thomas Modyford's reports, and Charles Modyford was called in, as his father's agent, to help compile a list of episodes where Spanish ships had seized British ones and ill-treated British subjects. Sir Thomas's habit of always reporting such cases to London, with properly-sworn depositions, now paid dividends, and always there was the knowledge that Sir Thomas's son Jack was still missing with the *Griffin* frigate.

The Privy Council eventually met a week before Christmas to consider the Spanish protest, which had been delivered four months earlier. The secretary read out the details of the individual episodes cited by Spain and described cases where Modyford complained about Spanish behaviour.

Some of them were bizarre. There was the case of Captain Edward Beckford, who hailed a ketch off the South Cays and found she had a Spanish crew who 'spread their bloody colours and fired a volley of small shot'. He captured her and discovered she was in fact owned by Alexander Soares, a Briton, who had sailed from New England a year and a half earlier and vanished with his ship and crew. Captain Robert Delander, with a mast of his ship damaged off Cuba, had asked permission to enter Havana for repairs. The Spanish governor had agreed, seized the ship, sold her and put Delander and his men in prison. Finally the Privy Council considered yet again the case of Jack Modyford and the *Griffin*. The latest information was a deposition by privateersmen describing how one of the Spanish men of war which chased them was the former *Griffin*, now flying a Spanish flag: they knew her well and recognized her without difficulty.

After calling various witnesses the Privy Council considered the whole position in the light of the Spanish note. All the members present – ranging from the King to the duke of Albemarle, and the secretary of State to the duke of York – decided that it was a simple case of six of one and half a dozen of the other. The minutes of the meeting show that they decided to send a memorial to the Spanish government pointing out that the ship 'chiefly insisted upon' by the Spanish ambassador had been taken before the last treaty between the two countries was ratified. The Spanish had likewise captured several English ships and 'insomuch that the violent and hostile actions of the Spaniards upon his Majesty's subjects in those parts do exceed those of the English upon the Spaniards, Lord Arlington and Sir John Trevor are instructed to acquaint the Spanish Ambassador herewith, and leave in his hands a memorial of the particulars' drawn up from the depositions and other evidence. Arlington and Trevor were to propose 'a total reciprocal amnesty and oblivion of all that is past, and a settlement of mutual good intelligence for the future, as to kind reception into the harbours and ports, affording all necessary refreshments of wood, water and victuals for their money'.

The reason the Privy Council had finally met on 18 December may well have been that news had just been received of Morgan's raid on Portobelo, and they wanted to get the Spanish to agree to the 'amnesty and oblivion' proposal before reports of the attack were received in Madrid. However, before a reply was received from Madrid the Spanish ambassador called on Lord Arlington again, this time with furious protests about an attack on Portobelo by Jamaica privateers who had been 'pillaging and committing outrages scarce heard of'. Before the English government had time to answer, the ambassador was visiting Arlington yet again with fresh evidence about the Portobelo raid. This concerned the ship *George and Samuel*, which had just arrived at an English port from Jamaica and, it seems, had taken part in the Portobelo expedition. Her bill of lading, the ambassador declared, showed that quite apart from the amount received by owners and merchants, 'the share [of the Portobelo purchase] of every soldier was 600 oz, or £80 at half a crown per ounce . . .' He demanded full satisfaction for Spain and punishment for the governor of Jamaica because he had broken the treaty of Madrid between Spain and England.

London was soon full of gossip and speculation about Portobelo; with the religious problem, any difficulty with Spain was seized on by zealots of each side. The Catholics soon put about the rumour that Modyford was to be re-called in disgrace and brought to a trial; those wanting a stick to belabour the duke of York's circle claimed that Modyford was justified; that he was responsible for the safety of the island and the Spanish were preparing an attack.

Among the ordinary and Protestant English the hero of the day was not Modyford, who had shown considerable courage by in effect declaring war on Spain in the Indies, but Harry Morgan. The Spanish, however, knew that although the Welshman knocked their castles down, Modyford signed the commission and sent him to sea. The man the Queen Regent of Spain wanted to see destroyed was Sir Thomas Modyford. With him and his planter policy gone, there was a good chance that Thomas Lynch and his merchants would come to power, and he could be relied on to stop all the provocations ...

Although Modyford was appalled at the destruction of the *Oxford* frigate after only a few weeks' service, the Spanish on the Main lit candles and murmured their thanks to the person they credited with having caused the ship's destruction. In Morgan's day as well as now, a ship approaching Cartagena sights Colina de la Popa, a wedge-shaped hill and the highest for miles around. A convent stood on top of the hill in Morgan's time, its walls white and forty feet high (today the ruin still remains and a huge cross is illuminated at night).

The convent honoured the city's patron saint, Nuestra Señora de la Popa, and is best described by William Dampier, the sailor who became a buccaneer and explorer (marooning Alexander Selkirk), and who knew the West Indies well. He described the lofty convent as, 'the very shrine of the West Indies: it hath innumerable miracles related to it. Any misfortune that befalls the privateers is attributed to this lady's doing, and the Spaniards report that she was abroad the night the *Oxford* man of war was blown up ... and that she came home all wet; as, belike, she often returns with her clothes dirty and torn with passing through woods and bad ways, when she had been out on any expedition ...'

Morgan's own feelings at losing his fine ship and so nearly losing his life are not recorded, but Leslie speaks for the buccaneers. They were in no way discouraged – 'while Morgan was safe they thought success sure ...' The Welshman soon had his small fleet reorganized, although this needed a good deal of tact. Because each ship was privately owned (often by a syndicate which stayed on shore) he could not arbitrarily take a deserving mate from one ship and give him command of another whose captain had perished in the *Oxford*: usually a mate would expect to succeed to the command if his captain was killed, but often such a man was not suitable.

With the *Oxford* and nearly three hundred men gone, Morgan's force was now too weak to attempt Cartagena, although he did not tell the buccaneers this immediately; instead he set a rendezvous for a month ahead and sent out another appeal for more ships. This time the rendezvous was four hundred miles dead to windward, at Saona Island, off the south-eastern tip of Hispaniola. The *Satisfaction* had to return to Jamaica – she was needed for an operation off Campeche – and she was told to pass the new date and position to any more Tortuga and Port Royal privateers wanting to join. Morgan estimated that he could rely on getting another half a dozen ships.

He left Cow Island with the ships he had, lost three weeks trying to get round False Cape and Punta Beata against the strong easterly wind, and, with food and water getting very short, 'spied an English vessel at a distance', according to Esquemeling. 'Having spoken with her, they found she came from England and brought of her for ready money some provisions they stood in need of.' They could only buy enough to last for a few more days, so Morgan decided to land near Santo Domingo 'to seek water and what provisions they could find'.

This involved several fights with Spanish troops but the buccaneers managed to kill many scores of cattle and with the beef salted away in casks Morgan ordered his little fleet to resume the weary beat to Saona Island. When the ships tacked into the anchorage some days later he was disappointed to find that no other privateer was waiting. Not only that, his force was now much weaker: apart from the *Oxford*, he had lost more ships, mostly because they could not stand up to weeks and miles of battering their way to windward. Sails chafed and stitching rotted in the alternate bright sun and heavy rain, hull planking spewed caulking, rigging stretched, chafed and parted, men became worn out, unable to remember a time when they were not crashing to windward, their ships rolling violently and pitching as though every wave was a cliff edge over which they were falling.

Now he had eight ships and about five hundred men. Most of the ships were small, one or two of them little more than large boats whose crew had to spend most of their time at the pumps or bailing with calabash shells when going to windward, their lives a misery because clothing was constantly soaking wet and provisions soon spoiled. In the past month, Morgan had been considering new targets, but his plans were based on finding more ships waiting at Saona. 'Having hitherto resolved to cruise upon the coasts of Caracas and plunder all the towns and villages he could meet, finding himself at present with such small forces, he changed his resolution by the advice of a French captain that belonged to his fleet,' wrote Esquemeling.

The French captain had been with the French buccaneer Francis L'Ollonais who, three years earlier, had attacked Maracaibo. They had eight ships and about 650 men for the raid, the French captain told Morgan, and 'he knew all the entries, passages, forces, and means how to put in execution the same again'.

The rest of Morgan's captains agreed with the admiral: the Frenchman's plan was excellent. Enough time had passed since L'Ollonais' raid for the Spanish to have relaxed again, regarding the attack as unique. 'Hereupon,' wrote one of the buccaneers, 'they weighed anchor and steered their course towards Curaçao.' The coast of what was then the province of Caracas (now

Venezuela) runs east and west, but at the western end, on the border with Colombia, there is the very deep Gulf of Venezuela which funnels down at its inshore side to become a narrow channel, like the neck of a flask, and then opens out again into the almost circular Lake of Maracaibo to complete the effect of a flask, or carafe, forming a vast inland sea.

Morgan was fortunate that fifty miles to the east of the exact centre of the entrance to the Gulf of Venezuela is the island of Aruba (called Ruba by the buccaneers), and another fifty miles east of that is the Dutch island of Curaçao. Many of the buccaneers could recognize either landmark. They covered the 400 miles from Saona, sighted Curaçao and bore away for Aruba, where Morgan anchored his fleet and stayed two days, buying meat and also wood, which his larger ships needed as fuel for the big coppers used for cooking.

He sailed at night so that any curious watchers in Aruba would not know the course he steered, and made for the western side of the Gulf, but with the French captain recognizing the peaks of the Sierra de Chamare he was able to keep well out into the Gulf, out of sight of the various Spanish watch towers. Entering the Gulf he made his way south, towards the narrowing neck of the flask forming the channel to Maracaibo. The coast here inside the Gulf is very low; long sandy beaches have surf breaking a mile offshore and there are no mountain peaks or hills to help the navigator find the channel. Finally they sighted a village three or four miles inland, which the French captain recognized as Sinamaica, and Morgan was able to anchor his ships for the night.

The channel was almost closed off by several islands, San Carlos, Bajo Seco and Zapara, which were low and sandy, fringed here and there with mangroves. The channel itself, with a depth of twelve feet or less, twisted in S-bends between Seco and San Carlos, then between San Carlos and Zapara. The key to the channel was Seco, little more than a sandy cay with a shallow bank of quicksands stretching to Zapara and on which the sea usually broke heavily. This area was referred to as the Bar of Maracaibo; it was the neck of the flask.

At dawn next morning Morgan led the ships down towards the three islands, but the buccaneers soon found that the Spanish had learned a lesson since the L'Ollonais raid, building a fort on San Carlos Island with its guns covering the channel. (Baja Seco Island has since disappeared and near its original position there is now an unnamed islet with a drying patch called Baja Seco Fort.) Morgan's force was sighted almost at once from the fort, which 'did now fire continually against the pirates'. There was no question of passing the fort while it was in Spanish hands – the channel was only three hundred yards away, well within range of its guns, and a boat had to row ahead of the ships with a hand lead, checking the depths and determining which way the channel went.

The admiral ordered men to land from boats to attack the fort, but there was little protection against the Spanish guns once they were on the almost flat, sandy cay: they had to shelter behind dunes as they worked their way close enough to the walls to open fire with their muskets and pistols.

They found it hot work: the eleventh parallel of latitude passes precisely through the tip of San Carlos where the fort is built. Then in the early afternoon the regular wind sprang up as the French captain had warned. By three o'clock half a gale was blowing out of a clear sky, whipping sand into their eyes, the locks of their muskets and pistols, and their food. It went on blowing until long after midnight, the so-called evening wind for which the Gulf is famous. 'The dispute continued very hot on both sides,' Esquemeling said, 'being managed with huge courage and valour from morning until dark night.'

Soon after it was dark Morgan crept across the dunes to get close under the walls of the fort. He worked his way round the walls and found an open gate. The fort was empty, 'the Spaniards having deserted it not long before'. Morgan called to his men and they joined him, lighting lanterns for a search. They had not gone far into the building before Morgan suddenly detected a familiar smell, shouted a warning and ran towards a slow match which was spluttering away, a fuse leading to a train of powder and then to the magazine, so that the fort would blow up within a few minutes. 'Captain Morgan prevented the mischief by snatching away the match with all speed, whereby he saved both his own and his companions' lives,' wrote Esquemeling. The match had been cut to give a burning time of fifteen minutes from the moment it was lit and had less than five minutes more to burn when Morgan pulled it away and stamped it out.

So the legend surrounding the admiral grew: more than two hundred of his men were in or close to the fort at the moment he recognized the smell of burning slow match; every one of those men knew they would have been blown to smithereens but for the quickness and bravery of their leader.

Morgan then continued his search of the fort. There were sixteen guns, some 12-pounders and the rest 24-pounders, 'a great quantity of powder ... also a great number of muskets and military provisions'. Then, after placing sentries, the buccaneers slept until daylight.

Soon after dawn a boat went out to tell the anchored ships to come through the channel and anchor as close as possible to the fort. Boats then ferried out powder, muskets and each ship's share of 'military provisions' – flints, slow and quickmatch, spare ramrods, rests for the muskets and holsters for the pistols. The fort's sixteen guns were spiked, or 'nailed' as it was then called, a nail being hammered into the touch hole to block it completely and the head cut off, making the gun useless until the nail was drilled out, a tedious task which usually led to the touchhole being damaged and made too large.

The look of a successful buccaneer: an embroidered and ermine-trimmed crimson coat with sapphire buckles worn over mail, a hat of matching crimson velvet lined with miniver and decorated with a heavily jewelled aigrette . . . This portrait, now untraceable, of a man in his late forties was for many years believed to be Sir Henry Morgan, painted by Rembrandt when the buccaneer visited Amsterdam in 1655. In fact this was the year that Morgan arrived in the West Indies, aged twenty. After that he visited England only once, under arrest as a State prisoner, in 1672 when he was thirty-seven and England was at war with Holland. (*Photograph: National Museum of Wales*)

Portuguese gold 2 Cruzados, 1642.
(*British Museum*)

Portuguese silver Cruzado,
Joad IV 1640–56.
(*British Museum*)

French Crown, Louis XIV 1643.
(*British Museum*)

Gold Spanish Doubloon,
Philip IV 1621–65.
(*British Museum*)

Mexico City Piece
of Eight, 8 Reales,
1659.
(*British Museum*)

Mexico City Piece of Eight, 8 Reales, Charles II 1681.   (*British Museum*)

The complete buccaneer as seen by a French artist. The only relics to be seen today are the clay pipes, most of them made in Holland, which can still be found on most of the islands of the Caribbean. (*British Library: Esquemeling French edition*)

The Earl of Arlington: Catholic and pro-Spanish, he did his best to thwart the buccaneers and privateers of Jamaica as they waged war against the Spaniards in Cuba and on the Main. (*National Portrait Gallery*)

Lord Vaughan, a Governor of Jamaica who detested Morgan, was regarded by Samuel Pepys as "one of the lewdest fellows of the age". (*National Portrait Gallery*)

George Monck, Cromwell's famous general who later brought Charles II back to the throne and became the first Duke of Albemarle. (*National Portrait Gallery*)

Christopher, second Duke of Albemarle, who continued the family friendship for the Morgans and succeeded in restoring Henry to favour. (*British Museum*)

Charles II, above, who had Henry Morgan brought back to England as a State prisoner and sent him back to the West Indies with a knighthood and a commission as Deputy Governor of Jamaica. (*National Portrait Gallery*)

From the Jamaica Government's accounts, showing entries ranging from "Paid Joseph Curtis Bricklayer for repairing the King's House . . . 12:10.0" (first line) to "Paid Sr Henry Morgan Charges in mounting Great Guns . . . 07:10.0" (eleventh line). (*British Library*)

Sir Henry's secretary wrote the body of the letter to Sir Leoline Jenkins on 22 August 1681, protesting at the disbanding of the Port Royal Regiment, and then Morgan himself wrote the last four much abbreviated lines beginning "Your Honn^{es} Most obedient hum[ble] . . ." and signing his name as one word, "HenMorgan". (*Public Record Office*)

Morgan and his buccaneers attack Puerto del Principe (now Camaguey) in Cuba. Despite its original name it is forty-five miles inland and yielded a disappointing "purchase" worth only 50,000 pieces of eight. (*Esquemeling Spanish edition*)

The capture of Portobelo, showing Morgan capturing Fort Triana. Buccaneers fight their way up scaling ladders (right middleground) while both defenders and attackers hurl grenades and stinkpots. This picture, approved by the Dutch buccaneer Esquemeling, is likely to be accurate. (*British Library: Esquemeling Dutch edition*)

Portobelo: buccaneers armed with sabres and daggers pursue fleeing Spanish soldiers. The two wounded men in the foreground and the fleeing soldier between them are wearing bandoliers on which are hung "Apostles", small cylindrical containers with caps, each holding sufficient gunpowder to load a musket or pistol. (*British Library: Esquemeling Dutch edition*)

One of the first buildings ever erected by the Spanish in Portobelo was the hospital, shown here as it appears today. (*Popperfoto*)

Three hundred years after Henry Morgan's attack on the Castillo de San Gerónimo, the cylindrical sentry box and seaward wall still guard Portobelo. Prince Maurice was reported to be imprisoned here, and in the dungeon Morgan found eleven Britons who had been in chains for two years. (*Popperfoto*)

Morgan's fighting retreat from Maracaibo: buccaneers in a fireship set ablaze the 48-gun Spanish frigate *Magdalen* (right) while Morgan attacks the *Marquesa* (above and beyond), and the rest of his squadron, laden with the "purchase", sail out to safety past the fort. The 38-gun *Santa Louisa*, whose captain cut the cable and ran her ashore, can be seen burning in front of the fort. (*Esquemeling Spanish edition*)

The Isthmus, which Morgan and his buccaneers had to cross to attack Panama. Landing at the mouth of the Chagres river (bottom centre, spelled Cagre), where he lost the *Satisfaction* on a reef, he led his men up the river as it twisted its way to Venta de Cruzes (centre left) and then marched to Panama city (left, below the compass rose). The Caribbean, known then as the North Sea, is to the north of the Isthmus, and the South Sea (Pacific) to the south of Panama. (*Esquemeling, Spanish edition*)

Morgan destroys the Spanish army and captures "the famous and antient city of Panama". This Spanish picture shows the Pacific and the city in the background with the tower of the cathedral of San Anastasius. The buccaneers attack from the right as a desperate Viceroy, Don Juan Perez de Guzman, orders "Two great herds of oxen and bulls" (shown coming from the left) to be driven against them.

(*Esquemeling Spanish edition*)

A Dutch version of the sack of Panama, showing the activity on the seaward side of the city. (*British Library: Esquemeling Dutch edition*)

The only convent in Panama had been named after San José and was one of the few stone buildings in the city. After being looted by buccaneers it was badly damaged by flames and today this is all that remains in Old Panama. (*Popperfoto*)

Eliz.th Cavendishe. 1.st
Daughter to Henry Duke
of Newcastle Married to
Christopher Monk 2.^d
Duke of Albemarle

The Duchess of Albemarle: a portrait by Sir Peter Lely, the famous seventeenth-century portrait painter. Highly strung, vivacious, gay and wilful, at the age of fourteen Lady Elizabeth Cavendish married one of the richest men in the kingdom. She is typical of the exquisitely dressed society beauties in the England of Morgan's day. (*Duke of Portland's Collection*)

A True and Perfect Relation of that moſt Sad and Terrible

EARTHQUAKE, at Port-Royal in JAMAICA,

Which happened on *Tueſday* the 7th. of *June*, 1692.

Where, in Two Minutes time the Town was Sunk under Ground, and Two Thouſand Souls Periſhed: With the manner of it at Large; in a Letter from thence, Written by Captain *Crocket*: As alſo of the *Earthquake* which happen'd in *England, Holland, Flanders, France, Germany, Zealand, &c.* And in moſt Parts of *Europe*: On *Thurſday* the *8th* of *September*. Being a Dreadful Warning to the Sleepy World: Or, God's heavy Judgments ſhewed on a Sinful People, as a Fore-runner of the Terrible Day of the Lord.

The EXPLANATION.

A. *The Houſes Falling.* B. *The Churches.* C. *The Sugar-Works.* D. *The Mills.* E. *The Bridges in the whole Country.* F. *The Rock and Mountains.* G. *Captain Ruden's Houſe ſunk firſt into the Earth, with his Wife, and Family.* H. *The Ground rolling under the Miniſter's Feet.* I. *The great Church and Tower falling.* K. *The Earth Opening and Swallowing Multitudes of People in Morgan's Fort.* L. *The Miniſter Kneeling down in a ring with the People in the Street at Prayers.* M. *The Wharf covered with the Sea.* N. *Dr. Heath going from Ship to Ship to Viſit the bruiſed People, and do his laſt Office to the dead Corpſes that lay Floating from the Point.* O. *Thieves Robbing and Breaking open both Dwelling Houſes and Ware-Houſes during the Earthquake.* P. *Dr. Trapham, a Doctor of Phyſick, hanging by the Hands on a Rack of the Chimney, and one of his Children hanging about his Neck ſeeing his Wife and the reſt of his Children a Sinking.* Q. *A Boat coming to ſave them.* R. *The Miniſter Preaching on a Tent to the People.* S. *The dead Bodies of ſome Hundreds floating about the Harbour.* T. *The Sea waſhing the dead Carkaſſes out of their Graves and Tombs, and daſhed to pieces by the Earthquake.* V. *People ſwallow'd up in the Earth, ſeveral as high as their Necks with their Heads above Ground.* W. *The Dogs eating of Dead Mens Heads.* X. *Several Ships Caſt away and driven into the very Town.* Y. *A Woman and her two Daughters beat to pieces one againſt the other.* Z. *Mr. Beckford his Diging out of the Ground.*

Port-Royal, in Jamaica, *June* 30. 1792.

Rack of a Chimney, and one of his Children hanging about his Neck, were both ſaved by a Boat; but his Wife and the reſt of his Children and Family, were all Loſt: Several People were Swallow'd up of the Earth, when the Sea breaking in

Captain *Wiſſon* and his Son, Mrs. *Robinſon*, Mrs. *Gifford*, Doctor *Trapham's* Family, Mrs. *Fuller*, Mr. *Fyanne*, Mr. *Braenue*, Mr. *Sexpiens*, Mrs. *Ignos* and his Wife, Mr. *Pryer*, Mr. *Lemdzbeere*, Mr. *dewell*, Mrs. *Raſhorn* and her Family, Mrs. *Rynors*

This broadsheet showing the earthquake destroying Port Royal was on sale in London within a few weeks "being a dreadful warning to the sleepy world". The more important things shown are: G, Captain Ruden's house sunk in the earth with his wife and family; I, St Peter's, the church built by Morgan and his friends, collapsing; K, the earth opening up in Morgan's Fort and swallowing "multitudes of people"; L, Dr Heath praying with people in a circle round him; O, thieves robbing houses; P, Dr Trapham hanging on to the chimney; S, the bodies of hundreds of people washed away as the land sank under the sea; V, people trapped up to their necks by cracks in the earth. (*British Library*)

'These things being done, they embarked again, to continue their course towards Maracaibo. But the waters were very low,' Esquemeling noted, 'whereby they could not pass a certain bank that lies at the entry of the lake.'

This bar was a quicksand, the most dangerous that the buccaneers faced in the whole of the Caribbean. Two hundred years later, in the last days of the sailing navy, the British Admiralty warned all mariners: 'Should a vessel unfortunately ground on the bar, as no dependence can be placed on anchors to heave off by, and being a quicksand, she will be placed in imminent danger.'

Maracaibo was another twenty miles down the channel, so the buccaneers 'were compelled to put themselves into canoes and small boats, with which they arrived the next day before Maracaibo, having no other defence but some small pieces [i.e. boat guns] which they could carry in the said boats'.

Nature was still an enemy – or, rather, Maracaibo's defence – because quite apart from the afternoon wind, squalls known as *chubascos*, lasting for up to an hour and blowing as hard as a strong gale, arrived in the afternoon with little or no warning. The buccaneers rowed steadily up into Maracaibo itself and, putting their boats and canoes ashore, they ran to the fort defending the city, 'which they found in like manner as the preceding, without any persons in it; for all were fled before them into the woods, leaving also the town without any people ...'

Morgan sent search parties through the town in case the Spaniards had hidden troops who would later attack the buccaneers unawares. Then, says Esquemeling, 'not finding anybody, every party, according as they came out of their several ships, chose what houses they pleased to themselves, the best they could find. The church was deputed for the common *corps de garde*, where they lived after their military manner, committing many insolent actions'.

A hundred buccaneers sent out to look for people who could be forced to reveal where they had hidden their valuables returned the next day with fifty mules 'laden with several good merchandise' and thirty people who, Esquemeling says, were tortured, some on the rack, until they told the buccaneers what they wanted to know. Although he obviously did not protest at the use of the rack at the time, he is rightly critical of the buccaneers for using it, although he fails to point out that the rack was already installed in Maracaibo – just as there was one or more in Portobelo and every other town on the Main and New Spain, as much part of a town's facilities as the plaza or water troughs, and there for the Spanish officials, lay and religious, to use on their own people.

As the days passed and Morgan questioned new prisoners he gradually collected 'about one hundred of the chiefest families with all their goods', and it became obvious that there were few left at large that mattered. After three weeks he decided to go farther into the Lake of Maracaibo to look for purchase. L'Ollonais had gone down as far as Gibraltar almost at the far end, and the French captain was confident he could pilot them. By now the ships of the fleet had managed to cross the bar and reach Maracaibo, where the loot was taken out daily in boats. Fresh provisions were also loaded, and Morgan had men killing cattle and salting the meat.

The move south needed a strong nerve: to the north, between Morgan and the Caribbean, was the narrow neck of the channel and the islands of San Carlos, Baja Seco and Zapara. The fort had been put out of action, but some well-placed batteries manned by determined men could stop the buccaneers ever getting out ...

Morgan then sorted out his prisoners: he sent on board his ships under guard a dozen of those who would be known in Gibraltar. They would be used as messengers because, from the accounts reaching him, all available Spanish troops were now concentrating in Gibraltar. It seemed certain he would have to fight for every bit of purchase there; it would not be abandoned like Maracaibo.

The little fleet weighed and headed for Gibraltar, but when they were still five or six miles away Morgan gave the order to anchor. A canoe was hoisted out, the dozen prisoners were put in and the buccaneers rowed down to the town under a flag of truce. Morgan had given the prisoners their instructions: they would be landed at Gibraltar and set free, but they must go immediately to the mayor or garrison commander with a simple warning: Gibraltar must surrender at once, 'otherwise Captain Morgan would certainly put them all to the sword without giving quarter to any person he should find alive'. They were to bring the mayor's answer back to the buccaneers waiting in the canoe.

The reply was defiant and Morgan gave the order to weigh and steered towards the town, intending to test the Spaniards. The moment the ships were in range of the batteries the guns opened fire, and Morgan promptly bore away, sailing just out of range and then anchoring. He saw that on one side of the town there was a large forest and that all the beaches were easy to reach in canoes. The problem was one he had faced many times before and which presented no real difficulty.

The attack is described by the Dutch buccaneer: 'The next day, very early in the morning, they landed all their men ... Guided by the Frenchman ... they marched towards the town, not by the common way but crossing through the woods, which way the Spaniards scarce thought they would have come.' But the Spanish had had a whole night to reflect on L'Ollonais' attack on them, and they decided that was enough. 'Hereupon were all fled out of the town as fast as they could, carrying with them all their goods and riches as also all the powder, and having nailed all the great guns.'

Morgan had already sent out search parties to look for inhabitants, just as he had in Maracaibo, but although it had yielded a good purchase there it failed here in Gibraltar: the people and their valuables were much better hidden, having had more time to get farther away to the woods. As soon as he realized this, Morgan divided his buccaneers into several parties and sent them off to search the plantations because the Spanish 'could not live upon what they found in the woods without coming now and then to seek provisions at their own country houses'.

There were soon about 250 prisoners collected at Morgan's headquarters, and he, Collier and John Morris were kept busy questioning them, always asking the same questions – where they had hidden their treasures, and if they knew where any of their countrymen were hiding. 'Such as would not confess were tormented after a most cruel and inhuman manner,' wrote Esquemeling.

Among the slaves there was a man who promised to lead Morgan to a river running into the lake, 'where he should find a ship and four boats richly laden with goods that belonged unto the inhabitants of Maracaibo. The same slave discovered [revealed] likewise the place where the Governor of Gibraltar lay hidden, together with the greatest part of the women of the town ...'

Morgan promptly sent off two hundred men in boats to look for the Maracaibo goods while he took another 250 men to seek the governor. 'This gentleman was retired into a small island seated in the middle of the river where he had built a little fort, after the best manner he could, for his defence. But hearing that Captain Morgan came in person with great forces to seek him, he retired farther off unto the top of a mountain ... unto which there was no ascent but by a very narrow passage.' Morgan and his men tried to follow but they were beaten by torrential rain.

The party that went after the Maracaibo goods were also unlucky because the Spaniards, hearing that they were coming, managed to unload most of the merchandise and hide it before they bolted, but 'they left both in the ship and boats great parcels of goods ... which the pirates seized and brought thereof a considerable booty unto Gibraltar. Thus after they had been in possession of the place five entire weeks, and committed there infinite number of murders, robberies, rapes and such like insolences, they concluded upon their departure'.

Morgan's last move was to demand a ransom for the town, saying that if it was not paid he would burn every house to the ground. Prisoners released to find friends hiding in the fields who still had money returned to tell Morgan that the few people they found said that the governor had forbidden them to pay any ransom. They pleaded with Morgan to have patience because they could collect about 5000 pieces of eight. In the meantime some townspeople would act as hostages for the rest, which would be paid by the time Morgan reached Maracaibo.

'Captain Morgan, having now been a long time absent from Maracaibo and knowing the Spaniards had had sufficient time wherein to fortify themselves and hinder his departure out of the Lake, granted them their proposition.' He released all the prisoners and the four people who were agreed upon for hostages handed themselves over.

Morgan had been in the lake for more than eight weeks. It was now the middle of April and he knew that news of his presence must have reached Panama, 550 miles away across several mountain ranges, let alone Cartagena, which was 250 miles away, over only two mountain ranges.

It took four days to sail back up to Maracaibo, his fleet increased by vessels he had captured, and as Morgan's own ship anchored he looked carefully over the town with his telescope. Nothing appeared to have changed: the fort was deserted, there was no one in the streets.

Buccaneers went on shore and finally came across 'a poor distressed old man, who was sick'. From him they discovered that 'three Spanish men of war were arrived at the entry of the lake, and there waited for the return of the pirates out of those parts. Moreover, that the castle [on San Carlos island] was again put into a good posture of defence, being well provided with guns and men and all sorts of ammunition.

'This relation of the old man,' Esquemeling reported with an unsuspected talent for understatement, 'could not choose but cause some disturbance in the mind of Captain Morgan, who now was careful how to get away through those narrow passages of the entry of the lake.'

He sent for the captain of the fastest vessel in his fleet and ordered him north at once to investigate. The ship returned next day and the captain reported to the admiral that indeed there were three ships; he had approached them so closely that he had been in danger from the shot they fired. The largest mounted thirty-six large and twelve small guns, the second one carried twenty-six large and twelve small and the smallest had sixteen large and eight small guns.

'These forces were much beyond those of Captain Morgan,' commented Esquemeling, 'and hence they caused a general consternation in all the pirates, whose biggest vessel had not above fourteen small guns. Every one judged Captain Morgan to be despond in his mind and be destitute of all manner of hopes, considering the difficulty either of passing safely his little fleet amidst those great ships and the fort, or that he must perish. How to escape any other way by sea or land they saw no opportunity nor convenience ...'

19

The Defeat of Don Alonso

If Esquemeling's words really described the buccaneers' fears, they had all underestimated Harry Morgan, who selected a reliable Spanish prisoner and sent him to Isla San Carlos with an important message for the admiral commanding the Spanish warships. The message was brief; it was a demand that the admiral pay a considerable sum as the price for dissuading Morgan from burning down Maracaibo. (Although Esquemeling does not mention it, he presumably also demanded a safe conduct for his ships.)

The buccaneers manned the fort at Maracaibo, guarding against a surprise attack overland, and two days later the prisoner came back with a reply from the Spanish admiral. He was Vice-Admiral Alonso del Campo y Espinosa, commanding the three ships which were all that now remained of the *armada de barlovento* (see page 138). His flagship was the 48-gun *Magdalen*.

His letter to Morgan was naturally written in Spanish, and it was hurriedly translated. Morgan then discovered that he was up against not just three ships of war but the threat of many half-decked boats coming from ports only a hundred miles or so to windward in the province of Caracas.

'Having understood from all our friends and neighbours the unexpected news that you have dared to attempt and commit hostilities in the countries ... belonging unto the dominions of his Catholic Majesty,' Don Alonso began, he was writing to tell Morgan that he had come to the castle 'which you took out of the hands of a parcel of cowards'. There he had now 'put things in a very good posture of defence and mounted again the artillery which you had nailed and dismounted.

'My intent,' he told Morgan flatly, 'is to dispute with you your passage out of the Lake, and follow and pursue you everywhere ...' He then offered Morgan some hope: if he would surrender everything he had captured, including slaves and prisoners, 'I will let you freely pass, without trouble or molestation, upon condition that you retire home presently unto your own country.' But if Morgan made any resistance, 'I will command boats to come from Caracas, wherein I will put my troops and, coming to Maracaibo, will cause you utterly to perish by putting you every man to the sword. This,' he warned, 'is my last and absolute resolution. Be prudent, therefore, and do not abuse my bounty with ingratitude.

'I have with me very good soldiers who desire nothing more ardently than to revenge on you and your people all the cruelties and base infamous actions you have committed upon the Spanish nation in America.' The letter was signed 'on board the Royal ship *Magdalen*, lying at anchor at the entry of the Lake of Maracaibo'.

If Don Alonso could make good even half his threats, Morgan and his buccaneers would not see the sun set on the day they met the Spaniards. Nor could Don Alonso's threats be dismissed as braggadocio: any two Spanish ships had more guns than Morgan's entire fleet, let alone the disparity in size, while they had another sixteen on the fort to help them – a total of 126, not counting boat guns, which totalled at least thirty more.

Morgan had taken a great risk in the first place in entering the lake, with its narrow neck; he had then dallied far too long at Maracaibo and Gibraltar. Now the Spanish had their fingers on the neck, waiting to squeeze.

Yet Morgan knew his men, for this was the secret of his leadership. He assembled them all in the dusty *plaza* at Maracaibo and under a blazing tropical sun told them of Don Alonso's arrival. He described the three ships waiting for them some twenty miles up the channel, and then he read them Don Alonso's letter. Now, he told them, he wanted 'their advice and resolutions upon the whole matter'. Would they rather surrender all they had so far purchased in order to buy their liberty or would they prefer to *fight* for it? 'They answered all unanimously: "They had rather fight and spill the last drop of blood they had in their veins than surrender so easily the booty they had gotten with so much danger to their lives." '

According to Esquemeling one of the buccaneers then spoke up, undertaking to sink the *Magdalen* with only twelve men by making a fireship out of the Spanish vessel captured in the river near Gibraltar. (Morgan later claimed that it was his own idea; that no one suggested it to him.) It would be important, the man is supposed to have emphasized, to disguise her so that the Spanish would not recognize her as a fireship.

Esquemeling then describes how the man proposed to do it. Standing vertically on her decks would be short logs with hats and *montero* (Spanish hunting) caps on top of them so that they looked like men. Other logs would protrude through the portholes to imitate cannon. 'At the stern,' the man said, 'we will hang out the English colours and persuade the enemy she is one of our best men of war that goes to fight them.' Far more important, the channel out of the lake turned to the north-west and then ran west for some distance before turning north into the Gulf of Venezuela. The Spanish ships were waiting there – which meant the fireship would have a following wind: she would not have to tack or wear, so there need be only enough men on board to steer her and escape by boat after setting her on fire when they were sure she would collide.

The buccaneers were all keen on the idea of a fireship, but many of them knew that they were bound to lose some of their ships if they had to fight their way out. Could they not bargain with Don Alonso? Admiral Morgan had originally demanded a ransom for Maracaibo and Don Alonso's reply had said nothing about it. There were still the four Spanish hostages being held until Gibraltar paid the outstanding ransom, and there were all the slaves taken at Gibraltar – slaves which were particularly valuable to the Spanish.

Yes, they could try to bargain: Morgan was shrewd enough to see he had something to offer Don Alonso. Next day he sent two men with his proposals: in return for a safe passage for his ships (and their booty, of course) Morgan would quit Maracaibo without doing any damage to the town and free the slaves without ransom. He would also free the four hostages without Gibraltar paying the ransom.

Don Alonso rejected the terms 'as being dishonourable for him to grant. Nor would he listen to any more proposals from the buccaneers, saying that unless they surrendered within two days, under the conditions offered in his letter, he would immediately come and force them to do it.'

Esquemeling records that no sooner had Morgan received this message than he prepared to fight,

resolving to get out of the Lake by main force and without surrendering anything. In the first place he commanded all the slaves and prisoners to be tied up and guarded very well. After this they gathered all the pitch, tar and brimstone they could find in the whole town wherewith to prepare the fireship ...

Likewise they made several inventions of powder and brimstone, with great quantities of palm leaves very well anointed. They covered very well their counterfeit cannon, laying under every piece thereof many pounds of powder. Besides which they cut down many outwarks belonging to the ship, to the end the powder might exert its [explosive] strength the better.

Thus they broke open also new portholes where, instead of guns, they placed little drums of which the negroes make use. Finally the decks were handsomely beset with many pieces of wood dressed up in the shape of men with hats, as *monteros*, and likewise armed with swords, muskets and bandoliers.

By 29 April Morgan was satisfied that his ships were ready; the eight privateers, a motley collection of vessels, some with single masts, others with two, were prepared for action. The man commanding the fireship had his orders – he would lead the way out to the north, sailing along the twenty-mile channel on the ebb so that he had both fair wind and tide. He would sail straight for the *Magdalen* and Morgan would follow to attack the second largest Spanish ship, the 38-gun *Santa Louisa*, while other privateers tackled the 24-gun *La Marquesa*.

Early on 30 April Morgan gave the signal and the squadron sailed, led by the fireship. They covered the twenty miles to find the Spanish ships anchored across the channel between San Carlos and Zapara and covered by the sixteen guns in the fort. As it was getting dark, Morgan signalled his ships to anchor for the night.

'The dawning of the day being come,' wrote Esquemeling, 'they weighed anchor and set sail again.' This time the fireship steered straight for the *Magdalen*, looking as though she was going alongside in a regular battle of broadsides. There was not a wisp of smoke nor a tongue of flame to give away her secret. There were fewer than a dozen men on board, and hanging on ropes from the ends of the yards were grapnels which were intended to catch in the *Magdalen*'s rigging, holding the two ships together. There was nothing unusual about that; ships going into battle and intending to board the enemy usually had grapnels rigged in just that way. There was a boat towing astern, too, but most of the privateers were towing canoes or boats – it was the best way of keeping them out of the way of roundshot or flying splinters.

The *Magdalen* fired a few shots at the approaching ship but was content to hold her full broadside until they were alongside each other. Then the enemy ship was only a few yards away and the horrified Spaniards saw smoke suddenly billowing up through her hatches. As the buccaneers on board ran aft to climb into their boat, spasmodic explosions began shaking the ship and pieces of wreckage covered with blazing tar and pitch were hurled into the air and landed on the *Magdalen*'s decks.

Frantically the Spaniards tried to boom her off but by now the explosions were rapid as flames reached the pile of powder beneath each log representing a gun or man. Then the flames reached the magazine and the whole ship blew apart, showering the *Magdalen* with jagged baulks of burning timber, flaming planks and smouldering cordage. The *Magdalen* was doomed, 'for the flame suddenly seized her timber and tackling and in a short space consumed all the stern, the forepart sinking into the sea'.

The *Santa Louisa*'s captain, seeing the *Magdalen* ablaze and not knowing if there were more fireships among the privateers coming towards him, promptly cut his anchor cable and sailed his ship straight for the beach in front of the fort. The moment she grounded he ordered his men to begin chopping holes through the hull and cutting away the rigging so the masts fell over the side. *La Marquesa* was less fortunate – the buccaneers swarmed on board before she could get under way and her 150 Spanish sailors and soldiers were made prisoners. Morgan ordered his boats to row round picking up survivors from the *Magdalen*, many of whom had leapt into the water to escape the flames and were now clutching pieces of floating wreckage.

Unknown to Morgan, the Spanish admiral, Don Alonso, had managed to get on shore and make his way to the castle.

'The pirates were extremely gladded at this signal victory, obtained in so short a time and with so great inequality of forces, whereby they conceived greater pride in their minds than they had before. Hereupon they all presently ran ashore, intending to take the castle. This they found very well provided with men, great cannon and ammunition – they having no other arms than muskets and a few fireballs in their hands.'

They spent the rest of the day firing at the garrison with muskets and at dusk tried to creep up to the walls to throw in fireballs, but the Spanish fire was too heavy. 'Thus, having experienced the obstinacy of the enemy and seeing thirty of their own men already dead and as many more wounded, they retired unto their ships.'

Admiral Morgan now moved to *La Marquesa*, his third flagship in a few weeks. She was fast and well-built, a little smaller than the *Oxford* but a great deal bigger and more weatherly than the 14-gun ship he had been using before and after the *Oxford*. He left the present siege of the fort to Collier and Morris: for the moment he was more anxious to question prisoners and find out the situation inside the fort. Among the prisoners Morgan soon found the former pilot of his new flagship; a man who was not Spanish and quite prepared to answer questions. Morgan had many to ask him – 'How many men did each of the three ships have on board? Are you expecting more ships to arrive? Where did the three ships sail from ... ?'

The pilot had no objection to telling Morgan what he knew, and he spoke the truth because it has been possible to check all the important facts he gave. *La Marquesa*, he said, was one of six ships sent out from Spain (to form the *armada de barlovento*) 'with instructions to cruise upon the English pirates and root them out from these parts'.

After they arrived in Cartagena the two largest ships were sent back to Spain – they were unsuitable for operations against the buccaneers – so that four were left under the command of the vice-admiral, who took them round to Campeche 'to seek out the English'. They were anchored there when a great norther blew, the pilot said, and the third largest of the ships, the 18-gun *Nuestra Señora del Carmen*, with a crew of 150, parted her anchor cable, blew ashore and was wrecked.

Don Alonso, the pilot told Morgan, then sailed for Santo Domingo. 'Here we received intelligence there had passed that way a fleet from Jamaica,. and that some men thereof having landed ... the inhabitants had taken one of them prisoner, who confessed their whole design was to go and pillage the city of Caracas.' Don Alonso promptly sailed for Caracas where he met a boat which reported the buccaneers were in the Lake of Maracaibo and had seven small ships and one boat. 'Upon this intelligence we arrived here [where we were told] that the English had taken the city of Maracaibo and that they were at present at the pillage of Gibraltar.'

Don Alonso ordered that all the guns saved from the wreck of the *Nuestra Señora del Carmen* should be put in the castle, with two more 18-pounder guns from his own ship, the *Magdalen*. The castle's original guns, nailed by the raiders, were to be drilled out and remounted on their carriages. He instructed the people at Maracaibo 'to repossess the [empty] castle and reinforce it with one hundred men more than it had before its being taken by the English'. The pilot told Morgan that the Spanish then received the news that the English were returning to Maracaibo from Gibraltar. The evening after Morgan's ransom demand arrived Don Alonso gave 'a very good supper unto all his people' and then 'persuaded them neither to take nor give any quarter unto the English that should fall into their hands'.

This explained to Morgan why it had been so difficult to rescue any men from the *Magdalen* or *Santa Louisa*. The pilot told him: 'This was the occasion of so many being drowned, who dared not crave any quarter for their lives, as knowing their own intentions of giving none.'

The pilot then gave Morgan news which showed him how close he had been to failure with the fireship: 'Two days before you came against us a certain negro came on board Don Alonso's ship, telling him: "Sir, be pleased to have great care of yourself, for the English have prepared a fireship with desire to burn your fleet." But Don Alonso would not believe this intelligence, his answer being: "How can that be? Have they, peradventure, wit enough to build a fireship? Or what instruments have they [to] do it withal?"'

The pilot's reward was his freedom and, regarding himself as 'very well used' by Morgan, he joined the buccaneers. He then told Morgan that there had been 'a great quantity of plate on board the *Magdalen* when she sank; he guessed the value at up to 40,000 pieces of eight...' Morgan promptly ordered one of his ships to anchor close to the wreck 'to watch all occasions of getting out the said vessel what plate they could'.

Morgan now turned his attention back to Don Alonso, who was still besieged in his fort and, with his ships gone, also marooned on the island of San Carlos. There was very little fighting, the buccaneers simply watching and their sharpshooters making sure that no one could walk round the battlements without getting a bullet in the head.

The Spanish and the buccaneers had reached a stalemate. Morgan and his ships were trapped in the lake by the guns of the fort; Don Alonso was trapped in his fort by the buccaneers. Morgan had spent the previous few days trying to turn his predicament to his advantage and decided that the only ace he had to play was Maracaibo itself, still deserted and thus in his hands. A messenger was sent to Don Alonso demanding a ransom for the town, otherwise Morgan 'would entirely consume and destroy it'.

One of the buccaneers wrote: 'The Spaniards, considering how unfortunate they had been all along with those pirates and not knowing after what manner to get rid of them, concluded among themselves to pay the said ransom, although Don Alonso would not consent unto it.'

They asked what ransom Morgan wanted and agreed to his demand – 20,000 pieces of eight and 500 beeves. The money was delivered with the cattle, which were promptly slaughtered, salted and taken on board the ships. Morgan then refused to deliver up all the hostages. He did not trust Don Alonso, who had not agreed to his fellow countrymen paying the ransom, and Morgan could imagine the fort suddenly opening fire as his fleet sailed past. The hostages would stay on board, he told the Spaniards, until all his ships had passed the fort safely and were anchored out of range on the Caribbean side of the channel.

In the meantime Morgan moved up in *La Marquesa* to rejoin the ship he had left to search for the plate in the sunken *Magdalen*. The buccaneers had been busy and met with success. 'He found her upon the place, with the sum of 15,000 pieces of eight, which they had purchased out of the wreck, besides many other pieces of plate, [such] as hilts of swords and other things of this kind; also great quantities of pieces of eight that were melted and run together by the force of the fire...'

However, the more his 'purchase' grew – without any fighting he had increased its value by 35,000 pieces of eight in less than a week – the more concerned Morgan became about Don Alonso and the fort. He thought that the Spanish admiral refused to agree to the Maracaibo ransom for one of two reasons: either he really was a zealous patriot, or he feared being ordered back to Spain under arrest to face charges of treachery or cowardice.

Don Alonso was in fact not prey to any conflicting thoughts: he knew quite well that if he was defeated he would be called to account in Madrid, and this governed everything he did – particularly the wording of dispatches, public statements and letters. His first letter to Morgan (a copy of which would be sent to Spain) condemned the Spaniards who had fled from San Carlos fort as 'a parcel of cowards' and went on to make windy statements about his duty and intentions.

Morgan's problem was, quite simply, that if the fort opened fire on him as he passed he had no aces left to play: Maracaibo would be astern and safe from him because returning there would mean having to pass the fort yet again. And obviously Don Alonso, having made it quite clear that he would sooner see Maracaibo go up in smoke than pay any ransom, would not care if Morgan executed his hostages because the fort opened fire...

Yet Morgan always liked to hold a trump card in his hand. For the moment he could think of no way of using surprise so, for the first time, he had been reduced to bargaining from an extremely weak position. Yet he had little choice; with all his ships and men bottled up in the lake it could be only a matter of time before Don Alonso received reinforcements – troops sent overland by the viceroy of Panama, and troops sent round in boats from Caracas ... Time was Don Alonso's ally and Morgan's enemy.

Morgan therefore worked on the hostages: they were told that unless they could make Don Alonso agree to the safe passage of the ships, 'he would certainly hang them all'. The prisoners promptly drew up a petition which was sent over to the fort, but Don Alonso would have none of it.

He 'gave them for answer a sharp reprehension of their cowardice, telling them: "If you had been as loyal unto your King in hindering the entry of these pirates as I shall do their going out, you [would have] never caused these troubles ... I shall never grant your request, but shall endeavour to maintain that respect which is due unto my King, according to my duty."' With Don Alonso talking such a gale of wind, 'the Spaniards returned to their fellow prisoners with much consternation of mind and no hopes of obtaining their requests...'

Morgan seemed unperturbed, giving orders to share out all the booty captured so far, 'fearing lest he might not have an opportunity of doing it in another place, if any tempest should arise and separate the ships'.

There was also another reason – as admiral of the Brethren of the Coast he was worried that any of the commanders 'might run away with the best part of the spoil which then did lie much more in one vessel than another'. There was, Morgan knew, sufficient loyalty among the buccaneers in getting the purchase; it was only after they had their hands on it that there was a risk of the purchase being more valuable than loyalty.

Esquemeling describes how 'they all brought in, according to their laws, and declared what they had; having beforehand made an oath not to conceal the least thing from the public. The accounts being cast up, they found to the value of 250,000 pieces of eight in money and jewels, besides the huge quantity of merchandise and slaves: all which purchase was divided into every ship or boat, according to its share'. The purchase was about the same as Morgan won at Portobelo, where he had nine ships and 450 men to share the purchase. Here at Maracaibo there were eight ships and five hundred men.

Yet this was no time for a buccaneer, be he a Morgan or a cabin boy, a Dutch captain or a French bosun, to gloat over his share: at the moment he was rich (rich again, in many cases) but apparently had little hope that he would live to be able to spend it. As Esquemeling wrote: 'The question still remained on foot how they should pass the castle and get out of the Lake.'

The two opponents, Harry Morgan and Don Alonso, were, curiously enough, men who were having to fight outside their real elements: the Spaniard was a sailor forced to be a soldier to defend the fort; the Welshman was a soldier whose attack apparently could be launched only from ships.

Finally, Morgan apparently put himself in Don Alonso's position and decided that the Spaniard was expecting a full-scale attack on the fort from seaward. All his guns were facing the sea, more than thirty of them. Fourteen were those salvaged from the *Nuestra Señora del Carmen*, wrecked off Campeche; two more were 18-pounders from the *Magdalen*; the rest were the original guns remounted.

On a gun-for-gun basis, the fort could fire thirty-two guns, all of a heavy calibre. Her largest opponent would be *La Marquesa*, with a broadside of eight medium and four light guns; after that there would be Morgan's former ship, with seven light guns. The guns of the rest of the privateers were of no concern to such a fort.

Then Morgan decided on the most ingenious plan of his buccaneering career. To Don Alonso, a large number of buccaneers landing on the island obviously indicated a night attack on the fort, scaling the walls. Equally obvious, such an attack would be made on the landward side of the fort, because the buccaneers knew that all the guns were on the seaward side.

The privateers, led by *La Marquesa*, anchored out of range of the fort but close to the shore, where mangroves grew a dozen feet high in thick tangles of roots and branches. Morgan chose a place where the boats were in sight of the fort right up to the mangroves, but where the low bulk of the mangrove trees, with their dark green, thick foliage, would hide the men as they climbed over the roots after scrambling out of the boats.

Don Alonso and his men watched and counted for the whole day as boats full of men armed with pikes, swords and muskets left the privateers, rowed to the shore and at once unloaded their men, rowed back to the privateers and filled up again. One hundred ... two hundred ... three hundred. Morgan was obviously going to make a full-scale attack; only a few men would be left on board the ships. The attack would come as soon as it was dark – the buccaneers would not take the unnecessary risk of a daylight assault – and Don Alonso set his garrison to work pushing and hauling the guns to the inshore side of the fort, so that they could sweep the ground over which the buccaneers would have to attack.

Darkness came with its usual tropical suddenness, and the Spanish waited anxiously, expecting any moment to hear musket shots and the crash of scaling ladders being pushed against the walls. Instead they suddenly heard a distant cannon firing from seaward; then another and another, until seven shots had been fired. Then they saw in the darkness that Morgan's fleet had passed in the darkness and was now anchored well out of range on the seaward side of the channel with nothing to stop it leaving the Gulf. There was nothing Don Alonso could do; he had been completely hood-winked by Morgan, who had got his fleet past the fort without the Spanish firing a shot – and without hanging a hostage.

Morgan had in fact decided to take a great risk. He waited until the tide began ebbing (after dark), running northwards along the channel from the Lake of Maracaibo into the Gulf of Venezuela. As soon as the current was flowing at more than a knot, first *La Marquesa* and then the rest of the privateers weighed anchor but did not at first set sails, just drifting towards the channel. As they approached the fort and the narrowing channel they let fall their sails because although a current usually flows strongest in the deepest part of the channel there was little chance of them grounding. As each of the privateers came abreast the fort she fired a single parting shot, there being no reason why she should not be heard even if she could not be seen.

Meanwhile the Spanish were still waiting for the attack on the landward side of the fort, thinking that the privateers were being sailed with skeleton crews – Don Alonso and his officers had after all spent most of the day watching hundreds of buccaneers come on shore in boats. When the attack did not come Don Alonso ordered the guns to be dragged back to the seaward side and as soon as they were in position they began a heavy fire into the darkness. Morgan, with his ship anchored safely out of range and the rest of the privateers now close round him, watched and laughed and no doubt drank a toast.

The four or five hundred buccaneers for whom Don Alonso was nervously waiting were in fact on board the privateers, which the majority of them had never left. Morgan's trick had worked perfectly. The boats had rowed to the mangroves crowded with buccaneers sitting upright and obvious on the thwarts. Those men had climbed up into the mangroves and – apparently – scrambled on shore. What Don Alonso and his officers had not seen was the same men crawling out again along the boughs of the mangroves and dropping back into the boats, lying flat and on top of each other while the oarsmen rowed seemingly empty boats back out to the privateers to collect 'more' men, when once more they sat up on the thwarts. Instead of the boats taking out many scores of men, they kept rowing the same few back and forth, comfortably seated on the thwarts one way, lying flat on the bottom boards the other.

Next day Morgan decided to return the hostages he was holding for Maracaibo: the people had paid the ransom to save their city and there was no reason to keep them. They were sent down to the fort by canoe, under a flag of truce, and to Don Alonso's credit he gave them a boat 'that every one might return to his own home'. There were several Spaniards whom Morgan kept prisoner on board *La Marquesa*: they were the hostages from Gibraltar, which still had not paid its ransom.

20

Spain Retaliates

On 17 May 1669 Port Royal went mad: the cheering and yelling, cracking of muskets and echoing boom of cannons firing salutes from Fort Charles and the batteries were like the beginning of a Spanish fiesta. Hundreds of people stood on the beaches watching the admiral's triumphant return.

They knew the *Oxford* frigate had blown up, but they now saw that his flag-bedecked little fleet was led by a frigate quite as large. Those seamen with sharp eyes recognized that Morgan's flagship had a Spanish sheer and the cut of her sails was Spanish – their first news that not only had Harry Morgan successfully raided some port on the Main but captured a Spanish frigate as well. And not only a frigate: as they counted the vessels they soon realized that he had many prizes.

While Morgan went on shore and was taken by carriage round to Spanish Town to report to Sir Thomas Modyford, the wounded among the buccaneers were carried to Port Royal for treatment by doctors. Customs and Excise men went out to make up their lists; traders boarded ships to make offers for jewellery and plate.

The people of Port Royal had given the buccaneers a hearty welcome because most of them were tradesmen or the families of the seamen, but conspicuously absent from the quays were Sir Thomas Modyford and members of the Council, and although Morgan would have guessed the main reason he did not learn the details until he arrived at the King's House and met the Governor.

The two men's conversation was not very cheering because each man's news made the other's blacker. Morgan told Modyford that he had raided not Cartagena – he had not enough men for that – but Maracaibo and Gibraltar. Modyford then had to warn the admiral that as soon as the government in London heard about it the King would probably be furious, saying that a raid on Cartagena itself might have been justified because a Spanish attack on Jamaica might be mounted from there, but Maracaibo and Gibraltar could by no stretch of the imagination be regarded as threats.

When the *Isabella* arrived from England several weeks before, Modyford told Morgan, she had brought letters from his son Charles Modyford describing Spanish protests and saying that when the *Isabella* sailed it seemed likely the government would disavow the Portobelo raid. Both men knew that this would probably involve recalling the governor or withdrawing his commission.

In the meantime the buccaneers were roistering in Port Royal's streets: hundreds of men of various nationalities were making sure that it lived up to its reputation of being the most sinful city in the world. A local historian recorded that they would roll a pipe of wine into the street 'and oblige everyone that passed to drink'. Staid citizens were forced to swill tankards of wine before they could go about their business. The buccaneers would also scatter the wine 'in vast quantities, thinking it excellent diversion to wet the ladies' clothes as they went along and force them to run from the showers of wine'.

Modyford was thankful for one aspect of the Maracaibo raid – the destruction of the *armada de barlovento*, which was a double victory because not only were the Spanish deprived of their three ships of war, but capturing *La Marquesa* meant that Jamaica still had a frigate, despite the loss of the *Oxford*. England's offer of an 'amnesty and oblivion' had in fact been rejected out of hand in Madrid. Any hope of it being accepted had been washed away in the flood of anger over the Portobelo raid for which, the Spanish government told Lord Arlington, the Queen Regent demanded full satisfaction and the dismissal of Sir Thomas Modyford.

The King and Privy Council were now in a difficult position. The pro-Spanish faction was furious that Modyford should have allowed Morgan to make such attacks; but there was no question of making an abject apology to Spain and disgracing Modyford. The result was inaction in London, caused by an inability to decide what to do. In Madrid however it was interpreted as indifference, and with the reluctant agreement of the Council of the Indies an angry government decided to retaliate.

Letters went out to all the governors and viceroys in the Indies telling them that the Queen Regent commanded each of them 'to cause war to be published against that nation, and to execute all the hostilities which are permitted in war, by taking possession of [British] ships, islands, places and ports...' As soon as they received the letter, the governors in Cuba, Hispaniola, New Spain and the Spanish Main began issuing commissions to any Spanish ship that would sail as a privateer.

Ironically enough the British knew nothing of all this for many months, until a copy of a commission signed by the governor of Santiago was captured in the *San Nicolas de Tolentino* privateer. The reason was not hard to find – the British and French were so used to being attacked on sight by Spanish ships (and attacking them too) that possession of a commission by a Spanish ship merely legalized a situation that always existed.

In Jamaica Modyford waited until all the celebration had died – which happened only when the buccaneers ran out of money – and then on 14 June the town crier marched through the streets of Spanish Town behind a drummer who beat a ruffle at every crossroads. With many an 'Oyez' and 'Hear ye', he read a proclamation by Sir Thomas withdrawing the admiral's commission of 'Colonel Henry Morgan' and all the privateers. Then he went on to Port Royal and read it there. The reception he was given by the buccaneers, whose pockets were now empty, is not recorded, but Colonel Beeston noted in his diary: 'Nevertheless the privateers went in and out but not with commissions.'

A month later, when a ship brought more letters from his son warning Modyford that the King was extremely angry with him, the governor decided that his best defence was a description of his activities from the day he first arrived in Jamaica as governor, and he settled down to write it. The narrative was brief until he reached the time when he received permission from the duke of Albemarle to issue commissions. He still did not issue any, he wrote, until March 1666, when the Jamaica Council voted that they were necessary for the defence of the island. But, he emphasized, the only commissions he issued were 'for taking ships, and none for landing'.

'I always reproved them for so acting, especially in the business of Puerto Bello and Maracay [sic]; to which they made their defence in writing, which I sent home but never received any answer to.' Later, he wrote, 'receiving an intimation of his Majesty's sense ... and also advice of the Spaniard's intention to attempt us, the galleons being daily expected in the Indies and the New Spain fleet already there, in order to detain the privateers on the island I repealed all their powers'.

He commented on the 'unreasonable rumours of the great wealth these privateers are said to get' – the Portobelo 'business' cleared them £60 per head and 'the fight with Don Alonso at Maracay [sic] £30'. This 'the common sort spent immediately in arms, clothing, and drink, and some of the officers and civiller sort are settling plantations, and the owners of ships spend their shares in refitting, so that they are from hand to mouth, and have little or nothing left.

'His Majesty's fifteenths [shares] I keep to be employed in fortifications, which may be about £600, and his Royal Highness's tenths I have always sent home ... for his account. To myself they [the privateersmen] gave only £20 for their commissions, which in all has never exceeded £300.' He challenged 'the boldest maligners and rash talkers' to disprove the truth of his claim.

Modyford was shrewd; one can see the wisdom of holding back the King's £600 and spending it on fortifications: His Majesty grumbled about the privateers but always accepted his share of the prize money. However, since he disapproved of the privateers' recent activities he could hardly complain if the governor diverted his share to help pay for the defence of Jamaica.

The summer of 1669 was a long holiday for Morgan; for the whole of the hurricane season he stayed on shore, spending his time with Elizabeth and travelling round the countryside looking for land suitable for another plantation. He already had the one bought from Lawrence Prince, which had been cleared. Now he was looking for several hundred acres which no one owned and which could then be granted to him. He finally found what he wanted, 836 acres of hilly land in the parish of Clarendon, bounded on one side by the Minho River. Near Chapelton village in the Rio Minho valley, it is still called 'Morgan's Valley', and woods nearby were known as 'Morgan's Forest'. In 1669 the land was part of the new frontier, at the very edge of the plantations, and the letter patent describes the northern boundary as being 'waste hilly woodland'.

The patent refers to 'Collo. Henry Morgan' who 'hath transported himself together with his servants unto our Island of Jamaica', and the grant was made to him in the King's name 'for his better encouragement for being one of our planters there and for diverse other good causes'. The actual wording was not significant; it was a stylized rendering used with slight variations for all such grants.

Although Morgan was already a planter and only extending his lands (at no cost to himself in this case, apart from the usual stamp duties), another leading buccaneer had also decided to apply for a grant of land, thus joining Morgan, Lawrence Prince and John Morris as landowners. He was Captain Edward Collier, who had been with Morgan on most of the expeditions and was one of the handful of survivors from the *Oxford*. He became a neighbour of Morgan's, choosing a thousand acres in Clarendon parish.

The grant of land to Morgan was the first reward he had ever received from the Crown or the government of Jamaica. The grant was dated 30 November. By a macabre coincidence the duke of Albemarle died in bizarre circumstances three days later, leaving both Sir Thomas Modyford and Harry Morgan without a patron or a powerful friend at Court.

In the meantime Vice-Admiral Don Alonso del Campo y Espinosa, the former commander of the *armada de barlovento* and Fort San Carlos, was under arrest. The viceroy and captain-general of Tierra Firma, Don Juan Perez de Guzman, decided to send him as a prisoner to Spain, accused of a variety of crimes, following Morgan's raid on Maracaibo and Gibraltar and the loss of the *armada de barlovento*. (When Don Alonso reached Spain he was taken before a *junta de guerra* which, as soon as it heard Don Juan's charges and Don Alonso's defence, cleared the admiral and commended him for his bravery.)

Don Alonso was not the only important visitor to Spain in the autumn of 1669: Sir William Godolphin arrived in Madrid as the King's representative with widespread powers to negotiate. His mission was, in effect, to bring about the 'amnesty and oblivion' suggested by Britain at the beginning of the year and recognition that Jamaica was now British. The proposals were practical but, from the Spanish point of view, meant that Madrid was making all the concessions because France, Holland and England were trespassers, even though they held all the islands of the Lesser Antilles. They were nations which had flagrantly ignored papal authority and crossed the Line.

Any treaty between Britain and Spain would have to ensure that privateering stopped, all past injuries be forgotten, sovereignty over the territory held by Britain be recognized by Spain, and trading be allowed. Sir William's task was to reduce all this – and much more – to a treaty and get the Spanish to sign it.

The delicacy of such negotiations was well understood by Modyford and his planters, but despite visits to London by the more influential of them, it seemed impossible to make the King and the Privy Council understand that while the talking was going on in Madrid, Jamaica was defenceless; that all round her was Spanish territory, with Spain steadfastly refusing to admit that Britain owned Jamaica.

In Jamaica only the merchants were hopeful about the eventual result of negotiations. Every merchant dreamed of riches, selling slaves and hardware the length of the Main and New Spain, and he so little understood the Spanish mind that he considered that the Jamaica privateers were the people that continually wrecked everything. No Jamaica merchant, totting up his books at the end of a year's trading, could appreciate that the real problem was that Spain's claim that she alone had any right to territory and trade 'Beyond the Line', maintained for nearly two hundred years, was supported by the Spanish government, Church, Council of the Indies and merchants.

In London the pro-Spanish faction at Court was loud in its criticism of Modyford, Morgan and the buccaneers, but Charles II was conscious that although he had spent his early years in the courts of Catholic France and Spain, the majority of his subjects were Protestant, and he tried to find a middle road.

As far as the ordinary people were concerned, Harry Morgan was a hero in an England that needed one. There had been the humiliation of the two Dutch wars, with Dutch ships actually sailing up the Thames and blockading London – a memory less than two years old. The only cheerful news had come from Jamaica and it had always concerned Harry Morgan who, like Drake and Ralegh before him, knew how to singe the Dons' beards, wielding cutlass and pistol against great odds and bringing back pieces of eight by the trunkful. And here, or so it seemed, was the King criticizing him . . .

The fact that Henry Morgan and Edward Collier received substantial grants of land justified Modyford telling the duke of Albemarle (who died four days after Modyford signed the letter) that some of the 'best-monied' of the privateers had become planters, while others were trading with the local Indians along the coast of Central America. At the same time he admitted that a few privateersmen – he called them 'knaves' – were still attacking Spanish ships, landing their purchase at various outlying harbours in Jamaica that Modyford could not control.

The year ended in London with Charles Modyford giving the secretary of State the usual annual report, which showed there were 1500 privateersmen on the island, serving in twenty ships. Apart from them there were 3000 other men who could bear arms, as well as 1200 women and children and 2500 slaves.

Christmas and New Year's Eve of 1669 were cheerful times for the Morgans. Harry had been busy for many weeks securing his grant; now he had to get more slaves and put in overseers to start clearing the land, even though the grant would not be formally registered in the island's record office for several more weeks. Money would never again be a worry. By now Elizabeth's two brothers had the estate left by their father working profitably. Had he lived, Colonel Edward Morgan would have been gratified to see how the Morgans had rallied round to help each other.

As the eldest of the daughters Elizabeth had become almost the matriarch of the family. Anne was occupied with her first son, Thomas, now a year old, and she was pregnant again. Young Thomas became his Uncle Harry's favourite (and would be a trustee of his will) but having the boy at Lawrence-field with his mother and nurse emphasized that Elizabeth still had no children. Colonel Edward Morgan had had six children, the Byndloss family was to comprise eight, and after she had married Henry Archbold, Johanna Wilhelmina would have four sons. Yet Harry Morgan and his wife tried unsuccessfully to start a family. The buccaneer leader wanted desperately to have a son, a boy who would continue the name of Morgan and to whom he could leave the plantations.

Although they did not realize it, 1669 was the last year in which Harry Morgan's luck was entirely good; he had been both skilled in battle and lucky, and there had been no repercussions from London that mattered – expressions of His Majesty's wrath were distressing, but so far they had not affected Harry's share of the purchase. Harry Morgan's standing with the governor could not be higher and the planters looked up to him as the only man who could effectively defend Jamaica. The privateersmen who had elected him their admiral clearly never regretted their choice. The only group in the island who were less than enthusiastic about Harry Morgan were the merchants, under the leadership of Thomas Lynch.

Still, there appeared little to bother Morgan: the planters had the power. In London there was certainly a pro-Spanish clique at Court gathered round

Lord Arlington but so far they had been unable to play a card that could not be trumped by the duke of Albemarle. As they celebrated the New Year, Modyford, Morgan and the planters did not know that there was already a ship crossing the Atlantic to bring them news that the duke was dead. Arlington and his group now had the power in the Privy Council, a power considerably increased by the King's known sympathy for Catholicism.

The year 1670 began quietly. It was also the year in which William Congreve was born, to become the playwright chronicling Restoration England. His phrase 'The Devil watches all opportunities' might have been written to describe this time in the West Indies. Early in January 1670, as if to draw attention to the truce he was trying to enforce, Modyford decided to free some Spanish prisoners and, at the same time, send a friendly letter to the governor of Cuba. He chose a Jamaica ship, the *Mary and Jane*, whose master was a Dutchman, Bernard Claeson Speirdyck, popular in Port Royal as a former privateer commander and usually known as 'Captain Bernard' or 'Bart'.

Bernard took on a cargo of goods he knew would be in demand in Cuba and sailed with the prisoners to Manzanillo, handing over the prisoners to the mayor and asking permission to trade. The ship was searched three times before he was given permission to sell his cargo. As soon as this was done – there was no difficulty in disposing of the goods; everything was in short supply at Manzanillo – Bernard sailed again to return to Jamaica. On the way the *Mary and Jane* sighted a ship which hoisted English colours. Following the peacetime custom, Bernard hove-to the *Mary and Jane* and sent over two men in a boat to hear the latest news. As they climbed on board, the strange ship steered for the *Mary and Jane* and fired a broadside into her. She was no passing British ship but the *San Pedro y la Fama*, a 14-gun Spanish privateer commanded by a lively braggart named Manuel Rivera Pardal, who had ninety-six men on board.

Bernard had only sixteen men left in the *Mary and Jane* to handle her six guns, but for the next three hours, until it was dark, the Dutchman managed to fight off the *San Pedro*. It was not a dark night, so Captain Bernard could not escape, and at daylight the Spaniards attacked again. Cornelius Carstens, who was both purser and cook on board the *Mary and Jane*, said that the fight went on for another four hours, by which time 'the good old Captain and several of his crew' had been killed and the ship set on fire. Finally she was captured by the *San Pedro*. According to Carstens a jubilant Rivera told his prisoners that he had a Spanish commission valid for five years 'through the whole West Indies', and that it had been granted for 'satisfaction of the Jamaicans taking Puerto Bello'.

Rivera put nine of the prisoners, including Carstens, in a boat, gave them food and water and the course for Jamaica, and sailed on for the Main with his prize. There was uproar in Port Royal when the nine survivors arrived and told their story. As soon as Carstens revealed Rivera's boast that he had a five-year Spanish commission, and that it was issued in retaliation for the Portobelo raid, he was taken to the governor, and Sir Thomas heard the whole story at first hand.

As far as the governor was concerned, this was the equivalent of a declaration of war in the West Indies by Spain – and yet he had, only a few months ago, publicly withdrawn Colonel Morgan's commission as admiral and the commissions of all the privateers ... He discussed the situation with Morgan, and they agreed they could not act on Rivera's reported word alone: they needed to capture a ship and find a commission on board. One signed by a Spanish governor would be all the evidence needed to send to the Privy Council and justify Sir Thomas once again issuing commissions in Jamaica.

In the meantime Sir Thomas had to deal with the case of Captain Robert Searle – and it had arisen just at the wrong time. Captain Searle had been the privateer captain who four years earlier had to return captured specie and ships (see page 106). Now he was to be punished for his part in a straightforward piece of tit-for-tat.

Searle and his ship the *Cagway* had been in the Bahamas when, soon after Morgan's Maracaibo raid, Spaniards from Florida sailed down the chain of Bahama islands to New Providence (not to be confused with Old Providence, off the Nicaragua coast) and sacked the English settlement there. This led to several angry privateersmen, among them Searle, sailing for Florida and sacking St Augustine, on the north-east coast. Coming so soon after Modyford's proclamation withdrawing all commissions, and so obviously intended as revenge, the governor decided that he would have to punish the leader, who by general consent was Searle. When he returned to Jamaica, Searle guessed that he might be out of favour; instead of sailing into Port Royal he took the *Cagway* to a bay at the eastern end of the island out of the governor's reach.

'There arrived also at Port Morant,' Sir Thomas reported to Lord Arlington, 'the *Cagway*, Captain Searle, with seventy stout men, who hearing that I was much incensed against him for that action of St Augustine, went to Macary [sic: Macarry] Bay, and there rides out of [my] command. I will use the best ways to apprehend him, without driving his men to despair.'

The presence of Spanish commissions was soon confirmed. Another Spanish ship, the *San Nicolas de Tolentino* – Modyford called her a consort of Rivera – found two small Jamaican ships off the north-eastern tip of the Yucatàn Peninsula, bound for Campeche to pick up logwood. However, the crews were former privateersmen who had been forced to serve in trading vessels because of the withdrawal of commissions, and instead of the *San Nicolas* returning to Cuba with two prizes she found herself captured by her intended victims, along with her papers.

The two merchant ships took the *San Nicolas* back to Port Royal, handing over her papers as proof of what the Spaniards had been doing. Among them was a commission which read:

Whereas the Queen Regent of Spain by an order dated 20th April, 1669, was pleased to inform Don Pedro Bayona y Villa Nueva, Captain General of the Province of Paraguay and Governor of the city of Santiago de Cuba, that relation being made to her of the hostilities which the French and English made in the West Indies, she had made complaint thereof to the King of Great Britain, giving him notice of the peace celebrated in 1667, to which his Majesty answered that his subjects had no peace in the Indies, upon which the Queen commanded Don Pedro to cause war to be published against that nation, and to execute all the hostilities which are permitted in war, by taking possession of the ships, islands, places and ports ... with which object this commission has been granted.

It was unambiguous and quite genuine, and told Modyford that Spain had been at war with Britain in the West Indies for the last eleven months. Thanks to the wretchedly inefficient Spanish bureaucracy, it had taken months for the Queen Regent's *cedula* to reach the various governors and captains-general, and many weeks for the order to be turned into action. Questioning the captain of the *San Nicolas* then revealed even more alarming news: ships of war were due from Spain, and more private ships were due with commissions.

Quite apart from what Modyford and the Council might now decide, the Brethren in Port Royal had made up their minds as soon as they heard of the death of Bernard, one of their favourite captains. They were sailing, whether or not the governor granted commissions. The attack, Modyford told Lord Arlington, 'has so incensed the whole body of privateers that I hear they meditate revenge and have appointed a general rendezvous at Caimanos [the Cayman islands] next month, where', Modyford added, writing before the *San Nicolas* commission had been discovered, 'I will send to divert them or moderate their councils'.

If the Brethren were vengeful, the planters and merchants were frightened: the Queen Regent's order eleven months ago – now confirmed by a warning letter to Modyford from the Dutch governor of Curaçao, who had also seen one – seemed to be part of a much bigger move against Jamaica and perhaps the other British islands of the Lesser Antilles. Even now they pictured a Spanish fleet at sea, carrying enough troops to seize and garrison Jamaica.

Scores of men, be they plantation owners like Modyford and his brother James or merchants like Thomas Lynch (who also owned a large plantation), faced complete ruin. The attitude of both planters and merchants was summed up by Sir James Modyford in a letter to Thomas Lynch, who was on a prolonged visit to England. The governor's brother was writing on 18 March, within two or three days of the discovery of the *San Nicolas*'s commission:

> I could wish I were not so deeply engaged in planting, especially now that I see the Spaniards begin to take the right course to ruin us. They have denounced [i.e. declared] war against us in Cartagena ... They tell us plainly that they have daily in expectation twelve frigates from Europe ... who have commissions (as all ships shall have that come to the Indies) to take all the English they can light on.
>
> I wish you had your plantation with you and that it were not too big to be sold; mine, if possible, I'll dispose of and leave this warm sun for your God's blessing; for the Duke of Albemarle's death, this war, our making a blind peace [i.e. in 1667], no frigates [from England] or orders coming out gives us cruel apprehensions and makes many remiss.

The activities of the *San Pedro* and *San Nicolas* had been only the beginning. A former privateer commanded by Captain Thomas Rogers brought a Spanish prize into Port Royal. The Spaniards, Rogers reported, had attacked him and the only way he could save himself was to board and capture the Spanish ship, which he did without much trouble. He was checking through the prisoners when he found an English renegade who had adopted Spanish nationality and religion and lived in Cartagena. On questioning him, Rogers was startled to be told that 'war against Jamaica' had been proclaimed in Cartagena.

Modyford then received a report from another Englishman at Curaçao that officers of a Spanish ship there had told him that a similar proclamation had been made at Portobelo, and no quarter would be given to English ships, 'merchant or man of war'. Soon after that Modyford was warned that a Spanish ship had captured the *Amity*, a British ship from Bristol, off Grenada, in the Windward Islands, and taken her into the Dutch island of Curaçao to land her crew.

In sending a report to Lord Arlington describing several of these episodes (as well as enclosing a copy of the Spanish commission and many depositions) Modyford asked for latitude to retaliate 'in case the Spaniards act hostilities against us'. Jamaica could deal with any attack arising in the West Indies, he wrote, and would not need assistance from England 'unless the Spaniards send forces from Europe'.

There was then a lull for a month: apart from the capture of the *Amity*, May passed quietly, with little more than the angry threats of privateersmen in Port Royal and planters meeting of an evening over their glasses of punch. Then a rider galloped into the capital with alarming news: parties of

Spaniards, landing from two ships, were attacking villages and plantations along the north coast. Many houses had been set ablaze and settlers and slaves taken prisoner. By the time the nearest militia force could be collected and sent over the mountains the two Spanish ships had vanished.

A few days later three ships (one a French prize) were sighted off Port Royal and more militia were called out, galloping along the coast trying to keep level with the intruders as they sailed westward. The Spaniards came in close and anchored, as if intending to attack a big plantation nearby, but weighed and sailed as soon as the militia arrived. Next day they landed farther down the coast and burned two houses.

Nothing more was seen of the ships for a week; then a messenger arrived carrying a rolled-up canvas placard which was delivered to Sir Thomas Modyford, who read it and promptly called the Council and showed it to them. Dated 5 July, it said in Spanish and in English:

I, Captain Manuel Rivera Pardal to the chief of the squadron of privateers in Jamaica.

I am he who this year have done that which follows. I went on shore at Caimanos [Caymans] and burnt twenty houses and fought with Captain Ary and took from him a catch [ketch] laden with provisions and a canoa.

I am he who took Captain Baines [Bernard] and did carry the prize to Cartagena, and am now arrived at this coast and have burnt it.

And I am come to seek Admiral Morgan, with two ships of war of twenty guns, and having seen this, I crave he would come out upon the coast and seek me, that he might see the valour of the Spaniards.

And because I had no time I did not come to the mouth of Port Royal to speak by word of mouth in the name of my King, whom God preserve.

With planters and privateersmen protesting that their hands were tied while the Spanish did as they pleased, Modyford was waiting anxiously for news from London before he made up his mind. Godolphin's negotiations in Madrid were dragging on and on, and every week Modyford hoped that a ship would arrive with news that a new treaty had been signed or that a state of war existed – in Europe as well as in the West Indies.

But no word came; Arlington was taking refuge in silence. Modyford knew no more of the government's hopes and fears in June 1670 than he did in June a year earlier, when he had to deprive Morgan of his commission by proclamation through the streets. Yet Rivera's attacks on Jamaica could not be ignored. Quite apart from the damage already done, they might well be a reconnaissance; now Rivera saw how easy it was to burn plantations and vanish again, he might return with many more ships.

Modyford decided it was time to call the Council and, for lack of instructions from London, let the island's leaders decide what should be done. Ten members attended its meeting on 29 June – all of them planters; the merchants stayed away – and there were many reports to be considered. For the second time during Modyford's governorship they had to make a decision to ensure the island's safety. For the second time they read reports, discussed the problems – and turned to Harry Morgan.

The mild drama of that Council meeting held in the King's House at Spanish Town on 29 June 1670 is best described by the minutes of a resolution which was passed unanimously. The minutes were written so that a copy could be sent at once to the King and began by referring to the copy of a Spanish commission sent to Jamaica by Wilhelm Birk, the governor of Curaçao, in which the Queen Regent of Spain commanded her governors 'to make open war against the subjects of our Sovereign Lord the King in these parts'.

Spaniards from Cuba had landed in Jamaica, burning houses, killing people and taking prisoners and, the Council noted, had arranged a rendez-vous at Santiago 'for the speedy invasion of this island'. Repelling this invasion would mean the plantations 'will run to ruin, our cattle and other stock run wild, our slaves take to the woods...' They would eventually beat the enemy but they would be 'put to begin the world again, to our in-supportable loss and most infinite damage to his Majesty's service'.

The King's latest orders to Modyford were then quoted, particularly the provision that 'forasmuch there are many things incident to that government there [in Jamaica] for which it is not easy for us to prescribe such rules and directions for you' as the situation might require, 'instead of them you are with the advice of the Council to take care therein as fully and effectually as if you were instructed by us...'

Having established that in an emergency not covered by previous orders the Council was to advise the governor, the Council then recorded its advice:

That Commission be granted to Admiral Henry Morgan to be Admiral and Commander-in-Chief of all the ships of war belonging to this harbour, and of all the officers, soldiers, and seamen belonging to the same, requiring him with all possible speed to draw into one fleet, and with them put to sea for the security of the coast of this Island and of the merchant ships and other vessels trading to and about the same. And to attain, seize and destroy all the enemy's vessels that shall come within his reach; and also for destroying all the stores and magazines laid up for this war, and dispersing such forces as are or may be brought together for prosecuting the same.

He shall have power to land in the enemy's country as many of his men as he shall think needful; and with them to march to such places as he shall be informed the said magazines or forces are, and then accordingly take, destroy and dispose of; and to do and perform all manner of exploits which may tend to the preservation and quiet of this Island, being his Majesty's chief interest in the Indies.

There was little money in the island's treasury (certainly not enough to pay for the hire of a score of ships and at least a thousand men who were expected to volunteer) and the Council decided there was no need to depart from the usual method of reward. 'There is no other pay for the encouragement of the said fleet [but] that they shall have all the goods and merchandise that shall be gotten in this expedition, to be divided among them according to their usual rules.' No one in the fleet, they resolved, 'shall be molested for his debts'. When an 'extraordinary alarm' was raised, all owners of slaves in the island were to bring their men, 'furnished with bills, axes and other necessary tools' ready for building huts, clearing tracks 'and such other necessary work'.

So once again the governor and Council of Jamaica put the safety of the island squarely on the shoulders of Harry Morgan and the buccaneers. This time, however, his instructions could be widely interpreted – no doubt intentionally – and gave justification for Morgan landing more or less wherever he pleased.

On 2 July a drummer marched once again through Spanish Town and then Port Royal, followed by the town crier, who warned the people that the island was in danger and that volunteers were needed to man the ships while all members of the various defence forces were to report to their depots. The Port Royal Volunteers were quickly mobilized under Robert Byndloss, now a lieutenant-colonel. One of his young officers was his wife's brother Charles.

The excitement among the privateersmen was intense; they had not forgotten Captain Bernard's death at the hands of Rivera, nor Rivera's recent poster, which they regarded as an insult not just to their admiral but to all Jamaican privateersmen.

Although Morgan had not yet received his commission from the governor he set about recruiting his force. With England at peace with France he could rely on the Tortuga buccaneers once more and use the island as a rendezvous, which was set for 24 October. Esquemeling informs us:

With this resolution, he wrote diverse letters to all the ancient and expert pirates there inhabiting, as also to the governor of the said isle [Tortuga], and to the planters and hunters of Hispaniola giving them to understand his intentions, and desiring their appearance at the said place, in case they intended to go with him.

All these people had no sooner understood his design but they flocked unto the place assigned in huge numbers, with ships, canoes, and boats, being desirous to obey his commands. Many who had not the convenience of coming unto him by sea traversed the woods of Hispaniola, and with no small difficulty arrived there by land...

Morgan's immediate problem in Port Royal was that many of the ships were already at sea. He wanted to hoist his flag in the 22-gun *Satisfaction*, the former French pirate *Le Cerf Volant*, but she was away on a long cruise and no one knew where she was. Captain John Morris – a survivor from the *Oxford* explosion – promised to bring the *Dolphin*, having increased her armament to ten guns, and he signed on a crew of sixty.

Captain Lawrence Prince agreed to sail again and his *Pearl* also had her armament increased to ten guns. He signed on fifty men. The enterprising Captain Robert Searle and the *Cagway* were absent: Searle had unwisely ventured into Port Royal, been seized by the governor, and now waited in jail under arrest until word came from England about how he should be punished for the St Augustine raid.

Although Morgan knew nothing of it, he soon had an extra ship that would later cause him trouble. Dr George Holmes was the owner of the 50-ton *Port Royal*. Holmes wanted nothing to do with privateering; he preferred a smaller but assured profit at the minimum risk and gave orders to the *Port Royal*'s regular captain, Humphrey Thurston, to sail to Campeche for a cargo of logwood. But Port Royal was so full of martial fervour and activity that sailing for logwood struck Thurston as a mundane affair. Without a word to his cautious owner, he put more guns in the *Port Royal* so that she had a total of twelve, signed on fifty-five of the toughest privateersmen he could find, and sailed on an expedition of his own, a trial voyage, as it were, before joining the admiral.

Within a very short time Thurston had captured a 50-ton Spanish ship which he decided to turn into another privateer, without bothering to take her to Port Royal and going through all the tedious formalities of having her condemned as a prize (and explaining to Dr Holmes why the *Port Royal* was now a ship of war). The prize was the same tonnage but faster and handier than the *Port Royal*, mounting eight guns. Thurston decided he preferred the prize, so he renamed her the *Thomas* and took her over. He gave the command of the *Port Royal* to James Delliatt, who signed on fifty-five men, and the two ships sailed for Admiral Morgan's rendezvous at Tortuga.

Morgan's commission was not issued until 22 July (Modyford wisely waited until the last moment, hoping that instructions would arrive from England) and with it were commissions for the ten privateer captains who so far had agreed to sail. Given by 'Sir Thomas Modyford, Baronet, Governor ... Vice-admiral to his Royal Highness the Duke of York in the

American Seas ...', it was addressed to 'Admiral Henry Morgan, Esq.'. It referred to the Queen-Regent's *'shadula'*, and said that the Spanish governors were 'diligently gathering forces together to be sent to St Jago de Cuba, their general rendezvous and place of magazine, and from thence as the most opportune place to be transported for a thoro' invasion and final conquest (as they hope) of this island ...'

Morgan was appointed admiral and commander-in-chief of 'all the ships, barques, and other vessels now fitted or which hereafter shall be fitted' for the defence of the island, and it required him 'to use your best endeavours to get the vessels into one body or fleet, and to cause them to be well manned, fitted, armed and victualled, and by the first opportunity, wind and weather permitting, to put to sea for the guard and defence of this island ...'

So much for the commission. Morgan received his orders from the governor two days later – eleven instructions which covered every possible eventuality. They are of particular interest because they concern a fleet that would eventually comprise twenty-eight British ships and more than 1300 men, quite apart from eight French ships and more than five hundred Frenchmen.

Morgan was to 'advise your fleet and soldiers that you are on the old pleasing account of "no purchase, no pay", and therefore that all which is got shall be divided amongst them according to accustomed rules'.

If he should 'find it prudential' to get to Santiago 'and God blessing you with victory', he was to hold the city and wait for further orders from Modyford. Bitter experience and the pile of depositions in his files led Modyford to frame the seventh instruction with care: 'You are to inquire what usage our prisoners have had, and what quarter hath been given by the enemy ... and, being well informed, you are to give the same, or rather our custom is to exceed in civility and humanity ...' Morgan was empowered to grant commissions 'according to the form I have used, taking security of £1000 for the performance of the same'.

By now Modyford had done all he could to safeguard Jamaica. A ship was already on its way across the Atlantic to London, carrying the minutes of the Council meeting of 29 June, and with them was an urgent letter to Lord Arlington. 'It is possible that the Spaniards with their great ships of forty and sixty guns may be masters of the seas and impede our trade,' Modyford told Arlington, 'in which case we must implore the assistance of his Majesty's frigates; but on shore we fear them not, but hope in time to fix the war in their own country, to which your Lordship's advice and favour would greatly encourage.'

Arlington had contrived to give Modyford no instructions for more than six months; since the duke of Albemarle died at the beginning of December, Modyford had received only routine letters from England. As Modyford, Morgan and the planters had feared, the duke's death had left them without friends in the Privy Council, without protection in the West Indies, and so far without any agreement with the Spanish.

Morgan was angry that the *Satisfaction*, one of the largest and most powerful of the Jamaica ships, still had not come in. She had been sent back to Port Royal from Cow Island in January 1669, and after victualling and watering she had sailed with orders to patrol off Campeche, where apparently she had been ever since. Finally, in July 1670, Modyford had word that she was in the Cayman Islands and ordered her back to Port Royal at once. She arrived at the beginning of August, fortunately before Morgan had left for Tortuga in Captain Bradley's *Mayflower*. Surgeon Browne was still in the ship and thoroughly bored by a cruise lasting more than a year and a half with 'a dull and sluggish commander'. Admiral Morgan must have had a high regard for Browne, who wrote from Port Royal to the under-secretary of State, Sir Joseph Williamson, on 7 August saying that the *Satisfaction* returned to find 1500 men and their ships assembling there 'for some notable design on land'. Morgan had appointed him surgeon-general to the expedition, he added.

Commenting that a Spanish attack on a Bermuda ship had left that island so angry that scores of men were offering to join any expedition from Jamaica, Browne told Sir Joseph that 'fifteen or twenty sail of third, fourth or even fifth rate frigates could overrun the whole Indies in a very short time and add a splendid jewel to his sacred Majesty's Crown'. However, he warned, Jamaica would be in great danger once Morgan sailed, and the islanders wished frigates had arrived from England.

Sir Thomas Modyford was in the meanwhile as full of doubts as any imaginative man could be after having for the second time in his life personally declared war on the Spanish in the West Indies. It could be argued that the Council had advised him but the fact was that the King would blame, sack or even jail him if necessary, not the Council. By August, when Admiral Morgan and the *Satisfaction* (with Captain Edward Collier in command) led the Jamaica privateers out of Port Royal, Modyford still had no news of Godolphin's negotiations in Madrid. All he knew was what his son Charles could glean in London: that with the old duke of Albemarle dead, Modyford had no champion in the Privy Council. Power lay with the Cabal which, although deriving from the Jewish word *cabala* (occult or secret knowledge), represented the initials of the five men who had most influence with the King at this time.

Modyford had to decide on the man in the Cabal most likely to be sympathetic towards Jamaica's present plight. Obviously not Clifford, who was a Catholic, nor Arlington. The duke of Buckingham – well, at this point it was hard to see what he stood for. He had often opposed the King's party in Parliament, but had joined the Cabal in 1667. That left Ashley and

Lauderdale. The earl [later duke] of Lauderdale was secretary for Scotland and unlikely to be interested in the affairs of a distant island. Lord Ashley (later earl of Shaftesbury), like most of the leading men in the country, had changed sides in the Civil War, but from Modyford's point of view he was the only member of the Cabal likely to read any letter with a sympathetic eye.

'Knowing the great respect your Lordship hath always borne to righteous causes,' Modyford wrote, his son Charles would deliver documents 'in which there are many reasons for the present justice of our arms against the Spaniard; yet because it may be looked on as a fond rash action for a petty governor without money to make war with the richest, and not long since the powerfullest prince of Europe, I have thought it reasonable to give your Lordship a short and true view of affairs here'. The documents ranged from copies of the Queen Regent's *cedula* to the minutes of the Jamaica Council's meeting.

The Spanish possessions were large but thinly populated, Modyford wrote. The Indians, Negroes and slaves were indifferent to their masters and he gave Cuba as an example. It was 'in length 600 miles and not above six towns on it, and those so far distant from each other that they cannot be any relief to themselves'. He pointed out:

> The country abounds with cattle, hogs &c, and by this means our private men of war careen, refit, and victual without more charge than a gang of hunters and dogs, and expect no other pay than what they get from the enemy.
>
> These are men, who [totalling] about 1500, never will be planters. I have employed them to keep the war in their own country, and judge you, my Lord, in this exigent, what course could be more frugal, more prudential, more hopeful – the men volunteers, the ships, arms, ammunition their own, their victuals and pay the enemy's, and such enemies as they have always beaten.

Spain had been preparing for the war since April 1669, and probably longer, but as a result of his actions he hoped that 'there will be a good foundation laid for a great increase of his Majesty's dominions in these parts'.

Lord Ashley's rôle in all this, so far as Modyford was concerned, was to persuade the King that the governor had acted reasonably – he now had the documents to prove that – and obtain the King's approval.

When Morgan led the privateers out of Port Royal on 14 August he was concerned at first to get the men away from the taverns and brothels, so he anchored at Bluefields Bay, at the western end of the island, and there the seamen hurried on with splicing and setting up rigging, stitching sails and re-paying the decks, careening the ships and cleaning the bottoms of weed and barnacles.

Four days later a ship arrived in Port Royal direct from England with a letter for Modyford from Lord Arlington. Written on 12 June, it had taken just two months to reach Jamaica. In chilling words the secretary of State said that Godolphin's negotiations with Spain continued, and news was 'daily expected' from Madrid of an agreement which would let them all 'live like good neighbours in the West Indies, they affording us a safe retreat in their ports, and wood, water and refreshments for money, forbearing to ask freedom of trade, which neither we in our Leeward plantations nor they in any part of America, according to their ancient constitutions, can admit of; this they could hardly agree to, such have been their resentments for what the privateers have done, and such their demands for reparations'.

This curious letter ended with an order: 'His Majesty's pleasure is that in what state soever the privateers are at the receipt of this letter, you keep them so, till we have a final answer from Spain, with condition only that you oblige them to forebear all hostilities at land.'

Arlington said he had received Modyford's dispatches up to 20 March, so that he knew of the capture of the *Mary and Jane*, and death of Captain Bernard, an episode he dismissed as 'not to be wondered at after such hostilities as your men have acted upon their territories'. He made no suggestions about how the island should defend itself and completely ignored Modyford's earlier requests for frigates. Yet apart from the gift of the *Oxford*, His Majesty had not spent a penny on the island for years but continued giving away land to his favourites – the 3000 acres granted to the earl of Clarendon were the latest example, the worthy earl never having visited the island.

Modyford could place little reliance on Arlington's letter because it said almost nothing. Far from telling Modyford that, in return for an end to privateering, Arlington hoped for a proper treaty in which Spain recognized Britain's ownership of Jamaica, he merely hoped for 'some articles that might make them live like good neighbours in the West Indies'. And he told Modyford, in the tones a cardinal might adopt to an erring acolyte, that he could not expect the Spanish to allow Jamaica to trade because they were offended by the privateers.

The Jamaican people had fought Nature and the jungle for almost every square foot of plantation, paid for every building, church and highway and captured nearly all the cannon which were now mounted in the fort and batteries they had built at Port Royal. Except for a brief period when Commodore Mings was in the area, they had defended themselves. Lord Arlington was being as optimistic as only a politician can afford to be if he thought Modyford and the Council in their plight would pay too much attention to his words.

However, Modyford could – and did – obey his instructions. The privateers were to be kept 'in what state soever' they were when Modyford received the letter. Very well, they were at sea, and they could stay there. And Modyford was 'to oblige them to forebear all hostilities at land'. Very well, a ship should be sent to bring back Admiral Morgan so that he could be told of the King's prohibition.

Morgan came back from Bluefields Bay and, Arlington was told, the governor informed him of the King's instructions, 'strictly charging him to observe the same, and behave with all moderation in carrying on this war'. He answered that he would observe the orders as far as possible 'but necessity would compel him to land in the Spaniards' country for wood, water and provisions', or otherwise he would have to 'desert the service'. However, unless Morgan had assured himself that Spanish towns had laid up stores intended for the destruction of Jamaica 'he would not attempt any of them'. With that Morgan returned to his ships.

Sir Thomas in his reply to Lord Arlington, which was frank and concealed nothing (it reveals much about Arlington's knowledge that a governor had to write in such terms), said that 'had that reputed most wise Council of Spain suspended their resentment [against Jamaica] but two years longer, most of our privateers [would have] betaken themselves to another way of living, for their rigging, sails and ships were almost worn out, and their owners disheartened for want of commissions, so that the better sort daily came on shore to settle, and the seamen who will never settle began to dispose themselves on merchant voyages'.

He ended bluntly:

Could the Council of Spain be well informed of their want of men to defend their large possessions in these parts, they would conclude themselves incapable of destroying Jamaica and make peace; but they are borne up by false measures of their strength and have plunged themselves into this war and so slight the application of Sir William Godolphin; but a little more suffering will inform them of their condition and force them to capitulations more suitable to the sociableness of man's nature ...

Rattling the Bars

With his ten ships refitted Morgan sailed from Bluefields Bay and headed north to begin operations off Cuba. There was no enemy ship among the South Cays or near Manzanillo, so he left Captain Morris and the *Dolphin* in the area as a lookout and sailed eastwards to Santiago, but the harbour was empty and Morgan contented himself with rattling the bars along the coast. The news that nearly a dozen British ships were in the area would make sure the Spanish stayed at home.

With the date of his rendezvous drawing near, Morgan and his little fleet headed for Tortuga, two hundred miles to the eastward, but they had not crossed the Windward Passage before bad weather hit them. Morgan had been taking a risk ever since he sailed because September – which was only a few days off – is the height of the hurricane season. Fortunately they had only storm-force winds, and although the fleet was scattered none was lost. By 2 September they had all reached Tortuga.

The storm blew fortune into the lap of John Morris and the *Dolphin*. After combing the South Cays and the nearby coast without finding a Spanish ship that would yield a prisoner and thus intelligence, he made for a sheltered bay on the Cuba shore when the heavy weather arrived. There he found a Spanish man-of-war at anchor – and she was commanded by Manuel Rivera Pardal, the poster artist. Compared with the *Dolphin*'s ten guns and sixty men she was armed with fourteen guns and 'double-manned, having taken on board eighty musketeers and good stores of ammunition, grenadoes and stinkpots'. The story was related to Sir Joseph Williamson by Surgeon Browne, who said that at the *Dolphin*'s first broadside the Spaniards all panicked and bolted from the guns. Rivera was killed while trying to control them and of the scores of men on board only five were taken prisoner by the *Dolphin*.

When Captain Morris went through the Spanish warship's papers he found three more Spanish commissions, which were sent on to Port Royal. Mody-ford forwarded them to Arlington with news of Rivera's death, pointing out that he was 'a person of great value amongst them and empowered to carry the royal standard at the maintop'. Modyford also sent Rivera's canvas poster with the challenge to Morgan so that the secretary of State could make 'a guess of the man's vanity'.

John Morris arrived at the rendezvous to find ten ships anchored in the channel between the lofty island of Tortuga and the shore of Hispaniola: the *Satisfaction* was there with Admiral Morgan on board and Captain Collier in command; nearby was Lawrence Prince's *Pearl*. Among the smaller privateers were Charles Swan's tiny *Endeavour* and Patrick Dunbar's 10-ton *Prosperous*.

Morgan saw that, with late arrivals, his fleet might eventually comprise more than thirty ships and 1500 men, and few of them would have enough provisions on board for a lengthy cruise, so he called a council of all the captains present to discuss the problem of food. The main shortage was grain; they would need a lot of it to grind into flour, and none was available in Hispaniola. Few ships had nearly enough meat, either salt or *boucan*. Clearly the first priority for the whole fleet was obtaining provisions.

The Spanish had plenty of grain so the easiest source was the Main. It was decided to send four ships and a large boat under Captain Collier to the best area for maize, the towns and villages near Riohacha, halfway between the entrance to the Gulf of Venezuela and Cartagena. Collier was also to capture prisoners who would yield intelligence.

'In the meanwhile,' Esquemeling recorded, 'Captain Morgan sent another party of his men to hunt in the woods [of Hispaniola, now Haiti], who killed there a huge number of beasts, and salted them. The rest of his companions remained in the ships to clean, fit and rig them out [for] sea, so that at the return of those who were sent abroad all things might be in readiness to weigh anchor...'

Another storm hit Morgan's anchored fleet on 7 October and within a few hours ten of the Jamaica privateers were aground after dragging their anchors or parting their cables. Only the *Satisfaction* remained afloat when the weather cleared. Morgan made an inspection of the ships and although all were damaged eight could be refloated after a lot of work and made ready for sea. That left Morgan with the large crews from the three that were wrecked. He divided them among the other ships but wrote to Modyford appealing for more vessels, explaining that he was at the moment in the absurd position of having too many men. Slowly more ships joined him: at the end of October Modyford sent over three privateers (including Captain Bradley) who had just come in to Port Royal after a successful attack on Nicaragua; then three French privateers arrived, each with seventy men.

Morgan reported to Modyford at the beginning of November that he had 1100 men, with more expected, and he hoped to begin the expedition by the end of the month. He had heard a rumour that Prince Rupert was due in the West Indies with a large fleet, although Surgeon Browne's comment to Sir Joseph Williamson was apt: Rupert's fleet might conquer the West Indies 'but without Admiral Morgan and his old privateers, things cannot be as successful as expected; for they know every creek, and the Spaniards' mode of fighting, and be a town ever so well fortified and the numbers never so unequal, if money or plunder be in the case, they will either win it manfully or die courageously'. Browne then made an interesting judgment on Morgan, with whom he had been serving for some time: 'Admiral Morgan has been in the Indies eleven or twelve years, and from a private gentleman by his valour has raised himself to what he now is, and no one can give so clear an account of the Spanish force.'

Days became weeks, and then a month had passed since Collier's ships left for Riohacha and the maize – a long delay which, said Esquemeling, 'occasioned Captain Morgan almost to despair of their return, as fearing lest they were fallen into the hands of the Spaniards'. It also occurred to Morgan that they might have 'made some great fortune in that voyage, and with it escaped to some other place'. Finally, after five weeks, Morgan saw not five ships returning but seven. One was clearly a heavily-laden merchant ship, another a Spanish privateer prize, and the buccaneers' ships were also carrying cargo.

The story that Collier had to tell Morgan was a good one. His little squadron had arrived at Riohacha after being delayed by calms and captured a ship from Cartagena which was nearly full of maize. He then ransomed the town for another 5000 bushels of maize and sailed for Tortuga with his prize. On the way back they sighted and captured a Spanish privateer, and when Collier examined her captain he found she was the *Galliardena*, an 80-ton ship armed with ten guns. More questioning revealed that the buccaneers' revenge on the boastful Rivera was now complete because the *Galliardena* had been the second ship with Rivera when he attacked the north coast of Jamaica, firing plantations and putting up his poster.

The *Galliardena*'s crew of thirty-eight gave Collier information of vital importance to the admiral and as soon as the squadron arrived in Tortuga they were taken over to the *Satisfaction* for Morgan to question. Some of them had information of such significance that John Peake, Morgan's secretary, took it down in writing. The *Galliardena*'s captain, in a statement he signed, said that in Cartagena (whence the ship had just sailed) the people were 'in arms offensive against the English' and the president of Panama, Don Juan Perez de Guzman, had issued commissions against the English to several ships, which had since taken English prizes. Don Juan had given the Spaniards 'great encouragement against the island of Jamaica, and the more by reason of a fleet fitted out of Old Spain for these parts under the command of one Don Alonso'.

The rumour about Prince Rupert was not the only one to reach Jamaica. The second one had a chilling ring of possibility about it, particularly because of the known policy of Lord Arlington and his pro-Spanish colleagues and the chance that Godolphin's mission in Madrid might well have been told to produce a treaty at almost any price.

Modyford wrote to Arlington that he was very worried at the rumour that 'Jamaica was to be sold to the Spaniard, or at least there was working to that purpose'. The report probably reached Modyford from his son Charles, and it is an indication of the distrust between Arlington and Jamaica that the planters could well visualize the secretary of State and the King sacrificing the island for the sake of a one-sided accord with Spain.

Modyford also told Arlington in a later letter that one of the Jamaica privateer captains had just brought back information from Nicaragua that the governor of Panama was 'much blamed' by Madrid 'for having done nothing all this time' in the war against Jamaica and similar letters had been sent to the other Spanish governors, 'by which your Lordship may have some aim at the violence of their intentions and the little force they have to execute them'.

By 23 November, when Morgan sent one of his regular reports to Sir Thomas Modyford, so many more Frenchmen had joined him that he was now short of ships for them. These men were true *boucaniers* who for years had been living in Hispaniola, shooting cattle and hogs and trading hides and tallow for powder and shot.

Morgan's relationship with the French in Tortuga was now excellent: seven French ships had come in so far, the largest being Captain Tribetor's 14-gun *St Catherine* with a crew of 110. However, the remaining French ships could carry no more extra men – the 10-gun *St Pierre* had ninety on board; even the tiny sloop *Le Cerf*, hard put to carry two guns, carried forty men. Yet sleeping on the beach were several score tough *boucaniers* who had their own muskets; men who were crack shots and would be invaluable when besieging a Spanish fort or fighting through rough country, although useless as seamen.

The Spanish prize, the 80-ton *Galliardena*, was still at anchor and un-manned. A 10-gun ship was a valuable addition to the fleet, so Morgan handed her over to the French (there was no time to send her to Port Royal to be condemned in the prize court) and Captain Gascoine was put in command. He signed on eighty of his fellow countrymen.

The time had come to make the first move, and the Dutch buccaneer reveals how careful was Morgan, dispelling any idea of a half-drunken swash-buckler who relied on a bullying manner and bluster to get his way: 'After Captain Morgan had divided the maize, as also the flesh which the hunters brought in, among all the ships according to the number of men that were in every vessel, he concluded upon the departure, having viewed beforehand every ship, and observed their being well-equipped and clean. Thus he set sail and directed his course towards Cape Tiburon, where he determined to take his measures and resolutions of what enterprise he should take in hand.'

A stretch of the coast at the south-western tip of Hispaniola between Cape Donna Maria and Cape Tiburon – a striking peninsula of white cliffs – provides many sheltered bays, and geographically it is well placed as an anchorage whether ships are bound for Cuba, Jamaica, the Main or the Mosquito Coast. By the time his ships were anchored round him in the lee of Cape Tiburon, a total of thirty-six and manned by 1846 men, Morgan had assembled the largest fleet of privateers the Indies had ever seen, twenty-eight of them British and eight French. Morgan decided the fleet was too unwieldy – buccaneers were neither trained nor temperamentally suited to answer signals – so he divided it into two squadrons, appointing Edward Collier to be the vice-admiral commanding the second squadron.

The ships and captains represented a cosmopolitan selection hard to find anywhere but in the Caribbean. By far the largest was Morgan's flagship, the 22-gun *Satisfaction*. Thirteen ships mounted ten or more guns, but five of the Jamaica vessels were so small that they had no guns at all. Patrick Dunbar's 10-ton *Prosperous* was the smallest, carrying sixteen men, while Roger Kelly's *Free Gift* at 15 tons managed to mount two guns and, although only the size of a small fishing smack, forty privateersmen had signed on. William Curzon's 12-ton sloop *Betty*, which the admiral had been using to carry dispatches, had twenty-five men, two more than Roger Taylor's 20-ton *Bonaventure*.

Humphrey Thurston was of course present with his prize the *Thomas*, and unbeknown to Dr George Holmes the *Port Royal* was also there under her new captain, James Delliat. The most important thing for success was that the really experienced privateer captains were in the expedition – apart from people like Morris, Prince and Bradley, there were men such as Richard Norman, who had been at Maracaibo with his 10-gun *Lily*, and Thomas Rogers, also at Maracaibo and now ready to sail with his 12-gun *Gift*.

Men were far more important than the actual broadsides of their ships because they all knew from long experience that most buccaneer battles were fought on land. Thus John Barnett's 50-ton *Virgin Queen* was welcome because although she had no guns she could carry thirty men and ample provisions. With the possible exception of the *Satisfaction* and the *Galliardena*, not one of the ships had been designed as a ship of war; the vast majority were little more than crudely-fashioned boxes designed to carry as much cargo as possible.

There was a good deal of paper work for Morgan to complete now the whole fleet was finally assembled at Cape Tiburon. First, every captain, English or French, had to have a commission giving his name and the name of his ship. Then Morgan called all the captains together on board the *Satisfaction*. He had decided that an expedition on the present grand scale was worthy of a new agreement, one which gave better terms for almost everyone, but particularly the wounded, the captains – and himself. He had prepared articles of agreement which laid down a different division of the purchase.

The King had his usual fifteenth share and the duke of York his tenth; after that Morgan received one per cent while each captain received the shares of eight men for the use of his ship and the same again for himself. Beside his normal share the surgeon was to get 200 pieces of eight (£50) for the use of his medicine chest and the carpenter one hundred.

The compensation for wounds was considerably increased. Payment for the loss of a leg went up from 400 pieces of eight for the left or 500 for the right to 600 (£150) for either. The loss of one hand meant compensation of 600 pieces of eight, but a man who lost both received 1800 (£450). The rate for an eye remained the same, 100 pieces of eight (£25). In each case the compensation was listed as cash or slaves at the rate of 100 pieces of eight per slave. At the current rate a piece of eight was equal to five shillings, so a slave was valued at £25.

Quite apart from wounds, Morgan had worked out a system of rewards for bravery which, like the compensation, was to be the first charge on any purchase. 'Unto him that in any battle should signalise himself, either by entering the first any castle, or taking down the Spanish colours and setting up the English', there was a reward of 50 pieces of eight.

With commissions issued and agreements signed, Morgan and his captains then had to decide where they should attack. It is very easy to say that they were deciding as buccaneers where to raid; choosing the city that would give them most purchase. That was undoubtedly the attitude of most captains, but it did not account entirely for the attitude of Morgan or his senior officers. Morgan had a wife and two large plantations, three sisters-in-law, three brothers-in-law and all his friends living in Jamaica; his whole future, fame and prosperity was as wrapped up in the island as the years that had passed. Edward Collier had just been granted an estate of a thousand acres; Lawrence Prince, John Morris and Joseph Bradley were also substantial planters. Even Morgan's secretary, John Peake, had a future in the island: he later became a planter and speaker of the House of Assembly.

To the leaders of Jamaica it seemed that not only had they no friends in the Privy Council but the man with most power as far as Jamaica was concerned, the secretary of State, was almost as much their enemy as the Court of Spain. To people in Jamaica, be they planter or apothecary, merchant or fisherman, wife of a privateersman or one of the scores of trollops living in Port Royal, the threat from Spain was real and it was immediate. It was all very well for Arlington deliberately to avoid giving the governor any information or directions for more than six months, but he was living safely in London, his life in danger only if he fell down the stairs or contracted some disease. His property was safe unless he hazarded it at the gaming table. He would not, for instance, suddenly see a group of Rivera's men racing up to his house with pikes and pistols, shooting his slaves and taking his wife and children and himself prisoner, to rot in a jail in Cartagena for the next few years, with an occasional spell on the rack to make them change their religion.

The fear of raiding ships appearing over the horizon was what everyone was living with in Jamaica. They all knew that their defence depended not upon the British government and the cold words of Lord Arlington but on the ships that sailed in and out of Port Royal.

Modyford's attitude was obviously a great deal more high-minded than Morgan's, but the latter knew the risks he ran if he went too far: he could bring Modyford down, as well as discrediting himself. He also knew what would happen if Modyford's commission as governor was withdrawn by the King: the merchants would have the power, with one of the leading merchants getting the job. All these factors were in Henry Morgan's mind on board the *Satisfaction* on 2 December 1670, as he faced his captains and his vice-admiral.

Henry Morgan was a great leader but it is significant that, unless he was acting under direct orders from the governor, he always discussed with his captains where they should next attack and, although he used his exceptional powers of persuasion, he always did what the majority decided. There is no evidence that he ever persuaded the buccaneers to attack a place against their will, which leads to the conclusion that he led by their consent.

Admiral Morgan, Vice-Admiral Collier and thirty-six captains gathered on the quarterdeck of the *Satisfaction*, the greatest meeting of privateersmen the West Indies was ever to see. Yet some of the captains, men like Humphrey Thurston, were attending their first council of war and were excited and talkative, anxious to have their say while they had the ear of Admiral Morgan. The proceedings were slow because of the need to translate for the benefit of the French captains. Morgan began, he later told Modyford, by asking the captains' advice on which Spanish port or city 'it was fittest to attain for his Majesty's honour and the preservation of Jamaica and to put the greatest curb on the insolencies of the enemy'.

He told them that his orders mentioned Santiago de Cuba, but various captains suggested other towns. Several mentioned Panama, notoriously the richest city in the Indies; one or two suggested Cartagena; Vera Cruz was popular with some because the capital of New Spain and the centre for the riches of Mexico had never been raided on a large scale.

With thirty-six captains, all rugged individualists, it was obvious the council was likely to last all night so they elected a committee of the most experienced who would make recommendations to a full council. There was no argument about who should form the committee – Edward Collier, John

Morris and Joseph Bradley were immediate choices; two French captains represented the Tortuga privateers, and they all agreed to eleven others.

They began by considering Santiago de Cuba, then called St Jago, and they were able to question several Englishmen who had recently escaped from there, including Captain Richard Powell who, Morgan said, 'had not been above twenty days from St Jago'. It was late in the year for an attack on any open coast on Cuba; the Trade winds would be blowing strongly and there was always the risk of northers. In addition, Morgan told Modyford, 'it was impossible for us to attempt that place without hazard of the whole party, and the certain loss of most, if not all our vessels by foul weather; all the knowing prisoners examined affirming the same, upon which we abandoned that design'.

The committee then considered Cartagena, but they all knew that it, like Havana, was almost impregnable, the entrance so covered by forts that only a combined assault from seaward by large ships of war and overland by a strong army could guarantee success.

Next the captains considered Panama. To the buccaneers it was a magic name, synonymous with the gold and silver of the Indies. There came all the riches of the mines of Peru; there lived wealthy merchants in great luxury. Panama was rich, so there would be a good purchase, but it was powerful, and with a march of more than fifty miles across jungle and over mountains the buccaneers could not hope for a surprise attack.

If Cartagena, Portobelo, Old Providence, Santa Marta, Maracaibo and other towns and cities were the limbs of the Spanish Main, the city of Panama was its heart. If Panama was taken, would the limbs wither and easily fall? From the Spanish point of view the city was safe from attack, with the almost impassable mountains, rivers and jungle of the Isthmus separating it from the buccaneers swarming the North Sea. Only one man had ever tried to attack it, and that had been Drake scores of years ago. The jungle was thick and the single track from Portobelo could be so easily guarded that the Spanish considered that Panama's only possible danger – and that very remote – would be an attack from the South Sea, by pirates who made the terrible voyage round Cape Horn.

When Morgan, Collier, Bradley and the other buccaneer leaders viewed the idea from the Spanish point of view, Panama began to look promising. Certainly the thick jungle and high mountains were enormously difficult for newly-arrived hidalgos from Spain, but to true *boucaniers* who for so many years had scraped a living and evaded Spanish patrols across the similar jungles and mountains of western Hispaniola, they presented no problems – providing there was a good purchase at the other end ...

The committee finally agreed unanimously and the full council of war was called again, when Morgan told the captains (and later reported to Modyford): 'that it stand most for the good of Jamaica and the safety of

us all to take Panama, the President thereof having granted several commissions against the English, to the great annoyance of Jamaica and our
merchantmen'.

Panama was the one Spanish city in the Indies about which the buccaneers knew nothing, so it was important to find reliable guides, quite apart
from prisoners who could be interrogated for more information. The council
of war had no doubts about where both could be found – they voted for
first capturing the island of Providence, 'being the King's ancient property
and the people there being from Panama, no place could be more fit'.

Next day, on 3 December, Morgan sent a sloop to Jamaica with a dispatch for Sir Thomas reporting that he 'was under sail with thirty-six ships
and 1800 men', and enclosing a list of all the ships, their captains, tonnages,
armament and number of men on board. Morgan purposely did not mention
his fleet's destination, saying only that prisoners revealed that the Spanish
were assembling troops at Cartagena, Portobelo and Panama ready for the
arrival of the galleons, which would be used to transport them 'against
this island'. His fleet actually sailed from Cape Tiburon for the tiny speck
of land that was Old Providence, 575 miles to the south-west, on 8 December.

In Europe events had begun to speed up in the last half of 1670. On 11
July a treaty of 'alliance and commerce' was signed with Denmark, and
seven days later 'Gulielmo Godolphin' in Madrid signed on behalf of Britain
the treaty with Spain for which he had been working for so long. Written
in Latin and comprising sixteen sections, it represented something of a
triumph for Sir William. After claiming for nearly two hundred years that
only she could possess the land beyond the Line, Spain finally agreed that
Britain could own the lands in the New World that she already occupied.
At long last she had given up her claim to Jamaica. There was no mention
of reciprocal trade agreements, but both nations agreed to abstain from
hostile acts. In future it was up to Britain to stop buccaneering because
such raids would be regarded as acts of war.

The treaty was immediately sent to London for ratification. Four months
were allowed for this – until 18 November – and another eight months
allowed for its publication in the colonies. This meant that the treaty did not
come into force in the West Indies until 18 July 1671, exactly one year after
Godolphin signed it in Madrid. Once the treaty had been ratified in London,
neither the King nor Arlington hesitated to deal with Sir Thomas Modyford.
There was no difficulty about sacking him, but who could be made governor
in his place?

Thomas Lynch had been living in England for the past five years, ever
since Modyford had sacked him from his post of chief justice, although he
still owned a large plantation in Jamaica. Fourth son of a family from Cran-
brook in Kent, and grandson of a former bishop of London, Lynch was

thirty-eight years old and, like Henry Morgan, had gone out to Jamaica with Venables' expedition. He seemed the ideal man to Lord Arlington and he was notified in late September that he would be appointed lieutenant-governor. This was a shrewd move because there had been no lieutenant-governor since Colonel Edward Morgan died. Lynch could thus be appointed while Modyford still remained governor.

It was usual for governors to have knighthoods, a custom which is still continued, although rapid communications have reduced the recipients to little more than clerks, and on 3 December Thomas Lynch attended the King at Whitehall to receive his knighthood. By a bizarre coincidence it was also the day that Morgan told Modyford that he was 'under sail with thirty-six ships'.

Lynch was engaged to Vere, the daughter of Sir Edward Herbert and sister of the earl of Torrington, and they were married a few days after the ceremony in anticipation of the move to Jamaica. Parliament voted £1000 for Lynch's 'equipage and expenses in going to Jamaica'. Lynch then received his commission and the revocation of Modyford's commission, but both documents were dated a month later.

As the finishing touches were put to Lynch's instructions in London on 20 December, Modyford sat down in Jamaica to write to Lord Arlington. He was now very worried because a ship coming into Port Royal brought private letters mentioning the possibility that a new treaty was about to be signed in Madrid, or had been signed and was likely to be ratified, and giving the terms. But the ship did not bring any word from Arlington.

Although the treaty had been signed in July and ratified in London by the end of August, Arlington had not told Modyford, with the result that four months later (although the voyage from England to Jamaica usually took two months) Modyford knew nothing officially; his only knowledge was little more than gossip. However, he had acted quickly, as he told Arlington: 'I had despatched to the Admiral [Morgan], before the first of these expresses arrived, a copy of the articles of peace with Spain, intimating that though I had them from private hands and no orders to call him in, I thought fit to let him see them, and to advise him to mind your Lordship's letter of the 12th of June and do nothing that might prevent the accomplishment of his Majesty's peaceful intentions.'

That letter of 12 June, now six months old, was the one that said the privateers were to remain as they were when the letter arrived. However, Modyford was unlucky, because 'the vessel returned with my letters, having missed him at his old rendezvous; however, I have returned her to the Main with strict instructions to find the Admiral out'.

Yet for all the rumour of peace and talk of treaties, Modyford was only too aware that he was governor of Jamaica and therefore responsible for its defence; a responsibility vastly different from that of ministers in the cloistered quiet of Whitehall, because if Modyford mismanaged the island's defence against a Spanish invasion it would be his own plantation that was burned, and himself and his wife would be taken off to a Spanish jail . . .

The voyage of Morgan's fleet from Cape Tiburon to Old Providence, 575 miles, was one that the buccaneers undertook without a moment's thought, but finding the tiny island with the charts and instruments then in use would make many a modern navigator despair. The navigator of Morgan's day could find his latitude – his distance north or south – by taking a sight of the sun, measuring the angle with a backstaff, the forerunner of the modern sextant, but his knowledge of longitude, the distance east or west, depended then on an accurate measurement of the distance he had sailed from a known position.

The important thing for him to know was the latitude of the destination, and as the latitude of Old Providence was known the fleet sailed south until their backstaffs showed they had reached it. Then they turned westward and sailed along that latitude ('Running their westing down') until they sighted the island.

It was the way that ships crossed the Atlantic, as Sir Henry Colt described so graphically, but there was always the danger of hitting the destination in the darkness. In the Caribbean, and particularly in the passage from Hispaniola to Providence, this danger is greatly increased by the currents – those off Providence are described in the latest sailing directions as 'strong and irregular . . . passing vessels should take the utmost precautions'.

The charts that Morgan and his captains possessed – mostly drawn by themselves in their voyages, or old ones to which they made additions as they visited new places – bore little relation to modern charts, either in the shape of the islands or their names. The chart of 'The Cariby Islands' drawn by William Hack about ten years after Morgan's voyage is one of the most detailed, covering the area from Trinidad to west of Cartagena, the Lesser Antilles and most of the Greater. Many of the islands have curious shapes because of the problem of finding the right longitude. Thus islands are often too long or too short in an east-west direction, although they are usually approximately the right 'height' in a north-south direction. The buccaneers' island of Tortuga is written Turtugas; Curaçao is Quirasao. Grenada, at the south end of the Windward Islands, still has its Spanish spelling of Granada and is shown upside down; Nevis is still the Nieves of Columbus' day. The Spanish Main is shown as four provinces, Cartagena, Santa Marta, Venezuela and Nova Andalusia.

Morgan's fleet made a fast passage considering the smallness of many of the ships. They were six days out of Cape Tiburon when the three peaks of Old Providence came in sight soon after daybreak. It soon became clear that the Spanish had strengthened the island's defences and a battery of four guns now covered the buccaneers' favourite anchorage, although they did not open fire. Morgan wasted no time and within a couple of hours of the ships anchoring a thousand men had landed by boat and formed up, ready to fight their way across the island – but there was no sign of the enemy.

As Morgan worked his way across the mountainous island he discovered that the Spanish had evacuated the whole place and were now concentrated in Santa Catalina, the tiny adjoining island. Esquemeling's first sight of it after the long march the length of Providence was not encouraging. The drawbridge was removed and it was 'so well fortified with forts and batteries round about it as might seem impregnable'.

The Spaniards 'began to fire upon them so furiously' that the buccaneers could not advance the first day 'but were contented to retreat a little, and take up their rest upon the grass in the open fields, which afforded no strange beds to these people. What most afflicted them was hunger, having not eaten the least thing that whole day.' A careful reconnaissance showed that the Spanish had built nine forts and batteries, the largest of which, San Gerónimo, was built of stone with twenty guns, ranging from eighteen to six pounds, and surrounded by a ditch twenty feet deep.

That night, with a thousand buccaneers asleep in the fields, their muskets, pistols, and swords beside them, heavy clouds built up from the east and 'about midnight it began to rain so hard that those miserable people had much ado to resist so much hardship, the greater part of them having no other clothes than a pair of seaman's trousers or breeches and a shirt, without either shoes or stockings'. Soon they were 'in such condition that one hundred men, indifferently well armed, might easily that night have torn them all in pieces'.

The rain continued all next day 'as if the skies were melted into waters' and, wrote Esquemeling, 'the pirates were now reduced unto great affliction and danger of their lives through the hardness of the weather, their own nakedness, and the great hunger they sustained'. At this point the buccaneers' morale was extremely low, and Esquemeling gives a revealing picture of Morgan as the leader, showing that it was his force of character that kept control of the men. When Morgan heard many of them say they would return on board the ships,

he thought it convenient to use some sudden and almost unexpected remedy: unto this effect he commanded a canoe to be rigged in all haste and colours of truce to be hanged out of it.

This canoe he sent to the Spanish Governor of the island with this message: 'That if within a few hours he delivered not himself and all his men unto his [Morgan's] hands, he did by that messenger swear unto him,

and all those that were in his company, he would most certainly put them all
to the sword, without granting quarter to any.'

Although he had a thousand men, they were armed only with muskets
and pistols, pikes and swords against forty-nine cannon and, as they were
to discover later, more than 1200 muskets in the forts. Since Santa Catalina
was a bristling fortress surrounded by the sea, Morgan's threat to 'put them
all to the sword' was a colossal bluff, but he was obviously relying on the
effect that his own name and the buccaneers' reputation would have on the
governor and his garrison. An hour or two later the canoe returned with a
tantalizing answer: the governor wanted two hours to deliberate in a council
of war; after that he would answer Morgan's message.

The rain stopped and the buccaneers managed to get their weapons
dried out. Powder had remained dry in flasks, but the slow match used with
the matchlock muskets and pistols had been soaked. Now lengths were put
up to dry in the sun, thin snakes hanging down from the branches of
bushes.

Two hours later the governor's two emissaries landed with a very delicate
proposition to put forward. Shorn of all euphemisms, it meant that the
governor was prepared to surrender the island but needed Morgan to join
in a charade which would make sure the governor was not sent to Spain
and subsequently shot or garotted for cowardice. Their governor 'desired
that Captain Morgan should be pleased to use a certain stratagem of war
for the better saving of his own credit and the reputation of his officers . . .'
He had worked out all the details – first, Morgan and some of his troops
should come to the bridge at night and attack the San Gerónimo fort and at
the same time all of Morgan's ships should open fire on another fort, Santa
Teresa, and land troops on the beach near a battery.

The governor would then go from Santa Teresa to San Gerónimo, and
the buccaneers who had landed from the ships would then capture him and
pretend ('using the formality') to force him to surrender San Gerónimo. It
was also agreed, noted Esquemeling, 'that on one side and t'other there
should be continual firing at one another, but without bullets, at least into
the air, so that no side might receive any harm by this device'.

On the day after the surrender the buccaneers lined up and counted all
the prisoners. There were 190 soldiers, forty married inhabitants of the island
with forty-three children, exactly one hundred slaves and thirty-four of their
children. 'The pirates disarmed all the Spaniards and sent them out immediately unto the plantations to seek for provisions, leaving the women in the
church, there to exercise their devotions.'

The buccaneers then began counting up the arms in the forts. Apart from
forty-nine cannon, 1220 muskets, and many pistols, flints and coils of slow
match, there were more than thirteen tons of gunpowder in the magazine.

The casks of powder were rowed out and distributed among the ships, with many muskets and pistols. 'All the guns were stopped and nailed, and the fortresses demolished, excepting that of San Gerónimo, where the pirates kept their guard and residence.'

While this was going on Morgan, Collier, Bradley and Morris were busy making plans for the next part of the operation. They now had a base only three hundred miles from Chagres, the point on the Isthmus where they would begin their march on Panama, but they needed guides and, as Esquemeling had already commented, the buccaneers knew that among the garrison the Spanish had 'employed many banditti and outlaws belonging to Panama and neighbouring places, who are very expert in the knowledge of all that country'.

Morgan's first move was therefore to inquire 'if any banditti were there from Panama ... and hereupon three were brought before him who pretended [i.e. claimed] to be very expert in all the avenues of these parts. He asked them if they would be his guides and show him the securest ways and passages unto Panama; which, if they performed, he promised them equal shares in all they should pillage and rob in that expedition.'

Morgan's offer, not surprisingly, 'pleased the banditti very well', and they promised to 'serve him faithfully in all he should desire, especially one of the three, who was the greatest rogue, thief and assassin among them and who', Esquemeling said, 'had deserved for his crimes rather to be broken alive upon the wheel than punished with serving in a garrison'.

While the work on the islands was being completed, Morgan decided to send some ships to prepare the way for the buccaneers' landing. At this time there were two ways across the Isthmus. The first was going by boat from the coastal town of Chagres up the twisting and turning Chagres River to Venta de Cruz, about halfway, then changing to a mule, after which it was a day's ride to Panama. The second route, used only during the dry season, was by land along a track from Portobelo to Venta de Cruz, then picking up the road to Panama. Venta de Cruz was the meeting place of the river route to Chagres and the land route to Portobelo and had a customs house. The gold and silver now always went by horse or mule all the way to Portobelo (the authorities would not risk it being lost because of a boat sinking) but ordinary cargo for Panama came up the river by boat to Venta de Cruz in the rainy season and transferred to mules for the last part of the journey. There were warehouses in which cargo could be stored in the dry.

Venta de Cruz was described by an Englishman a few years later as 'a small village of inns and storehouses', while the surrounding country was 'savannah and woodland intermixed, with thick short hills, especially

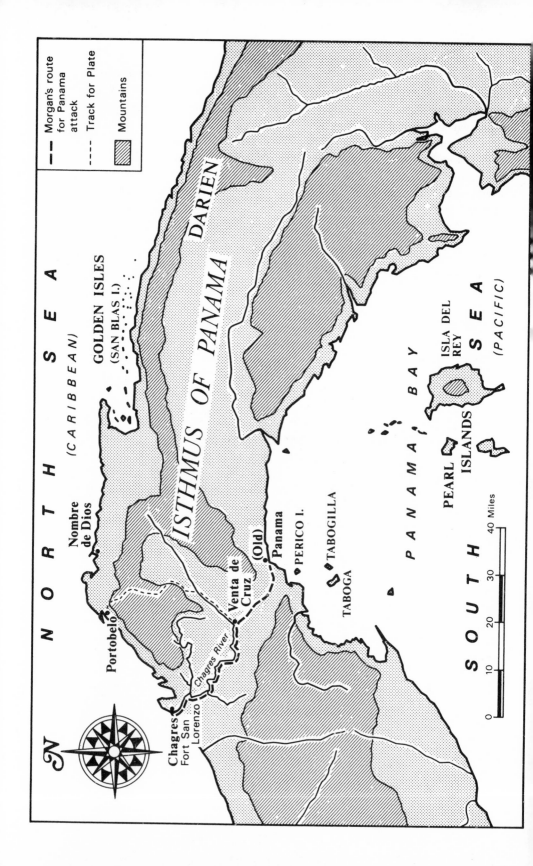

towards Panama'. Either route to Venta de Cruz, by river or overland, went through thick forests where lofty trunks towered up from tangled bush and, if there was no track, men had to cut their way through, yard by yard, with machetes. Mountains cross the route with the passes rising five hundred feet or more. During the wet season – which lasts eight months – the rain is torrential for hours at a time and leeches and mosquitoes make the traveller's journey a nightmare.

Morgan had no choice over the route: using the Portobelo track meant capturing the city first, and he knew that the Spanish defences had probably been extended since he had last captured the city and the garrison increased considerably, with the certainty that a horseman would warn Panama. The Chagres River route, which meant they could go by boat more than halfway to Venta de Cruz, had only one obstacle, the San Lorenzo castle at the river mouth.

The entrance to the Chagres River, with three high peninsulas on the north side like fat fingers, had a long, low beach on the south side. In the middle of the entrance was the Laja Reef, a rocky ledge below the water, so the channel into the river and up to Chagres town was to one side or other of the Reef. On top of the first peninsula and guarding the entrance was the castle of San Lorenzo, described by Esquemeling as 'built upon a high mountain at the entry of the river, and surrounded on all sides with strong palisades, or wooden walls'. These walls were double, the space between filled with earth, 'which renders them as secure as the best walls made of stone or brick'.

The top of the mountain was divided into two sections, with the castle built on one side and the division forming a ditch some thirty feet deep. There was only one entrance to the castle, by a drawbridge over the ditch. 'That part which looks towards the south [seaward] is totally in-accessible and impossible to be climbed [and] the north side is surrounded by the river ... At the foot of the said castle, or rather mountain, is seated a strong fort, with eight great guns, which commands and impedes the entry of the river. Not much lower are to be seen two other batteries, whereof each has six pieces of cannon.'

Morgan wasted few words in his report to Modyford in describing his next move. Some Spanish soldiers 'took up arms with us and by them under-standing that the castle of Changra [Chagres] blocked our way, the Admiral called a council of all the chief and forthwith there was dispatched 470 men in three ships under the command of Lieutenant-colonel Bradley'.

Leaving Old Providence on 18 December the three ships, led by Bradley's *Mayflower* and including the 10-gun *Lily*, were unlucky, running into strong south-easterly winds, so that they spent Christmas Day at sea and did not sight the three peninsulas at the entrance to the River Chagres until the next day. The Spanish were expecting them: the governor of Panama had warned

three weeks earlier that Morgan and his buccaneers were at Hispaniola, preparing for an attack on the Main. The governor had discovered this when a
deserter from Collier's little squadron at Riohacha went to the Spanish
and told them all he knew – the size of the squadron assembling in Tortuga
and the latest gossip about its target.

Don Juan was a sick man at this time, suffering from a painful attack of
erysipelas, but he acted at once. Knowing that Morgan could attack
Panama only by way of Portobelo or Chagres, he sent two hundred men to
reinforce the Portobelo garrison, although he guessed that Morgan would
attack through Chagres.

The commander of Chagres castle, Don Pedro de Lisardo, had complete
confidence in the strength of San Lorenzo, the fort below, which was commanded by Don Francisco de Saludo, and the batteries; he had often told
Don Juan that he could hold Chagres against all comers – 'although six
thousand men should come against them, he should with the fortification
and men he had, be able to secure himself and destroy them'.

Nevertheless, Don Juan sent him another 164 men to reinforce the 150
men he already had. In addition Don Juan sent companies to set up
ambushes at various points along the River Chagres just in case any of the
buccaneers managed to pass San Lorenzo in the darkness. For the defence
of Panama, in the unlikely event of the buccaneers getting through, he
had mobilized 3600 men, infantry, cavalry and artillery.

When the *Mayflower* and her two consorts arrived off the River Chagres
the Spanish 'began to fire incessantly at them with the biggest of their
guns', according to one of the buccaneers. It was obvious to Bradley that
he could achieve nothing with his ships; his guns were completely out-
ranged by those of San Lorenzo and the fort. It was a task for the buccaneers
in their rôle as soldiers, not sailors, and it is significant that before leaving
Hispaniola Morgan had given his captains alternative army ranks which
they would use on land. All captains of ships would be at least majors; some,
like Joseph Bradley, were colonels, because of their experience or the fact
that they held the rank in one of the Jamaica regiments.

A look at San Lorenzo with a telescope convinced Bradley that there
was no chance of climbing the cliff on the seaward side: the rock was bare
and sheer and even cactus and small shrubs had a hard time clinging on.
Guessing that there must be a gateway on the landward side he sailed down
the coast to a sheltered bay, anchored his ships and took four hundred men
on a tedious march through thick jungle and over rocky hills towards San
Lorenzo.

The three peninsulas made ridges over which they had to climb and hack
their way and 'although their guides served them exactly', they suddenly
and unexpectedly came out in front of San Lorenzo, where alert sentries
opened fire. 'They lost so many of their men with shot from the guns, they

being in an open place where nothing could cover nor defend them,' wrote Esquemeling.

Yet Bradley's men had to get close if his method of attack was to succeed. He had seen from the *Mayflower* that the strength of San Lorenzo was in its double wall of wooden planks with a thick layer of earth in between. This was immensely strong against cannon fire, the earth absorbing the shot, but Bradley's plan was to set fire to the planking, making it all collapse and leave breaches through which his buccaneers could storm the garrison. The men had therefore brought with them dozens of fireballs, which were round bottles of pottery or cast iron filled with combustible material, the cork being a wad of cloth which was lit just before the fireball was thrown.

The first attack failed because the fireballs did not set enough of the planking ablaze. At nightfall the buccaneers attacked again, some of them firing at the Spanish defenders with muskets while others hurled fireballs at the wooden palisades and the gate. Suddenly a fire started inside the castle, lighting up first the walls and then the hills and the river entrance. It is not sure how it began. One anonymous buccaneer wrote that 'one of our men being shot in the back with an arrow which pierced his body, [he] instantly pulled it out at his breast and, wrapping some cotton about it, shot it back [with his musket] into the fort, the cotton kindling in the discharge'. The flaming arrow then landed on a house thatched with palm leaves and set them on fire which, 'meeting with a heap of gunpowder before it was perceived, blew it up, to no small surprise of the besieged.

'As they wanted water, they were more busied and perplexed in extinguishing it, and we taking the advantage, set fire to the palisades in several places at once, so that the Spaniards now saw themselves surrounded by flames.' As the palisades burned and great heaps of earth fell into the ditches, the buccaneers tried to scramble up into the castle, 'notwithstanding that some Spaniards who were not busied about the fire cast down upon them many flaming pots, full of combustible matter and odious smells, which occasioned the loss of many of the English'.

The Spaniards could not prevent the palisades being entirely burned down by midnight. The buccaneers continued to try to get into the castle, 'although the fire was great they would creep upon the ground as nigh unto it as they could and shoot amidst the flames against the Spaniards they could perceive on the other side, and thus came many to fall dead from the walls'.

When daylight came they could see right into the castle, the great piles of earth making tumbled causeways across the ditch. But the Spanish commander, Pedro de Lisardo, had ordered his guns to be hauled round so that they covered the gaps. One party of buccaneer sharpshooters concentrated on picking off the Spanish gunners and 'about noon the English happened to gain a breach, which the governor himself defended with twenty-five soldiers. Here was performed a very courageous and warlike resistance by the Spaniards, both with muskets, pikes, stones and swords'. Eventually the governor was killed, along with the majority of his men.

Harry Morgan gave the credit to the buccaneers' fireballs breaching the walls, 'where our men courageously stormed and the enemy as bravely defended to the last man, refusing quarter, which cost them the lives of 360 men, and of our side was lost thirty outright, one captain and one lieutenant, and seventy-six wounded'.

When the buccaneers sorted out their few prisoners ('whereof scarce ten were not wounded') they were told that eight or nine Spanish soldiers had 'deserted their colours and were gone to Panama to carry news of their arrival and invasion'. The capture of San Lorenzo had given the buccaneers one of their bitterest battles. With 106 dead and wounded, Bradley had lost a quarter of the men he had landed from the *Mayflower* and the other two ships. The buccaneers did the best they could to treat the wounded, among them Colonel Bradley, who was in great pain with a danger of gangrene setting in. His only hope was that Morgan would arrive in time with the *Satisfaction* so that Richard Browne, the surgeon-general, could treat him.

In the meantime the surviving buccaneers rounded up slaves from the town of Chagres, farther up the river, and put them to work with the unwounded prisoners to repair the castle. The whole of Morgan's fleet was to be left anchored in the River Chagres while the buccaneers went on to Panama, and an important part of the plan was that small crews would be left in the ships and the San Lorenzo castle would be garrisoned to defend them. The garrison of the lower fort, commanded by Don Francisco de Saludo, had fled while San Lorenzo burned.

Days which would normally have been spent in celebration passed in a fog of heat and weariness; nights that would normally have been spent drinking and toasting were passed at Chagres on guard against a surprise Spanish counter-attack, or trying to sleep amid the whine and nip of mosquitoes. It was far worse for the wounded; flies attracted by the smell of blood buzzed round them, even though slaves fanned with palm fronds.

San Lorenzo had finally surrendered on 28 December and slaves and prisoners were at work replacing the palisades and shovelling the earth back into position from the 29th onwards. New Year's Eve was spent cutting wood and shovelling earth and the first day of 1671 saw San Lorenzo looking a little more like a castle. By then the *Mayflower* had led the other two ships into the river, carefully rounding the Laja Reef, to anchor under the guns of the castle, fort and batteries.

Colonel Bradley's condition was worsening; the terrible leg wounds were becoming gangrenous and he was feverish. Captain Richard Norman, who had assumed the rank of major once he stepped on shore, took over command of the buccaneers and waited impatiently for Morgan and Surgeon Browne: there seemed little doubt that Bradley was slowly dying. Finally, on 2 January, the lookouts on the walls of San Lorenzo gave a hail: Admiral Morgan's ships were in sight. Major Norman at once had an English flag run up on the flagpole of San Lorenzo – the prearranged signal to the admiral that the castle had been taken – and very soon the *Satisfaction* and several other ships were heading in for the river entrance.

From the castle walls the Laja Reef could be seen clearly below the surface in the middle of the channel and Major Norman and his men watched, expecting to see the *Satisfaction* passing it to one side or the other. Close behind her was the 12-gun *Port Royal* and two other ships, the rest of the fleet being a mile or two astern.

Morgan's flagship looked a fine sight as she ran in towards the river entrance with a following wind, with more than thirty ships following astern. Suddenly Norman realized that the *Satisfaction* was heading straight for the Laja Reef: unless she trimmed her yards and put her helm up or down in the next few moments the flagship would be wrecked on the ledge of the rock across which the sea often broke in a continuous series of rollers.

Before there was any chance of warning Morgan, the *Satisfaction* hit the reef, her masts crashing over the bow as the shock of the impact parted the rigging. The following seas began to slew her round and almost at the same time the *Port Royal* hit the reef, followed by two more ships, all of which broached. All were heavily laden; before leaving Old Providence eight days earlier, Morgan had ordered that much of Santa Catalina's provisions should be taken to Chagres for the garrison he intended to leave there.

While the men in the four ships scrambled into boats the rest of the fleet managed to keep clear of the reef and reached the river safely. The wind gradually veering to the north brought in a heavy swell, and there was no chance of refloating the *Satisfaction* or the other three ships. Fortunately there was time for the boats of the fleet to save much of the provisions and powder.

'Captain Morgan was brought into the castle with great acclamations of triumph and joy of all the pirates, both of those who were within and also them that were but newly come,' wrote one of the men. Morgan wasted no time in preparing for the journey to Panama. There were several small Spanish vessels anchored in the river, each armed with two iron guns and four smaller ones of brass, and used to carry cargo up and down the river. These and four other small craft were seized, along with many large canoes.

Morgan now worked out the best way of using his forces. He had left Hispaniola with 1846 men, and his first real casualties had been the hundred here at Chagres. He had not left a garrison at Old Providence, guessing the Spanish would soon be too occupied to worry about retaking it. He would leave Major Norman and four hundred men at San Lorenzo castle, and 140 men on board the privateers, so that he would have 1200 men for the expedition to Panama. In the meantime he had to bury his old friend Colonel Bradley.

The River Chagres was low; the rainy season was now over and according to prisoners there were at least five places on the way to Venta de Cruz where the boats would have to be unloaded to reduce their draught enough so they could be hauled over rapids. Weight was going to be critical; every man would carry a musket or pistol, as well as a pike or cutlass. He had to have shot, powder, and slow match, a blanket for sleeping – not for warmth but to cover him against mosquitoes and leeches – and a tarred jacket which helped keep him dry when it rained but, much more important, protected powder and match. In the heat it would have been enough for men to march with musket and cutlass, but each would have to carry water and food. Yet too much weight would mean that the boats would draw more water and might well go aground at other places, causing more long delays. They had to travel light: that was certain. Morgan decided that food and water would have to be sacrificed. It was a critical decision, but they would have to rely on foraging at the villages along the side of the river.

At De Los Barcos they had their first disappointment: swarming on shore Harry Morgan and his 1200 men left Chagres on 8 January, travelling up the river in a motley collection of craft. The luckier ones were in the cargo-carriers, single-masted vessels with large sails and oars; those in the canoes – which were up to forty feet long and carved from a single tree trunk – had to row.

The river twisted and turned to an almost unbelievable degree; its length from Chagres to Venta de Cruz (much of it now obscured by the Panama Canal) was three times the direct distance. Often the buccaneers, not knowing how the river turned back on itself, would be passing only a mile or two from a stretch they had traversed hours before. The great problem for strangers was knowing for sure which was the main river. Scores of tributaries poured through narrow valleys to join it; wide branches trended away to become other rivers and often the buccaneers came to a fork and, but for their guides, would have taken the wrong one. In the first eighteen miles, to the village of De Los Barcos, the Chagres had been joined by eight rivers, and there was usually an Indian village where they met.

to find food, they discovered that the Spanish had fled and taken their provisions with them. 'This day, being the first of their journey, there was amongst them such scarcity of victuals that the greatest part were forced to pass with only a pipe of tobacco, without any other refreshment.'

Although they found no food, there was no sign of the enemy either, so their muskets could remain well smeared with lard and wrapped in greasy cloths, their powder in corked bottles and their slow match coiled into glass jars against the torrential rain squalls that came up in a few minutes, poured for half an hour and then travelled on, to leave blue skies, scorching sun and steaming jungle. Morgan was now considerably less optimistic: the boats were frequently grounding where, according to the guides, there should have been enough water; the roots of mangroves, like thousands of long, rusty-red arthritic fingers, were showing up well below the normal level of the river at this time of the year.

At dawn next morning they started off again, the river getting narrower and shallower. The earlier heavy torrents of the rainy season had torn away trees up in the hills and washed them down to the Chagres, stranding them in the shallows, where their trunks, with branches still attached, blocked the channel in several places. They struggled through the day, paddling, hauling tree trunks and catching drinking water in the rain showers. Just before the sun set they saw a large cross built on the right-hand side of the river: the village of Cruz de Juan Gallego.

'Here they were compelled to leave their boats and canoes, by reason the river was very dry for want of rain and the many obstacles of trees that were fallen into it,' wrote Esquemeling. Morgan questioned the guides, who assured him that the tangled undergrowth along the river banks cleared away in another twelve miles, so that marching overland would then be much easier. The admiral knew that all the boats would be needed for the return to Chagres, but Spanish troops might try to capture or sink them. He therefore chose 160 men to stay behind as guards.

With that the rest of the men, 1040 in all, began the march, if that was not too grandiose a word for what was a sweaty fight through thick jungle, machetes slashing, feet slipping, the twisting roots of bushes ripping off the crude boots of skin and string which was all that many of the Tortuga *boucaniers* wore.

Esquemeling wrote:

Having this morning [10 January, the third day] begun their march, they found the ways so dirty and irksome that Captain Morgan thought it more convenient to transport some of the men in canoes (though it could not be done without great labour) to a place farther up the river called Cedro Bueno.

Thus they re-embarked, and the canoes returned for the rest that were left behind ... The pirates were extremely desirous to meet any Spaniards or Indians, hoping to fill their bellies with what provisions they should take from them, for now they were reduced to the very extremity of hunger.

*　　*　　*

At Cedro Bueno the jungle seemed thinner, much to Morgan's relief. When there was enough water in the river the journey to Venta de Cruz took five or six days at the most, but up to now they had covered only a third of the way in three days. At this point many buccaneers wanted to cut their way through overland, tired of the continual paddling and lifting the heavy craft over the shallows. Morgan agreed, and the fourth day began with the majority of the buccaneers on land, led by one of the guides.

'The rest went by water, farther up with the canoes, being conducted by another guide, who always went before them with two of the said canoes, to discover on both sides the river the ambuscades of the Spaniards.' Morgan and his men wanted to be ambushed, and as they approached one village 'the guide of the canoes began to cry aloud he perceived an ambuscade. His voice caused infinite joy unto all the pirates, as persuading themselves they should find some provisions wherewith to satiate their hunger, which was very great'.

They were disappointed: there had been an ambush but the Spanish had fled at the last moment, leaving nothing behind but 'a small number of leather bags, all empty, and a few crumbs of bread scattered upon the ground where they had eaten'. The starving buccaneers 'fell to eating the leathern bags, as being desirous to afford something to the ferment of their stomachs, which now was grown so sharp that it did gnaw their very bowels, having nothing else to prey upon. Thus they made a huge banquet upon those bags of leather, which doubtless had been more grateful to them if divers quarrels had not arisen concerning who should have the greatest share'.

The buccaneers marched on, arriving just before nightfall at Torna Munni, where it was obvious that the Spanish had planned another ambush but again fled at the last moment. Here each buccaneer 'was happy that had reserved since noon any small piece of leather whereof to make his supper, drinking after it a good draught of water for his greatest comfort'. Esquemeling described how the leather was first sliced into pieces. 'Then they did beat it between two stones and rub it, often dipping it in the water of the river to render it by these means supple and tender. Lastly they scraped off the hair, and roasted or broiled it upon the fire. And, being thus cooked, they cut it into small morsels and eat it, helping it down with frequent gulps of water ...'

They reached Barbacoa on the fifth day, searched for food and finally 'found a certain grotto which seemed but lately hewn out of a rock, in which they found two sacks of meal, wheat and like things, with two great jars of wine'. Barbacoa is two thirds of the way to Venta de Cruz, and by then the movement of the buccaneers resembled the rout of a defeated army rather than an advance to the attack. When they began on the sixth day, some marching and others paddling the canoes, they were eating 'leaves of trees and green herbs or grass such as they could pick, for such was the miserable condition they were in', according to Esquemeling. Then, at noon, 'they arrived at a plantation, where they found a barn full of maize. Immediately they beat down the doors and fell to eating of it dry, as much as they could devour. Afterwards they distributed great quantity, giving unto every man a good allowance thereof'. Carrying as much as they could, they continued the journey, but when they camped at the tiny village of Santa Cruz 'great murmurings were heard that night in the camp, many complaining of Captain Morgan and his conduct in that enterprise and being desirous to return home. On the contrary, others would rather die there than go back one step from what they had undertaken. But others who had greater courage than any of these two parties did laugh and joke at all their discourses'. They knew they would reach Venta de Cruz next day and before starting 'they all made clean their arms, and every one discharged his pistol or musket, without bullet, to examine the security of their firelocks'.

They were still some distance from the town when they saw buildings and then smoke coming from chimneys, and hunger drove them on to cover the last few miles in record time. But when they arrived there 'in great haste, all sweating and panting', they found the town deserted, 'nor anything that was eatable wherewith to refresh themselves, unless it were good fires to warm themselves, which they wanted not. For the Spaniards before their departure had every one set fire to his own house, excepting only the storehouses and stables belonging to the King'.

When they searched the King's stables – left by the Spanish because none dared to take the responsibility of ordering their destruction – they found 'fifteen or sixteen jars of Peru wine and a leather sack full of bread'. All this wine after days of living on strips of leather, leaves from trees and then dried maize soon made the men very ill, which 'caused a new consternation in the whole camp'. Although Morgan guessed that the reason was 'their huge want of sustenance . . . and the manifold sorts of trash which they had eaten', he told his men the wine was poisoned, and ordered the rest to be poured away. 'January 15,' he reported to Modyford, 'we arrived at Venta Cruces . . . where we thought we might be relieved [of our hunger], having marched three days without victuals, but it was as the rest all on fire, and they fled.'

At Venta de Cruz the River Chagres turned away to the north-east and Panama was twenty-five miles to the south. The canoes could go no farther, and all the men who had been travelling in them had to be landed, 'though never so weak in their bodies'. Morgan did not want to weaken his force by leaving men behind to guard the canoes, so he ordered all but one of them to be sent back down the river to join the boats. The one canoe was hidden carefully, ready to carry orders down the river should the need arise.

Many of the men were so weak after the bout with the Peruvian wine that Morgan ordered his force to spend the day, 14 January, resting in the town, but next day the march continued towards Panama.

Panama Burns

Panama was not at all the romantic city of legend as Morgan and his 1040 buccaneers marched towards it. Although the most important port on the coast of the South Sea, it was detested by shipmasters because it was already shallow and now silting rapidly. Unlike the comparatively tideless North Sea, the South Sea at Panama had a rise and fall of twenty feet, and a ship alongside the quay at the top of the tide was likely to dry out and sit on the mud at low water. Large ships preferred to use Perico, six miles to the west (and the site of modern Panama), transferring their cargoes to small sloops which carried them to the city.

The city that prepared to drive off Morgan's buccaneers had its streets running with geometrical precision north and south and east and west, but only the most important of them were cobbled. The population was about seven thousand, but the city had changed little in the last fifty years, from the time that Thomas Gage, who spent several years there, wrote that its houses 'are of the least strength of any place that I had entered in; for lime and stone is hard to come by, and therefore for that reason, and for the great heat there, most of the houses are built of timber and are but boards ... which serve for stone and brick and for tiles to cover the roof'.

The stagnation of Panama was due to the lack of trade: galleons from Spain were by now visiting Portobelo only once every two or three years, and then more to collect the plate than to deliver cargoes for Panama and the ports and mines to the south. However, a legacy from earlier and wealthier days, when rich penitents were free with endowments, there were seven monasteries, a convent, a cathedral, several churches, and a hospital run by forty-five monks and twenty-four nuns. There were less than a dozen stone buildings, and these included the supreme court and the headquarters of the town council, half a dozen private houses belonging to rich merchants, and the cathedral of San Anastasius, whose tower was the highest building in the city.

A recent report sent to Madrid showed that about thirty of Panama's citizens were wholesale merchants and twenty retail, while a number of people owned large droves of mules, a profitable investment because they had a monopoly of the transport to and from Venta de Cruz, Portobelo, Perico and several other towns. There were more than a thousand mules, and one stable owned seventy-five. The problem of getting cargoes to Panama from the North Sea coast, restricted as it was to the land route by mule from Portobelo or the river to Venta de Cruz, had long since led to several suggestions for linking the North and South seas by a canal, using one of the rivers for most of the way. Alvaro de Saavedra Ceron, a relative of Cortés, who died in 1528, was one of the first to see the possibilities of the Chagres, and then in 1616 Philip III gave orders for a survey to be made to see if a canal could join the seas by way of the Gulf of Darien and the Atrato river. (The Panama Canal was finally opened in 1914.)

Perhaps the most pretentious buildings in Panama, after the supreme court and the viceroy's palace, were the King's stables. Built of stone and wood, they housed the royal horses which were used to carry the King's share of the plate to Portobelo, and to draw the viceroy's carriage.

Although it had not grown in recent years Panama was still one of the richest cities in the world; the older Spanish families living there formed a firmly-rooted and wealthy colonial nobility who passed their lives as a court round the governor and viceroy. The bishop of Panama was a powerful figure and this year was looking towards celebrating the 150th anniversary of the founding of the bishopric: Panama had had a bishop seventeen years before a court of justice was established. The churches and cathedral were as full of gold and silver crucifixes and candlesticks, richly-wrought altar pieces and ornaments as became the city which was the crossroads for the gold and silver of the Indies. The houses of many of the wealthier merchants, although dismissed by Thomas Gage as made of 'boards', were in fact built of cedar, large and airy with richly carved and ornamental balconies round the upper floors, designed in an early version of what would later be called the Spanish Colonial style.

The wealthier Spaniards lived a life which was little more than aping the Court ceremonial they believed existed in Spain; the week was spent attending the cathedral and paying visits to each other. The dresses to be worn and the elegance of carriages and horses were of great consequence. Life in such an enclosed community changed little in the course of a decade. A visit to Spain was not only extremely perilous but took at least two years because of the uncertain dates of ships coming out again to Portobelo or Cartagena.

The pattern of commercial life had not changed either. The ships came up from Arica and other ports to the south with the plate and unloaded at Perico, whence the sloops brought it over to Panama, where the harbour continued to silt up and masters of ships regularly grumbled, pointing out that no vessel of more than sixty tons could now get alongside the jetty. Every couple of years – rarely more frequently these days – word came from the governor of Cartagena that the galleons were coming. Then the merchants would prepare for the fair at Portobelo, though the wealthier ones now sent their assistants instead, for fear of pestilence.

In recent years there had been increasingly bad news from the North Sea of the *corsaros*. It had been a great shock when they had raided Portobelo, a town so many of the merchants knew well, and even worse when they attacked Maracaibo. For scores of years the people of Panama had slept soundly in their beds knowing that the pestilential jungle and the high Cordillera de San Blas protected them from the ravages of the *corsaros*. Then, a month ago, the viceroy had received almost unbelievable rumours. The *corsaro* Morgan was at Hispaniola with more than a thousand men and a great fleet, and one of the places he was reported to be considering as a target was Panama.

Since then it had been like hearing the distant rumbles of a rapidly approaching storm: messengers had arrived in the city to report Providence and Santa Catalina captured; then that the impregnable castle of San Lorenzo at Chagres had fallen. Then that a thousand buccaneers had been sighted paddling up the Chagres and had passed De Los Barcos and Cruz de Juan Gallego ... Spanish troops sent out to ambush them had failed and they had reached Cedro Bueno ... More troops ordered to halt them had fled and they were at Torna Cavallos. More reinforcements had been sent to hold them at Venta de Cruz – and now word had come that the town had been left a smoking ruin and Morgan and his *corsaros* were on the march for Panama...

The viceroy rallied troops and left the city to be ready to fight the buccaneers on the flatter land towards Venta de Cruz and reported:

The Images of the Pure and Immaculate Conception ever since the day of the battle of Chagres Castle had been carried out in general procession attended by all the religious and the fraternity of St Francis, that of the nuns of our Lady of Rosario, those of San Domingo and those of the Mercedes, together with all the saints and patrons of the religious. And always the Most Holy Sacrament in all churches was uncovered and exposed to public view.

Masses were constantly said for my happy success. I parted with all my jewels and relics, collected in my pilgrimage, presenting them to the aforesaid images, saints and patrons.

For all that, there was little to cheer Don Juan Perez de Guzman as his carriage took him to Guibal, the place he had chosen for the forth-coming battle. Still in pain from erysipelas and faint because his doctor had bled him three times, he was depressed because the reports he had been receiving showed that his officers and men had so far proved poltroons. First there was Tiris de Castillo, a captain who commanded a company of mulatto troops. The commander of the fort at Chagres, Don Francisco de Saludo (not to be confused with Don Pedro de Lisardo, who commanded the castle), had ordered Tiris de Castillo to defend the village of Cerro Colorado, many miles up the River Chagres.

However, Indian scouts and Spanish soldiers no sooner arrived at Cerro Colorado to report that the English were eight miles down the river than Tiris de Castillo burned down the village he was supposed to defend and hurriedly retreated up the river to Barbacoa. There he was startled to find Saludo, who had escaped from his fort at Chagres while the buccaneers were still battering away at the castle on the hill above him. As soon as he heard Tiris de Castillo's story, Saludo also lost his nerve and the two men decided to retreat at once to Venta de Cruz. This, the viceroy realized only too well, meant that the English had been able to get all the way up the River Chagres without meeting any opposition.

Then another officer had persuaded the viceroy to give him a hundred men, swearing with suitable rhetoric that he would either retake the castle of San Lorenzo at Chagres or 'disorder the enemy' if they tried to get up the river. Don Juan had given him 250 of his best men and since then heard that they bolted the moment they met the English.

The viceroy reached Guibal. There he announced that he dare not go any farther from Panama in case the English, breaking out across the savannah, managed to outflank him and reach the city.

Morgan and his men continued their advance towards Panama, finding the countryside a mixture of sharp-sided gorges and smooth peaks, thick forests and rough plains. After an early start on the eighth day they had by early afternoon begun to pass through a narrow gorge between high cliffs when 'all on a sudden, three or four thousand arrows were shot at them'. The arrows seemed to drop almost vertically out of a cloudy sky and as the buccaneers scrambled for cover they could not see where their attackers were hiding.

As they loaded their muskets and pistols they waited for another shower of arrows, but none came. Morgan gave the order for the march to continue and soon they approached a wood. They saw one group of Indians running away but careful to keep an eye on the route the buccaneers were taking, but a second group waited, obviously 'with full design to fight and defend themselves. This combat they performed with huge courage', wrote one of the buccaneers, 'till such time as their captain fell to the ground...'

Progress was now much faster because the buccaneers were following the rough but well-used mule trail from Venta de Cruz to Panama: Morgan told Modyford of 'the enemy constantly galling us with ambuscades and small parties, and we still beating of them for a league together, although they had all the advantage that could be of use, the way being so narrow that we could not but march four abreast, and such a deep hollow [i.e.

along a deep valley] that the enemy lay over our heads'.

Finally they reached the beginning of the great plain that stretched to Panama and the shores of the South Sea, and darkness fell, heavy rain soaking the buccaneers. Next day, 17 January and the ninth since they had left Chagres, saw Morgan getting his men off to an early start. Soon after noon the track climbed a steep hill and 'they discovered from the top thereof the South Sea. This happy sight, as if it were the end of their labours, caused infinite joy among all the pirates...' Out at sea they could see a ship under sail and six boats, which were making for the nearby island of Taboga and probably carrying refugees.

As they went down the other side the buccaneers found a great number of cattle and Morgan immediately ordered a halt, the buccaneers hurriedly setting to work slaughtering the animals. One of them wrote:

> While some were employed in killing and flaying of cows, horses, bulls and chiefly asses, of which there was greatest number, others busied themselves in kindling of fires and getting wood wherewith to roast them. Thus cutting the flesh of these animals into convenient pieces, or goblets, they threw them into the fire and, half-carbonadoed or roasted, they devoured them with incredible haste and appetite. For such was their hunger, that they more resembled cannibals than Europeans at this banquet, the blood many times running down from their beards unto the middle of their bodies.

The march continued, with Morgan sending out fifty men to take prisoners, 'for he seemed now to be much concerned that in nine days' time he could not meet one person who might inform him of the condition and forces of the Spaniards'.

Soon after that they could see the steeple of the highest building in Panama, the cathedral of San Anastasius:

> This steeple they no sooner had discovered but they began to show signs of extreme joy, casting up their hats into the air, leaping for mirth, and shouting, even just as if they had already obtained the victory.
>
> All their trumpets were sounded and every drum beaten, in token of this universal acclamation and huge alacrity of their minds. Thus they pitched their camp for that night with general content of the whole army, waiting with impatience for the morning, at which time they intended to attack the city.

That evening a troop of cavalry came almost within musket shot but after shouting a few threats at the buccaneers the majority rode off towards the city, leaving seven or eight horsemen to keep a watch.

The viceroy had pitched his camp three miles from the gates of Panama. Admiral Morgan noted that he sighted the enemy 'where he lay in battaglia with 2100 foot and 600 horse, but finding the day far spent we thought it not fit to engage, but took up our quarters within three miles of them, where we lay very quiet, not being so much as once alarmed'.

In the Spanish camp Don Juan Perez de Guzman was finding that every decision to be made in Panama city was being brought to him, and the people demanding audiences and offering advice ranged from priests to cavalry officers. Following a report that two thousand English were advancing, Don Juan was being besieged by officers pleading with him to break camp and march back to Panama. They made expansive oaths that once there they would defend the city to their last drop of blood, but Don Juan refused to change his mind: this was the place to defend the city, he declared, out on the plain at Guibal. The city itself could not be defended – 'it being impossible then to fortify it, it having many entrances, and the houses all made of wood, so soon as the enemy should once make a breach, we should quickly be exposed to their fury, and forced miserably to shift for ourselves'.

Don Juan went to bed, a weary man and a sick one, because his surgeon was continuing to bleed him. But when he woke next morning he discovered that barely a third of his men were still in the camp: the rest had deserted during the night. He had no choice but to make for Panama, hoping the buccaneers would not attack before he arrived. Fortunately for him Morgan's men still had not taken a reliable prisoner, so Morgan had no idea of the Spanish strength, apart from what he could see through a telescope.

It took Don Juan nearly all day to get back to the city and he wrote:

I arrived on Saturday night at Panama, and Sunday morning went to the great church, where having received the Holy Communion, before our blessed Lady of the Immaculate Conception with great devotion, I went to the principal guard, and to all that were present I expressed myself to this effect:

'That all those who were true Catholics, Defenders of the Faith and devotos [sic] of our Lady of the Pure and Immaculate Conception, should follow my person, being that same day at four o'clock in the afternoon, resolved to march out to seek the enemy and with this caution that he that should refuse to do it, should be held for infamous and a coward, basely slighting so precise an obligation.'

All proferred me their assistance except those that had slunk from me at Guibal; and when I had drawn them up in order I carried the chief of them to the great church, where in the presence of our Lady of the Pure and Immaculate Conception, I made an oath to die in her defence. And I gave her a diamond ring of the value of 4,000 pieces of eight, in token of compliance with my word and heartily invoked her aid.

After this, I marched with my army about a league from Panama, having with me three field pieces covered with leather and charged. And from that place I ordered another party with two other guns, of the men which came from the River [Saludo's men from Venta de Cruz], being above three hundred, to advance towards the enemy, which neither did any good.

The comparison between the leaders of the opposing forces is an interesting one. Henry Morgan was now thirty-five years old and at the height of his fame. He had successfully attacked most of the major towns on the Spanish Main, except Cartagena; the name 'Morgan' had replaced 'El Draco' as a threat to recalcitrant Spanish children. Don Juan Perez was an old soldier, a veteran of the bitter Netherlands campaigns, and he had been captain general and viceroy of Panama for the whole of the time covered by Morgan's career as a buccaneer, the name Henry Morgan pursuing him like the memory of an unconfessed mortal sin.

Now, on Sunday, 19 January, the two men faced each other with their armies. The Spaniard relied on his men's military discipline, allegiance to the King and devotion to their Church and saints. The Welshman had drawn up his men knowing that discipline in the usual sense did not exist; that two or three hundred, the true *boucaniers* from Hispaniola, were superb marksmen; and that every one of them was driven on by greed and nothing else. Purchase, not patriotism, was the spur.

The Spaniard's leadership was backed up by the King's writ; mutiny, cowardice, slothfulness – these could be punished by the due process of the law. In contrast the Welshman knew that his leadership, his control over the army, rested only on his tongue, and on the results he produced. The moment the buccaneers were not persuaded by his words or actions, they would go back to their ships. They wanted purchase as greedily as any sovereign imposed taxes or a bishop sought converts, and they were equally ruthless.

The position Perez chose for his army was a good one: to the right there was a ravine with a hill beyond that would help guard that flank. He commanded the centre, with the cannon in front; Don Juan Portando Bergueno commanded the right wing and Don Alonso de Alcandete the left. One squadron of cavalry covered his left flank, another under Don Francisco de Haro his right.

He had unusual reinforcements which he described as 'two great herds of oxen and bulls, drove thither by fifty cow keepers on purpose to disorder the enemy'. He had ordered that one herd should be ready on the left of his army and the other on the right, and he planned to have them driven in at a critical stage in the battle, hundreds of bellowing and frightened animals stampeding their way through the buccaneers' positions.

His force outnumbered the buccaneers by more than five hundred but they seemed to frighten Perez more than the enemy because he wrote: 'This body of men which I had thus brought with me was composed of two sorts, valiant military men and faint hearted cowards, many of them having all their estates and pay due them left in the castle of Chagres and Portobelo, and a great part of my men were Negroes, mulattos and Indians to the number of about 1200, besides about 300 more belonging to the *Asiento* [i.e. slave importers].

'Our firearms were few and bad in comparison with those the enemy brought,' he went on, without mentioning that the buccaneers had carried theirs on their backs or in canoes the width of the Isthmus. 'For ours were carbines, arquebuses and fowling pieces but few muskets for they likewise had been left in Portobelo and Chagres.'

Don Juan planned a set-piece battle: the vanguard of the buccaneers would storm his centre and be cut to pieces by his artillery. Then his cavalry would charge with their lances and completely disorganize the buccaneers. Finally the herds of oxen and bullocks, goaded into a frenzy by their keepers, would thunder in from left and right and complete the rout of the enemy. Thus would Panama be saved: not by the thunder of cannon but the thunder of hooves.

The buccaneers made an early start on this Sunday morning. They had been roused out and ordered to stand-to some two hours before dawn because Morgan expected a surprise attack from Perez's army, and as he watched the darkness turn to the grey of dawn he did not know that the Spanish camp opposite him was by now deserted and at that moment Don Juan Perez was preparing for holy communion in the distant cathedral.

They still had plenty of meat from the previous day: some cattle which had been kept alive were now slaughtered to give them a breakfast of enormous steaks of rare roast beef, the kind of meal that turned the mildest matelot into a bellicose cut-throat, and each man packed some pieces of roast meat in his satchel to eat later.

It was a fine day; the cloud had gone to leave a clear sky with a light breeze and the promise of scorching temperatures. Behind them in the distance was the small mountain from which they had first seen the South Sea (still known as El Cerro de los Buccaneros); in front of them were the towers and steeples of Panama city.

Admiral Harry Morgan was about to fight his first regular land battle. Previously he had commanded sieges or raids on towns and cities: never before had he faced an enemy on an open battlefield and, in this case, one equipped with cavalry and two squadrons of bulls. He had drawn up his order of battle with care, and the buccaneer leaders were now being addressed by their equivalent military ranks. He had given command of the vanguard of three hundred men – which included the sharpshooters from among the *boucaniers* – to Lieutenant-Colonel Lawrence Prince, and made Major John Morris its second-in-command.

The main body, Morgan said in his report to Modyford, was made up of about six hundred men, and divided in two, with the left wing commanded by Colonel Edward Collier and the right 'by the General', Morgan himself, now using the military equivalent of his rank of admiral. A rearguard of three hundred men was led by Colonel Bledry Morgan, who had joined the buccaneers at Providence, bringing a message from Modyford for the admiral, to whom he does not seem to have been related.

As soon as the men had finished their breakfast Morgan inspected them, made a rousing speech, and ordered them to begin the march on the Spanish camp and, when that was found to be deserted, on to Panama, six miles away. The Spanish army was sighted in the early afternoon, drawn up in front of the city. Morgan noticed a hill to his left, helping to cover the Spanish right flank, with a ravine beyond it. Their cannon, which soon opened fire on Lawrence Prince's vanguard, were placed directly in front of the main Spanish force. Morgan then saw that the light westerly wind was blowing the smoke from these guns across the Spanish positions, cutting down their view, and the sun was in their eyes.

Despite all that, he saw that a direct attack on the Spanish would fail. Yet he spotted a weakness in Perez's defence – the hill did not really protect the Spanish right flank because Perez apparently did not realize that the ravine limited the reinforcements he could send over to Don Juan Portando Bergueno. Morgan immediately decided to turn the Spanish right flank. He gave orders that Collier's three hundred men out on the left wing 'should wheel their bodies to the left and gain a hill that was hard by, which if gained we should have forced the enemy to fight to their disadvantage by reason that he could not bring out of his great body more men to fight at a time than we could cut out of our small body...'

The Spanish troops were ready and Don Juan had earlier given the infantry very strict orders how they were to meet the buccaneers' attack. For a start, no troops were to move without an order from him, but as the buccaneers came within range 'the first three ranks should fire on their knees and after this [discharge] they should give place to the rear to come up and fire, and that although they should chance to see any fall dead or wounded, they should not quit their stations but to the last extremity observe these orders'.

The Spaniards watched the clouds of dust which marked the English advance across the savannah and the five cannon kept up as heavy a fire as possible, aiming at Prince's vanguard, which was now approaching rapidly while Collier's left wing made for the hill and was, for a while, hidden from the viceroy's sight.

Francisco de Haro, commanding the squadron of cavalry on the right wing, then led his men in a furious charge on Prince's vanguard, little knowing that by chance he had chosen the one body of buccaneers not carrying pikes, the very weapons for fighting off cavalry. The moment Prince realized he was going to receive the full attack he formed his men into a square, determined to make the best use of his sharpshooters but ordering them not to fire until he gave the word.

With Haro leading, the cavalry came racing towards the square of men, who blew on the match of their muskets to make sure it was glowing well, and waited. When the leading Spaniards were only thirty or forty yards away, Prince gave the order to fire. Each of the sharpshooters had aimed carefully and a good half of the cavalrymen were killed or wounded, Haro himself falling from his horse only a few yards from the nearest buccaneers.

The survivors of his shattered squadron swung away and bolted, but companies of infantry from the Spanish vanguard had then arrived to attack what they expected to be the remnants of the enemy force. Prince's men were hastily reloading their muskets and many of them began to fight with cutlasses.

In the meantime Collier's men had captured the hill without much opposition, seen Prince's men disperse the cavalry and observed Morgan beginning to attack the Spanish left wing under Alcandete. At once Collier wheeled his men to the right, down the hill, to help Prince drive off the Spanish infantry. Very soon, as Morgan later told Modyford, 'the enemy's retreat came to plain running'.

Meanwhile Morgan's own right wing was attacking the Spanish left wing and Don Juan wrote:

I was at this time in the right wing of the vanguard, watching the enemy's motion, which was hasty, by the foot of a hill in a narrow place, above three musket shot [distance] of the left wing of our army, when on a sudden I heard a loud clamour, crying: 'Fall on! Fall on! For they fly!' at which Don Alonso de Alcandete was not able to keep them [his men] in their ranks, nor stop them from running, though he cut them with his sword, but they fell into disorder. And I, well knowing the fatality of this, gave command that they should drive up the herds of cattle and charge with the horse.

So, putting myself at the head of the squadron of the right wing saying 'Come along, boys! There is no other remedy now but to conquer or die! Follow me!' I went directly to the enemy, and hardly did our men see some fall dead and others wounded, but they turned their backs and fled, leaving me there with only one Negro and one servant that followed me.

Yet I went forward to comply with my word to the Virgin, which was to die in her defence, received a shot in the staff I carried in my hand

upright close to my cheek. At which moment came up to me a priest
of the [Cathedral] called Juan de Dios (who was wont to say mass in
my house), beseeching me to retire and save myself, who I twice sharply
reprehended.

But the third time he persisted, telling me that it was mere desperation
to die in that manner and not like a Christian. With that I retired, it
being a miracle of the Virgin to bring me off safe among so many thousand
bullets.

The cattle stampede was a fiasco: most of the animals, terrified by the
noise of gunfire and met with a hail of shot from the buccaneers which killed
the leading animals, turned back and trampled first the cow keepers and
then some companies of Spanish troops which had not fled until that moment.

The battle was then over: Perez's 1700 men were either dead or wounded,
or had bolted for the temporary safety of the city, pursued by the
buccaneers. Morgan's plan had worked perfectly. He described the end of
it to Modyford:

Although they worked such a stratagem that hath been seldom or never
heard, that is when the [infantry] engaged in the flank, he attempted
to drive two droves of cattle of 1500 apiece into the right and left angles
of the rear, but all come to one effect, and helped nothing for their flight
to the city...

[There] they had 200 fresh men and two forts, one with six brass guns,
the other with eight, and the streets barricadoed, and great guns in every
street, which in all amounted to thirty-two brass guns, but instead of
fighting [the viceroy] commanded the city to be fired, and his chief
forts to be blown up, the which was in such haste that they blew up forty
of his soldiers in it. We followed into the town, where in the market place
they made some resistance and fired some great guns, killed us four men
and wounded five.

Once the viceroy had reached the city ahead of the buccaneers he tried
to rally his men but failed, reporting that:

I endeavoured with all my industry to persuade the soldiers to turn and
face our enemies but it was impossible; so that nothing hindering them,
they entered the city to which the slave and owners of the houses had
set fire, and being all of boards and timber, was most of it quickly burnt,
except the *Audiencia*, the Governor's House, the convent of the Mercedes,
San Joseph, the suburbs of Malambo and Pier de Vidas, at which they
say the enemy fretted very much, being disappointed of their plunder
and because they brought with them an Englishman, whom they called

the Prince, with intent there to crown him King of the Tierra Firma.

The 'Prince' was, of course, Colonel Lawrence Prince, the privateer captain who now commanded the vanguard. Don Juan or other Spaniards must have heard his name mentioned, believed it was a title, and drawn the absurd conclusion.

The important point is Don Juan's description of how and why the city burned. Morgan was subsequently accused by people having considerably more prejudice than intelligence of setting fire to the city, although why buccaneers should want to burn down a city before they had a chance of looting it and staying in comfort in its luxurious houses for a few days has never been explained. However, on the written authority of Panama's viceroy and governor, the city burned because the owners of the houses and their slaves set it ablaze.

Morgan said: 'At three of the clock in the afternoon we had quiet possession of the city, although on fire, with no more loss on our side in this day's work than five men killed and ten wounded, and of the enemy about 400.' He then wrote what was in fact the city's epitaph, because the Spanish never rebuilt it. Instead they erected a new city along the coast at Perico, leaving the jungle to claim the ruins of the old:

> There we were forced to put out the fires of the enemy's houses; but it was in vain, for by 12 at night it was all consumed that might be called the City; but of the suburbs was saved two churches and about 300 houses; thus was consumed that famous and antient City of Panama, which is the greatest mart for silver and gold in the whole world, for it receives the goods into it that comes from Old Spain in the King's great Fleet, and likewise delivers to the Fleet all the silver and gold that comes from the mines of Peru and Potosi.

Morgan, Collier and the other buccaneer leaders had struggled hard to stop the flames spreading through the city because every house that blazed meant the destruction of silk furnishings and valuables; silver plate and cutlery, candlesticks and other ornaments were lost in the flames and debris. Using kegs of gunpowder left at the batteries, they blasted breaks in the rows of houses in the hope that the flames would not leap the gaps, but the buildings were dry and sparks carried by the breeze continued spreading the blaze.

As important as saving the buildings was preventing any Spanish ships escaping. Captain Robert Searle, released from prison at the last moment by Modyford to join Morgan, led the group of buccaneers who had been given orders to seize every boat and ship in the port and then go on to Perico and do the same there.

By daylight on Monday morning the city was a smoking ruin and the buccaneers began their search for loot. The city had received so much warning that the buccaneers were assuming that many tons of valuables had been sent by ship to Arica and Lima. The priests had removed most of the valuables from the churches and cathedral, and the nuns had emptied the convent, all of them then sailing in a ship reported to be called *La Santissima Trinidada*. A large gold altar in one church, too big to be moved, was said later to have been painted black so that the buccaneers would think it was age-darkened wood.

The rich families of Panama had hidden their valuables or packed them in panniers on mules, and fled over the hills. The city's great warehouses, however, were untouched. They were far from full because the galleons had not come to Cartagena and Portobelo for many months, but they contained several tons of silk, lace, linen and other expensive cloths. The King's warehouses where the bullion was stored under guard were empty: the plate had been loaded on board a ship and sent back to Lima. Don Juan Perez had escaped from the burning city and taken to the hills with a few score men, and for many miles round the city small groups of soldiers, with or without officers, roamed the countryside, looking for food and careful to keep out of the hands of the buccaneers.

Esquemeling tells stories of scores of women being raped by the buccaneers, and he goes into great detail about an alleged incident concerning Morgan and a young Spanish woman, the wife of a rich merchant 'and her beauty so great as peradventure I may doubt whether in all Europe any could be found to surpass her perfections either of comeliness or honesty'. He then takes up more than three times the space he devoted to Morgan's attack on Panama to Morgan's attack on her virtue – 'he used all the means he could both of rigour and mildness, to bend her to his lascivious will and pleasure...'

Morgan's attentions allegedly provoked the following plea from the lady, quoted verbatim by Esquemeling, presumably hiding within earshot of the boudoir: 'Sir, my life is in your hands; but, as to my body in relation to that which you persuade me unto, my soul shall sooner be separated from it, through the violence of your arms, than I shall condescend to your request.' It was a story sure to bring tears to maidens' eyes – but another which Esquemeling's publishers had later to deny.

Seven months after the Panama raid, and at a time when he was angry with Morgan, the expedition's surgeon-general, Richard Browne, wrote to Sir Joseph Williamson about stories he had heard of the cruelties said to have been committed in Panama: 'The report from England is very high, and a great deal worse than it was: what was done in fight and heat of pursuit of a flying enemy, I presume is pardonable; as to their women I know nor ever heard of anything offered beyond their wills; something I know was cruelly executed by Captain Collier in killing a friar in the field after quarter given; but for the Admiral he was noble enough to the vanquished enemy.'

In his report Morgan told Modyford: 'Here in this city we stayed twenty days, making daily incursions upon the enemy for twenty miles around about, without having so much as one gun shot at us in anger, although we took in this time near 3000 prisoners of all sorts, and kept likewise barques in the South Seas, cruising and fetching of prisoners that had fled to the islands with their goods and families.'

The largest ship the buccaneers managed to press into service was a barque which was alongside the quay 'although', complained the viceroy, 'I had given orders that there should be none. Yet had they not complied with my command, and when they would have set it on fire, the enemy came fast and put it out, and with it [the ship] they did us great damage, for they took three more with it, and made great havoc of all they found in the islands ... taking and bringing from thence many prisoners'.

Morgan gave command of the first barque to Searle, who hurriedly repaired her and put to sea to scour the islands which stretched offshore in an almost straight line – the Perico Islands, just off the port, Taboga and Toboguilla, and Otoque, the most distant before reaching the Pearl Islands (Las Islas del Rey). He was looking primarily for ships and vessels (particularly *La Santissima Trinidada*) which, laden with valuables, were hiding in various anchorages along the Panama coast or among the islands. After taking the three barques referred to by the viceroy, Searle sailed over to Taboga Island and landed with his men, looking for refugees. Instead they found a store of wine and the seamen promptly started drinking heavily and by evening most of them were drunk.

They were far too drunk to notice a large Spanish ship come in from seaward and anchor; nor did they notice a boat being lowered and rowed for the shore full of casks. The first they knew of all this was when the boat's crew were captured as they looked for fresh water. The Spaniards were taken to Searle, who started questioning them – and discovered that the ship was none other than *La Santissima Trinidada*, which was carrying all the gold, silver and jewels which the government, private citizens and the Church in Panama had shipped out for safety. Instead of sailing for Lima, her captain, Don Francisco Peralta, had simply put to sea, apparently intending to return to Panama with his cargo and passengers (who included all the nuns from the convent) after the buccaneers had left, because as far as he knew they had no ships.

Searle at once gave orders to his men to capture *La Santissima Trinidada*, but they would not leave their wine. Peralta, alarmed when his men did not return and suspicious of the barque, weighed anchor and fled with his ship, being out of sight by daybreak.

Meanwhile the buccaneers in the city were searching the wreckage and slowly finding hurriedly hidden riches. They lowered themselves down wells and rainwater cisterns and found gold and silver objects thrown in for safety by their fleeing owners; they found boxes of gems hidden in ceilings and under floorboards. Prisoners were brought in and forced to reveal hiding places and pay ransoms.

As the days went by the purchase piled up. One of the barques taken over by the buccaneers captured a cargo ship from Peru whose captain was blissfully unaware that Panama had changed hands. The ship was carrying a mundane cargo, except for 'twenty thousand pieces of eight in ready money'.

Finally Morgan set 14 February as the date for leaving Panama. All available mules were brought to the main square, 175 in all, and loaded with the purchase; hundreds of slaves were formed up; and all the wealthy prisoners whose ransom had not been paid were assembled under guard.

There had been heavy rain on the North Sea side of the Isthmus while the buccaneers had been in Panama and the water had swollen the River Chagres so that the boats could get all the way up to Venta de Cruz, where they were now waiting for Morgan to arrive. One of the buccaneers said that when the expedition left the city of Panama the 175 mules were 'laden with silver, gold and other precious things, besides 600 prisoners, more or less, between men, women, children and slaves'.

When the long convoy finally reached Venta de Cruz Morgan announced they would wait there several days. Many of the prisoners had not yet been able to arrange for their ransom to be paid and Morgan wanted to collect the money and free his hostages. 'He commanded an order to be published among the prisoners,' said Esquemeling, 'that within the space of three days every one of them should bring in his ransom, under the penalty ... of being transported unto Jamaica.'

The journey continued with the unransomed prisoners and slaves put in the boats under guard. At one of the villages halfway to Chagres, where the expedition camped for a rest, Morgan ordered all the buccaneers to parade:

according to custom, and caused every one to be sworn that they had reserved nor concealed nothing privately to themselves, even not so much as the value of a sixpence.

This being done, Captain Morgan having had some experience that those lewd fellows would not stickle to swear falsely in points of interest, he commanded every one to be searched very strictly, both in their clothes and satchels and everywhere it might be presumed they had reserved anything. Yet, to the intent this order might not be ill taken by his companions, he permitted himself to be searched, even to the very soles of his shoes.

By common consent, one man from each company was chosen as a searcher, and the wisdom of Morgan's precaution is shown by the fact that the ring which Don Juan Perez had given to the Madonna in the cathedral, worth 4000 pieces of eight, could have been tucked into any man's beard. The Frenchmen among the buccaneers, however, 'were not well satisfied with this new custom of searching, yet their numbers being less than that of the English, they were forced to submit unto it'. With the search over and the purchase under guard, the expedition boarded the boats and canoes again and went on to Chagres.

There the purchase was totalled up. Gold and silver, whether ingots or ornaments, was valued by weight, and gems by consent. Coins were included at their face value because Spanish coinage was, of course, valid currency in Jamaica following Morgan's raid on Portobelo. Slaves were valued at the price they would fetch in Jamaica, usually about £20 each. The total value was estimated at about 400,000 pieces of eight, nearly twice the Maracaibo purchase.

Feeling among the buccaneers was (on the sole authority of Esquemeling) beginning to run against Morgan, perhaps because the purchase from Panama was smaller than expected. This was mainly due to the failure to capture La Santissima Trinidada, and of course the real riches of Panama, the silver ingots from Potosí, had been shipped out of the city.

There had been talk of buccaneers leaving Morgan at Panama and sailing off with the captured barques to take up piracy in the South Sea but Morgan had put an end to any such move by having the masts of the barques cut away when he had no further use for the ships. The man said to be planning to start roaming the South Sea on his own account was Charles Swan, the veteran privateersman who commanded the tiny Endeavour, one of the smallest vessels in the expedition, who remained a friend of Morgan's but several years later went to the South Sea by way of Cape Horn.

Esquemeling says that many men grumbled when they received their share of the purchase 'and feared not to tell him openly to his face' that Morgan had reserved the best jewels to himself. The buccaneers, Esquemeling said, 'judged it impossible that no greater share should belong to them than 200 pieces of eight [£50] per capita . . .' No other buccaneer ever accused Morgan of cheating, and with more than fifteen hundred watching the division it is unlikely Morgan could have succeeded in cheating even if he had tried.

With the purchase divided out Morgan released the Spanish prisoners whose ransom had not been paid, ordered all the guns from San Lorenzo to be carried out to the ships so that they could be used to defend Port Royal, and then had the castle wrecked.

By now, in late March, one or two small ships had arrived in Chagres from Jamaica with stories that a new treaty had been signed between England and Spain; that commissions were being withdrawn, and that there was talk among certain people in Jamaica that the buccaneers would be punished. This was quite enough to decide several of the captains that they would give Jamaica a wide berth until the situation became clearer; they had a living to make and a profit to earn, and they were already well placed to sail north, along the Mosquito Coast, capturing coasting vessels and raiding towns in Nicaragua and Honduras.

Morgan sailed from Chagres to Port Royal with only four ships in company. Eight French ships sailed for Tortuga, and Esquemeling's ship went north to Costa Rica and then on to the Isle of Pines, at the western end of Cuba, before finally returning to Port Royal.

Prisoner of State

In Panama city the Spanish looked at the ruins and also considered how Nature was slowly spoiling the anchorage by washing in silt. They decided to leave the old city and begin building a new one at Perico. As the months went by the ruins of what had once been the most fabulous city in the New World slowly disappeared under creeping vines and bushes, and termites devoured the wood because in the Tropics nothing ever stands still. The rectangular tower of the cathedral dedicated to Saint Anastasius, once the tallest building in the New World, began to sprout cactus from the cracks between the stones.

In the past six years, between 1665 and 1671, buccaneers and pirates had attacked and plundered eighteen cities, four towns and thirty-five villages on the Main and in New Spain. Ironically the single raid on the greatest city had destroyed it completely, yet places like Maracaibo and Gibraltar had been raided twice, Riohacha five times, Santa Marta and Campeche thrice and Tolu (south of Cartagena) eight times. Various other towns and villages in Cuba, Hispaniola and Puerto Rico within thirty miles or so from the sea had been raided innumerable times by the French, British and Dutch; by men who were legitimate privateersmen or greedy pirates, by well-organized expeditions or single ships whose captains and crews needed food, liquor or women.

On 23 February 1671 a newsletter published in England told a startled London that a letter just arrived from Jamaica and dated 15 December said that a fleet led by Admiral Morgan had sailed a fortnight earlier to sack Panama. The fleet, said the newsletter, consisted of thirty English and French ships and the men were going to Panama 'which they intend to plunder'. The ship taking that letter to England had made a fast passage from Jamaica because only forty-four days elapsed between writing it and the publication of the newsletter, but given favourable weather it was possible.

Jamaica's new lieutenant-governor, Sir Thomas Lynch, still had not sailed for the West Indies. Publication of the newsletter gave him plenty of food for thought and a furious Privy Council, secretary of State and King waited for the first protest from the Spanish ambassador.

Morgan arrived back in Port Royal early in April on board the late

Colonel Bradley's *Mayflower*, with Lawrence Prince in the *Pearl*, John Morris in the *Dolphin* and Thomas Harris in the *Mary*. As usual, Port Royal went wild, but there were barely five hundred men with Morgan, instead of the 1300 known to have taken part in the expedition. However, from the point of view of the owners of taverns and brothels, the arrival of five hundred buccaneers just after the sharing of a purchase was welcome enough; the seamen alone were worth £25,000 and most of them intended to spend their share.

There was gossip about the expedition and rumour galore, but the facts spoke for themselves: yes, the admiral had lost the *Satisfaction* on a reef, but the Jamaica militia was standing by to guard a great deal of gold and silver waiting to be unloaded from the ships. Yes, the French had made many accusations against the admiral, but he had led them all across the Isthmus to the South Sea and captured Panama with the loss of less than a score of men, and the ships had brought back hundreds of slaves, each worth £20 or so. Yes, *La Santissima Trinidada* had escaped from Panama with the city's riches – but that was not the admiral's fault; his orders for her capture had been disobeyed.

Those who wanted to criticize Morgan had to look hard for listeners because the hard-headed shopkeepers and traders in Port Royal judged on results, and in the last thirty months Morgan and his men had brought in 50,000 pieces of eight from the raid on Puerto Principe, 250,000 from Portobelo, 250,000 from Maracaibo and Gibraltar, and now 400,000 from Panama, a total of 950,000, which was equal to £237,500. By comparison, the total value of the exports from England to all the colonies in the West Indies for 1669 was less than half that amount, £107,791.

It is not known how much Harry Morgan made out of the expedition, but if the figure of 400,000 pieces of eight for the Panama raid is correct, the duke of York's share would have been 40,000 (£10,000), the King's 26,666 (£6666) and, under the terms of the articles the captains signed, Morgan had one per cent, 4000 (£1000). From Esquemeling it is known that an ordinary seaman received 200 pieces of eight (£50).

Back at Lawrencefield and reunited with Elizabeth, Morgan settled down on 20 April to write the final draft of his report to Modyford describing the whole expedition. The governor had told him of the private letters and rumours from England about the treaty but neither knew that within a few days of Morgan beginning to draft his report Sir Thomas Lynch and his bride had at last sailed from England in the *Assistance* frigate, knowing from the newsletter that an expedition led by Morgan had gone off to attack Panama.

The King's instructions to Lynch were harsh and drafted on the basis that Modyford might refuse to give up his power. With the King and Arlington jubilant at the new treaty, Modyford had no hope that anyone in London would appreciate the problems caused by the long delays in getting information to or from Jamaica.

Now that the treaty was signed the Spanish were even louder in their protests against Modyford, Morgan and the buccaneers, and Lynch was told that Modyford had 'contrary to the King's express commands, made many depredations and hostilities against the subjects of His Majesty's good brother the Catholic King'. It was, of course, untrue to refer to 'the King's express commands', as Arlington's letters already cited prove beyond doubt, but although secretaries of State might be witless they could do no wrong, and Arlington and the King needed a scapegoat to placate the Spanish ambassador.

Lynch's instructions said that as soon as he had arrived in the island and taken possession of Jamaica's 'government and fortress, so as not to apprehend any ill-consequence thereupon', he was to arrest Sir Thomas Modyford and send him back to England as a prisoner. Lynch was also told to publish the treaty of Madrid within eight months, agreeing with the Spanish governors on a particular day. And he was to call in all the privateers.

The frigate taking Lynch out was to bring Modyford back a prisoner, and the duke of York told Captain John Hubbart, commanding the ship, that if there was any opposition by Modyford's friends, Hubbart was to help Lynch 'with his utmost force, by annoying by all ways the island, and particularly by destroying the privateers'.

In the meantime Modyford's son Charles was arrested and put in a cell in the Tower of London as Lord Arlington's security for the good behaviour of his father. At this point, Arlington's attitude towards Modyford would have been no different had the governor committed an act of treason. The Tower of London had a particular significance as a jail; another anti-Spaniard, Sir Walter Ralegh, had been executed there only fifty-two years earlier.

Sir Thomas Modyford and Morgan were anxious to send a garrison over to Old Providence to secure it before the Spanish returned. The governor's brother, Sir James Modyford, had been appointed the lieutenant-governor when Edward Mansfield had captured it, but the Spanish had returned before he could take up his post. Now, Sir James wrote to Sir Joseph Williamson, he proposed going over and taking possession in the name of the King.

At the end of May 1671 the Jamaica Council met to hear Morgan's report on his execution of the Council's order of the previous year. 'Admiral Morgan gave the Governor and Council relation of his voyage to Penamaw [sic],' the minutes recorded, 'and the Board do give him many thanks for executing his last commission, and approves very well of his acting therein.'

Modyford received his first official news of the new treaty with Spain in May, within a week of reading Morgan's report, and it came not from London but in a letter from the governor of Puerto Rico, dated 30 April. He told Modyford that he had received from Madrid a copy of the new treaty and instructions to arrange with the governors of English islands a suitable date for publishing the treaty simultaneously. For himself, he proposed 'the Vespers of St John' as a suitable day and if he heard nothing from Modyford by that date would publish it, repeating it later on the day suggested by Modyford, commenting 'good news doth never weary'.

Although by the beginning of June this letter was the only official document he had received about the new treaty, Modyford sat down on 7 June to give Lord Arlington his reasons for acting against Spain in the West Indies. Modyford still had no official news that he was about to be replaced by Lynch (although as he began to write Lynch was only eight days' sailing from Port Royal) but he drafted a lengthy document explaining his recent actions. It was headed 'Considerations from Sir Thomas Modyford which moved him to give his consent for fitting out privateers against the Spaniard' and cited the Spanish commissions and the attacks by Rivera. He had the King's instructions allowing the governor, in extraordinary cases and with the advice of the Council, to 'use extraordinary remedies'. Morgan's commission was 'solely to avenge' the Spanish affronts, and the commissions to privateer captains were 'only to execute Morgan's orders whereby it is evident that nothing was in design but his Majesty's service'.

It might be objected that Morgan's fleet could have been recalled after the coast had been secured, and thus 'the mischief of Panama prevented', Modyford wrote, but the privateers who were providing ships, arms, ammunition and provisions at their own expense would not have obeyed such orders. They would have expected, 'as the late Lord General [the duke of Albemarle], that great master of war, adviseth, the soldier to look on the enemy as the surest pay'.

If he was to be censured for granting the commission to Morgan, Modyford wrote, then 'this fatal doctrine' must follow: that if the French, Dutch or Spanish made war on Jamaica, the governor 'must not take up any offensive arms until he had advised the King and received His Majesty's order to proceed'. This warning to the King, 'if it escape the enemy and all sea hazards', could not arrive in London in under three months. The King would need three months to decide and the answer might reach Jamaica three months after that – 'which makes nine months, during which the pressure of the enemy must be endured'.

To anyone who knew the islands and the delays caused by weather in the North Atlantic and the normal hazards of the sea, Modyford's argument was sound, and he wrote that 'my humble request to your Lordships [the Privy Council] is to be sure of a prudent and loyal person for the Government, and then trust him with that commission which the wise Romans gave their generals ... so well did they understand that rule of trusting him that was on the place, who clearly sees what cannot be imagined by much wiser men at so great a distance'.

The first anyone in Jamaica knew that something unusual was happening was on 25 June, when the lookouts at Fort Charles reported that two frigates were in sight, steering for the entrance to Port Royal. A messenger was sent hurrying off to Sir Thomas in the capital, and the ships were later identified as British frigates, and then named as the *Assistance* and *Welcome*.

As soon as they anchored the usual Customs and harbour authorities went on board and were startled to find that Thomas Lynch was returning to the island after an absence of several years. Not only that, but he had recently received a knighthood and had brought his new wife with him. At the moment, at the age of thirty-eight, he had a particularly painful attack of gout.

Lynch then paid an official call on Sir Thomas Modyford, receiving the governor's regrets over the gout, introducing Lady Lynch, showing him his commission as lieutenant-governor, and telling him of the new treaty and the instructions Lynch had been given for publishing it. He treated Modyford as the governor; he was careful to keep secret the fact that in his baggage were the documents which removed Modyford from office, put him under arrest and ensured that he was sent back to England as a prisoner of State destined for the Tower in the wake of Ralegh.

Lynch left his honour in his baggage, too. Because there was no official residence for a lieutenant-governor and no suitable house available for him, Modyford at once invited the Lynches to stay as his guests at his residence, the King's House. Soon their baggage was brought up from the *Assistance* and Modyford began giving a series of receptions for the man who had, on the face of it, replaced the long-dead Colonel Edward Morgan. Lynch in the meantime found the gout so painful that, as he wrote later to Lord Arlington, he had kept his bed four days out of the seven he had been in Jamaica.

The first thing to be arranged with the Spanish authorities was the publication of the treaty, and of all the Spanish possessions in the West Indies the most important was Cartagena. Modyford and Lynch decided to send the two frigates there 'and in them Major Beeston and Captain Reid to carry the articles of peace, &c, and to bring away the English prisoners', Beeston recorded in his journal. The two frigates sailed on 16 July but they were hardly out of sight of Jamaica before Captain Hubbart, commanding the *Assistance*, fell ill. Lieutenant John Willgress had to take over the command and three days later Hubbart died. The two frigates arrived at Cartagena on 23 July and arrangements were made for publication of the treaty and prisoners were released.

Lynch was soon discussing with his friends the activities of the privateers, and making no secret that Modyford and Morgan were out of favour in London. The gossip about the Panama raid, too, was spreading through the island as more of the privateers returned, and Lynch soon sat down to write his first report to Lord Arlington. As far as the privateers were concerned, he wrote, the Panama expedition 'has mightily lessened and humbled them, and they would take it as a compliment to be severe with Morgan whom they rail horribly for starving, cheating and deserting them'. He considered that the *Assistance* frigate and a ketch would be enough 'to awe the privateers and reduce the refractory'.

That was written on 2 July, seven days after arriving in Port Royal, and he was soon reporting that 'four-fifths of the men' who had gone with Morgan to Panama had been lost, a blatant untruth because nearly half of the Jamaica men had returned with Morgan in the four ships, and more were arriving each week, including Esquemeling.

One ship coming into Port Royal brought interesting papers for Morgan – Don Juan Perez de Guzman's official report to Madrid on the capture of Panama and Chagres, which had been captured by one of the privateers. Morgan had it translated and gave copies to Modyford and Lynch. The new lieutenant-governor sent a copy to Sir Joseph Williamson with a complaint that the Jamaica treasury was empty, the cocoa harvest blighted and the sugar crop ruined for the lack of rain.

Before the *Assistance* and *Welcome* arrived back from Cartagena with the released prisoners, many of whom had been kept in irons for two or three years and others used as slaves to work on fortifications, Harry Morgan had fallen ill with a fever, probably an illness picked up on the journey to or from Panama. There had been no criticism of him in Port Royal from when he arrived back until July, when Lynch arrived, but from then on rumours began to make the rounds of drawing rooms and taverns that Morgan, Collier and the other leaders had cheated many of the buccaneers. By late August, Browne, the man whom Morgan had made surgeon-general of the expedition, had decided that, even at that late date, it would be wise to turn against Morgan despite having praised him in earlier letters. Browne had come back in Morgan's ship, and for nearly five months he had not written any criticism of the admiral to Sir Joseph Williamson, but on 21 August he wrote that at Chagres Morgan and his officers 'gave what they pleased, for which [the buccaneers] must be content or else clapped in irons, and after staying there a week the Admiral and four or five more [ships] stood for Jamaica being like to starve in that ten days run, and the rest for want of provisions were forced to leeward, where hundreds were lost, starved, which is half the undoing of this island'.

Browne did not explain why none of the other ships also took a chance like Morgan and made for Jamaica, even though he says quite flatly that Morgan and 'four or five more' were 'like to starve' on the voyage. The truth was that all the ships were short of provisions, but many of the privateers, having heard that Modyford was withdrawing commissions, decided to stay away from Port Royal and continue attacks on the Spanish, and later it was convenient to put a different interpretation on their actions. Esquemeling was back in Port Royal by July, his ship having been attacking the Spanish along the Mosquito Coast and Cuba...

'There have been very great complaints by the wronged seamen in Sir Thomas Modyford's time against Admiral Morgan, Collier and other commanders, but nothing was done, but since Sir Thomas Lynch's arrival they are left to the law,' Browne wrote. 'The commanders dare but seldom appear, the widows, orphans, and injured inhabitants, who have so freely advanced [money] upon hopes of a glorious design, being now ruined through fitting out the privateers.'

One phrase of Browne's reveals why he wrote such a letter to Williamson at this late date – 'in *Sir Thomas Modyford's time*'. For the past week Modyford had been under arrest on board the *Assistance*. After waiting nearly five weeks Lynch had finally carried out his orders; his host for more than a month was now locked up in a cabin in the frigate. The way he had done it showed cunning, if not courage. On 15 August he had invited Modyford and the Council on board the *Assistance*. The unsuspecting Modyford and some of the Council came on board and were greeted by Lynch. Harry Morgan was not present; he was at home in bed, a very sick man, and several members of the Council had not accepted the invitation. But the *Assistance*'s captain and his ship's company were ready in case there should be trouble.

With the Council members present, Lynch then told Modyford that he had orders to send him back to England 'as a prisoner of State'. Describing the affair later, Lynch said that some members of the Council had not come on board the *Assistance* 'fearing that surprise or fear might occasion some rash actions, but God be thanked, all remained quiet, only by some in secret I was [later] traduced as a trapan [sic: a decoy], and one that had betrayed the good general'.

Once he had told Modyford that he was under arrest, he assured him and the Council members (apparently on the strength of Lord Arlington's word) that his 'life and fortune were in no danger and that he had orders to pardon all, which was a mark that Sir Thomas Modyford was not such a capital offender, but there was a necessity of the King's making this resentment for such an unseasonable iruption'.

With Modyford locked up on board the *Assistance* and no sign of disorder in Spanish Town or Port Royal, Lynch called another Council meeting, the most crowded in the island's history. Lynch showed the members his orders to arrest Modyford and told them flatly that they were not to be disputed, although he admitted 'his manner of doing it might privately be censured'. The Council was far from sympathetic with Lynch, and when they insisted on passing a resolution confirming the commission they had originally given Harry Morgan, Lynch had to agree and a copy of it was sent to London with Modyford.

Earlier, Lynch had Modyford transferred to another ship, the *Jamaica Merchant*, commanded by Joseph Knapman. Modyford's second son, Thomas, was desperately ill at the time of his father's arrest, and when Modyford asked permission to go on shore to visit him Lynch refused, fearing trouble in both Port Royal and Spanish Town, where the former governor was popular. The *Jamaica Merchant* sailed for England on 25 August.

By an ironic coincidence the admiral commanding the latest *flota* from New Spain had just been sent to prison for six years. Don José Cenleno had arrived off San Lucár, at the mouth of the Guadalquivir, and found that his flagship drew too much water to cross the bar. His orders said that in case of difficulty he was to make for a port in Galicia or Cantabria, but hearing enemy ships were in that area he went into Cadiz. This led to him being sentenced to six years in jail at Oran, a penal settlement.

In Port Royal and Spanish Town after the *Jamaica Merchant* had sailed, affairs quietened down and Lady Lynch presented her husband with a son, who was christened Charles.

Harry Morgan, still a very sick man, met an unexpected problem. One of the privateers which had not returned to Port Royal was the *Thomas*, the former Spanish ship captured by Captain Humphrey Thurston while he was commanding the *Port Royal*. Dr George Holmes had discovered that although he had sent his *Port Royal* to Campeche for logwood, her captain had gone off on his own account, and now the worthy doctor complained to the Council in a petition in which he had the facts wrong, thinking the *Thomas* had been wrecked while following Morgan and the *Satisfaction* into Chagres, whereas it was the *Port Royal*.

The *Port Royal* was worth £300, Holmes told the Council, and her Spanish prize had been laden with wine and silk. Admiral Morgan, he continued, had been paid £1000 for the loss of the *Satisfaction*, and the buccaneers had agreed on compensation for any ship that was lost. Holmes had asked for his compensation but had received nothing, and now he requested the Council to call Admiral Morgan. The Council agreed and an order was made for Morgan to attend the next meeting so that a decision could be made 'as shall be agreeable to law and equity'. Whether or not there was some private agreement between Morgan and Holmes is not known; the matter never came before the Council again.

The buccaneers who had not come back to Port Royal soon confirmed their fears that Jamaica under her new governor was a dangerous place for them, and Esquemeling finally gave the reason why so many ships had not returned. The new governor, wrote Esquemeling, 'gave notice unto all the ports [of the island] by several boats' saying that he had received from the King 'strict and severe orders not to permit any pirates whatsoever to set forth from Jamaica to commit any hostility or depredation upon the Spanish nation or dominions, or any other people of those neighbouring islands'. As soon as they heard this, the privateers 'dared not return home'. Esquemeling added that Lynch 'apprehended several of the chief actors herein, and condemned them to be hanged, which was accordingly done. From this severity many others still remaining abroad took warning and retired to the island of Tortuga, lest they should fall into his hands. Here they joined in society with the French pirates...'

In London there was little at home or abroad to cheer the King, Arlington or the rest of the Cabal. The West Indies were in fact a tiny mirror which reflected what was now an increasingly turbulent picture in Europe. Although Britain had signed a new treaty with the Dutch within days of the one negotiated with Madrid, relations with Holland were still so bad that Charles II and Arlington were considering Spain as an ally should a third Dutch war break out.

Yet in Spain the young King (also Charles II, known as *El Hechizado*), warped and twisted in both mind and body, was an idiot unlikely to produce an heir. Louis XIV of France, anticipating the day when this doltish Habsburg died, wanted his throne and looked to England for agreement. France too was getting close to war with the Dutch, and by the time Lynch arrived in Port Royal the British King had signed a secret treaty with Louis XIV which in effect backed Louis' claim to the Spanish throne and agreed to support France – in return for a handsome subsidy – in a war against the Dutch.

While Charles II walked a tightrope in London, anxious to offend neither the Spanish nor the French, and hurriedly trying to fit out a fleet which could destroy the Dutch fleet and allow her colonies to be seized, reports began to arrive from the West Indies, Spain and Holland of a remarkable English victory.

In an England where Francis Drake had been dead for only seventy-five years and many a young man had been told stirring tales by his father about how he fought the Spanish Armada all the way up the Channel, the Spanish were still the natural enemies; stories of singeing the Dons' beards were popular, particularly because the King and his brother so favoured the Roman Catholics ... By the end of June it was clear that Harry Morgan, the hero of Portobelo and Maracaibo, had now crossed the Isthmus and destroyed the legendary city of Panama, a task which had defeated Drake.

The King and his ministers were appalled. Although newsletters were publishing accounts of the expedition, no word had arrived from Modyford. When the Spanish ambassador delivered a violent protest, Arlington could only reply that he had no dispatch about it, Sir Thomas Modyford had in any case been sacked, was by now under arrest, and would soon arrive in London as a prisoner of State. Spain had for years been demanding the punishment of Modyford, and the ambassador was soon reporting that Madrid was unimpressed by this overdue move. The city of Panama had been entirely destroyed, the losses were enormous, and the man who had done all this was Henry Morgan, who was not being punished.

When a dispatch finally arrived the Privy Council met and, a contemporary diarist noted in August: 'The letters of Sir Thomas Modyford were read giving relation of the exploit at Panama, which was very brave, they took, burnt and pillaged the town of vast treasures but the best of the booty had been shipped off and lay at anchor in the South Sea, so that after our men had ranged the country for sixty miles about, they went back to Nombre de Dios [sic: Chagres] and embarked for Jamaica. Such an action had not been done since the famous Drake.'

Although the *Jamaica Merchant* was expected in England any moment, when the sight of Modyford being marched off to the Tower of London might do something to placate the Spanish ambassador, the Spanish government was adopting a considerably more threatening tone as extra details of the Panama raid became available. Reports to London from various European capitals said that Spain was even considering war.

This was enough for fresh orders to be sent off to Lynch: Henry Morgan was to be arrested and sent to England at once as a prisoner of State. The King and Arlington hoped that with the two main figures of the Panama raid lodged in the Tower the Spanish protests would die down.

The order to arrest Morgan had only just left London as Sir Thomas Lynch was forced to call a council of war. He had been in Jamaica only five months before the wheel had turned full circle and he was facing the same kind of crisis that Modyford had dealt with a year and a half earlier. 'The Church and Grandees of Spain', he wrote to Lord Arlington on 29 November, had decided to recapture Jamaica, and they intended to use an army of five thousand men, to be carried in a fleet of thirty-six ships. This news had reached merchants in Jamaica in letters from Holland, Spain and London.

He had immediately declared martial law and called a council of war to plan the defence of the island. Because there was no money in the island's treasury, it would be defended 'upon my own credit', and the fortifications would be strengthened as much as he could afford.

He sent a copy of the minutes of the council of war but said that 'this noise of war makes me more strict in observing the peace, people being too apt to wish for a rupture to satisfy their own designs, and I cannot think it is for the Spaniards' interest to break it lest we should bring the war again into their own quarters'. To confuse Lord Arlington even more he added: 'I will never do this without positive instructions, for I had rather maintain the charge of the whole nation in Jamaica than of one ambassador [sic] in the Tower, though I am told it will check these people mightily to know that they must only fight like baited bears within the length of their chain.'

In direct contrast to the calm contradictions of Lynch's letter to Arlington, the minutes of the council of war show that its members took a far more serious view of 'the noise of war'. Harry Morgan was conspicuously absent, although it is not entirely clear whether this was due to Lynch deliberately ignoring him or if he was too ill: the fever that had sent him to his bed was to last several more months. However, his second-in-command for the Panama raid, Edward Collier, was given a prominent rôle in the defence plans, which were under the command of Major-General Bannister, a former governor of Surinam.

When the council of war met again on 9 November the first item on the agenda concerned not the Spanish but the effect of martial law on certain people in Jamaica. The Act originally laid down that a trooper had to provide himself with a horse worth £5 but now the council, noting that 'the price of horses is much raised', ordered that a trooper 'shall appear on an exercising day' with a horse worth £10.

Having dealt with the inflation as it affected the cavalry, the council then gave instructions in case of invasion. They ordered that 'the appearance of five ships makes an alarm', and laid down the chain of command. Finally the council ordered that 'the chief officer residing in Port Royal has, in case of invasion, full power to burn down any house, press ships and do anything for the preservation of the place, and be indemnified by this order'.

As the council of war finished its meeting, Sir Thomas Modyford was completing his first month as a prisoner in the Tower of London. His son had been released after being held there as a hostage for more than six months. But the former governor was not closely confined and could have visitors.

Within a few days the order arrived in Jamaica from London for the arrest of Morgan and, from Lynch's point of view, it could hardly have come at a worse time because he was having great difficulty in persuading the leaders of the island that his defensive policy was correct. Under Modyford they had seen that the best form of defence was attack.

Lynch told Lord Arlington on 17 December that he was afraid 'the sending home Morgan might make all the privateers apprehend they should be so dealt with, notwithstanding the King's proclamation of pardon'. However, he wrote:

I shall send him home so as he shall not be much disgusted, yet the order obeyed, and the Spaniards satisfied. I cannot do it now, for he is sick and there is no opportunity, but I hope the *Welcome* will be ready to bring him in six weeks.

To speak the truth of him, he's an honest brave fellow, and had both Sir T.M and the Council's commission and instructions, which they thought he obeyed and followed so well that they gave him public thanks, which is recorded in the Council books. However, it must be confessed that the privateers did divers barbarous acts, which they lay to his Vice-admiral's [Collier's] charge.

There was little to cheer Harry Morgan, although he did not know that he too was to be arrested. However, another of the Morgan girls was married on 30 November 1671, as though the banns had been called at St Catherine's Church as soon as the new crisis began. Johanna Wilhelmina, the youngest of old Colonel Edward's daughters, finally married Colonel Henry Archbold, whose plantation was on the mainland opposite Port Royal (where Kingston now stands).

Robert and Anna Petronilla now had two sons. Young Thomas Byndloss, the first of the new generation, would inherit from his father Robert, and Henry and Elizabeth, recognizing they would never have children, appear to have decided very early that the second, Charles, would inherit from Henry. This would be a considerable legacy – quite apart from Lawrence-field, which was flourishing, a considerable amount of work had now been done on the new estate at Morgan Valley.

Harry Morgan, Byndloss and Archbold now formed a significant section of the politically active planters, and all three brothers-in-law were close friends of Thomas Ballard, an 'Old Stander' from the Venables expedition and a member of the Council.

Lynch had done one thing which was likely to change the way the island was run in the future. Modyford had not called the House of Assembly for more than six years but on 1 December writs were issued for new elections. Next day, Harry Morgan had to go into the capital to swear an affidavit, and this document is the only one that gives definite information about the year of his birth because he gave his age as 'thirty-six years or thereabouts'.

The only other person of consequence in Port Royal whose life underwent a considerable change in December 1671 was Captain Willgress, the former lieutenant now commanding the *Assistance* frigate in place of Hubbart. Willgress had been drinking heavily long before he crossed the Atlantic with the new governor, and the Tropics had their usual effect. He was soon continually drunk and Lynch removed him and put Captain Thomas Beeston in command. He reported this to Lord Arlington in the middle of January when he said that the *Assistance* would be leaving for England with Henry Morgan as soon as she returned from a cruise off Cuba. He wanted to keep the *Welcome* until another frigate came out from England – without a ship of war, he admitted, the people 'would neither keep the peace nor defend themselves from pirates or from the insults of their neighbours'.

When she returned from her cruise off Cuba, the *Assistance* came into Port Royal with two prizes following astern. Captain Beeston was soon reporting to the governor that one was English, commanded by Captain Francis Witherboon, and the other French, and both captains had 'committed great violence against the Spaniards'. They were both charged with piracy and sentenced to death, a bizarre process since the island was still under martial law in fear of the arrival of a Spanish invasion fleet.

The *Assistance*'s success as a pirate hunter – she was the faster and more powerful of his two frigates – led Lynch to change his mind about sending her to England with Morgan: instead the *Welcome* should take him. Originally a prize, the *Welcome* was an old 36-gun frigate which had been sunk to block the Thames in 1667 when the Dutch attacked. She was later raised and made into a fireship, being hurriedly changed back to a fifth-rate to accompany Lynch to the West Indies.

Arresting Morgan and sending him to England was only one of many problems for Lynch. The new House of Assembly met for the first time in February 1672, when the members refused to vote any cash for repairs to Port Royal's defences. It was the Crown's duty, they said, to pay for the defence of the island. The immediate effect on Lynch was that none of the £2500 he had spent of his own money could be repaid. Lynch was also angry about Modyford and told Lord Arlington that Modyford's representation that Lynch had promised him 'security of life and fortune' was 'a damned untruth'. (He had forgotten that he had earlier reported to Arlington that he had told Modyford his 'life and fortune were in no danger'.)

On 4 April 1672, not knowing that Britain and France had just declared war on the Dutch, Lynch wrote the formal orders for Captain John Keene of the *Welcome* to take on board Colonel Henry Morgan as 'his Majesty's prisoner' and sail at once. He was also to take Captain Francis Witherboon to England as a prisoner: he had just been sentenced to death for piracy, after being captured by the *Assistance*. Lynch did not waste the opportunity of making up a small convoy which the *Welcome* could escort, and Keene was ordered to take three ships with him. Two of them were small, so that the voyage would take exactly three months.

Richard Browne, the former surgeon-general of the Panama expedition, called on Captain Keene and tried to get a passage to England. On the day the *Welcome* sailed he wrote to Williamson complaining bitterly: 'I cannot find myself in any way obliged to Admiral Morgan, for if he had been just to his word I had come off [i.e. sailed for England], but God grant that he may find as few friends as I; but mine and others' gold in his pocket may do something. I find myself little obliged to Captain Keene of the

Welcome, a span new captain of the last edition, who denied my [application for] a passage to England.'

Major-General Bannister, the former governor of Surinam and now in charge of Jamaica's land defences, wrote to Lord Arlington on 30 March about Morgan:

> The bearer, Admiral Morgan, is sent home confined to the *Welcome* frigate to appear, as is suspected, on account of his proceedings against the Spaniard. I know not what approbation he may find there, but he received here a very high and honourable applause for his noble service therein, both from Sir Thomas Modyford and the Council that commissioned him.
>
> I hope without offence I may say he is a very well deserving person, and one of great courage, who may, with his Majesty's pleasure, perform good public service at home or be very advantageous to this island if war should break forth with the Spaniard ...

Three months to the day after sailing from Port Royal the *Welcome* anchored at Spithead. She was in poor condition, with a leaky hull and leaky decks (as soon as the Navy Board surveyed her she reverted to being a fireship). Morgan's condition after being confined in a damp cabin for twelve weeks can be imagined: for several months he had been ill with a fever, then he had been taken on board a ship which had sailed for England on a course which meant that as she approached Bermuda the temperature was dropping one degree a day until the average of eighty degrees to which Morgan was accustomed was more than twenty degrees lower. Captain Keene reported to London on 4 July 1672 that both prisoners were 'much tried' by their long confinement, 'especially Colonel Morgan, who is very sickly'.

'Arise, Sir Henry'

Sir Thomas Lynch, the man who for years had preached in England of trade with Spain in the West Indies and had been listened to by ministers who neither understood Spanish policy 'beyond the Line' nor wanted it explained to them because it contradicted their aim of friendship with Catholic Spain, now lived in the King's House in Spanish Town with one of his enemies safely imprisoned in the Tower of London and the other locked up in a cabin on board a leaky old frigate. With the signing of the new treaty the way should have been clear for profitable trade with all the Spanish colonies, and for all this the people of Jamaica should have been duly grateful.

Unfortunately they were not. The alarm over the Spanish threat had not subsided before Lynch heard of the war with the Dutch and on 6 July 1672, two days after Captain Keene wrote to London from Spithead saying that the *Welcome* had arrived with a 'very sickly' Morgan on board, Lynch was so frightened about the island's immediate future that he wrote directly to the King for help. He 'feared all may be lost if we have not a frigate or two to defend the island. It is impossible to raise privateers against the Dutch that have neither country nor merchants to take'.

In his agitation, Lynch was telling His Majesty an outright lie. Far from the Dutch having 'neither country nor merchants', Curaçao handled as much trade as Port Royal and was the centre for all the illicit slave trade with the Main and New Spain, as well as supplying most of the slaves for the British and French islands. Lynch, in other words, was looking for excuses why the privateers would have nothing to do with the island's new lieutenant-governor, yet he had to look no farther than the Point, where the bodies of privateersmen just condemned for piracy swung from gibbets, or recall that Harry Morgan's fellow prisoner was a privateer captain charged with piracy and condemned to death.

At no time in his life, then or later, did Lynch hint that he ever understood why Modyford had for so long played a very wary game with the privateers; careful always to keep them under some control in peace yet ensuring that they would be available in war. Lynch's own reports show that he had no policy other than the naïve and unrealistic belief that free trade with Spain depended on Jamaica, and the letters he sent back during the first year reveal a muddled, puzzled and frightened man. Lynch understood only what he preached, appeasement. He could not understand that it was like blackmail – the more he paid the more was demanded.

His first letter, written within a week or two of arriving in July 1671, said the treasury was empty and the cocoa and sugar cane crops blighted, and that a frigate and ketch would 'awe the privateers'. By November he was reporting martial law and a council of war in face of a Spanish invasion threat and begging for 'positive instructions'. In December he hoped for 'a little underhand trade' with the Spanish. By February 1672 his first Assembly was refusing money for fortifications, and despite that in March he reported: 'People all seem satisfied, trade is increased.' By the second July, though, he feared, 'All may be lost if we have not a frigate or two to defend the island' against the Dutch because the privateers would not help him.

The beginning of the hurricane season was a bad time for Lynch, who was in constant pain from gout. In September 1672, with Morgan and Modyford in London, Jamaica was hit by a hurricane, the first in the seventeen years that the English had been on the island. By November the Privy Council was writing to warn Lynch that they feared 'the Dutch meditate an attack on Jamaica' and that he was to protect himself as best he could.

Modyford remained in the Tower and during the first weeks of his stay the Privy Council had considered a petition to the King on his behalf, signed a year earlier by most of the leading planters in Jamaica, when the first rumours reached the island that he might be recalled. The first name on the petition was Henry Morgan, followed by Colonel Cary and Robert Byndloss, as well as seven majors, seventeen captains, thirty-three leading merchants and 251 freeholders (the latest returns showed that land was owned by 717 families).

The petition made no difference. The man it concerned was already a mile or so down the Thames from the Privy Council offices, getting used to living in the cold, damp stone room allocated to him in the Tower after twenty-five years spent living in the Tropics. 'Read in Council, November 9th, 1670, and rejected', Sir Joseph Williamson noted on a corner of the first page.

Although Modyford's imprisonment was not strict, his confinement satisfied the Spanish ambassador, who could rejoice that thanks to Lord Arlington one of the men regarded in Madrid as among Spain's worst enemies was undergoing the same imprisonment which had been inflicted on an earlier enemy, Sir Walter Ralegh.

Harry Morgan was more fortunate. He was sent up to London in August 1672 but not imprisoned. Sir Thomas Dalby, in a history of the West Indies published a few years later, wrote:

Without being charged with any crime, or even brought to a hearing, he was kept here at his own great expense above three years, not only to the wasting of some thousands he was then worth, but to the hindrance of his planting, and improvement of his fortune by his industry ... so that under those difficulties and the perpetual malice of a prevailing court faction, he wasted the remaining part of his life, oppressed not only by those but by a lingering consumption, the coldness of this climate and his vexations had brought him into, when he was forced to stay here.

Dalby could have added that although Modyford spent two years in the Tower he was never accused of a crime.

As a youth Harry Morgan had left a Puritan country; he returned seventeen years later to Restoration England. The new London was rising to Christopher Wren's designs from the ashes of the Great Fire, and it was a London that in the late summer of 1672 was lively and corrupt, gay and glittering. Samuel Pepys was within months of being appointed Secretary of the Admiralty office, and at Court the powerful Cabal was slowly losing its grip on power, and would be brought crashing by the Commons' determination to have done with Catholicism.

Once he arrived in London many people came to Morgan's help, and from unexpected quarters. William Morgan, a relative and deputy lieutenant for Monmouth, wrote to the Privy Council pleading for 'Colonel Henry Morgan of Jamaica', a relation and formerly a neighbour, 'as I have a very good character of him, and in the management of the late business to Panama he behaved with as much prudence, fidelity and resolution as could be reasonably expected ... and all good men would be troubled if a person of his loyalty and consideration as to his Majesty's affairs in those parts should fall for want of friends to assist him'.

The one thing that kept Morgan out of the Tower was probably the Test Act. Although various legends say Morgan joined Modyford (as though being incarcerated in the Tower was a necessary part of becoming a hero) the Tower of London records do not mention the name of Henry Morgan, and he can be thankful that his illness had delayed his arrival in an England which was just going through what is best described as a quiet but determined revolution.

The war against the Dutch had started off badly, with the King scraping together every penny to prepare the fleet, although the first great battle against the Dutch in Sole Bay, beginning on 28 May 1672, was one of those bloody stalemates where each side could claim victory. In the meantime the French attacked the Dutch by land, advancing so fast that England became alarmed as the French armies advanced on the Scheldt, for centuries regarded as the sally port for an enemy invasion fleet.

Harry Morgan had arrived in England in the summer of 1672 at a time of curious change; the French ally was beginning to look more like the traditional enemy she had been for so long; the idea of a Catholic nation holding the coastline from the Pyrenees to the Texel was just the ammunition wanted by the strong Protestant majority among the English people. With winter the war lost momentum; the Dutch people found new strength and a rousing leader in the young Prince of Orange; mud and flooded dykes slowed down the French army; fleets were laid up until early spring.

At the end of February 1673 the Lord High Admiral, the duke of York, was brought toppling in a sequence of events that had started with the King's Declaration of Indulgence. This, suspending penal laws where ecclesiastical affairs were concerned, was regarded as the first step in bringing the country back to Catholicism. The country decided the King had gone too far; it was in no mood to indulge kings or Catholics; certainly not while the French, albeit allies, were advancing along the Channel coast. When the House of Commons met in February it insisted the King withdraw the Declaration and in its place passed the Test Act. This laid down that every holder of a public office should receive the sacrament according to the Church of England, make a declaration against transubstantiation, and take an oath of supremacy. No Catholic, in other words, could hold public office.

On the following Sunday the King received Communion at the Chapel Royal but the duke did not, nor did two of the five men who had formed the Cabal, Clifford and Ashley. No new Lord High Admiral was appointed; instead fifteen commissioners were chosen to carry out the task – the Board of Admiralty – and Samuel Pepys was appointed the Board's secretary.

Harry Morgan, maintaining himself at his own expense, was at least free to meet and talk with whom he pleased, and although he had not been in England since he was a youth there were many people with interests in Jamaica who were in powerful positions. There also was the duke of Albemarle, the son of 'the Great General', a relative of Thomas Modyford and one of the leading younger figures of Restoration England. Christopher Monck, the second duke of Albemarle, was twenty years old in August 1673 and a close friend of the King. He had been born in an attic above a tailor's shop in the Strand, the son of George Monck and the former Anne Clarges, a farrier's daughter and the widow of a milliner. Christopher had received the usual favours that came to the son of one of the most powerful men in the kingdom: by the age of thirteen he was captain of a regiment, a little later a member of Parliament.

The Albemarles were a strange family, and the title passed from the general to his son in a scene which lacked only owls hooting in a storm amid bolts of lightning for the ultimate dramatic effect: while the old duke was dying in one room and the duchess in another, his son and heir, aged sixteen, was in a third marrying the fourteen-year-old Lady Elizabeth Cavendish. Yet for all the bizarre timing it was a marriage of love between a beautiful girl and a youth who, inheriting the dukedom, became one of the richest men in the kingdom.

With the King his friend, life at Court for the young duke was a glittering and exciting affair. His wife was highly-strung and vivacious, keeping abreast of her husband in pursuing gaiety and gambling. Lely, the great portrait artist of the day, painted her with 'a curious haunting kind of beauty', it was noted at the time, with 'sleepy eyes and a tiny mouth, the whole surrounded by chestnut curls'. She had her own private income and the duke added £1200 a year, much of which went on the gambling tables. Yet although Albemarle loved luxury and extravagance he could leave both aside when necessary. He commanded one of the regiments raised to fight the Dutch; he served in Prince Rupert's flagship, the *Sovereign*.

In later years, when the King had a yacht built, Albemarle ordered one, too. However, following fashions set by the King was an expensive business, even for the *nouveau riche*, and before long he was plagued with money troubles. The duchess too ran up enormous bills and a contemporary noted that he 'ruended her by letting her have her own will'. But the days when Albemarle House would have to be sold to quieten creditors and the duchess's whimsies would be recognized as approaching madness were still in the distant future when Harry Morgan joined their circle. For the moment it was more important that the duke was a Privy Councillor and one of the Lords of Trade and Plantations who had the King's ear.

Merely as a nephew of Major-General Sir Thomas Morgan, who had been regarded on the battlefields as 'second only to the Great General', Harry Morgan would have been a welcome visitor to Albemarle House, but in an age seeking sensation and amusement he was particularly welcome as the person about whom London had been chatting: the man who led the buccaneers to sack Maracaibo, Portobelo, Granada and Panama. In salons where the rich had otherwise to find excitement in the turn of a card or the click of dice, the arrival of a tall and bearded Morgan, still suntanned but gaunt from illness, obviously a man of action, was more than welcome: the fashionable hostesses had a genuine swashbuckler available.

Morgan might lack social polish but he told a good tale – a tale making an exciting and welcome change from the grumbles of merchants who had lost ships to the Dutch or could not get their bills paid by the Navy or Army, of smokers unable to get their tobacco from Holland or ladies whose lace had been taken by Dutch privateers on its way over from France. Leaving the dice to listen to a story of a buccaneer seizing a smoking fuse leading to a Spanish powder magazine, or a description of the governor of Panama driving out an army of hundreds of bulls and oxen in a vain attempt to save his city – these were stories that won Morgan the hearts of ladies and the envy of other men. Yet the stories he told impressed his listeners as well as thrilled them because they were not the wild tales of an excitable bravo – they were accounts of well-planned expeditions.

In August 1673, when Prince Rupert fought the Dutch in yet another indecisive battle, the Privy Council was having to consider the West Indies. Sir Thomas Lynch had asked for more ships but none was available. Even the leaky *Welcome* had disappeared in a sheet of flame as she was sent against the Dutch. Lynch had only the *Assistance*, and his desperate plea for more frigates made it clear he could get no help from the privateers. Yet Modyford, the man in the Tower, had always made do with privateers, and Henry Morgan had taken them to sea. The comparison was easy to make and it was valid. Now the King and Arlington faced the consequences of their earlier policy. To placate Spain they had sent out Lynch, put Modyford in the Tower and brought home Morgan. As a result they now risked losing Jamaica to the Dutch.

What should be done? What could be done? What *had* to be done? Lord Arlington had many questions, but he was far from sure who could answer them in time. The King had no such doubts: he had heard from Albemarle all about Morgan and his ideas for Jamaica.

There is no evidence that His Majesty had ever received Morgan up to then, but at the end of July 1673, while Modyford was still in the Tower and Morgan a prisoner of State, Arlington requested that the man who was the admiral of the Brethren submit a memorandum for the King's attention describing what he considered necessary for Jamaica's defence.

Quite what His Majesty had said is not known, but Morgan's memorandum referred to the King's 'commands and promise concerning Jamaica', and from his suggestions it seems probable that there had been more than a hint that Morgan should return to the island in a position of authority. Certainly this is how Morgan interpreted it, because he said that twenty iron guns, with powder and shot, were needed at once for the new batteries at Port Royal, and he asked for a fifth-rate frigate to take him back . . .

In the West Indies a French attack on the Dutch island of Curaçao early in the year failed and by April 1673 Lynch was reporting that the people of Jamaica were now 'apt to be over-secure than fearful'. The new House of Assembly was still refusing him money for fortifications even though he read out a letter from the King advising the danger the island was in. The furious governor, 'considering it necessary the several officers should with all speed repair to their respective commands', dissolved the Assembly, his third and last. Work had to stop on a new fort that Lynch had started at Port Royal, one worthy to stand near Fort Charles and which he intended to name James, after the duke of York.

The rest of the year in Jamaica was comparatively quiet. On 19 October France declared war against Spain, but the news took time to reach the West Indies. Among the bits and pieces of gossip circulating among the fashionable London drawing rooms as 1673 came to a close, the report that the earl of Winchelsea was going to be the new Governor of Jamaica was wrong, but it was an indication that the King and Privy Council were dissatisfied with Lynch. From Arlington's point of view Lynch had been the man for the time: given that the policy was then to placate Spain there could have been no better choice. Now, though, Arlington finally understood that if Jamaica's defence had to be left to the privateers – and with England so heavily in debt and the fleet in poor condition there was no choice – the governor had to be a circus tightrope walker like Modyford, not a barker like Lynch.

Henry Morgan's memorandum of the previous August had impressed the King, and there is no doubt that the colonel – for in London most people still referred to him either as Colonel or Admiral and always as Harry – had by now a reputation as a shrewd administrator and leader, as well as a bold fighter. More important, from the King's point of view, was that policy would very soon be undergoing another change because peace negotiations with the Dutch were proceeding satisfactorily and there was every hope that signatures would soon be put to a treaty between England and the United Provinces.

When the Council of Trade and Plantations met on 23 January 1674, Lord Arlington told them that Lynch was being recalled and that the new governor of Jamaica would be the earl of Carlisle. The deputy governor, he added, would be Colonel Henry Morgan ...

Morgan's commission was drawn up first, although the matter was not treated with any urgency. The peace treaty with Holland was signed on 19 February, and a month later the new deputy governor was given his commission and instructions to go out to the island. Significantly the phrase 'deputy governor' was used, not lieutenant-governor, although later either title was used in referring to him. Carlisle finally refused the appointment, and on 3 April Lord Vaughan was given the post. Thirty-four years old (five years younger than Morgan) and the son of the earl of Carbery, he was a patron of the arts (one of Dryden's earliest patrons) and a poet. The broad-minded Samuel Pepys regarded him as 'one of the lewdest fellows of the age', and the man who wrote the prologue to Dryden's *Conquest of Granada* proved to have nothing in common with a man who had sacked the Granada of New Spain with a sword in his hand, even though he was a fellow Welshman.

Vaughan's instructions said in no uncertain terms that he was not to declare war without the King's command. As far as legislation in Jamaica was concerned, he was not to allow any laws to be re-enacted which had expired because they had not been confirmed by the Council in London within two years, unless there was a 'very urgent occasion'. Vaughan then began a long argument with the King and Privy Council about the appointment of Morgan. Much of this was verbal, but it soon became clear that the elegant heir to an earldom who was a lively figure in the limbo of literary London had a distaste for the buccaneer leader, although later he claimed he had not objected to the appointment but the way the responsibilities were allocated. He did not want Morgan to be called the deputy governor; he wanted him described as the lieutenant-governor.

Unknown to the British government or to Lynch in Jamaica, the Spanish government had agreed in February to requests from governors in the West Indies to grant *patentes de corso*, or commissions. The governors had been complaining that their coasts were defenceless after Morgan's destruction of the *armada de barlovento* at Maracaibo, and the French had been attacking them. Undoubtedly the English privateers would go to Tortuga and get French commissions.

Coinciding with these requests had come reports from their ambassador in London that Harry Morgan, far from being out of favour with the British government, was now advising the King in matters concerning Jamaica. Spanish shipowners from ports along the Bay of Biscay had twice before failed to get commissions, but with the *cedula* of February the way was clear. Privateers left at once to base themselves on ports in Puerto Rico, Hispaniola and Cuba. Soon the word 'Biscayner' became common at Port Royal, meaning any privateer from Old Spain, not just one from a Spanish port on the Biscay coast.

While the Biscayners began their raids, Vaughan and Morgan still remained in London and Modyford was freed from the Tower. Morgan was approached by John Gadham, the astronomer, who had published the first edition of his *Jamaica Almanack* in 1672 and wanted to dedicate the 1675 edition to the buccaneer leader. He also met the diarist John Evelyn, who recorded the only known personal reference to Morgan during his stay in England. They met on 20 September 1674, when it was well known that Morgan was due to return to Jamaica:

At Lord Berkeley's I discoursed with Sir Thomas Modyford, late Governor of Jamaica, and with Col. Morgan, who undertook that gallant exploit from Nombre de Dios to Panama on the continent of America; he told me 10,000 men would easily conquer all the Spanish Indies they were so secure [sic].

They took great booty, and much greater had been taken, had they not been betrayed and so discovered before their approach, by which the Spaniards had time to carry their vast treasure on board ships that put off to sea in sight of our men, who had no boats to follow. They set fire to Panama and ravaged the country for sixty miles about. The Spaniards were so supine and unexercised that they were afraid to fire a great gun.

Meanwhile Lynch was fuming in Jamaica because ships arriving in Port

Royal during the last half of 1674 brought letters with the latest news for planters and merchants from their friends and business associates in England, and Morgan himself wrote frequently to his relatives. No one was at all reticent about what was happening in Whitehall; but the Council of Plantations told Lynch nothing.

He wrote on 20 November to Sir Joseph Williamson, who had replaced Lord Arlington as secretary of State, and began by saying: 'The Spaniards expect the galleons in two or three months with twenty Biscayners, Ostenders and Flushingers, which are likely to clear the Indies of all that infests them ... One of the reasons of their coming is the noise of the Admiral's [Morgan's] favour at Court and return to the Indies, which much alarmed the Spaniards and caused [their] King to be at vast charges fortifying in the South Seas ...'

He then looked back over the last three years that he had been governor and commented that Jamaica had improved 'to a marvel' and the people were as contented 'as the English can be'. He then wrote frankly: 'I wonder that I have not been made acquainted with Lord Vaughan's coming that I might have done all that is possible for his reception, for provision is not suddenly made, and Admiral Morgan's letters have long since declared first Lord Carlisle, then himself for Governor; others [say] Lord Vaughan or Sir Ed. Ford, and by this [latest] ship says a stop was put to Lord Vaughan's and Lieutenant General Morgan's commissions.'

The complex situation in the West Indies, where France was at war with Spain and Holland, but England was officially at peace with everyone, led to unexpected problems in Jamaica, where the marquis de Maintenon, commanding a French warship, brought a Spanish prize into Port Royal and wanted to sell it. Lynch was anxious not to offend either the man who was the nephew of a duchess, or the French government, but he knew such a sale would certainly upset the Spanish government so, as he reported to Whitehall, he had treated the marquis 'with all respect possible', and refused permission.

Lynch's commission was formally revoked in London on 3 November and three days later new commissions were drawn up for Vaughan and Morgan containing certain changes resulting from Vaughan's complaints about his deputy governor. Vaughan's instructions, written the following month, had an extra paragraph: if – as the King had been told – the Spanish governors were in fact issuing commissions, thus breaking the treaty, Vaughan was to claim compensation for any damage done. If the Spanish refused to pay, he was 'to give out commissions to privateers sufficient to redress the injury and satisfy those endamaged'.

One last thing remained before the two men left for Jamaica. In official documents Henry Morgan was referred to as 'Colonel'. It was customary for a governor to be given a title, although not always a deputy or lieutenant-governor. The King decided, however, that Morgan should have a knight-hood, although it is not clear whether this was in effect a warning to the Spanish or further proof of the King's 'particular confidence in your loyalty, prudence and courage and long experience of the colony' referred to in Morgan's commission.

So just before Christmas Colonel Henry Morgan, the elected admiral of the Brethren of the Coast and the future lieutenant-governor of the island of Jamaica, attended the King and with the ritual of being tapped on the shoulders with a sword became Sir Henry Morgan, Knight.

By New Year's Day 1676, the *Foresight* frigate was at anchor in the Downs, the great anchorage for Channel shipping inside the Goodwin Sands off Deal, and nearby was a tubby merchant ship, the *Jamaica Merchant*, which had brought Sir Thomas Modyford back to England as a prisoner and was still commanded by Joseph Knapman. Stowed in the *Jamaica Merchant*'s holds were the twenty iron guns specified by Sir Harry Morgan, along with powder, shot and slow match. The passenger accommodation had been cleaned up and prepared for Sir Harry, who was expected any day to join the ship from London.

The accommodation of the *Foresight* had been changed considerably in the past few weeks because she too was expecting passengers – Lord Vaughan (whose wife had recently died), his physician Dr Trapham, and his chaplain and various servants, and also Sir Thomas Modyford, who had chosen her for his return to Jamaica instead of taking a more comfortable passage with Morgan in the *Jamaica Merchant*.

Lord Vaughan had already given Sir Harry written orders about the voyage to Jamaica, obviously suspicious of his deputy because under the terms of his commission Morgan could act as governor in Vaughan's absence. He later claimed that Morgan had told several people in London that he intended to get to the island first. He told Morgan 'to keep me in company and in no case be separated from me but by stress of weather'.

Vaughan was an optimist. The 522-ton *Foresight* was fresh out of the dockyard with a clean bottom, so she was a much faster ship than the bulky and smaller *Jamaica Merchant*, but Sir Harry was a practical man; he could not write two lines that rhymed, let alone a long prologue to a Dryden comedy, but there is little doubt that if he wanted to lose the *Foresight* he and Captain Joseph Knapman could find a way.

Yet it is highly probable that Vaughan and the *Foresight*'s captain saved him the bother: when the two ships weighed in the Downs the frigate, with her larger ship's company, was the first to get her anchors up, and she was under sail and passing the South Foreland before the *Jamaica Merchant*'s anchors had broken the surface. By the time Captain Knapman was passing the Foreland the *Foresight* was out of sight down the Channel. It is unlikely that Morgan had intended this to happen because, far from sailing on alone to make a fast passage to the West Indies, the *Jamaica Merchant* then joined a convoy sailing south and commanded by Sir Roger Strickland. Vaughan later claimed that the *Jamaica Merchant* only stayed with the convoy until she had sea room – probably until clear of Finisterre – before setting a course for Jamaica. In the meantime the *Foresight* 'lay by expecting five or six days'.

Captain Knapman passed clear of Madeira (whose governor later refused the *Foresight* any provisions), picked up the north-east trades, and steered for the Leeward Islands. He made a fast crossing and by the end of February the *Jamaica Merchant* was sailing along the south-western coast of Hispaniola, within two hundred miles of Jamaica. Quite why the ship should be so close to Île-à-Vache, the Cow Island which had so often been the buccaneers' rendezvous, has never been explained, but there was a sudden grinding beneath the *Jamaica Merchant*'s keel. Her bow rose and wind and waves slewed her round: she was aground on a reef close to the island. Knapman swore later he did not know what evil genius had led him there 'and never was any man more surprised considering the course they had steered'.

The ship came off the reef but began sinking fast, taking with her the guns, powder and shot intended for Port Royal's defences. Boats were hoisted out and all the passengers and crew were rowed over to Île-à-Vache, and the badly-damaged *Jamaica Merchant* finally sank in shallow water, not far from where the wreckage of the *Oxford* was scattered over the sea bed.

For the next few days Sir Harry Morgan fretted on the island: there were no privateers there and the only things they had been able to get from the *Jamaica Merchant* before she sank were food and water, muskets and documents. Finally a ship came in sight and Morgan recognized her as the 40-ton *Gift*, commanded by Captain Thomas Rogers, who had been with him on the Panama expedition and was now sailing with a French commission against the Spanish.

Rogers was startled to find his old chief – last seen just before he was taken off in the *Welcome* as a prisoner of State – stranded on the beach at Île-à-Vache, but for all that now a knight and the new lieutenant-governor of Jamaica.

On 6 March the *Gift* sailed into Port Royal, flying a British flag in place of the French, in honour of the occasion, and Sir Harry Morgan landed once again in Jamaica after an absence of almost exactly three years. Next day the Council met under Lynch and Sir Harry presented his documents. The first was the order revoking Sir Thomas's commission and the second was his own commission appointing him lieutenant-governor and saying that, in the absence of the new governor, he was to assume the powers. The Council agreed all was in order and Lynch handed over the island's administration.

Elizabeth Morgan had not gone to England to join her husband, so the reunion at Lawrencefield can be imagined, and one of the first things she discovered was that she was now Lady Morgan – her husband had received his knighthood within a few days of sailing from the Downs, so that despite being shipwrecked he had still arrived before any other ship that could have brought her the news.

There had been many changes: Elizabeth told him of the progress that had been made in clearing and planting on the new estate, and they had another nephew – Johanna and Henry Archbold had a son, although he was a weakly child. The two Byndloss boys, Thomas and Charles, were now lively youngsters, talking and sturdy, lucky to have survived the fevers that made childhood in the Tropics a gamble. And Anna Petronilla was expecting her third child.

Sir Henry's first days back in the island were a prolonged celebration: the planters saw his knighthood and commission as the King's tardy approval of the policies they had always advocated. There was still no sign of the *Foresight* and Lord Vaughan. Morgan inspected the island's defences and from people like Captain Rogers he had already heard that the Spanish had not changed their ways. Biscayners and Dutch privateers were busy along most coasts, armed with Spanish commissions. There were good pickings against the Spanish and Dutch for ships with French commissions, Rogers had told him, and the privateers' only fear at Tortuga was that a Dutch fleet might arrive – a distinct possibility now that England had signed a treaty with the United Provinces.

Morgan found Port Royal's fortifications crumbling, the regiments short of men and rarely exercised, and few ships available to defend the island. The defences were a monument to an unfortunate conjunction of Lynch's quarrels with the Assembly and his hopes for accord with the Spanish. As the man who had planned the early fortifications and knew better than any-one else how to mobilize the island's defences, Morgan decided to make a start. He called a Council on 11 March and the members ordered that as he was the commander-in-chief the great Seal should be placed in his hands, thus giving him the authority to act.

Finally, late on 12 March, the word came from the lookouts on Morant Point that the *Foresight* was at last approaching, and Sir Harry prepared his welcome as though he intended to leave no grounds for complaint from Lord Vaughan and was determined to show the elegant man from Restoration London that Jamaica was not backward in the social graces. The guns of Fort Charles and the batteries had been inspected and their crews were ready; flags were hoisted at every flagpole; Lynch, the members of the Council and the island's leading planters and merchants were warned to stand by. At the King's House in Port Royal – the original official residence, but unused for years – beds had been prepared with fresh linen and the servants had the menu for the governor's first dinner, because he would stay there a day or two before going on to his official residence in Spanish Town.

Early on 13 March the *Foresight* came into the harbour as the guns began booming out the long salute to the new governor. Morgan went out to greet Vaughan, but unfortunately there is no account of the meeting. Vaughan learned that not only had Morgan beaten him by a week, but had already been proclaimed through the streets as lieutenant-governor – and had been shipwrecked as well.

His Lordship's views on various island personalities were soon made known in his reports to London, but there is no record of how the islanders regarded their new governor. He was not a man whose appearance inspired confidence. He was obviously a sensualist; he had a fleshy face with thick lips and heavy jowls, the nose large with a wide bridge and the eyes set far apart. His hands were slender with long narrow fingers although now, as he ate and drank his way through these early days in the Tropics, they were spent mopping his face which perspired heavily under a long wig that reached below his shoulders.

On 17 March the Council met under Vaughan to start the serious business of government. The most important item on the agenda, normally a routine matter with a change of governor, was to receive from Lynch an account of the revenue. Sir Harry, reporting to the secretary of State in London in his capacity as commander-in-chief of the island's forces, said that the money in the treasury was found to be 'very short, and likewise his Majesty's stores so exhausted that there was found in all the stores but fourteen barrels of powder, which on occasion would not last three hours. Nevertheless, that shall not daunt me, for before I shall lose his Majesty's fortifications I will lose myself and a great many brave men more that will stand and fall by me in his Majesty's service; though they grumble much that their powder has been sold to the Spaniards by the late governor'.

Although the former governor had known he was to be superseded, Vaughan had arrived so unexpectedly that Lynch's accounts were far from up to date, and at the next Council meeting he had to ask for extra time. Vaughan agreed, but in these early days he was not impressed by his predecessor. He appointed a committee of three to audit the accounts, and two of them were certainly on Lynch's short list of enemies – Morgan and his brother-in-law, Robert Byndloss.

The coolness between Vaughan and Lynch very soon turned into a quarrel. Lynch had chartered the *Thomas and Francis* the previous year and put Captain George Gallop in command with a commission against the Dutch, sending her to sea with the *Flying Horse* privateer. Within a very short time they were back in Port Royal with a Dutch prize carrying 544 slaves. Shortly after that, Lynch had reported to London that several hundred slaves had just been sold in Jamaica for £22 each (presumably from the Dutch prize). Morgan later estimated that Captain Gallop and the commander of the privateer had made £7000.

Before there was any distribution of profits, however, a fifteenth of the value should have been set aside for the King and a tenth for the duke of York (who was, at this time, still Lord High Admiral). The trouble began for Lynch when the treasury accounts made no mention of the royal shares. No one criticized Lynch for chartering a ship and sending her off privateering; that he was later party to selling several hundred slaves captured from the Dutch raised no eyebrows. However, finding that the King and duke had been cheated was a convenient weapon for Lynch's enemies.

Sir Henry wasted no time in telling the secretary of State: 'The face of all things is most changed, and things go but indifferently between the General [Vaughan] and Sir Thos Lynch; nor can any one blame the General for there is the greatest cheat in the world intended to be put on the King about Captain Gallop's negro prize ... The General demanding the reason, Sir Thos answered he kept it for Captain Gallop, but,' Morgan commented acidly, 'if Gallop had come he would have answered it was condemned to the King. To keep people in the dark there was no registry kept of the fees of the condemnation ...'

Yet within a month Vaughan and Lynch had patched up their quarrel. There is no record about how it happened or how the missing money was recovered, but by 18 May Lord Vaughan was telling the secretary of State that he was very well satisfied with Lynch's 'prudent government and conduct of affairs'. Not only had the two men patched up their quarrel but both did their best to damage Morgan, Vaughan telling the secretary of State to refer to Lynch – who was returning to England – for details of recent events in the island. Lynch, he said, would also describe the 'unlucky shipwreck of Sir Henry Morgan and the loss of the King's stores occasioned by his particular ill conduct and wilful breach of his positive and written orders, and his behaviour and weakness since the meeting of the Assembly, which, with other follies, have so tired me that I am perfectly weary of him and think it for the King's service that he should be removed and the charge of so useless an officer saved'. If he had been given the authority to appoint a deputy, Vaughan wrote, he would choose Sir Thomas Lynch 'in preference to any other person'.

Lynch left for England on 24 May, taking Vaughan's dispatches with him, and no doubt satisfied that what had at first been a most unpromising encounter had later turned to his own advantage: he was delivering to London the letters from Lord Vaughan which he was sure would prove to the King and the secretary of State what a mistake they had made in appointing Morgan.

Sir Harry was happy enough to be back in Jamaica. Governors came and governors went, but he had two plantations, plenty of friends, bonny nephews and soon perhaps some nieces. He had a knighthood and behind him lay the fame that made him known as 'Morgan of Maracaibo' and then 'Morgan of Panama', and word had just been received from Cuba that the Queen Regent was to be warned as soon as he returned to the Indies. But for all that he had no children. Anna and Johanna were having children at regular intervals, but their eldest sister remained childless.

As he settled down again into the life of a plantation owner, Morgan saw that Sir Thomas Modyford had just been appointed the chief justice and his friends occupied most of the places on the Council, and because of this he became careless; he forgot that the sharp-eyed Vaughan was watching closely, waiting for the slightest mistake; that such men can always rely on tale-bearers. Nor were eyes only on Morgan; his close friends and relatives were also being watched.

Now they knew that he was back in Jamaica as lieutenant-governor, Sir Harry's old buccaneering friends were naturally anxious to see him again and relive old battles over a jug of rum, but many still held French commissions or had other reasons for being cautious about sailing into Port Royal. One such man was Captain John Edmunds, who had been with Sir Harry on various expeditions, although he had missed Panama. He sent a cautious note of inquiry and in return received a reply signed by Sir Harry assuring him in friendly terms of a welcome in any of the island's harbours and that Edmunds 'would receive all the privileges he could expect from him'. That letter never reached Edmunds; instead it ended up in Vaughan's hands, and he sent it to the secretary of State with another concerning Sir Harry's brother-in-law, Robert Byndloss.

The French governor of Tortuga, Bertrand d'Ogeron, was issuing French commissions against the Spanish and Dutch to any privateers requesting them, and as an *ex officio* admiral of France he was entitled to a share of any purchase. The privateersmen, however, were smart enough to sell what they could in Jamaica. The open sale of prizes was forbidden, but there were enough quiet harbours and sheltered bays for privateers to unload slaves, liquor, tobacco, cloth – indeed, any articles with a ready sale in Port Royal.

By using Port Royal the privateers were avoiding paying d'Ogeron his share, and as he was shortly returning to France for a visit he wrote to Robert Byndloss, who had trained as a lawyer, asking him to collect his shares and giving him power of attorney. A copy of that letter was soon in Lord Vaughan's hands.

Vaughan's strength in the island lay in the fact that he alone appointed the members of the Council and he could expel them too. He had been instructed to increase its size to twelve, and he had been careful not to appoint Morgan a member. However, when he reported to London the death of Major-General Bannister, the Council president, he was instructed to appoint Morgan in his place.

Those instructions arrived in September and Vaughan immediately wrote a heated reply to Sir Joseph Williamson.'I am every day more convinced of [Sir Henry's] imprudence and unfitness to have anything to do with the civil government, and of what hazards the island may run in so dangerous a succession,' he told the secretary of State. 'Sir Henry has made himself and his authority so cheap at the Port, drinking and gaming at the taverns, that I intend to remove there speedily myself for the reputation of the island and the security of that place, though I pretend it is only to change the air, having lately had a fever.'

Morgan had drunk and gamed at Port Royal's taverns regularly for seventeen of the last twenty years; with little more than a wave of the hand he could send Port Royal's able-bodied men tumbling on board the privateers to follow him anywhere. Now Vaughan, the man characterized as 'one of the lewdest fellows of the age' by Pepys (a broad-minded but shrewd judge), was about to remove himself to the King's House at Port Royal, to improve the moral tone of authority, if not of the town itself. 'His Majesty's speedy resolution of what I have proposed would exceedingly satisfy all the sober and wealthy people, who are very doubtful of what may happen in case of my death or absence,' Vaughan concluded.

By December the secretary of State's reply told Vaughan that he should make up his differences with Morgan and, Sir Joseph said, he was writing to give Morgan the same advice. The result was that Sir Harry attended the Council's next meeting and was sworn in as a member, a satisfying Christmas present. By coincidence Vaughan read out a letter just received from the King: all privateers with French commissions against Spain were to be recalled. There was no alternative but for the Council to order proclamations to this effect to be read at Spanish Town and Port Royal.

It was another case of Whitehall's unerring instinct for bad timing, and the Council's secretary, Peter Beckford, wrote at once to the secretary of State to warn him that: 'My Lord's great trouble is to carry himself even with the Spaniards, for they are daily taking all the ships they can master, and are very high,' and 'were not the French from Tortuga daily galling them with privateers, we should conclude ourselves in some danger ...' The blow hot, blow cold instructions from London left Vaughan in a difficult position: he had come out with orders to issue commissions if he could get no compensation from the Spanish; now he was told to recall the very Port Royal ships which were defending the island, albeit under French flags.

Most of Vaughan's domestic problems were, by now, coming from the Assembly. The new speaker was Samuel Long, who ..ad been removed as chief justice to make room for Modyford. He and fellow members had a procedural dispute with Vaughan which resulted in the governor proroguing the Assembly for six months. Vaughan clearly considered that the King, House of Lords and House of Commons in England had a parallel in Jamaica – governor, Council and Assembly. His autocratic attitude resulting from this naturally made him very unpopular, and it was very obvious that he 'made haste to grow as rich as his Government would let him'.

At the beginning of February 1676 Sir Harry had received a letter from the secretary of State asking him various questions concerning the island. The letter was very delayed and at the time Sir Joseph wrote he had no idea how bad the relationship between Morgan and Vaughan had become. The buccaneer's reply was bland. For the letter and all other favours, he wrote:

> I render your honour all the humble thanks that a loyal and obliging heart can express. I am very sorry that I cannot answer your commands therein expressed; for truly the little share I have in the Government makes me incapable of giving your honour any perfect account of the state of the island which his Excellency hath not as yet been pleased to give me leave to see; and as for corresponding with our neighbours the French and Spaniards, he hath positively commanded the contrary and I have ever loved obedience to my superior, therefore never will presume to break his orders: but if your honour thinks it may be, as I am apt to believe for his Majesty's service, be pleased to let me receive his orders therein by your honour.

In the meantime Morgan was looking round for yet another estate. Lawrencefield and the larger plantation at Morgan Valley were prospering, probably because he employed good overseers, and he finally decided to apply for 4000 acres in the parish of St Elizabeth, flatter land than any he owned and better suited for planting sugar.

By now his sister-in-law Anna was pregnant for the fourth time, after having had her third child, a daughter, who was named Anna Maria, the first name after her mother, grandmother and great grandmother. The Archbolds had their second son, and he was called Henry. Sir Harry and Lady Morgan were the godparents, and the baby, although not born with a silver spoon in his mouth, had the next best thing: he, like Robert Byndloss's second son, had been born under the doting eye of the admiral of the Brethren of the Coast, and the two second sons would inherit his wealth while their elder brothers would inherit from their fathers. As if to emphasize the personal tragedy of Henry and Elizabeth Morgan's childless-ness – a longing reflected in his will – Johanna announced that she was expecting her third child and soon all the Morgans, Byndlosses and Archbolds would be driving in their coaches to St Catherine's Church for the christenings.

Lord Vaughan was angry about the privateers: it galled him to think that ships owned in Port Royal and commanded by local men were sailing under French flags and with Tortuga commissions. It was illegal; it was in defiance of the King's proclamation recalling the ships. But Vaughan, like the majority of men of limited intelligence who spend years in politics without realizing they are merely dabbling, failed to understand that for practical purposes if a law cannot be enforced it should be erased from the statute books; that having town criers bellowing proclamations was merely crying 'wolf' with a ruffle of drums.

Yet Vaughan's personality would not allow him to be anything but an autocrat: he saw himself as in effect the king of his island; the Council and Assembly existed to enforce his orders, although the privateers ignored him. The Spanish did not behave much better: he tried to establish friendly arrangements with the governor of Cuba, for example, but every week brought news of Spanish privateers and Biscayners capturing British ships and taking prisoners to Havana, executing many for alleged piracy and condemning others to a life of slavery.

Vaughan ordered the confiscation of a Jamaica ship accused of landing goods without reporting to custom officials, and this was followed by an action on behalf of the Royal African Company. A ship from West Africa with three hundred slaves on board was seized at sea and brought into Port Royal, where it was found she did not have a licence from the Company. Vaughan ordered her to be condemned as a prize, which meant that the case had to come before the Admiralty Court, which comprised Sir Henry Morgan, Colonel Beeston and Robert Byndloss. They heard the evidence – and dismissed the case. A furious Vaughan ordered a new trial.

Vaughan now produced what he no doubt considered a strong card against Sir Harry. In a letter to the secretary of State he said flatly: 'What I most resent, and which I consider as part of my duty to lay before your honour, is that I find Sir Henry, contrary to his duty and trust, endeavours to set up privateering, and has obstructed all my designs and purposes as to those who do use that curse of life.'

Describing how privateers had gone to Tortuga and taken French commissions, he claimed that Morgan had recommended certain of them to d'Ogeron. Not only that, Vaughan claimed, but he had given his brother-in-law, Robert Byndloss, the task of collecting the French government's percentage of the prizes.

He then told the secretary of State about Captain John Deane. The *St David* had arrived in Port Royal after a long absence under the command of Captain Deane. The governor, noting that he 'had the impertinence to come to town', promptly had him arrested and charged with piracy. Vaughan decided to take no more chances with the Admiralty Court of which he was, as governor, the chief judge. So he tried Deane himself and, perhaps not surprisingly, found him guilty of piracy and sentenced him to death. There was an immediate outcry in Port Royal, both at the way that the trial had been conducted and the actual treatment of Deane. It alarmed Vaughan because it came from the shop owners and tavernkeepers, planters and merchants. Yet there was no question in his mind that he might have been wrong: the protests echoing round Port Royal and Spanish Town must, therefore, be inspired by Sir Harry and Byndloss.

For all that, it would be up to the Lords of Trade to decide whether or not John Deane ended up hanged from a gibbet, condemned as a pirate, and all the depositions and court records were sent to London (where they probably did as much as anything to cause Lord Vaughan's sudden replacement).

Vaughan continued collecting what evidence he could against Morgan and Byndloss, planning a showdown in which he hoped to have the Council's backing. By July he was ready and he chose an ordinary Council meeting. Sir Henry was not told of the meeting, so did not attend, but Byndloss was warned to be present because the Council would want to question him about his rôle as agent for the governor of Tortuga in Port Royal.

Eleven members attended and Vaughan presided. He had on the table in front of him certified copies of documents, originals of letters and depositions. He then played what he regarded as his trump cards: he told the Council that Morgan had been cooperating with privateers – he had the documents to prove it – and writing letters to them using the governor's name and authority without permission. With that, Vaughan produced a copy of a letter he alleged had been written to Captain Thomas Rogers, who had rescued Morgan and the rest of the survivors from the *Jamaica Merchant*. He claimed that similar letters had also been sent to Captain John Barnett, who had also taken his little *Virgin Queen* on the Panama raid, and to Captains Edward Neville, George Wright and several others.

These letters, Vaughan told the Council, were signed by Sir Harry and said that he was commanded by the governor (referred to in the letters as the captain-general) to tell all privateers, French as well as English, that they would find as much freedom as before in Port Royal and they could visit 'with abundance of safety'. Not only that, but Sir Henry's former secretary, Charles Barré, had sailed off to see the various privateers and do business with them. Lord Vaughan then ordered Barré to appear for questioning. Barré told the Council that while working for Sir Henry he had indeed copied the letters to Barnett and others. There were actually two letters, one to Barnett and a second for the other captains. But Barré denied ever negotiating with privateersmen on behalf of Sir Henry.

Sir Harry was brought in as soon as Vaughan finished his accusations. Morgan had no idea what had been going on: knowing nothing of a Council meeting, he had been told to wait upon the governor at a particular time. Now Vaughan asked him a series of questions and Peter Beckford carefully noted his replies. Not surprisingly, Sir Harry was furious: he had no chance to cross-examine Charles Barré in front of the Council and was not told of any particular charges. He could see that Vaughan intended to send the minutes of the Council meeting to the Lords of Trade as both charge and evidence.

Sir Henry said very little: he answered Vaughan's questions but made no defence to the Council. 'I can only say, it not being in my power to make my Lord prove it,' Morgan wrote later to the new secretary of the Lords of Trade, Sir Henry Coventry, 'that I never since I came back here wrote a line to any of the privateers; therefore the copies sent [to London] are forged on purpose to my prejudice ...'

As soon as he had finished questioning Morgan, the governor made his charges against Byndloss, telling the Council that Byndloss was acting for the governor of Tortuga. Vaughan then asked Byndloss for a written answer, regarded his behaviour in refusing as insolent, and ordered the provost marshal to arrest him. Byndloss finally handed over a written defence to avoid being taken into custody.

'As for Colonel Byndloss,' Sir Harry told Coventry, 'I know nothing of crime in him, but his being related to me, for he lives twenty miles from Port Royal, has a wife and five or six children, and one of the best estates in the island, therefore he is an understanding man and would not venture that hazard and estate against nothing.' He concluded: 'My unhappiness is that I serve a superior here that is jealous of all my action and puts himself to study my ruin.'

With Vaughan's charges made, the Council adjourned and Morgan and Byndloss prepared their defence. This would take the form of letters to the Lords of Trade, with depositions. All the documents, the two men decided, would be taken to London in the next ship by Byndloss's brother John: he would then be available to answer any of Their Lordships' questions.

The first thing Sir Harry did was to get hold of Charles Barré. It then transpired that although Barré had told Vaughan and the Council the truth it was only part of the story. It is not clear whether the rest of it had been ignored by the governor or Barré, but the former secretary promptly made a deposition, duly signed before a magistrate. This said that Sir Harry had drafted the letters to Barnett, Rogers and the others, and then passed them to Vaughan for approval, which the governor withheld, so they were never sent. In other words, the letters which Vaughan had produced to the Council were simply drafts.

Morgan then wrote to Coventry asking the Lords of Trade to suspend judgment until papers establishing his innocence arrived in the next ship from Jamaica. Knowing how various influences worked at Court, he added: 'But if His Majesty should be deaf to all, and these things should give his Majesty occasion to put me out, I hope he will be graciously pleased to order that I may be tried here at the Court of King's Bench, where the witnesses are.'

Governor Morgan

Lord Vaughan was soon very concerned with the actual safety of Jamaica. At a time when he had no privateers and only one frigate, the *Foresight*, to defend the island he heard that Vice-Admiral Jacob Binkes had re-captured Cayenne from the French on 9 May. Binkes had seven ships of the line, five frigates and a fireship. Where would his fleet go next after such a success? Did Britain's treaty with the United Provinces still hold? And the French: they would send out a large fleet to retake Cayenne, but could Vaughan be sure of French intentions? Meanwhile the Spanish continued capturing British ships, ignoring Vaughan's repeated protests.

By this time Vaughan was becoming increasingly concerned about his influence in England. Despite his various grumbles, complaints and sugges-tions, the Lords of Trade took very little notice of him. His early references to Morgan had resulted in almost a snub from the secretary of State. Now in Jamaica itself he was facing trouble from people signing petitions for clemency on behalf of Captain John Deane, who was still in jail and under sentence of death. The leading planters had already protested, but Vaughan decided they could be discounted as friends of Morgan. Then the petitions from the ordinary folk in Spanish Town and Port Royal began to arrive at the governor's residence. He knew that if a group of people took it into their heads to break down the jail doors and set Deane free, there was little to stop them.

Finally Vaughan granted Deane a pardon (which, as governor, he was entitled to do), saying that this was due to the man's repentance and the number of petitions. He seemed unaware that he had now acted as prose-cutor, jury, judge and finally governor – rôles which not even the King could combine.

A month later he received a letter from the Lords of Trade telling him flatly that the papers describing the case against Deane showed the trial was 'not warranted by the laws of England'. Pirates, they said, should be tried by a commission of oyer and terminer, not by civil law. The King had been advised that Captain Deane's execution should be stopped. Vaughan could only reply very lamely that the trial had led to the 'reclaiming' of several privateers, and that anyway he had pardoned Deane a month earlier. 'If I was not right in the law, no great harm is done, it being very prudential and seasonable at that time to do what I did,' he added.

He counted the weeks until he should hear from Their Lordships about his charges in Council against Sir Henry Morgan, but his luck was out: the Privy Council read the record of the case and referred it to the Lords of Trade, requesting a report. This was the standard procedure in such cases and normally Their Lordships would request more facts if necessary.

John Byndloss asked to be allowed to be present when it was discussed and his petition was read at a meeting on 2 November. That was all Their Lordships did until October a year later, when they decided they would have to make 'a further examination of the whole matter'.

A resident of Jamaica writing to the earl of Carlisle blamed Vaughan's troubles with the Assembly on his 'closing with Sir Thomas Modyford and neglecting Sir Henry Morgan and his brother [in-law] Byndloss', and said that from then on 'all things went heavy that concerned him there, and forced upon him little violences, which have aggravated matters against him'. This letter shows the great mistake that Vaughan had made when he first set foot in Jamaica in showing that he had been influenced by Modyford – with whom he had sailed from England – because the Assembly could remember only too well that while he was governor Modyford had not called elections for years, ignoring the Assembly completely.

At the end of September, Sir Harry Morgan acquired his third plantation when the patent was drawn up for the 4000 acres he had requested in St Elizabeth's parish. Slaves were bought, overseers appointed, and the task of clearing the virgin land and preparing it for growing sugar began – work which cost between £2 and £3 an acre. By now, owning nearly 6000 acres, Sir Harry had become a considerable landowner, although by far the most property was owned at this time by the Modyfords, with Sir Thomas Modyford's late brother, Sir James, having been granted 5300 acres, while one of Sir Thomas's sons had 6000. Lord Vaughan was also very busy acquiring land: by the time he left the island he was its largest landowner.

While Sir Harry increased his landholdings, both Byndloss and Archbold increased their families. Anna Byndloss's fourth child was another daughter, who was called Catherina Mary, the second name being in honour of her godmother, although Lady Morgan was better known as Dame Elizabeth. Johanna Archbold's third child was another son.

Sir Harry and Lady Morgan had also been the godparents of another baby, Richard, the first son of a couple who had recently settled in the island, Roger and Ann Elletson. A barrister, Elletson had arrived in Jamaica with a letter of recommendation to Lord Vaughan from the secretary of State, but he had not formed part of Lord Vaughan's 'court' and was soon doing much of the legal work of the planters. By the time his son was three years old, he was the island's attorney-general; by the time the boy was eleven, Elletson was the chief justice.

It was not long before her sisters were telling Lady Morgan that they were pregnant yet again – Anna expecting her fifth child, and Johanna her fourth. With seven children among two sisters, five of them boys, Sir Harry and Lady Morgan can be forgiven for any bitterness they felt at their own lack of offspring.

The new year, 1677, began with little change in the international scene, (although the word 'international' would not come into use for another 103 years when it appeared in Jeremy Bentham's *Principles of Morals and Legislation*). Despite his attempts to get on good terms with the Spanish, suppress the privateers and hang the pirates, Vaughan was soon writing yet again to tell the Lords of Trade that British ships were being plundered on the high seas by Spanish vessels. For months he had been collecting depositions sworn by Britons, mostly escaped seamen, which gave a grim picture of the waters of the Greater Antilles. The villain, according to Vaughan, was the governor of Havana, who was ordering the captures and holding crews as slaves, treating them barbarously.

These reports from Vaughan and the depositions, combined with protests from shipowners in London and Bristol, slowly had an effect on the King and Privy Council, who realized that their policy of attempting a friendship with Spain in the West Indies was collapsing not because of any failure on their part but because of deliberate action in Madrid. They saw that the policy started by Sir Thomas Lynch in November five years earlier had resulted in Spain assuming she had a free hand to harass and humbug British ships in the West Indies. In the island itself the people had long since lost faith in Whitehall; now, with the permanent quarrel between the Assembly and Vaughan, they had also lost faith in the governor's ability to protect Jamaica.

It was equally clear that Vaughan understood none of this. On the one hand he wrote heated protests about Spanish captures and the villainy of the governor of Havana; on the other, in the name of friendship with Spain, he antagonized the planters and accused many of the sea captains – who could, in an emergency, provide the privateers to defend the island – of piracy.

A series of events finally stirred the King and Privy Council into action. It began when the owners of a Liverpool ship, the *Diligence*, protested directly to the Privy Council. Their ship had gone to the Bay of Campeche, loaded with logwood and cocoa and sailed again. She had then been stopped on the high seas by a Spanish ship which took her cargo and provisions and stripped her rigging. This was such a clear breach of the treaty that the Privy Council acted at once, ordering the ambassador in Madrid to make a protest and demanding an explanation from the Spanish ambassador in London.

The ambassador was indignant when the secretary of State tackled him about the *Diligence*: what about the *Buen Jesus de las Almas*? he asked. She had just been seized by a British ship commanded by Captain John Barnett while on her way to Hispaniola, and 46,000 pieces of eight (worth £11,500) had been taken.

Sir Joseph knew nothing about the *Buen Jesus* and requested a report from Sir Thomas Lynch, who had just returned from Jamaica. Lynch replied that the affair had nothing to do with Jamaica. The privateersmen 'were not English nor came into any port of Jamaica to the knowledge of the Governor. Barnett had Frenchmen on board the said privateer, a French commission, fought under French colours, had the prize condemned and divided in a French port, when at the same time the Governor of Jamaica was taking great pains and was at great charge to retrieve her in order to [make] a restitution.'

By the time the Privy Council received Lynch's reply many more reports had arrived from Vaughan and they had also heard the views of one of their members, the earl of Carlisle, the man who was to have replaced Lynch, and was now being considered as Vaughan's possible successor.

Carlisle had received from a planter a long and well-reasoned letter which said: 'I remember upon our discourse of it, Sir Henry Morgan did always say to Colonel Byndloss, and the men with us, that if he were now a privateer for the Spaniards, as he had been against them, he would not doubt to ruin the whole country, by burning and destroying the sea-coast plantations ...' He urged the earl to come out as governor if offered the post, saying that Morgan and Byndloss 'are the men who have the true and most prevalent interest in the country; Sir Henry from his eminent and famed exploits in those parts, together with his generous and undesigned way of conversing with them, Colonel Byndloss by the same generosity and frankness of conversation, mixed with one of the most able understandings I have ever met with ...'

He went on to give a remarkably prescient warning of the danger from the French 'who, since Sir Henry Morgan showed them the way to take Panama, are the only people in these parts we should fear ... I must confess I think there is no difference at our being at war with Spain, and suffering others effectually to be so; for should Panama fall into French hands, the manufacturers of France would supply the South Sea, and all the world would be theirs ...' Although Carlisle's correspondent was alarmed by a powerful French fleet in the West Indies the Privy Council were not concerned at this time that France had any greater aim than holding what they already had.

By 11 July the Privy Council, considering it had enough information to take action, decided that the Spanish ambassador should be warned that 'if some speedy action' was not taken the King would be 'forced by the clamours of his subjects to use such means for the reparation as honour and justice obliges him to . . .' The logwood ships were suffering worst, and the secretary of State told the ambassador 'that his Majesty's subjects may have free liberty of trading in logwood' which was not contraband and frequently sold to British subjects 'by the Spaniards in those parts'.

Sir Henry Coventry had an unsatisfactory reply from the Spanish ambassador and sent orders to the ambassador in Madrid to demand satisfaction on behalf of the logwood ships and to say that unless compensation was paid in the case of the *Virgin*, the latest ship seized, the King was considering 'granting them letters of reprisal and must give effectual order therein, if speedy justice be not done therein'.

This hardening of the government's attitude followed orders which were already on their way to Vaughan from the Lords of Trade: he was to apply to Havana for the release of any English prisoners held there. A similar request was sent to the Spanish government through Godolphin.

Unaware of the slow change of policy in London, Vaughan continued writing his reports. In an annual survey of Jamaica's trade he noted that several merchants in Port Royal 'have correspondents at Bristol, Chester, Plymouth, Southampton, who supply servants, coarse cloths, provisions, iron-work'. It was in the interest of Jamaica to encourage the trade of Ireland and 'to disappoint those of New England, who never bring any servants or will take off any goods, but in exchange for their fish, peas and pork carry away our plate and pieces of eight'. However, the island was beginning to get a good store of meat and 'they begin to leave off that trade. No vessel comes from New York these two months'.

The Customs reports for the year 1676–7 show the extent of the trade between colonies and London. Barbados was by far the most important – eighty-five ships had arrived with 9880 tons of cargo, while forty had sailed. Jamaica came next, sending thirty-five ships with 2900 tons while twenty-seven left London. The exports from Jamaica to other places told a vastly different story: large quantities of sugar were sent to Virginia, Campeche and Carolina; tobacco was shipped to Campeche and Curaçao, cotton to New England and fustick to New York.

A new cloud on Vaughan's horizon was the need to call an Assembly. The laws passed two years earlier had been sent to London but since then, despite frequent reminders, he had not received the sanction from the Lords of Trade to continue them, so another Assembly would have to pass them again. He called it in April and ran into trouble almost immediately over the procedure which the Assembly wanted to follow but which Vaughan ruled was unparliamentary. The Assembly retaliated by refusing to pass a money bill, which meant that Vaughan had no funds with which to run his administration.

An exasperated Vaughan wrote to London in May requesting powers to suspend members of the Council – at the moment the Council itself had to agree before this could be done – and, he wrote, most of them were 'Old Standers and officers of Cromwell's army'. He said that if he was given seven or eight months' leave of absence to return to England he could explain matters to the King.

He had just written that letter and sent it off with the returning *Foresight* when his troubles with pirates began once again, with a cosmopolitan vengeance. He discovered that several owners of coastal plantations had recently bought 150 slaves from a privateer which had landed them secretly. He promptly seized the slaves while inquiries were made. The planters immediately protested that the governor had no right to take them, and Vaughan gradually managed to piece the story together. A British ship commanded by Captain James Browne, a Scot, had sailed from Port Royal with a French commission against the Dutch. Close to Curaçao he had sighted and captured a Dutch ship, the *Golden Sun*, which was carrying slaves. He took off 150, selling them in Jamaica.

Vaughan decided that the slaves were 'goods piratically taken' and instructed the Admiralty Court to condemn them. Once he could get his hands on Browne, the Scot would also be charged with breaking the Royal African Company's monopoly of the slave trade – only six months earlier Vaughan had been reminded officially of the Company's monopoly and that no one without a licence could import into Jamaica any 'blacks, gold, elephants' teeth, malagetta or any other commodities'.

Almost overnight Vaughan found that most of the Assembly and Council were against him. They did not sympathize with Browne taking a Dutch ship but they disagreed with Vaughan's seizure of slaves for which the planters had paid. Vaughan was determined to restore the slaves to their rightful Dutch owners, though for the time being it was hard to determine who they were because the captain of the *Golden Sun* had been killed when Browne captured the ship. The argument between Vaughan and the planters went on for several weeks until the middle of July.

Over on the Spanish Main at Santa Marta, just north of Cartagena, the bishop was a man famous in Spain's New World, Dr Lucas Fernández y Piedrahita, who was a creole. Born in Bogotá, in New Granada (now Colombia), he had just been appointed to the See of Panama, and in June 1677 he was packing all his possessions ready to begin the journey. Suddenly a squadron of privateers arrived off the town and within a few hours they had captured it. Their leader was a Frenchman, Captain Lagarde, but with him were two English captains, John Coxon and William Barnes, who had French commissions. Coxon had been a privateersman all his life; Peter Beckford had already reported to Whitehall that Coxon was 'hovering' round the coast of Jamaica and attempts to capture him had failed (within two years he led an expedition overland to attack Panama).

With the city in their hands, the privateersmen demanded a ransom, taking the bishop as a hostage, but before the ransom was paid three Spanish ships arrived from Cartagena with five hundred soldiers, so the pirates had to fight their way back to their ships with what purchase they had, and their hostage.

France was at war with Spain, so Captain Lagarde had broken no laws, and Coxon and Barnes had French commissions and were sailing under French flags. They all decided, for reasons far from clear, to make for Port Royal, where they arrived early in July apparently expecting to be welcomed as heroes. Instead Vaughan ordered the ships to leave the island after releasing the bishop, who was taken to the governor's residence as a guest while a ship was found to take him back to Santa Marta. Sir Harry Morgan, equally anxious to show him courtesy, presented the bishop with some richly-worked pontifical robes which he had seized in his raid on Panama.

To Vaughan's relief, the raid on Santa Marta outraged the Jamaica planters, although it was probably the arrival of Dr Lucas that brought home the danger of having British captains sailing with French commissions, attacking Spanish cities and bringing their purchase to Port Royal. The Assembly met and passed a hurriedly-drafted law forbidding anyone from Jamaica to serve under 'a foreign prince' against a country with which England was at peace. The penalty for breaking the law was death, but the Assembly allowed a period of three months during which privateersmen could return and receive a pardon. When the terms were made known in Tortuga, scores of privateersmen came back. Many of them had been on the recent Santa Marta raid, although Captain John Coxon was not among them because he was already planning a raid on Panama and the South Sea.

Vaughan was then informed that Captain James Browne, who had captured the Dutch *Golden Sun* and sold the slaves, had sailed into Port Royal, having heard of the new law and pardons. He at once had Browne and eight of his men arrested and charged with piracy. Within two or three days they were all found guilty and sentenced to death, despite their plea of immunity under the new law. Browne was Vaughan's real target, so he reprieved the eight seamen and signed the warrant so that Browne could be hanged the next day.

The Scottish captain, who had come into Port Royal in good faith, promptly appealed to the Assembly – which happened to be in session – claiming his life and freedom under their new Act. The Assembly elected a committee to go to the governor and request a week's stay of execution, so that they could consider Browne's petition.

Lord Vaughan would not receive them. The Assembly debated this snub and then sent its committee back to repeat the request. Vaughan then gave them his answer in writing, and it showed he was determined not to give an inch. He had just pardoned eight of the men, he wrote, but 'cannot in justice think Captain Browne a fit object of mercy'. He believed that 'hindering the sentence of execution will be of evil example and bad consequence'.

Yet it was the consequences rather than the actual execution that alarmed the Assembly, who immediately warned Vaughan in writing that if the execution took place 'all our privateers [who are still] out may think this Act a snare, and possibly it may make those already in [Port Royal] go out again, as they do not enjoy the security they expected and so become most dangerous enemies'. In the whole of his time in Jamaica Vaughan had shown neither flexibility of mind nor wisdom, and his reply, concerning his honour, was typical: he had already given his decision in writing and did not share the Assembly's 'fear of discouraging the privateers'.

The thoroughly enraged Assembly then realized that Browne had said that the court had ignored his plea for immunity under the Assembly's new Act. That was enough to allow the Assembly to act. A resolution was promptly passed ordering that the execution be delayed. Colonel Beeston, the speaker, issued his warrant to the provost marshal ordering him 'in the King's name' not to carry out the execution 'notwithstanding any warrant issued'. The chief justice granted a writ of habeas corpus and the speaker instructed the provost marshal to obey the writ and produce Browne.

Vaughan, determined that Browne should not escape, whatever the Assembly and the chief justice should decide, sent orders to the jail where Browne was held, 'Whereupon', the Assembly's journal recorded, 'the fellow was hanged half an hour after'.

Sir Thomas Lynch wrote to the secretary of State: 'The [provost] marshal came with an order signed by the Speaker to observe the chief justice's writ of habeas corpus which had been granted, but superseded by the Governor's order [for the execution]. My Lord resented this proceeding and immediately sent for the Assembly, after which reproving he dissolved.'

Lord Vaughan had done things that were beyond the power of the King and which were more in keeping with the actions of a vicious child, quite apart from the fact that he did not have the authority to try Browne in the first place – a view taken by the chief justice and the Assembly. The execution was perilously close to judicial murder.

When the Privy Council debated the Jamaica Assembly's act which led to privateers coming in, it had doubts and delayed giving its approval, deciding that the Act should be laid aside 'because thereby the privateers would be terrified from coming in'. This meant that not being confirmed within two years, it would lapse. The decision on this Act was, however, a very minor one for the Lords of Trade because far-reaching decisions had just been made about Jamaica's future which would bring the island close to revolt by removing its right to pass its own laws. The present constitution was far from efficient but it was the best one possible in the circumstances; an acceptable compromise between time, distance and local needs. When a governor quarrelled with the Assembly, the House sometimes passed quirkish acts, but each counterbalanced the other, with the Lords of Trade always in the background as a referee.

Some of the Assembly's laws passed during Vaughan's governorship were, however, too quirkish for Their Lordships, who did not realize that they were deliberate attempts to aggravate the governor. Nor was the Privy Council's understanding of the situation helped by their frequent consultations with Sir Thomas Lynch.

Their Lordships had to look no farther than Ireland to find what seemed to them a perfect solution to the constitutional problem, although their reasoning appears not to have gone beyond the conclusion that since Ireland was an island and Jamaica was an island, both could and should be ruled in the same way. In Ireland, Poynings' Law, which had been passed in 1494, ensured that the colonists had no power of their own; their parliament could consider and pass only acts sent to them from London by the Privy Council.

This reversal of the present situation in Jamaica had one crippling drawback: the acts sent out would have little or no relevance to the situation in the tropical island; they would be drafted by tired time-servers in Whitehall, shuffling their way to their pensions, knowing nothing of Jamaica's problems. And, of course, acts suggested by the governor and drafted in London, would be subject to the same delays as under the old system.

Having decided that in future Jamaica's laws would be made in England, the Lords of Trade made a start on the forty or so which Vaughan had sent to London during the last two years and which had not yet been sanctioned. An immediate stylistic alteration to delight the bureaucratic mind was made – instead of beginning acts with 'Governor, Council and Representatives assembled', the phrase would now refer to the 'King's Most Excellent Majesty by and with the consent of the General Assembly ...' Sir Thomas Lynch was consulted about the new system and, when he advised against it, telling the Lords of Trade that the people of Jamaica would oppose it, he was ignored.

Their Lordships realized that the running battle between Vaughan and the Assembly was a permanent part of the Jamaican political scene and he would have to be replaced. They considered once again the earl of Carlisle, who was far from enthusiastic. It was one thing to be going out as governor four years ago with Sir Harry Morgan as his deputy; it was quite another to go out with the task of forcing Poynings' Law on the colonists. Sir

Edward Poynings had been solving quite a different problem in Ireland nearly two hundred years earlier ...

Carlisle was forty-nine years old and a man of considerably more experience in international affairs than Vaughan: he had spent two years as ambassador to Russia, Denmark and Sweden, had fought with the Roundheads, been made a peer by Cromwell (Baron Gisland and Viscount Morpeth) and was now Deputy Earl Marshal of England. Finally he agreed to go out, and he also agreed to Sir Harry continuing as lieutenant-governor. The Lords of Trade no doubt realized that Morgan was by far the most popular man on the island, and Carlisle would need every available ally to get the new constitution accepted.

Meanwhile the warnings about France in the West Indies given by the earl of Carlisle's correspondent began to take on a significance. Relations which were already strained became almost inflamed when in November the duke of York's eldest daughter, Princess Mary, married William, Prince of Orange, who was the French King's most determined enemy. The duke of York was the heir to the throne, and Louis could see the possibility of William and Mary succeeding in eventually uniting Holland and England in a powerful alliance against France.

The French fleet under Count d'Estrées, which had recaptured Cayenne and lost an action against Vice-Admiral Binkes at Tobago, had come back across the Atlantic in late September and was reported in London to be refitting in Brest. There was talk of twenty large ships, with many privateers, and the fleet would be carrying 1500 soldiers. When it sailed from Brest on 7 October it was only too clear in Whitehall that it could easily capture Barbados, Antigua, Nevis, St Kitts and Montserrat on the way out and Jamaica and Bermuda on the way back, particularly since it could rouse out the Tortuga privateers as well as those sailing with it from Brest. The Lords of Trade sent out warnings to the islands but they could only guess at d'Estrées' orders. Barbados soon heard that the ships had arrived off Tobago.

While Their Lordships hurried on with the task of revising the forty acts, the country's relations with France were growing worse – Lord Carlisle was later to comment on 'my departure much pressing upon the expectation of war'. His commission as governor was signed on 1 March, and it was decided to send out two companies of men with him, one raised by a commission given to Carlisle, the other by a commission to Morgan. Carlisle was then given a warrant allowing him 'to cause drums to be beat about the city of London for raising two hundred men for service in Jamaica'.

The Navy Board prepared the 40-gun frigate *Jersey* to carry out the earl and his wife Anne. The *Jersey* was the same size as the *Assistance* and had been built at Maldon twenty-four years earlier. A second frigate would carry the bulk of the troops, and both ships would stay in Jamaica during the present emergency.

In Jamaica the first few weeks of the year 1678 had been uneventful, but they were the quiet before the storm. Vaughan had little to do, apart from listen to occasional disturbing reports of the French. He had sent the Assembly packing – one of its last acts was to cut Sir Harry Morgan's salary from £600 a year to £300 – and Vaughan busied himself with making sure that his plantations were being cleared properly. By now he was the island's largest landowner – he had 7737 acres, all in the parish of St Mary.

By February Vaughan received a hint from London that he might be replaced and he made his plans accordingly. Documents had to be drawn up under the Great Seal, and for reasons best known to himself he wanted to keep everything secret, as though to make a play of it with the success of the last act depending on the timing.(Dryden's comedy *The Kind Keeper of Limberham*, produced this year, was in fact dedicated to Vaughan.)

He called a meeting of the Council on 11 March and told the eight startled members who were present that he was leaving for England almost at once and he had given the deputy governor his instructions. Then, as if feeling the need for explanations, Vaughan said that since March no quit rents had been received (in Carlisle's first year these would amount to £913) and for eleven months he had received nothing for his administration's expenses. With that he left the room. Three days later, on 14 March, his ship sailed for England, three years to the day after he had first set foot on the wharf at Port Royal.

The French are Coming

Sir Harry Morgan, now forty-three, had been in his post as acting governor of Jamaica for less than three weeks when the warning arrived from the Lords of Trade in London that there was danger of a French attack. The news came late on 1 April 1678 and Morgan called a Council meeting for the next day, when every member was present to hear him take the oath as commander-in-chief and to discuss the major item on the agenda, 'the apprehension of a foreign enemy'.

A council of war to decide on the defences of the island was called for 5 April and all field officers were ordered to attend. The Council also put an embargo on anyone leaving the island. By the time the council of war met, Morgan knew exactly what he wanted to do, and his plan for the defence of Port Royal included building two new forts, even though the treasury was empty. Seventeen militia officers were present and, with Sir Harry presiding, they quickly declared martial law, adopted the articles of war and suspended civil law for twenty days.

The commandant of the forts was told to make an immediate inventory of all the muskets, sporting guns, pistols, powder and shot held in stock by Port Royal's merchants so that in an emergency they could be commandeered. While various companies were put on duty for the defence of Spanish Town and Port Royal, both places were patrolled at night by troops of cavalry. No boat was allowed to land at Port Royal between ten o'clock at night and sunrise, particularly the canoes carrying over water from Passage Fort. Finally, one in every ten Negroes on the island had to work on the fortifications.

The two new forts planned by Sir Harry were clearly inspired by experience gained in his attacks on Santiago, Portobelo and Maracaibo. The Port Royal of his day was in effect a large foot connected to the mainland by a long, thin ankle, with the instep and toes facing the sea and the sole and heel resting in the great harbour (see chart on page 314). Fort Charles had been built on the toes to cover the entrance to the harbour, with the Morgan Battery on the instep and Fort James protecting the channel across to Passage Fort. What was needed was protection that would prevent enemy ships forcing their way into the anchorage and strong defences to stop an attack on Port Royal by land along the ankle. Here Morgan was drawing from his own experiences.

The slaves began building one fort on the ankle, called Rupert, after the King's cousin, and another nearer the heel, later named Carlisle. Two batteries were extended and guns put in position, and most of the time Colonel Carey, Byndloss or Morgan rode round, making sure the work was done at top speed. Morgan's move in getting a tenth of the island's slaves put to work on the fortifications was one that avoided the problem of the empty treasury: the plantation owners lost the use of one man in ten but none complained: all could picture the sails of Count d'Estrées' fleet lifting over the horizon.

Eight days after the council of war a ship came into Port Royal with news that when she left London the capital was expecting war with France any day. It was also said that the earl of Carlisle would be sailing for Jamaica within a week or two. The twenty-day suspension of civil law ended on 25 April and Sir Harry called his second council of war to extend martial law until 10 June. He reported on the progress of the forts and batteries but could provide no answer to the question everyone was asking: 'Where is the French fleet?'

Three days later a ship arrived in from Barbados, and although her captain knew nothing of d'Estrées' whereabouts he had news which showed that the acting governor's energy was justified: all the British islands in the Lesser Antilles were hurriedly preparing their defences. Sir Harry then decided to send a ship to Hispaniola to seek more news and chose the *Advice* sloop, commanded by Captain Thomas Wigfall. A meeting of old privateering comrades at Tortuga or Île-à-Vache was likely to yield all the information known at either place. Meanwhile lookouts were placed along the south coast of Jamaica, each linked to the other by men on horseback.

Work at the fortifications 'went on vigorously' during May, but as the days went by more merchant ships were coming into Port Royal and loading with cargoes. Each of them would normally sail for England when ready, but Morgan knew they had to pass through the Windward Passage, almost within sight of Tortuga. If the French had later information from Europe or (more likely) the French privateers were prepared to anticipate a declaration of war, then all the ships would probably be captured.

Morgan called his third council of war on 31 May and explained his fears. Although the members listened, they did not at once adopt his proposal – to put an embargo on all ships sailing for Europe during the next two weeks, and then send them off in a large convoy – because many of them were shipping goods to England. The hard fact of an exporter's life meant that the first cargo landed at the marketplace fetched the highest price. If a merchant was lucky his ship arrived with, say, several tons of cocoa just when it was becoming scarce in London or Bristol. Another ship arriving with cocoa a week or two later would find the price had dropped considerably. Sending ships in convoy meant that with all the cargoes arriving at once, a scarcity could overnight become a glut ...

Sir Harry's warning was both short and simple: if the ships sailed alone they were unlikely to reach the marketplace at all. If the Tortuga privateers did not get them in the Windward Passage, then Frenchmen sailing out of the Channel ports certainly would. Morgan had his way; there would be an embargo until 14 June, by which time 'a good fleet of merchantmen' would be assembled.

The members of the Council had scarcely reached their homes before the lookouts along the coast reported a ship coming in from the east: the *Advice* was returning. Next day, 1 June, the little sloop arrived in Port Royal and Captain Wigfall immediately reported to Sir Harry news which must have seemed like a miracle, even to a hardened campaigner: most of Count d'Estrées' fleet had just been wrecked on Aves Island while on its way to attack Curaçao ...

Few seamen doubted the report for a moment: the tiny Aves, or Bird Island, might have been placed by a wilful Nature for the sole purpose of wrecking sailing ships. Formed by coral, only eighteen feet high, uninhabited, bare of trees and surrounded on three sides by a reef, Aves is a trap for ships passing from one group of islands to another – from Guadeloupe to Curaçao for instance, from Martinique to Puerto Rico or from the Virgin Islands to the Windwards.

Count d'Estrées had been sailing south-westward bound for Curaçao with a powerful fleet – eight ships of the line, eight frigates, three transports laden with five hundred guns, powder and shot, and a dozen or more privateers, including one commanded by de Grammont, one of the most famous of the French buccaneers. On the night of 4 May d'Estrées' flagship, the 70-gun *Terrible*, was leading the long column of ships when suddenly breakers were seen ahead, but before she could alter course the flagship ran up on one of the reefs of Aves. The Count immediately ordered warning guns to be fired but before the first gun could be prepared the ship of the line immediately astern had also smashed up on the reef in the darkness. The moment the flagship's guns began firing other ships mistook the warning for the standard signal for a council of war and promptly steered for the flash of the muzzles.

By daylight seven ships of the line, including the *Terrible*, the 64-gun *Tonnant*, 54-gun *Défenseur* and 52-gun *Hercule*, none of which was more than eight years old, the three transports and three frigates were stranded on the reef and rapidly being smashed up by the swell waves. More than five hundred seamen drowned, although d'Estrées escaped and eventually managed to get on board the only ship of the line that avoided the reef. The privateers took what they could from the wrecks and went off on their own while d'Estrées made his way to Hispaniola – he could not face the beat to windward to make Martinique. One group under de Grammont made for the Gulf of Venezuela and sacked Maracaibo and Gibraltar once again; others raided towns in Cuba.

D'Estrées arrived at Petit Goaves, in Hispaniola, on 10 May. The news of his disaster soon reached Tortuga and eventually the alert ears of Captain Wigfall, who also discovered that d'Estrées intended sailing for France with his remaining ships as soon as they had provisioned and taken on water.

The threat to Jamaica was over. Colonel Beeston thankfully noted in his journal that Wigfall's news ended all 'our present fears of the French'. Sir Harry called a meeting of the Council at Port Royal which ended martial law, gave permission for the ships waiting in Port Royal to sail for England, paid £20 for the hire of the *Advice* and voted a £10 reward to Captain Wigfall, noting his 'good service and readiness to obey the Governor's orders'. As Jamaica relaxed Sir Harry was thankful he had hurried the construction of the forts and emplacements: they were all completed with guns mounted and ready for the next emergency.

Sir Harry returned to Lawrencefield and his wife and once again was hailed as Jamaica's hero: for the third time in his life he had answered the alarm when the colony was threatened. The erosion that his reputation had suffered during his long absence in England was now repaired and the sycophants who surround power gathered round him like the mosquitoes that emerged at dusk.

Once again he was congratulating his brothers-in-law on additions to ˌneir families. Robert and Anna had their fifth child and third son who was christened Pöllnitz, which was Anna's mother's maiden name. The Archbolds had yet another son, so that Sir Harry had six nephews, not one of whom bore the surname Morgan.

On 17 July two frigates were sighted from Point Morant and by next day, when they arrived off Port Royal, they had been identified as British. Sir Harry, guessing that the new governor had arrived, had the gunners ready to fire a salute, the Port Royal Volunteers paraded, and the Council waited at the wharf to greet the earl.

Carlisle had not enjoyed the voyage in the *Jersey*: his gout had been bad the whole time and the constant rolling and pitching had caused him great pain. He had brought out Lord Vaughan's letter of recall and was thankful that Vaughan had left Jamaica six weeks before Carlisle had sailed from England. Then Sir Harry told him of the wreck of the French fleet, a disaster which Carlisle realized would go far towards easing the tension between London and Paris. The two hundred soldiers who had been recruited in London were landed, and it was decided that the earl's company would be stationed at Spanish Town while Sir Harry's would remain in Port Royal and be called the Port Royal Regiment.

The *Jersey* and her consort had brought out more guns, powder and shot, and Morgan was quick to ask Carlisle to send a frigate to recover the guns lost in the *Jamaica Merchant* (they were lying in 'five and nine feet of water'), a suggestion which Vaughan had resisted for three years, as if to emphasize Morgan's carelessness in losing the ship in the first place.

The earl's first letter to Sir Henry Coventry told the secretary how he had recovered from the gout as soon as he landed in Jamaica – indeed, he had done more walking in the last twelve days than in months before leaving England – and then reported on what he had found. He praised Morgan for strengthening Port Royal's defences and noted that British privateers with French commissions had come into port in anticipation of war with France, so that he was now worried about finding employment for them unless they could carry logwood – which depended on the Spanish.

The earl soon called the Assembly to consider the new constitution and after it met on 2 September he told Coventry that the members 'are so dissatisfied at the alteration of the government that I question whether they will pass any of these laws ...' He said he had given them copies of fifteen acts and 'gave them liberty to compare them with the originals'. He warned that some people were agreeing with the leading members of the Assembly in finding arguments against the new system of government rather than trying to 'accommodate things under it'. For the next five weeks the Assembly and the governor discussed, argued and finally quarrelled bitterly. The Assembly stuck to its argument that it should pass its own acts and Lord Carlisle was clearly bitter at having to argue a case for which he had little liking.

By 12 October the Assembly had been dissolved by the earl, and Colonel Beeston was noting in his journal: 'In this Assembly and the other that followed his Lordship was pleased very often, on several occasions, to call them fools, asses, beggars, cowards, and many other appellations, which management they took so ill from a wise Lord, considering the capacity they were then in, doing their King and country service, that it sets their hearts against him, and did no good to the public affairs.'

The speaker's bitterness was understandable, but however much Carlisle might have abused them when the House was in session, he was more than fair in giving their side of the argument in his letters to London. His report to Coventry after dissolving the Assembly said: 'I have met with the difficulties here I foresaw but could neither avoid nor prevent in England.' The members were 'much dissatisfied' in losing 'their deliberative part of power in altering and amending laws'. As a result they had thrown out all forty acts sent from England. Without actually telling the Lords of Trade flatly that the new system would not work, Carlisle's letters were the frankest they had ever received in Jamaica's brief history. In a letter to the secretary of State, the most powerful minister in England, he said: 'It rests now with the King and those about him to consider whether you will gratify the people in reverting to the former way.'

By the beginning of November, after only four months in the island, Carlisle was so concerned that he decided to send a detailed report to London with someone who could then be questioned in person by the Lords of Trade. His idea probably began when the Assembly presented the governor with nine reasons against the new system. The most important of these was that being English subjects they were entitled to be governed as such. All British colonies, they wrote, had assemblies in which their laws originated. 'The Irish method', now proposed for Jamaica was intended to support the English against the Irish, 'but they in Jamaica were all English.'

One of the acts thrown out by the Assembly was to continue a good way of making the ships using Port Royal contribute to its defence because a ship from England had to pay 'for every tunn such ship shall contayne, one pound of good and new gunpowder'. Ships from elsewhere paid 1s 3d 'of current money of this island' if from north of the Tropic of Cancer and '1s 3d once every year and no more' if from south of it, which meant that local shipping paid an annual duty. The next year's accounts for the island would, incidentally, include a bill for £3, 'Sir Henry Morgan's charges in mounting great guns', while 'powder money' for the year yielded the island £85 13s 3d.

The *Jersey* frigate came back from Île-à-Vache after her salvage work on the wreck of the *Jamaica Merchant* having recovered all twenty-two guns on board, as well as 212 shot. The guns were soon mounted on the new forts and in an emplacement on the coast called 'Morgan's Lines', which would eventually form the flanks of Morgan's Fort. They had just been put in position – bringing Port Royal's total to a hundred – when news reached the island that a peace treaty had been signed between France and Holland. In fact Holland had signed a treaty with Spain in August and with France a month later.

While Carlisle still presented to the Assembly the picture of an irascible and unbending aristocrat – he was the first peer of such rank to visit the island – he continued to argue the island's case with honesty and determination. In yet another letter to Coventry he said it was 'very advisable and requisite that there should be leave and power from the King to make laws (not relating to his Majesty's power and prerogative) to endure for some term till his royal approbation may be had therein ...' In other words, the Lords of Trade should return to the old system.

While the earl of Carlisle waited patiently for the reply from the Lords of Trade, the people of Holland were able to read an exciting new book just published in Amsterdam and called *De Americaensche Zeerovers*. It was written by a Dutchman using the pen-name of Alexander Oliver Oexmelin,

who had spent the past few years as a buccaneer and whose account, under
the English pen-name of Esquemeling, has already been quoted. Here, for
the first time, was a detailed story of his life in the West Indies – including
a description of Morgan's Panama raid.

The book was written in three parts. The first described Tortuga and
Hispaniola in some detail and how Oexmelin had twice been sold as a slave.
The second told of the activities of the famous French buccaneer François
L'Ollonais, and then went on to describe the early days of Henry Morgan
– his raids on Puerto Principe, Portobelo, Maracaibo and Gibraltar. The
details he gave showed that Oexmelin had sailed on most, if not all these
expeditions. The final part of the book described the Panama raid from
its very beginning – the rendezvous at Tortuga, the capture of Old Providence and Santa Catalina, and the seizure of the castle of Chagres. The
author must have gone on the long journey up the river to Venta de Cruz
and on to Panama: his accounts of all the villages and towns are correct,
and his description of the battle matches the Spanish.

For three years the Dutch were the only people to read the story of 'The
Buccaneers of America', but then the Spanish realized that a little judicious
manipulation in translation would provide them with a long book detailing
the atrocities of the English 'pirates', Henry Morgan in particular, and the
nobility and bravery of various Spanish governors, viceroys and admirals.
By 1681 the Spanish were able to read *Piratas de la America*, an amazing
story of rape and robbery, treachery and treason, pillage by land and sea,
and (because the translator knew what was required of him) in which every
foreigner was a scoundrel and nearly always an English one. Of course every
Spanish woman was a model of beauty and virtue, every priest a man of
unblemished piety and every Spanish governor a hero.

While Oexmelin's Dutch readers mulled over the depravity of the buccaneers – perhaps likening them to the seamen coming on shore at Amsterdam when the East India fleet reached the Texel – the Lords of Trade mulled
over Carlisle's recommendations, discussed them in the full Privy Council,
and by the spring of the next year, 1679, made up their minds. Everything
that Carlisle had written, every argument that he put forward, was ignored.
The new system was to continue. If the Assembly still refused to accept the
new laws, Carlisle was told to continue the laws of 1677 by proclamation
'until his Majesty's pleasure be known'.

While this letter was on its way to Jamaica – it would not arrive until
halfway through the hurricane season – Carlisle had to deal with the usual
kind of trouble at Campeche, warning London that the logwood cutters
were among the toughest men in the West Indies and if the Spanish would
not grant logwood they 'must of necessity expose their gold and silver to
a number of English who are abroad and having nothing to live on but
the logwood trade'. In other words the men would go back to a life of piracy.

'The French,' he added, 'have lately sacked Marrikey [Maracaibo], Truxillo and another town of the Spaniards on the Main, and brought off great booty to Petit Gouaves in Hispaniola.' These raids were led by de Grammont, who had come out with d'Estrées and escaped being wrecked on Aves.

In February, the governor's first quiet month for more than a year, he told Coventry: 'Exposing myself late one evening in the savanna to the north wind, I took cold, which hath occasioned the gout gently to visit me for some days, but it is going off again.' His rest was brief, because within a few days there was something approaching uproar in Port Royal involving Sir Harry Morgan as president of the Admiralty Court.

It began when Captain Francis Mingham sailed in with the *Francis* and was accused by the Customs of deliberately failing to declare two butts of brandy and twenty casks of cherry brandy. For what Carlisle later described as 'his improvidence and reservations' to dodge the Customs men, the *Francis* and her cargo were seized, and Mingham was taken before the Admiralty Court, where Sir Harry ruled that the *Francis* was condemned.

This was the usual judgment in a customs fraud but Mingham, who had been trading in and out of Port Royal for several years and had to account to his owners, was furious and appealed to the governor. 'Notwithstanding my kindness, whereby she was prevented of being sold according to the condemnation,' Carlisle warned Coventry, 'he is still dissatisfied and I believe will incense his owners to attempt your ears to inform the King.'

Carlisle was correct and by October Mingham was in London, petitioning the Privy Council to have his case reheard and complaining that the receiver-general at Port Royal, Thomas Martin, had acted 'out of malice only to the petitioner' and had the help of Sir Henry Morgan in getting the ship condemned. The Privy Council ordered a new hearing to be held in London on 1 May the following year, 1680, and after securing summonses to make sure that Sir Henry and Martin came to England to give evidence Mingham sailed for Jamaica to have the summonses served.

Sir Harry had no sooner received his summons than he sued Mingham for libel and the lawyers on both sides prepared their clients' cases. Carlisle told Coventry: 'Mingham is a very ill man. He took upon himself (though there is no mention of me either in the petition or the order) to serve me too, as he had served Sir Henry Morgan and Martin, as if I had been concerned in what he so falsely and maliciously charges them with.'

Then, so that Their Lordships should be aware that Mingham's petition was not entirely correct, Carlisle told Coventry: 'His ship was condemned in the Admiralty Court and sold but for £300, whereas the petition says £800 and that it was divided between them [Morgan and Martin], whereas I do not believe that they ever turned a penny of it to their own use.

'Sir Henry as judge of the Admiralty Court has not yet even received his fees and Mr Martin has given his share for the encouragement of trade for the building of an Exchange at Port Royal. They are now engaged with Mingham in a trial before the Grand Court.'

The case soon started going against Mingham, who realized that damages awarded to the lieutenant-governor of Jamaica were likely to be heavy. At a time when a creditor could (and usually did) have a debtor sent to prison, he had manoeuvred himself into a dangerous position. If he lost the libel case in Jamaica, he would certainly lose his original case when it was reheard in London.

He consulted with his lawyer, Francis Hanson, and Carlisle was soon adding a postscript to his letter to Coventry: 'Since writing the above, Mingham's attorney asked me to dissuade Sir Henry Morgan from prosecuting his action, promising a written acknowledgment from Mingham that his petition was false and scandalous.' Sir Henry refused and the case continued 'and the jury has given him £2000 damages. Thereby your Lordships may see how easy it is at this distance to be reproachfully and scandalously traduced to you ...'

Sir Harry Morgan then wrote one of his rare letters to Their Lordships and also sent them all the written evidence presented to his Admiralty Court when the *Francis* was condemned. Commenting that Mingham had in the recent libel case made 'no conscience of swearing falsely', he told the Lords of Trade:

> There was no malice on my part or Mr Martin's in the trial before the Admiralty Court as Mingham falsely asserts, nor did covetousness enter into the matter.
>
> The office of Judge Admiral was not given to me for my understanding of the business better than others, nor for the profitableness thereof, for I left the schools too young to be a great proficient [sic] in that or other laws, and have been more used to the pike than the book; and as for profit there is no porter in this town but can get more money in the time than I got by this trial.
>
> But I was truly put in to maintain the honour of the court for his Majesty's service, without which the Acts of Navigation cannot be enforced, for it is hard to find unbiased juries in the Plantations for such cases ...

In case Their Lordships found this hard to believe, he gave an example: 'A ship came in here with several cases of Irish soap and was seized by His Majesty's Receiver. The case was tried in the Court of Common Pleas, and the jury found for the defendants with costs. One witness swore that soap was victuals, and that might live upon it for a month, which the jury readily believed and found the aforesaid verdict.' He concluded: 'I beg your lordships to believe that if I have erred at all in this matter it has been in judgment only. May God love me no longer than I love justice.'

Captain Mingham's real troubles now began, because he could not raise the £2000 damages and was sent to jail. The owners of the *Francis* had paid for the petition to London but had nothing to do with Morgan's libel case, and Mingham found himself likely to be in jail well into the foreseeable future because he had no capital and no source of income.

The next ship leaving for England carried another petition to the Privy Council, this time from Mingham's wife Dorothy. She complained of the oppression and imprisonment of her husband 'by reason of the undue proceedings against him by Sir Henry Morgan, knight, Deputy governor of Jamaica and Judge of Admiralty there, and Thomas Martin, Gentleman Customer [sic] at Port Royal.' This had been the result of Mingham petitioning the Privy Council 'against the condemnation of the pink *Francis* of London...' Now Mingham requested his liberty so that he could come to London and present his case. The Privy Council, which had by now gone through all the papers in the case, was not impressed: Mingham could be freed providing he put up a security for the £2000 owing to Sir Henry Morgan.

The Jamaica Assembly protested at the case being moved to England, and Morgan offered to compound the case if Mingham paid the costs and bought Lady Morgan a carriage and pair of horses – an offer Mingham refused.

An hour before midnight on 7 July 1679, while Captain Francis Mingham was on his way to London with his first petition, the thudding of warning guns brought the people of Port Royal tumbling out of their beds. Officers and men of the militia seized their weapons and ran to their posts, Sir Harry Morgan hurried from Lawrencefield and the small battery at Passage Fort fired more warning shots to carry the alarm to Spanish Town. The warning was urgent: the French had arrived – eight ships of war had been sighted in the offing – and it seemed likely, because of an incident a few days earlier, that they were going to attack.

The French had unwittingly chosen a good moment, because the earl of Carlisle was staying at Guanabo, twenty-two miles from Port Royal. While a messenger rode through the darkness to warn him, Morgan and his cousin Charles, recently appointed commandant of Fort Charles, hurriedly mobilized the defences. The Port Royal Regiment and the company of soldiers brought out by Carlisle stood to arms; the guns of the forts were loaded, cavalry patrols galloped along the coast, watching for any landings, and every man with a telescope looked to seaward.

Several days earlier two French men-of-war had sailed into Port Royal and failed to salute the British flag by striking their topsails. When it became obvious that the refusal was deliberate the commandant had ordered his gunners to open fire. 'The fort fired seven guns, two of which are believed to have struck the French hull,' Carlisle later reported to the Lords of Trade. 'Whereupon the Frenchmen, luffing, edged into the harbour, fired seven shotted guns through the harbour into the town, and so stood out to sea.'

The people of Port Royal, with seven roundshot whistling about their ears, were as puzzled as Carlisle and Morgan. Had war broken out with France? Were the two Frenchmen making a reconnaissance to see if there were any English frigates in the harbour? Was it a piece of bravado? Was Count d'Estrées back? There were many questions and no answers, but the lookouts were alert on the night of 7 July because the most likely explanation was that war had indeed broken out and a French fleet had arrived off Port Royal before an English frigate bringing a warning.

Lord Carlisle, roused out his bed at Guanabo, had a horse saddled and rode through the night 'and was in with the forces at their arms before day'. He rode straight out to the Point and found that Sir Harry already had it 'in a good condition of defending itself'. Daylight came and he and Morgan could see the fleet of French ships lying hove-to up to windward, dark and menacing as the sun rose behind them.

As he stood on the Point, with Fort Charles on his right and 'Morgan's Lines' stretching along the coast to his left, Sir Henry found himself in an unusual situation: never before had he stood on the walls of a town and waited on the defensive for a powerful enemy fleet to attack him. Always he had been the attacker who swept in from the sea ... The difference on this particular morning was a significant one, not just for Morgan but for every man who was standing to arms, whether a reformed privateer or portly planter armed with a sporting gun. Whatever fighting they had done before had been on foreign soil, and always attacking. Now they were standing by to defend their own homes.

If the French attacked and Morgan failed to drive them off, he knew better than most that the life of Lady Morgan would probably be forfeit; that the Byndlosses and the Archbolds would perish as their houses and plantations were put to the flame. It needed no imagination on his part to picture it in his mind; he had seen it all – indeed, ordered some of it – the breadth of the Caribbean.

With the sun now above the horizon Morgan and Carlisle saw a French frigate come in towards the harbour while the other seven ships stayed hove-to, the fleet making sail from time to time to get back up to windward after drifting to leeward. The frigate anchored and a boat containing several officers was rowed to the Point, whereupon the ship sailed again.

'I met there Count d'Evreaux, a Knight of Malta,' Carlisle wrote, 'with some other French officers who pretended to come from Count d'Estrées to ask leave to wood and water at Blewfields Bay, or Point Negril, one of the most leewardly points of this island. They said they had been bound for Cartagena to demand all French prisoners but 'being driven to this coast by violent breezes, were now bound to Havana to make the like demand; that they were unwilling to trust to Spanish courtesy for wood and water ... They told us they came from France fourteen sail but had left seven at Lisbon ... To what end these French are come here we cannot possibly learn; they say against the Spaniards, but the people distrust their speech.'

Lord Carlisle soon discovered that far from his guns being pitted against d'Estrées' ships, he had to spend the day acting as a gracious host to Count d'Evreaux and his fellow officers. He subsequently reported:

> They admired the island but said they should have a better in Cuba. They were respectfully treated from morning till evening, when a small frigate came into the harbour-mouth, took them aboard and, after saluting the port, stood off to the fleet, which was cruising all day about two leagues to windward of our port.
>
> The Point [i.e. Port Royal] was so alarmed that the inhabitants removed their goods and families for fear of a French descent; and several sloops coming in with advice that the French fleet was standing off to windward, this so increased their jealousies that I called a Council to the Point.

Count d'Estrées took his fleet to windward, a move which did not lessen the tension in Jamaica. The people, led by Carlisle and Morgan, were no more inclined to trust the French than they would have done a Spanish fleet, and when the Council met at Port Royal, using the King's House, it proclaimed martial law for thirty days. Carlisle wrote: 'The whole of the inhabitants, soldiers and slaves, were set to work to increase the fortifications I being very glad of the opportunity of carrying on work which would have otherwise have gone forward very slowly.' After a few days eight of the French ships were sighted well to leeward. 'The occurrence has done us more good than harm,' commented Carlisle, 'but the generality of people will not give up their opinion that the French fleet when reinforced [by the ships left in Lisbon] is designed against this island ... Pray move the Master of Ordnance to hasten to us gun carriages, powder and small arms; the alarm has occasioned the using of all we had in store ...'

On 19 August, a week after Carlisle wrote that, the new Assembly met for the first time, called on the governor's own authority because he had not received instructions from London. The first day was spent in formalities but by the second there was yet another crisis in the island. Word passed rapidly from Port Royal to Spanish Town that, as Colonel Beeston noted in his journal, Sir Thomas Modyford had received letters reporting that the island 'was sold to the French'. Coming on top of the visit of d'Estrées' fleet, many people believed the story. The Assembly's bitter fight against the new system of government seemed to make it likely that the King would sacrifice the island in some new treaty with Louis – few had forgotten that Charles had, while in exile, promised to return it to Spain, and only Jamaica was having the new system thrust on it.

The Assembly asked Carlisle what information he had, but the governor's answer was not very reassuring: he had been told of a letter written from Barbados by Colonel Hilliard to Sir Thomas Modyford 'that the French designed for this', the Assembly's journal recorded, 'but he believed we might have time to put ourselves in a better posture; for as we are he did not believe us safe, and that should they attack us now he would not give half a year's purchase for any man's estate on the island'.

Carlisle's warning led to the Council and Assembly appointing a joint committee next day to report on what more defences were needed. The chairman was Sir Harry Morgan, who promptly led the thirteen other members of the committee down to Port Royal, took them round all the fortifications and explained his proposals for keeping the French fleet out.

The most unusual of these was his plan for fireships. His single fireship had been most successful at Maracaibo and now he proposed having four – 'or at least the materials for them' – ready for use. Two other ships should be moored inside the tiny, almost enclosed bay at the harbour entrance, behind Fort Charles, so that their guns could fire across the low-lying ground and cover the entrance while the land protected the ships themselves. Sir Harry pointed out several places where trenches should be dug for the troops so that they could rake the beaches with small arms fire if the French attempted a landing from boats. Gun platforms should be laid where new emplacements had been built eastward of Fort Charles – and a new fort should be started.

The committee met again next day to draw up and sign the seven-point report. From its style it seems Sir Henry wrote it, and he was thinking not only of the present threat but any future ones, because work on the proposed new fort should be carried on 'as time and materials will allow us to proceed with the building'. (This fort, when completed, was called Fort Morgan, in the middle of 'Morgan's Lines' and facing seaward.)

Three days after the report was handed over to the governor a ship arrived from England with the long-awaited reply of the Lords of Trade to Carlisle's plea that the old system of government should continue. The governor was instructed to call another Assembly, tell them to accept the new system and, if they refused, continue governing by proclamation 'until his Majesty's pleasure be known'.

Although Carlisle knew that with the people preoccupied with the French threat this was not the time to resume the battle over the new system, his instructions gave him no choice and he called a Council for the next day. He told the members of his new instructions and then went to the Assembly, who discussed the matter and next day asked him either to prorogue the House or adjourn for two months because the members considered 'the present juncture of time insufficient to debate so great a business, being under apprehension of danger from the French fleet'. Carlisle told Coventry: 'Finding them warm and nettled I thought it discretion to let them take time to digest their thoughts.' He therefore prorogued them. 'The apprehension of the island from the French fleet is very great,' he added.

Sir Harry Morgan then took the governor on a long tour of the harbour area and the valleys leading to it and, Carlisle wrote, 'we observed the properest passes to secure ... in case of an attack by land'. The latest musters showed that the island had 'a little above 4000 fighting men', although Jamaica had a reputation among its neighbours for having 20,000, 'and thus are formidable to them'. Although there were now a hundred guns mounted at Port Royal they had only a hundred barrels of powder.

Next day, as if to emphasize the urgency, a sloop sailed into Port Royal from Hispaniola with news for Sir Harry – six French ships of war had passed Île-à-Vache on 10 September, four of them very large. 'Undoubtedly they come to join with Count d'Estrées according to first accounts,' Carlisle noted, remembering that Count d'Evreaux had said that seven of d'Estrées' ships had called at Lisbon.

Carlisle's letter to Coventry was far from cheering. Local reports said that d'Estrées' squadron, now supposed to be at Havana, was to 'rendezvous a month hence at Hispaniola'. He based his concern on the fact that 'their hunters there have orders to have such a supply of dried provisions ready for them as shows their purpose on us or the Spaniard'. Yet even while he was on guard against the French Carlisle pointed out the irony that:

We are less well treated by the Spaniards who have lately taken many of our ships laden with logwood and cacao ... One Paul Abney was lately taken, with his sloop and passengers, prisoner by a Spanish man-of-war belonging to a squadron of five called the Barlovento fleet, commanded by the Vice-admiral of Cartagena, and the sloop, having only cacao on board, was plundered.

Abney produced my pass to the Vice-admiral who wiped his breech with it and threw it at him again; converted the cargo of the sloop to his own use and forced him to sign a receipt of having received money for the same (which indeed he had not) or else not to be discharged. Abney has sworn that when on board with the Vice-admiral he saw five

other [British] masters of ships on board, lately taken prisoners by the
Spaniards, and one of them in irons.

When the Lords of Trade received this report they reacted violently,
although considering the hundreds of earlier complaints and depositions
which they had ignored one has to assume that it was the Spanish admiral's
vulgar gesture that finally roused their wrath. The secretary of State was
ordered to demand satisfaction from Madrid for these 'injuries and sufferings
of the English by the violence of the Spaniards'.

The sudden arrival of another frigate from England, the *Success*, meant
that Lord Carlisle could send the *Hunter* to Cartagena to protest about the
Spanish vice-admiral and secure the release of the British prisoners, but she
was soon back and a rueful Carlisle had to report: 'The Spanish governor
was so jealous that he refused the captain or any of his company admittance
within the gates, and received them in a tent pitched for the purpose on
the beach.' He denied that he had any prisoners and as for the complaint
against the vice-admiral, 'just satisfaction should be given' when he returned
to port.

As men worked hard on the new fortifications at Port Royal, the hurricane season came to an end and 28 October, the day when the Assembly
would meet again, rapidly approached. In the midst of this uncertainty Sir
Thomas Modyford died. He was buried at St Catherine's Church in Spanish
Town but within six weeks, before the masons had finished carving a tablet
commemorating the man who made Jamaica 'what it now is', his eldest
son Thomas died. The title then passed to Charles, who for some years had
acted as his father's agent in London.

When the Assembly met on 28 October it rejected all the new laws, giving
the governor an address to be presented to the King, along with a 'justification' which had been agreed to by all the members of the Council and
the Assembly except Samuel Long, the chief justice, whom, Carlisle
grumbled, 'I have found all along ... to be a most pertinacious abettor and
cherisher of the Assembly's stubbornness in opposing this new frame of
government.' Long then withdrew to his plantation, which was more than
thirty miles from Spanish Town, but he had underestimated Lord Carlisle,
who noted: 'I have sent him his *quietus* and appointed Colonel Robert
Byndloss chief justice in his place, of whose fidelity to the King's interest
I have many proofs.'

Carlisle, realizing that nothing more could be done in Jamaica, suspended Long from the Council 'to bring or send him, with six more of
the Assembly, to attend the King in council in England to support their
own opinions, reasons and Address'. The Council agreed with him unanimously 'that there is no other or better expedient for the settlement of this
government'.

There was still no sign of the French fleet, and by now reports were reaching Carlisle with an alarming frequency showing that the former privateersmen who had been working the logwood trade out of Campeche were so angry that the King would not support them that they were deliberately provoking the Spanish, and many were turning to piracy.

More alarming was the fact that Peter Harris, 'a privateer since the taking of Panama', had just captured a 28-gun Dutch ship and was now sailing in her. She was powerful enough to be a threat to anything but a man-of-war, so Carlisle sent the *Success* in pursuit. She found Harris off the south coast of Cuba and chased him into the South Cays, where the privateersmen knew every channel. Within a few hours the *Success* hit a reef and was wrecked, an error in navigation which resulted in her master, responsible for pilotage, being court-martialled. He was sentenced to be flogged, jailed for a year and barred from ever again serving in one of the King's ships.

By the end of 1679 Lord Carlisle realized that he would have to go to England and talk over the island's future with the Privy Council, and he wrote home for permission. In his one and a half years in Jamaica he had, despite the bitter arguments with the Assembly, become a well-liked and respected man. In contrast to Lord Vaughan, he worked well with Sir Harry Morgan: there is no trace of the slightest disagreement between the two men, despite their completely different personalities.

One of his last activities before leaving the island was to appoint a committee of nine under the chairmanship of Sir Harry to draw up a report on piracy and the protection of trading ships. This he wanted to present to the Privy Council when he arrived in London. As far as Morgan was concerned, the report was almost a family affair, because his brothers-in-law Byndloss and Archbold were also members of the committee. From the style it seems probable that Morgan wrote it: the points were made with the brisk clarity which is very noticeable in the letters he wrote while acting as governor.

Peace with Spain was desirable for trade, but 'though instructed by the King to this end, the Governor can do little from want of ships to reduce the privateers and of plain law to punish them', the report said.

'The vast duties' paid in Spain itself on English goods and the 'great advance made upon them' by the Spanish merchants meant that prices were very high by the time they reached the Spanish buyers in the West Indies. Encouraging the Spanish on the Main to buy goods much more cheaply from Jamaica would also encourage them 'not only to admit us to a private trade with their outports and creeks but also to come to us and bring us money and goods to purchase our English commodities'.

The work of the privateers came in for some hard words directed against 'the detestable depradations of some of our nation (who pass for inhabitants of Jamaica) under the colour of French commissions. How much greater would [the Spanish merchants'] confidence be in us could these ravenous vermin be destroyed'. The report pointed out that the privateers never wanted for 'specious pretexts for irreconcilable hostility' to the Spanish because of 'the horrid butcheries of their fellow subjects who have fallen into their power'. This in turn increased the number of privateers because 'any sailors that escape these cruelties forget their duty to God and man, and give themselves wholly up to implacable revenge [on the Spanish] having no hope of redress here or in Europe'.

As far as the privateers were concerned, Morgan and his colleagues suggested, 'the surest way of putting down these incorrigible robbers' would be to ratify the act already sent to London by the Assembly making it a felony without benefit of clergy 'to serve any foreign prince against any other foreign prince at amity with England without a licence from the governor'. This would give Jamaica the necessary legal weapon which it had always lacked.

To enforce this act 'we suggest the appointment of a couple of sixth-rate frigates or yatches [sic] which can follow them into shoal water, with a fifth-rate frigate to support them...' The buccaneers now had grown so strong 'that a smaller force will not suffice for the first year'. Their ships were 'all extraordinary well manned and much better armed than any of our European shipping'.

A few days after this report was signed the earl of Carlisle sailed for England, handing over to Sir Harry Morgan. Samuel Long and six members of the Assembly were warned to be ready to defend themselves in England before the Privy Council.

Port Royal's defences were now quite strong, but not all Sir Henry Morgan's enemies were on the Main or in New Spain. The moment it was known in London that Carlisle had left the administration of the island in Morgan's hands, Sir Thomas Lynch and Lord Vaughan redoubled their efforts with the Lords of Trade...

27

The Golden Age

At the age of forty-five, Sir Henry was now at the peak of his fame and power and once again acting governor with a long list of other titles – Lieutenant-General, Vice-Admiral, Colonel-Commandant of the Port Royal Regiment, judge of the Admiralty Court and Justice of the Peace.

As *custos rotulorum* of Port Royal he made sure that the records of births and deaths were kept up to date. Some of the births he recorded were of his own nieces and nephews – Anna Byndloss's seventh child had been a son, who was named Morgan. With four sons and three daughters, Anna had no more children, while Johanna had her fourth son in seven years of marriage.

Sir Henry was still tall and lean, but by now he had a pronounced paunch. He drank heavily but it was the drinking that went with his boisterous personality. For him the day ended thick with the smoke of Dutch tobacco smoked in long-stemmed clay pipes. He had had enough strange and exciting adventures always to be ready with a yarn, and although Lady Morgan was more than used to her husband being brought home in a drunken stupor it is unlikely that she ever had to reproach him for being unfaithful. Later, when Morgan had fallen from favour and his enemies were seizing every scrap of gossip with which to attack him, he was called a drunken roisterer and a friend of pirates, but there was never a hint that he was anything but a faithful husband.

He was by now the most powerful governor the island had seen, because his fame and skill as a fighter endeared him to the ordinary people while the planters supported him as one of themselves. His brother-in-law Byndloss was the chief justice, his close friend Elletson was the attorney-general, and both served on the Council with his other brother-in-law, Archbold. His cousin and brother-in-law Charles was commandant of Port Royal, an appointment made by Carlisle and which would eventually need to be confirmed by the King. Privateers were a nuisance but the island was prospering and the future looked bright; law was enforced with a reasonably light hand.

Morgan did not move to the governor's residence in Spanish Town, preferring to stay in Port Royal, using the King's House there when necessary. His first letter to the new secretary of State, Lord Sunderland, reported that

he had some Jamaica privateersmen in jail awaiting trial and 'the rest are
alarmed and, not daring to enter any of our ports, keep on the wing until
they can find some place to settle on ... Their numbers are increased by
the necessitous and unfortunate, and they are encouraged by the security
of the Spaniards and their pusillanimity under all their plenty'.

His second dispatch to Sunderland mentioned quite casually, halfway
through the letter, that 'sloops returned from coasting on Hispaniola report
the arrival of the French fleet, some say fourteen, some ten sail'. Undoubtedly they would call for wood and water, he added, 'and then they
will see how our defences have improved'. The defences had not only been
improved but they were gradually being paid for, and the Treasury finally
settled Sir Harry's small charge for 'mounting great guns'.

The island's annual statement of accounts for the previous year gives an
interesting picture of the sources of the money needed to run a colony.
Wine licences yielded £355 and prizes £316. 'Powder money' paid by
ships amounted to £85 while liquor duties produced £1546. Quit-rents
brought in £918 and there was a balance of £126 of liquor duties carried
over from the previous year.

The charges were varied and included £2000 for Lord Carlisle's salary
and £600 for Morgan. Two cryptic entries referred to the *Francis* pink –
'Paid charges of a non-suit in seizing Francis Mingham's liquors – £6 15s'
and then: 'Paid of a judgment obtained by John [sic] Mingham for seizing
his liquors – £22 6s 1d.' The account ended with the usual deficit: 'Total
charge, £3353 14s 9d; total discharge, £3997 17s 2½d.'

While yet another hurricane season passed, Jamaica was quiet except for
an occasional chase after a privateer or pirate. What Roger Elletson in the
Assembly was later to call 'the golden age' was in fact the year from the
time Carlisle left. There was no bitterness in the Assembly and Samuel Long
and his colleagues were in England facing the Privy Council. The Jamaica
Council was cooperating with the governor – hardly surprising because its
members were either related to Morgan or his close friends – and there was
no sign of the French, which was fortunate because Morgan was still waiting for a replacement for the *Hunter*.

The *Norwich* frigate, commanded by Captain Peter Heywood, arrived on
2 November bringing letters for the governor from the Lords of Trade, and
among them were instructions ordering the discharge from prison of Francis
Mingham. When Morgan reported the man's release he added: 'I am persuaded I could have given good reasons for keeping him there.' He thanked
them for insisting on Mingham giving a security for the £2000
damages before going to England and begged leave 'to present ... a true
state of the case, that you may see how your great goodness hath been abused,
both by his original petition and his printed case'. The 'true state of the
case' was a copy of the Council minutes of an inquiry which established

that the law had taken its normal course: Sir Harry had not interfered. Mingham's problems, the Council noted, were 'due more to his own imprudence and a malicious desire for revenge than to any purpose of Sir Henry Morgan'.

Mingham packed his bags to hurry once again to England. Like many scoundrels the world over he knew what could be achieved if, bad as his case was, he could get the ear of an unscrupulous politician with an axe to grind; some man of no consequence or ability in Commons or Lords who was looking for a cause to champion to achieve his own dubious ends. With Vaughan and Lynch in England, Mingham knew where to find sympathetic ears, but it is perhaps significant that his lawyer, Francis Hanson, would no longer act for him in Jamaica.

In a report to the Lords of Trade saying 'all is quiet here; grateful seasons of rain promise very bountiful crops', Morgan described the arrival in Port Royal of 'a ketch empty, with only two men on board'. The two men in a sworn statement said their ship had sailed from West Africa 'with negroes, elephant's teeth, and gold dust' for Nevis, in the West Indies. They called at St Martin's 'under the French Government, to wood and water, and were invited into the harbour with much friendship, but afterwards suddenly seized and the ship unloaded'. The master and mates stayed there to secure redress, Morgan wrote, 'but consented that these two men should advanture by stealth to this island'. Morgan said he was now investigating the affair more fully.

The episode is of particular interest here because it shows that the old story of Morgan going out to Barbados as an apprentice and later joining the buccaneers at St Kitts is sheer nonsense. No ship from West Africa bound for Nevis would ever call at St Martin's for wood and water – the islands are within sight of each other. Had Morgan ever visited St Kitts, which is separated from Nevis by a channel only a few hundred yards wide, he would obviously have questioned the men more closely.

Port Royal now had an imposing new church, thanks to 'Sir Henry Morgan and other gentlemen, by whose liberal contributions the said church was erected'. Called St Peter's, the church was very close to the very big new fort which had been started in the middle of 'Morgan's Lines'. It was by far the tallest building in Port Royal; its square stone tower had been built with gun loops in the upper part while the lower section had a parapet which was machicolated, so that in case of an attack the defenders could shoot down directly at the enemy below, pour scalding oil and hurl rocks at them. A flagstaff on top of the church had a flag many feet square and the tower provided the highest lookout point for the whole of Port Royal.

As befitted a church which had been specially designed to play a defensive rôle in time of war, St Peter's first vicar, the Reverend John Longworth,

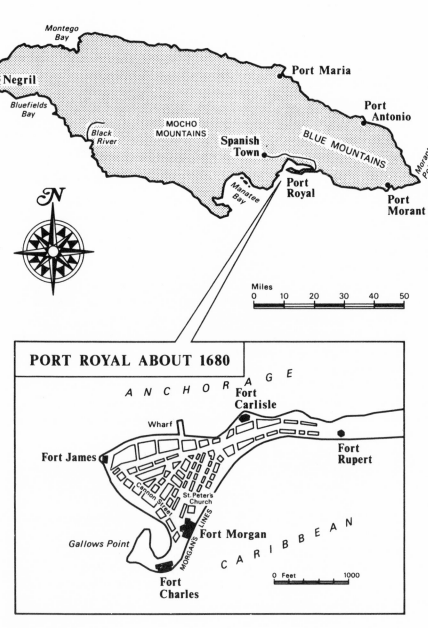

JAMAICA

Montego
Bay

Port Maria

Negril

Port
Antonio

Bluefields
Bay

Black
River

MOCHO
MOUNTAINS

Spanish
Town

BLUE MOUNTAINS

Morant
Point

Manatee
Bay

Port
Royal

Port
Morant

N

Miles

0   10   20   30   40   50

PORT ROYAL ABOUT 1680

A N C H O R A G E

Fort
Carlisle

Wharf

Fort James

Fort
Rupert

Cannon Street

St. Peter's
Church

Gallows Point

MORGAN'S LINES

Fort Morgan

C A R I B B E A N

Fort
Charles

0 Feet   1000

had the reputation of being a broad-minded parson who took a worldly view of privateering and privateersmen. It is unlikely that Sir Harry and his associates would have chosen a man who preached them a long sermon every Sunday promising fire and brimstone. Longworth's first text was 'Put off thy shoes from thy feet, for the place where thou standeth is holy ground', and the sermon so pleased his patrons that they had it printed.

Jamaica's whole future was decided in London during the autumn of 1680, and the only man of any consequence who was not in the capital while the arguments were going on was Sir Harry Morgan, although Charles Morgan arrived to look after his interests. With all the decisions to be made by the Privy Council the first move, made in September, was for Carlisle to bring his charges against Samuel Long, and once they had heard them the Council ordered Long to put up a bond of £1000 to ensure that he stayed in London. By way of reply, Long accused Carlisle of encouraging privateers and of corruption.

Six days later Carlisle was called before the Lords of Trade, who were considering a pile of protests from the Spanish ambassador about attacks on Spanish ships alleged to have been made by Jamaica 'pirates'. The complaints thoroughly angered Carlisle, who replied that the attacks by the privateers 'are committed by a sort of man without reach of government; but the injuries that we suffer from [the Spanish] are from men in office and public employ'. Not only that, but while he was in Jamaica his frigates had captured more privateers than the Spanish admiral for the whole time he had been stationed in Cartagena.

By now men like Long, Beeston and Beckford had delivered all their written arguments to the Lords of Trade and a committee of judges considering a constitution had heard a variety of witnesses. Then, on 30 October 1680, they were all called before the Lords of Trade and told the King's decision. It was an impressive meeting, with Prince Rupert present, as well as the young duke of Albemarle.

The decision was a complete victory for Samuel Long: His Majesty had decided that the island should have the same constitution as that in use at Barbados. This meant that Jamaica would pass her own laws and they would remain in force unless rejected by the Lords of Trade – a change from the old system whereby they expired after two years unless agreed by Their Lordships.

There was, of course, a price for all this. With the new constitution the island could not be taxed without the Assembly's agreement, but the King now asked for a fixed revenue. Their Lordships wanted no more arguing every year over a revenue bill.

Sir Harry soon heard that his enemies were at work in London, making accusations that also included Carlisle. The new secretary of State, Sir Leoline Jenkins, sent him a friendly warning, and both Carlisle and Charles Morgan wrote as frequently as ships allowed. The allegations were serious enough for Morgan to write a frank letter to Sir Leoline in which he pointed out that he had just received thanks 'from several Spanish governors on the Main for exerting so much care and vigilance in the suppression of privateers...' The complaints against Carlisle and himself 'have risen more from the desire of men to be popular than from their zeal for the King's service, valuing themselves of the frequent obstruction they give'.

Yet Morgan made one error: he mistook the allegations for the attack. Defending himself against the charges of not doing enough to get rid of pirates and privateers, he did not realize that the allegations were simply the most convenient weapons available to his enemies in London. He failed to appreciate that his enemies, mainly Vaughan and Lynch, were determined to ruin him to leave the way open in Jamaica for Lynch.

While Carlisle remained governor there was little they could do except gossip at Court. For the moment, then, Morgan's future hung on Carlisle. A change of governor might let in Lynch, and as the months passed the Royal African Company was gaining more influence in Jamaica. Its factors were often men of substance, and with the Company's monopoly of the slave trade it was changing the whole pattern of politics in the island. Within a few months the power would begin to slip from the hands of the planters and pass to the merchants – not the tradesmen of Port Royal, but the importers and exporters, the wealthy middlemen often living in England and controlling everything that was shipped in and out of the island, whether slaves or liquor, pots and pans or bags of flour.

This was all in the near future when, during 1680, Sir Henry began to build up a large estate around Port Maria, on the north side of the island. He did it by buying various pieces of land from other people – 300 acres for £70 from one couple, nearly 700 acres from Roger Elletson for £600, 200 acres from his friend Colonel Thomas Ballard, until finally he had some 1200 acres close to Port Maria. Once he had made it into one estate, he gave it a name – Llanrumney, a memorial to his birthplace in Wales. Then he built a large plantation house, something that befitted the man who had been the admiral of the Brethren and was now the acting governor of Jamaica.

One of the most active pirates in the West Indies was Captain Jacob Evertsen, a Dutchman who took a commission when he could and acted as a pirate when it suited him. His sole interest was in the size of the purchase; thoughts of danger, ethics and national interest he left to others. But he was elusive: frigates from Jamaica had searched for him without success and Spanish frigates from Cartagena had no better luck.

Then, soon after dark one Saturday night at the end of January 1681, just when Morgan had finished writing a letter to the secretary of State, a messenger arrived with the news that Evertsen's sloop was at anchor in a bay to leeward with a brigantine which he had just captured. Evertsen was lucky because the *Norwich* frigate was away on patrol and the vessels in Port Royal that Sir Harry could use were a sloop and several coasting wherries, unhandy craft hard to sail to windward and built to carry bulky cargoes between coastal villages and the ports.

Morgan promptly sent a company of soldiers from the Port Royal Regiment down to the wharf. Twenty-four of them were put on board the sloop, which had a crew of thirty-six, and the rest sent out to the wherries. He gave the captains their orders and by midnight the motley squadron had sailed to find Evertsen. They reached the bay at noon next day and, as Sir Harry had planned, Evertsen saw nothing alarming in the sight of a few wherries sailing in with a trading sloop in company. The bay was small enough for the wherries and sloop to tack in close to Evertsen's sloop.

Describing the next few minutes, Morgan wrote: 'Letting the King's jack fly, they boarded him.' The Dutchman was taken almost completely by surprise. 'They received three musket shot, slightly wounding one man, and returned a volley, killing some and wounding others of the privateers. Evertsen and several others jumped overboard and were shot in the sea near the shore.'

His sloop was then secured and 'twenty-six stout men' were taken prisoner and carried back to Port Royal, where they were questioned. When they revealed the names of the other men who had escaped overboard with Evertsen, Morgan issued warrants for their arrest. 'Such is the encouragement that privateers receive from my favour or the countenance of Government, whatever the reflection of the Spanish Ambassador,' Morgan told the secretary of State, pointing out that the Spanish, 'have this year [i.e. in January alone] captured twenty-two sail and absolutely ruined our Bay trade.' He commented that 'they have many English prisoners, we not one Spanish, and why should they have credit at Whitehall and we want it I leave to your Lordship'.

Evertsen had been sailing with a crew of seventy and, apart from six Spaniards, all were English. Morgan sent the Spaniards to Cartagena for the Spanish authorities to bring to trial and the rest of Evertsen's men were tried in the Admiralty Court on 14 March 1681, convicted of piracy and sentenced to death. 'But after deliberation and reflection that the General Assembly was to meet on the 18th following,' Morgan told the Lords of Trade, 'I thought it not fit to post them to execution, lest it should scare all others from returning to their allegiance.'

Morgan's fear that a mass execution at this time would frighten off returning privateers was because the Assembly was drafting a new bill –

which Morgan approved in May – for more severe penalties for privateers-men but allowing them a free pardon if they came in before September. The sight of a few dozen rotting corpses hanging in chains from the gibbets on Gallows Point was, with the memory of Lord Vaughan's execution of Captain Browne, hardly likely to lure in any men who were at last prepared to exchange the pike for a hoe.

In April 1681, Captain Francis Mingham made his final appeal before the Privy Council. Two years had passed since the *Francis* pink had been seized by the Customs in Port Royal and although the Council had been unreceptive to his first appeal the atmosphere had changed. The influence of men like Carlisle now counted for little or nothing; many rumours were circulating that he would not be returning to Jamaica and Morgan's enemies hurried to help Mingham plead his case.

The Privy Council's findings as reported to the King were remarkable. The condemnation of the *Francis* and her cargo 'was unwarranted, and the proceedings in the action [were] contemptuous towards your Majesty's Council Board [i.e. the Lords of Trade] and throughout oppressive and unjust'. The £300 for which the *Francis* had been sold should be repaid to Captain Mingham, the Council said. Having decided all that, thus restoring Captain Mingham's reputation as a fine upstanding gentleman who always paid his Customs dues and in consequence condemning Sir Henry Morgan, the Council, with the splendidly illogicality which is the breath of life to such august bodies, refused Mingham his costs because 'the seizure was colourable and the case had diverse circumstances of suspicion'.

The King, the Council continued, should 'express his displeasure' with Sir Henry and Thomas Martin, the receiver-general, because this would 'discourage the like proceedings to other persons in power'. As a final thrust at Morgan, Mingham was free to act if he wanted to sue for damages for the time he spent in prison. Francis Mingham, the man who smuggled brandy – for this had never been disputed – but who had managed to turn the routine condemnation of his ship into a personal fight with the governor, had been lucky because he had found the men at Court who could use him.

Within two or three weeks a letter was on its way to the British ambassador in Madrid, Sir Henry Goodricke, saying that 'his Majesty's presentations have gone so high against Sir H. Morgan as to name Sir Thomas Lynch to be Lieutenant-governor in his place. The Spanish Ambassador hath given his thanks with great solemnity for this mark of his friendship to the King of Spain, and he hath complimented the ministers likewise upon the occasion and it is certain that as he is satisfied Sir T. Lynch will be a good Governor for the satisfaction of the Spaniard so he will be a nursing father for the improvement of that Plantation'.

The Lords of Trade drew up a commission appointing Lynch the new governor at their meeting on 28 July 1681, and drafted his instructions. At the same time they recommended the King to revoke Morgan's commission not only as lieutenant-governor but as lieutenant-general, and likewise the commission that made Sir Francis Watson the island's major-general. The reason they gave for abolishing the offices (for this is what they were doing) had a curious detachment from reality – they were posts which 'we do not think of any further use to your Majesty's service in that colony.'

The King signed Sir Thomas's commission on 6 August, and to make sure he would have absolute power in the administration Lynch could not only suspend any member of the Council but declare that he could not hold any public office. This gave Lynch the weapon which, properly aimed, could eventually destroy Morgan and all his friends. The years of seeing Morgan applauded as the great buccaneer, the saviour of Jamaica, the man who could lead a swarm of cut-throats into battle against impossible odds by the persuasive power of his tongue – these were what Thomas Lynch, merchant, could not forgive or forget, and now he had a commission and authority which made sure that those years in the political wilderness would be revenged, providing he was patient.

At the end of October Sir Thomas and his wife Vere sailed in the *Sweepstakes* frigate, a 42-gun ship, but the first of the winter gales was soon sweeping the Channel and the *Sweepstakes* had to put into Plymouth for shelter. No sooner had one gale passed than another arrived, and by 20 December Lynch was grumbling that he had been weatherbound for eight weeks. Another eight weeks were to pass before the *Sweepstakes* could sail.

In Jamaica Sir Harry Morgan had heard nothing but rumours. In August, a few days after Lynch's commission was signed in London, he wrote to Sir Leoline Jenkins:

> I am by the public rumour possessed that the King hath disbanded the two companies here. [These were Carlisle's and Morgan's own, which had become the Port Royal Regiment.] It is said Colonel [Samuel] Long induced the King to dismiss the companies as being useless here. I am much startled by the Colonel's allegation, seeing that our daily experience proves the contrary. They are constantly employed either at sea or ashore. Twenty of the soldiers are at this moment on board the *Norwich* in pursuit of a powerful and desperate pirate, and I hear there has been an encounter and that some of them are wounded...

The situation with the new Assembly was far from satisfactory and Morgan still had to persuade it to pass the revenue bill, the condition the King had placed on granting the new constitution. Samuel Long was now back in the island, and a hero: almost single-handed, it seemed to the people, he had fought the Privy Council, made them abandon the use of Poynings'

Law and come back with a new constitution. However, Long still believed that granting a perpetual bill would destroy the Assembly's only weapon over a governor: if he had to depend on them for a revenue bill each year they had some control over him; they could force him to compromise. By 4 October Sir Harry was telling Sir Leoline that the Assembly's 'fears, jealousies and suspicions are such that, notwithstanding all my persuasions ... they drew up and passed a bill limiting the revenue to two years...' He had since argued with them and 'finding them somewhat startled and beginning to see their error, I remanded them to their own House, where they immediately threw out their two-years bill'. He then prorogued them for a month, hoping to get a seven-year bill.

A month later a jubilant Morgan wrote that things were 'brought to a lucky conclusion', because the Assembly had passed the Bill for seven years. Ironically, while the Privy Councillors abolished the posts of lieutenant-general and major-general, the Assembly for the first time voted £1000 a year to pay for fortifications.

It also passed an act against privateers which said that all treaties with other nations should be 'inviolably kept' while anyone from Jamaica who served 'in a hostile manner ... under any foreign prince, state or potentate shall be deemed a felon and, upon conviction, suffer death'.

Sir Thomas Lynch was a sick man when he arrived at Port Royal in the *Sweepstakes* on 14 May. With him was his five-year-old daughter Philadelphia, but he had been forced to leave his wife and son Charles behind in Madeira after waiting five weeks for them to recover from an illness.

The new governor had not been in Jamaica for five years, and even before he went on shore he was told that because he was not expected neither the King's House in Spanish Town nor the King's House in Port Royal was habitable. Sir Harry had been living in his own house, using the King's House in Port Royal for formal occasions, so Colonel Hender Molesworth, an old friend of Lynch's, invited him to stay. Not only was Lynch's residence uninhabitable but the treasury was bare. 'I am like to live here, as I am come, at my own charge,' he commented in a letter to London.

On the day he arrived, Lynch delivered the letter to Morgan cancelling his commission – the first official notice that the Welshman received – and took the oath of office. Whatever Morgan felt at being turned out without one word of explanation, he put a good face on it, telling his fellow Welshman Sir Leoline that he had received the King's order 'for my dismission from the commands of Lieutenant-governor and Lieutenant-general of Jamaica. I embrace them all with submission and obedience, but (though I speak it not from ambition of being continued, but from zeal for the King's service) I heartily hope the posts of Lieutenant [-general] and Major-general may prove as useless as they are represented to be. Sure I am that they have not appeared to be so hitherto...'

Although far from well and worried about his wife and son – he would eventually hear that both had died in Madeira – Lynch was soon heavily involved with the usual problems facing the island: piracy, relations with the Spanish and the defences of Port Royal. His first Council meeting was held on 27 May and his report to the Lords of Trade said: 'I ordered Captain Morgan to send me an account of the arms and stores ... I also ordered Sir Henry Morgan and others to take workmen, inspect the forts, and make agreement for their repair.'

The return of Samuel Long to the island, followed by Lynch, meant that the political groups – they were alliances of individuals rather than any party liaisons – now had their leaders and were ready for the bitter political fighting that lay ahead. Long, enjoying his hard-won popularity, was now the leader of most of the members of the Assembly and represented the 'Old Standers', supported by Beeston, Peter Beckford and the new speaker, Samuel Bernard.

A second group gathered round Lynch and were the majority in the Council. They differed little from Long in policy but represented the more influential of the merchants and were regarded by Morgan as pro-Spanish, men who would pay almost any price for friendship with Spain, knowing they would get it back a hundredfold from trade with the Main.

The third group and by far the smallest was formed by the planters gathered round Morgan. Byndloss, Archbold, Thomas Ballard, Sir Francis Watson and Morgan himself served on the Council but could be outvoted by the other seven members. Their only strength in the running of the island was now their membership of the Council, with Byndloss still the chief justice and Charles Morgan the commandant at Port Royal.

It took time for the three parties to prepare for the struggle that was bound to come. Lynch was in no hurry; he knew that Sir Harry and the men round him were impetuous. Elletson, though a brilliant lawyer, was hot-headed; Byndloss had an uncertain temper. Lynch judged that Morgan was by now a figurehead, doing what Elletson and Byndloss wanted. The aura of the great buccaneer that had surrounded him for so many years had faded; the time had come for new heroes, and for the moment the one who occupied people's thoughts in the island was Samuel Long.

So for the first few weeks Lynch was content to wait and carry on the day-to-day affairs of the island. Yet very soon he was showing the essential cynicism of his policy towards Spain. He was afraid that her reaction over privateers might harm the Jamaican smuggling sloops which were owned by local merchants. He told the Lords of Trade:

We have about twenty of these, from fifteen to forty-five tons; they are built here, admirable sailers, well-armed and treble-manned, some carrying twenty or thirty hands, who receive forty shillings a month.

They carry from here some few negroes and dry goods of all sorts, and sell them in the [Spanish] islands and all along the coast of the Main in bays, creeks and remote places, and sometimes even where there are governors, at St Jago [Santiago, Cuba] ... for they are bold where they are poor. But at Cartagena, Portobelo, Havana, &c, the Spaniards admit no one.

This trade were admirable were we not undersold by the great Dutch ships that haunt the coast of the Main and islands and were we not fearful of pirates, which is the reason why the ships are so strongly manned. Those and other expenses and hazards carry away much of the profit. This trade employs all the privateers that come in, and would bring in the rest had I your Lordships' order to connive at it.

Lynch's morality ran on mercantile lines. Smuggling goods into Spanish territory was regarded in Madrid as being as provocative as capturing her ships; a governor with motives as pious as those professed by Lynch over the treaty of Madrid should have tried to stop the Jamaica smugglers with the same zeal as he chased privateers and pirates. However, smuggling was something that was translated into a profit and loss account, and therefore he wished for official sanction so that he could 'connive at it'.

In September Sir Thomas had to turn his attention to the Assembly, telling the new session: 'Commonsense tells us we should not kick against the pricks' and that it was of the utmost importance that new laws were passed. He had in mind the revenue bill (Their Lordships had tossed out the seven-year one passed in Morgan's time). His intervention had an effect and the Assembly passed the bill without all the other clauses they had previously tacked on and to which Their Lordships had taken such objection. Lynch thanked them, saying that the 'disorders in my head and the misfortunes are somewhat alleviated' by the joy with which he saw the session end so happily.

The year 1682 ended with the King acting against the spirits. A proclamation of 13 December was aimed at getting rid of these earthly beings as well as forbidding anyone under the age of fourteen being carried in a ship without his parents. The proclamation referred to 'a lewd sort of people called spirits' and their activities 'in seducing many of his Majesty's subjects to go on shipboard', where they were seized and taken by force to serve in the plantations in the West Indies and America.

The words 'Tory' and 'Whig' were by now beginning to spread to Jamaica from England, and with them the strife and factionalism they represented. The King's hopes that the hatred of papists would slowly fade after the

Test Act were not realized; instead two groups had emerged to form the first political parties in the modern sense. The first group, the Tories, tended to be former Cavaliers who were strong monarchists, staunch Protestants and frequently landowners, with a detestation of dissenters. The Whigs, led by the earl of Shaftesbury, were often former Cromwellians and backed by the merchants who distrusted the King and accepted the rights of Protestant nonconformists.

With the backing of the ordinary people, Shaftesbury's party was powerful in London, and in 1681, during the time that Lynch was waiting to go out to Jamaica, the King had seized the opportunity of overthrowing Shaftesbury by calling a Parliament in Oxford. There, meeting in Christ Church Hall, the Lords and Commons suddenly found that Charles II had dissolved Parliament – something he would not have risked in London for fear of the mob. With the King then ruling without Parliament – which he did until his death four years later – the various factions discovered and fabricated even more plots: Titus Oates had been busy for a long time and many staunch Royalists were still terrified of the charge of Popery.

In Jamaica the island split along the same party lines: Morgan and his planter faction regarded themselves as Tories; they soon formed the Loyal Club and considered themselves the King's men, with the corollary that anyone who was against them was against the King. They were staunch Protestants – St Peter's Church towering over Port Royal and built with their money was a witness to that – and they hated Protestant dissenters and Catholics with equal ferocity. Long and his powerful group in the Assembly, and Lynch and his merchants, particularly Hender Molesworth, the agent of the Royal African Company, took over the role of the Whigs: there were still a large number of Cromwell's Old Standers in the island and many of them had become Port Royal's leading merchants with a monopoly of the slave trade.

The first flare-up between the two groups occurred in January 1683, when the Sessions met, and it was provoked by one of the Loyal Club, Roger Elletson, a former attorney-general during Morgan's time as governor. The episode was described by an indignant Lynch in a letter to London.

The justices were just seated but, before they could start their judicial business, Elletson asked leave to speak. 'Then, in a studied harangue, he pressed the justices to enforce the laws against dissenters. Everyone was much surprised and Colonel Molesworth answered that it was forbidden by our local laws and the King's repeated instructions.'

Lynch later discussed Elletson's demand with the Council and, deciding his conduct was malicious,

summoned him by warrant before us. He was asked whether the King could dispense with those laws. He would not answer. He was then asked whether he was not aware of the King's instructions to that effect, why he had not raised the question in Sir Henry Morgan's time, when he was Attorney-General, and whether the dissenters had done anything to forfeit the King's grace. To this he answered, 'No', and to the rest nothing ...

Elletson is an ill man. He was driven here by his crimes and necessities, and was the occasion of all the hard, inconvenient and illegal grants passed by Sir Henry Morgan, for which he is cursed and was told so before Sir Henry's face in the Council ... The Council putting all these things together, and judging that his last action was done from private malice and revenge, ordered him to be bound over to good behaviour, and an information laid against him at the Grand Court. He has since given in his submission, so I suppose we shall pardon him.

This incident was the opening shot in what was to become a bitter fight between Morgan's faction and Lynch's, and which was to degenerate into one between the planters and the merchants. For the time being, though, Lynch's main problem continued to be piracy, and the subject occupied most of the letters which described Elletson's attack on dissenters. He reported the loss of 'diverse vessels' with one ship, the *Trompeuse*, known to have captured sixteen or eighteen vessels off Hispaniola, 'so that at a moderate reckoning our losses, the Royal [African] Company's, and the English merchants' come to forty or fifty thousand pounds'.

For the next few months Lynch and the Lords of Trade were kept busy trying to control the piracy. Some of the ships involved were commanded by outright pirates, but other captains had French commissions issued in Tortuga. Lynch sent off to London lists of ships that had been robbed or captured and the secretary of State ordered protests to be made to the French government. Demands in Paris for compensation were ignored and finally the Lords of Trade gave Lynch permission to seize 'in the best manner you can such vessels and privateers as have injured our subjects, or shall disturb their lawful trade'.

During all this time Sir Harry Morgan remained out of public life, attending an occasional Council meeting but content to spend his time supervising the work on the Llanrumney plantation and occasionally travelling to Port Royal on visits which all too frequently turned into drunken carousals, going from one tavern to another with his friends and taking little care to keep his voice lowered as he made outspoken comments about anything that took his fancy.

Sir Harry's reputation was also suffering because of the behaviour of some of his friends and of his cousin Charles Morgan. Elletson's attack on dissenters had been ill judged and upset a number of people who had little sympathy for Lynch. Charles Morgan, still the commandant of Fort Charles, was a hot-headed young man and because some of his officers were followers of Lynch and Long there were frequent quarrels and arguments. Charles, drinking heavily and enjoying a martial life, left the running of the estate to his younger brother. Lynch, whose crest was a lynx passant, was content to wait.

News of the Rye House Plot reached Jamaica to add more fuel to the bitterness already existing between the Whigs and the Tories. The story of how Whig extremists had waited at Rye House, at Hoddesden in Hertfordshire, to assassinate the King and the duke of York as they returned to London from the Newmarket races had allowed the Tories to claim that they were the King's men, the true supporters of the Crown, leaving the Whigs in Jamaica to defend themselves against the charge of being republicans.

Into this volatile situation at Port Royal walked the irascible and erratic Captain Francis Mingham, still pursuing his vendetta against Sir Harry Morgan. Mingham had recovered the *Francis* and, with his son, was trading with her. Mingham was also an embittered man: his wife Dorothy, who had petitioned the Privy Council while her husband was in prison, had recently died and his son had grown up into a noisy and impetuous youth.

The *Falcon* frigate and the *Francis* were both anchored in Port Royal, and when Mingham's cooper left the ship after a quarrel he went over to the frigate, wanting to sign on. Captain Churchill, her commanding officer, was wary of taking a man from the *Francis* and wrote a letter which he sent across to Mingham asking if there was any objection. Mingham's answer was abusive: if Churchill had anything to say, Mingham wrote, he knew where to find him.

Churchill then sent a boat across to the *Francis* to get the cooper's box of tools and seabag and bring them back to the *Falcon*. Even though the cooper had signed off the *Francis*, Mingham regarded this as a direct insult and he and his son toured the taverns telling anyone who cared to listen what a scoundrel was Churchill. Already short of men, Churchill retaliated by sending a press gang on board the *Francis*, pressing five. Very soon there were near riots in the streets of Port Royal as Mingham and his son and mate roamed the taverns, provoking and insulting any of the *Falcon*'s seamen they could find. They were soon joined by the master of another merchant ship, Captain Wild, and his mate, William Flood.

The most violent of the five was apparently Mingham's mate, and as soon as he heard of the rumpus Captain Churchill sent his men to seize the mate and bring him on board the *Falcon* where, as punishment, he was hoisted on a rope from the foreyardarm. As soon as he saw the plight of the

Francis's mate, William Flood rowed out to the *Falcon* and boarded her, intending to rescue him. Whatever the rights and wrongs of the case up to now, the *Falcon* was a King's ship and Captain Churchill had so far ignored the fact that threats made against him were against a King's officer. He was therefore in no mood to argue the toss with Flood, who was seized, hoisted up to the yardarm in place of the mate, and ducked several times. Lowered down again, Flood was still full of energy and insults and began threatening Churchill on the deck of his own ship, which earned him a flogging.

Mingham's mate had by now left the *Falcon* while Mingham himself was trying to persuade Sir Thomas Lynch to take action. Lynch, perhaps realizing that the activities of Mingham and his cronies were perilously close to treason, would have nothing to do with it. Mingham and Wild then went to a justice of the peace and swore out depositions and took them to the judge advocate of Port Royal, who refused to do anything. In the meantime William Flood was released from the *Falcon*, with Mingham claiming that he was a very sick man.

Mingham, nearly demented, spent the next two days drawing up a petition to the Assembly (who rejected it, telling him to take it to the governor) and trying to take his revenge on his former cooper, whom he accused before a magistrate of being a mutinous seaman. The cooper was arrested, but before he could be taken to jail some of the *Falcon*'s seamen tried to rescue him – and found themselves in jail with the cooper, charged with rioting and disturbing the King's peace.

The situation now facing Sir Thomas Lynch was complex: Mingham's threats against Captain Churchill left him open to be charged with treason while Captain Wild's mate, Flood, was legally in peril for having boarded a King's ship and threatened her captain. Mingham's former cooper was in jail as a result of a charge by Mingham; several of the *Falcon*'s crew were now accused of rioting.

From Lynch's point of view, all this had played into Sir Harry Morgan's hands. Captain Churchill was a relative of John Churchill (the future duke of Marlborough), a close friend of the duke of York, and Mingham was not only a Whig but an avowed dissenter. All the trouble had occurred in Port Royal, where the Morgans were powerful, and clearly they would turn it to their advantage.

William Flood, who had been in his sick bed since the ducking and flogging, then died. Lynch had left Spanish Town and gone to Port Royal as soon as the trouble had begun – mainly in the hope of quietening the turbulent Mingham – and, as he later told the Lords of Trade, he was with Sir Harry when Captain Wild suddenly arrived and asked that the *Falcon* should be ordered not to sail until after the inquest. This was Lynch's first news of Flood's death, and he told Sir Harry 'to go down and ... do what was reasonable and legal. He went away with Wild and, God is my record, had no other orders by word, letter or message from me.'

Fifteen residents of Port Royal were warned to attend the coroner's inquest as jurors next morning, and promptly at seven the inquest began. Captains Mingham and Wild were there with their depositions, Mingham trying to persuade the jury to return a verdict of murder against Captain Churchill. Sir Harry was there with the attorney-general, Captain Simon Musgrave. It took the jury seven hours to reach a verdict that William Flood 'died of fever and natural death'.

The foreman and three of the jurymen then hurried round to Sir Thomas Lynch to complain about the presence at the inquest of Sir Harry and Captain Musgrave. Lynch told the Lords of Trade that the foreman claimed 'that evidence was transposed and the depositions not fairly taken ... I answered that it was not my habit to meddle with the ordinary course of justice; if they had returned their verdict they ought not to complain; they should have made their complaint at the opening of the inquest, now it was too late ...' Morgan and the attorney-general were at the inquest, Lynch added, 'to advise the coroner on points of law, and I concluded if the coroner had erred about, he had erred by their advice, and they knew he was not a man of skill in the law'.

Although the verdict saved Lynch from taking action against a relative of one of the duke of York's closest friends, the episode split the residents of Port Royal. Most of the merchants and shipowners were Whigs supporting Mingham; the tradesmen and innkeepers were torn between the Whigs and Morgan. For several days after the inquest there were brawls in the taverns and fights in the streets, but Captain Churchill stayed on board the *Falcon* out in the harbour, and after a while the Point quietened down.

The lull was brief and broken by Captain Charles Morgan. Every night a guard patrolled the streets of Port Royal under a captain, and on 2 October Captain Penhallow was in command. Penhallow was a Whig and, for reasons never brought out in the subsequent inquiry, he and his men met Charles Morgan in the street, started an argument and eventually began a fight which, according to the inquiry, developed into a riot. Next morning a complaint was made to Sir Harry Morgan, as the Port's justice of the peace. He heard the evidence and bound over Penhallow to keep the peace, making him find two sureties.

Following on the *Falcon* and Mingham affair, the riot was the last straw for Lynch: his information was that Captain Charles Morgan had started the riot in one of his drunken escapades, and Lynch realized that it was a good opportunity to show how Sir Harry had abused his position by shifting the blame to Penhallow.

Lynch called the Council, whose members ordered an inquiry in which the chief justice decided that Penhallow should be 'relieved from the recognisances required'. The chief justice at this time was Morgan's brother-in-law, Byndloss, who must have realized that releasing Penhallow was the quickest way of disposing of a case which did not bear too much investigation. All the depositions taken by Sir Harry were read to the inquiry, with several more sworn before other justices that contradicted them. These, with the chief justice's opinion, led the Council to decide that Sir Harry had acted without sufficient evidence.

That gave Lynch his chance to act on the authority given him in London to deal with Council members, and he moved swiftly. He called the Council again and asked the members a specific question: 'Whether the passions and irregularities of Sir Henry Morgan do not disqualify him from continuing in his offices under the Government?' The question was put down for debate next day.

Morgan made sure that all the members of the Council who were his friends – among them Sir Francis Watson and Colonel Thomas Ballard – were present, but he knew that the result was a foregone conclusion: Lynch and his followers had a majority. The Council's minutes describe in detail what happened. The governor 'acquainted Sir Henry Morgan that he and the Council, having considered the late disorders, passions and miscarriages at Port Royal, were of opinion that they happened chiefly by his means in countenancing the people that there were concerned therein to disturb the peace'.

If that was not sufficient, Lynch had several more shots in his locker. Sir Henry had 'on all occasions showed dislike and uneasiness under his government', as well as encouraging Elletson 'that formerly gave trouble to the Council and government'. Furthermore, he had 'countenanced' several men, including Archbold, 'that ridiculed and acted him [sic]', and his brother-in-law Archbold and others had 'opposed the King's interests and made parties against the Revenue Bill' to spite the governor. The minutes noted that the governor told Morgan 'of all that was sworn, which proved that he bound over as rioters Captain Penhallow, &c, that were sober and endeavoured to keep the peace, and not Captain Morgan, &c, that seemed to be the aggressors'.

Lynch said that Sir Henry had put about a story that there was a plot to kill Captain Churchill and Captain Morgan, 'swearing that as they would not kill the King because the Duke was not there [a reference to the Rye House plot], so they would not kill Morgan because Churchill was not there, and occasioning a dissention of Whigs and Tories'. Lynch then accused Morgan of 'cursing the Assembly and frequent reflection in his debaucheries on the [Governor] to the extreme hazard of the Government and disturbance of the people, especially at the Point'.

Once Sir Thomas had finished his accusations two of Sir Henry's friends, Sir Francis Watson and Colonel Ballard, began his defence and demanded to know what evidence there was to back the governor's charge that Morgan had cursed the Assembly. Sir Thomas produced a deposition by a Major Bache saying that a woman who owned a tavern recognized Sir Henry's voice as he passed one night, and he was cursing the Assembly. The Council sent for Bache, who told them it was reported to him by a Mrs Wollin. Mrs Wollin was then brought from her tavern, made to take the oath and told to describe what had happened. She 'declared that Sir Henry Morgan going by her door one night, with some others she did not know, she heard Sir Henry Morgan swear "God damn the Assembly"'.

After this evidence of a night in old Port Royal, Sir Henry was asked for his defence, and he made it as brief as his letters: 'Sir Henry only replied he hoped he should not be charged with others' faults; he had often chid them and never intended to offend the General [sic: governor-general].'

Lynch then put the all-important question to the Council: 'Whether it was consistent with the King's service and the peace and safety of the island, that Sir Henry Morgan should be continued in any employment.' Sir Francis Watson and Colonel Ballard said that he should be kept in the Council but relieved of all other commands, but the majority voted otherwise. 'It was accordingly ordered that Sir Henry Morgan be removed from all his offices and commands and suspended the Council.'

Morgan was forty-eight years old when his public life was brought to an abrupt end by that Council vote on 12 October 1683. His major fault was unwittingly summed up by a sentence in the Council minutes, when the governor 'repeated divers extravagant expressions of Sir Henry Morgan in his wine...' Once given the opportunity, Lynch had struck swiftly: only nine days had passed since Morgan took the evidence in the Penhallow affair.

Lynch and his friends spent the weekend preparing cases against the remaining three they wished to smash, Byndloss, Charles Morgan and Elletson. Of the three, Lynch was most concerned to ruin Byndloss – 'He is one of the worst men I know,' he told the Lords of Trade a few days later. 'When I was Governor before and he a Councillor, he took a pirate's false oath against me privately and sent it home by Lord Vaughan's secretary. I would not live if my credit came into the scale with such a man.'

Byndloss was the first to be accused before the Council, with Lynch producing depositions and charging that Byndloss was unfit to be the island's chief justice, a member of the Council, or an officer in the militia. The Council heard the evidence and voted to dismiss him from all public positions.

Then they called Captain Charles Morgan. Lynch's charge against the commandant of the fort were detailed – 'all the troubles and disorder at the Point' had been caused by the Captain, who had been protected by Sir Henry. He was a member of a special club that damned dissenters; he had almost killed the innocent Captain Penhallow ... and so the accusations went on. Lynch told the Council that he had already dismissed Morgan as commandant of the fort 'for violating the guards, beating the captain [Penhallow] and various other irregularities'.

When Charles Morgan was called upon to make his defence he used the same phrase as his cousin: he could not answer for the faults of others. The Council voted to revoke his commission.

Only Elletson remained, and he was called before the Council next day. His real crime in Lynch's eyes was the demand for action against dissenters, and his appearance at the sessions was described to the Council as 'malicious disturbances of the magistrates at sessions' while, for good measure, he was accused of something unlikely to be found in any penal code, 'consorting with lewd fellows'. The Council found him guilty: he could no longer appear in any of the island's courts as a lawyer, and they demanded bonds for his future good behaviour: he had to put up £1000, and two other sureties would have to provide another £1000.

Two days later Sir Thomas sat down to give Their Lordships a detailed indictment of Sir Henry and his friends. It was no more than what any politician in Jamaica could have written about his opponent: the man who had the power made the best of it. Nor had Lynch neglected to advance his own position as a landowner – he had been steadily acquiring plantations and by now owned as much land as any single man in the island, about 30,000 acres, but he was constantly buying and selling (at his death he owned 28,000 acres).

Lynch's report was long and rambling and began with a reference to Morgan on Lynch's arrival in Jamaica: 'Instead of uniting with me I found him little civil to me, mightily elated by hopes of my death and of governing in my stead.' Lynch had of course been ill for long periods; at one time, a month before this, he had apologized to the Assembly for 'the disorders of my head' which prevented him from making a lengthy speech. His report continued:

In his debauches which go on every day and night, he is much magnified and I criticized by the five or six little sycophants that share them. His particular creatures are one Cradock, Elletson and others who have broken the peace and affronted the government. He has always endeavoured to countenance and justify them within the Council and without.

In his drink Sir Henry reflects on the government, swears, damns and curses most extravagantly. He did so to the Assembly as appears by affidavits in Colonel Beeston's hands. Had you full knowledge of his behaviour while Lieutenant-governor of his excesses, passions and incapacity, you would marvel how he ever came to be employed, than why he is now turned out.

As for Charles Morgan:

He is so haughty, passionate and given to drink that it is impossible to serve him or use him. He was the author of the troubles at the Point, for some of which I was forced to deprive him of his commission as aide major. He has almost killed diverse sergeants by beating them, though they are not in pay; a woman has sworn that he killed her husband; officers at the Point will swear that no sergeant or soldier would go to the castle [Fort Charles] for fear of him; it is sworn that he never came to the castle till noon or later, and then so drunk and inflamed that he beat sergeants and soldiers immeasurably for no fault . . .

Yet at the end of it all Lynch was nervous at what he had done, asking the Lords of Trade: 'I beg that if you approve of the suspension of the Morgans, *you will send orders to that purpose*, otherwise there will be troubles in case I should die. These men are of great violence and no sense.' His report went to England by the last ship of the winter.

The Morgans did not leave Lynch to fire the only broadsides. Elletson made a sworn statement about the Port Royal riot and Henry Archbold made another denying that Sir Henry had ever cursed the Assembly as he passed Mrs Wollin's tavern. Charles Morgan swore to statements denying the charges against him, as did Sir Henry. They then decided that these documents, forming their appeal to the Lords of Trade against Lynch's charges, should be taken to London by Charles Morgan, Byndloss and Elletson. By chance the first ship of the year to leave for England – three months after Lynch's report – would be the *Falcon*, and Captain Churchill agreed to give them cabins.

Their departure, however, provided more ammunition for Lynch, because they were not about to let Captain Churchill sail without a party – a celebration in which the vicar of St Peter's, Dr John Longworth, cheerfully joined. Reporting Charles Morgan's departure in February 1684, Lynch told Their Lordships that 'he did his utmost to ruin his drinking friends and raise a riot at the Point, for all the night of his departure he and his drinking friends violated the guards and traduced the officers.

'He, Sir Henry and their party, a day or two before the *Falcon* sailed, secretly signed in attestation for Mr Langworth [sic], the parson of Port Royal, an ill man, who has drunk with them, to the scandal of his functions and the offence of his parish.'

The *Falcon* had no sooner left than a ship arrived with dispatches from London, among them a packet for Lynch enclosing a dormant commission which would make Hender Molesworth the island's lieutenant-governor. In thanking Their Lordships, Lynch said: 'It is certain that Sir Henry Morgan's hope of governing as first Councillor has buoyed up his little senseless party, and occasioned our late troubles.'

Hender Molesworth, the Royal African Company's chief agent in Jamaica, was very unpopular with the planters. Now forty-six years old, he had been in the island for eighteen years and had started off a career as a merchant by buying a share in the *Nuestra Señora de la Concepcion y San Joseph* when she was condemned as a prize in 1668. He had been a favourite of Lord Vaughan's and became a close friend of Lynch while in London for the hearing of Long's case.

Lynch had proposed the dormant commission because he was becoming more and more concerned with the prospect of dying. He had never recovered from the illness contracted on board the *Sweepstakes* and which had killed his wife and son Charles. Although it is not known what the illness was, there is no doubt it affected the whole period of his governorship, and at the time he wrote thanking Their Lordships for Molesworth's commission he had only six months to live.

Charles Morgan, Byndloss and Elletson arrived in England to find that the Lords of Trade had long since received Lynch's report and approved the dismissals. Charles presented their petition and after various delays Their Lordships heard the appeal early in June 1684, reporting to the Privy Council that there was no reason to change their decision.

When Lynch received word of the Lords of Trade's approval of the suspensions he had won the last round in his fight against Sir Harry Morgan which had really begun ten years earlier. But he had only two months to contemplate the victory. On 24 June he married Mary, the seventeen-year-old sister-in-law of the speaker of the Assembly, Samuel Bernard, and on 24 August he died, aged fifty-one. Colonel Hender Molesworth (who was to marry Lynch's widow four years later) took the oath as the island's new governor, and next day buried his old friend in the church at Spanish Town.

28

The Paths of Glory ...

Despite the political quarrels, Jamaica was prospering, with a bustling Port Royal full of ships and the planters getting high prices. But with a man who was Lynch's shadow now in the King's House, Sir Harry Morgan spent most of his time in his new home at Port Maria, consoling himself with rum punch and good company, awaiting news of his petition to the Privy Council and unaware that the people of England had just been given the chance of reading details of his exploits and those of the buccaneers.

Two enterprising London publishers had bought copies of *Piratas de la America y Luz a la defensa de las costas de India Occidentales*, the Spanish version, and the original Dutch edition of *De Americaensche Zee-Rovers* by Oexmelin, and had them translated into English, changing the author's name to Esquemeling.

The first version was brought out by William Crooke 'at the Green Dragon, without Temple Bar' with a long title, *Bucaniers of America; or a true Account of the Most Remarkable Assaults ... upon the Coasts of the West Indies by the Bucaniers ... both English and French, Wherein are contained ... the Unparallel'd Exploits of Sir Henry Morgan, our English Jamaican Hero. Who sack'd Puerto Velo, burnt Panama &C ...'* The second version was published by Thomas Malthus, who claimed his book was 'Made English from the Dutch copy'.

Copies of each book were bought by Charles Morgan, who was still in London, and he saw at once that they were extremely libellous: Sir Harry was referred to as a pirate, the author said Sir Harry had first gone out to the West Indies as an indentured servant, and accused him of committing many atrocities. Charles consulted with a lawyer, John Greene, and sent copies off to Jamaica.

When Sir Harry read through the books he was very angry but seems more concerned that he was wrongly described as having come out to the West Indies as an indentured servant (which was almost as bad as being transported) than being called a pirate. He very soon made up his mind what to do: he would sue William Crooke and Thomas Malthus for libel and claim £10,000 damages from each of them. In the meantime he listed the separate libels, with the page numbers, and sent them off to John Greene so that he could bring the cases in the King's Bench. On page 32 of Crooke's edition, for instance: a subsequent apology said that Morgan 'was a gentleman's son of good quality in the county of Monmouth, and never was a servant unto anybody in his life, unless unto his Majesty ... Neither did he ever sail but by commission from the Governor of those parts.'

There was no truth in alleged 'cruelties and barbarous usages of the Spaniards when at his mercy or his prisoners'. The account of blowing up the castle at Portobelo after locking the prisoners in a room was untrue 'for the castle was left standing and quarter given to all that yielded'. Nor was it credible, Crooke's apology said, that Morgan would allow the cruelties described, including the story 'that many Religious were pistolled; for no such persons were killed unless they were found in arms'.

Professional pride made Sir Henry deny one particular point, referring to the raid on Maracaibo: 'No advice was given to Admiral Morgan about the fireship mentioned on page 70; but rather it was entirely his own contrivance.' And, later on: 'the style of the letter of the Spanish Admiral is wrong; for he styled him "Captain Morgan, Head of the English Fleet", not "Commander of the Pirates".'

Far more important: 'The expedition performed by Admiral Morgan against Panama was not undertaken without commission from the then Governor of Jamaica, and it was upon account of new acts of hostility and fresh abuses by the Spaniards upon the King of England's subjects in Jamaica ...'

Both Crooke and Malthus settled out of court, and the *London Gazette* on 8 June reported that Sir Henry Morgan had recovered £200 damages in the King's Bench Court against each of the publishers whose books 'contained many false, scandalous and malicious reflections on the life and actions of Sir Henry Morgan of Jamaica, Kt'. Both publishers then printed new editions of their books with long apologetic prefaces. Thomas Malthus's preface admitted that 'to copy from a sophisticated copy of a sorry original is the Devil, and this has happened in the late translation of the *History of Bucaniers* ...'

About the same time as these new editions came out, a book describing Captain Bartholomew Sharp's buccaneering raid into the Pacific was published. It was written by Basil Ringrose, who was with Sharp, and published by 'P.A. Esq.', who managed to get another description of Morgan's Panama raid, which he added as a third section. He did this, he said, after reading *A History of the Bucaniers*, and with the idea that this account of Sir Harry's attack 'might in some measure rescue the honour of that incomparable soldier and seaman from the hands of such as would load him with the blackest infamy'.

Quite apart from that, 'P.A. Esq.' then went on to attack Esquemeling and some of his facts, printing instead material which may well have come from Morgan himself. 'To begin then with Sir Henry Morgan's parentage:

he [Esquemeling] makes him the son of a yeoman, and that he sold himself [i.e. as a servant] for Barbados; whereas it is sufficiently known that he was descended from an honourable family in Monmouthshire, and went at first out of England with the Army commanded by General Venables for Hispaniola and Jamaica.'

The most significant point about the apologies printed by Crooke and Malthus and the spirited defence by 'P.A. Esq.' is that although they appeared at a time when Morgan's numerous enemies in London were seizing anything with which to attack him, no word appeared in print to deny any statement in the apologies or defence; no one came forward claiming that the original allegations of torture, rape and robbery on Morgan's orders were true.

Esquemeling, the source of so much information on the buccaneers, was a man of many names during his literary career. The question of who he really was may never be answered, but the strongest contender is Hendrik Barentzoon Smeeks, a barber-surgeon from the town of Zwolle. He went to sea with the Dutch East India Company, survived a shipwreck – involving a voyage in an open boat from Western Australia to Java – and eventually went to Tortuga. After a lively career with the buccaneers he went back to the town where he was born, apparently writing his book, and from 1680 working as a barber-surgeon. He died in 1721.

The man about whom all the words were written stayed at Port Maria, content that his honour as a soldier had been cleared by the new editions of Esquemeling's book and the first edition of Ringrose's. Only one thing remained, and he would devote the rest of his life to it – he wanted to be restored to the Council. He drank heavily and stayed up well into the night, chatting with old friends. Former privateer captains, companions of past raids, came in to Port Maria and made their way up to Llanrumney. Reports reached Spanish Town that some of his visitors were men who had not given up privateering or piracy, but Governor Molesworth could never find proof.

Although he was childless, the house was usually full of young people. Byndloss's eldest son was now twenty while Charles, who would inherit much of Sir Henry's property, was a year younger. The youngest of the Byndloss children, Morgan, was now about ten years old, thoroughly spoiled by his three sisters. The four Archbold children were growing up – the second son, Henry, who would share Sir Harry's property with Charles Byndloss, was eleven years old.

Molesworth's first twelve months as governor followed the usual pattern of the past few years. In early March 1683 he heard that 'eight or nine hundred piratical English have possessed themselves of an island called Perico, a league and a half from Panama, where they have fortified themselves and maintained it against all the force the Spaniards could make against it ... Manta, near Lima, has been plundered by pirates and much damage done'.

His information was correct, and one of the leaders of the squadron of ships off Peru was Charles Swan, the indomitable buccaneer who had taken his thirty men in the 16-ton *Endeavour* when Sir Harry Morgan went to Panama. He had returned to England three years earlier and persuaded some merchants to back him in a venture to trade in the South Sea – 'trade' being a euphemism for smuggling. One of his officers in the ship, the *Cygnet*, was William Dampier.

Molesworth's letter to London reporting the Perico raid crossed with one saying that the King had died and been succeeded by the duke of York as James II. The news was a warning to Molesworth that he could expect to be replaced as soon as the new King had time to settle down, and within six months Sir Philip Howard was chosen. Molesworth was temporarily reprieved because Sir Philip died before leaving England. Once again Sir Harry Morgan had to try to guess who was likely to get the appointment. There seemed a good chance that the young duke of Albemarle might be interested, and if he came out Morgan knew that his appeal against suspension from public office was likely to succeed; the son of the 'Great General' had been friendly enough during Morgan's three years in England.

Sir Harry's friends were gradually regaining some of their political strength. Elletson, Thomas Ballard and Henry Archbold were all elected to the Assembly, and the rest of the planters made an effort to get seats. In the Assembly the leader of the Tories was Elletson, and among the acts for which Molesworth refused the Royal Assent was one that raised the value of a piece of eight to six shillings, and another that put an export tax on slaves.

Molesworth's problems continued, and he had to write to Their Lordships about pirates based on Cuba. The worst vessels were galleys, 'mostly manned by Greeks, but they are of all nations, rogues culled out for the villainies that they committ ... They lurk in the bushes by the shore, so that they see every passing ship without being seen. When our sloops are at anchor they set [sic] them by their compasses in the daytime and steal on them by night with so little noise that they are aboard before they are discovered'.

Not all Molesworth's troubles were with pirates; parsons sometimes gave him trouble. The Rev. Mr Gilbert, who arrived in Jamaica as the *Guernsey* frigate's chaplain, had been made the rector of St Dorothy's by Sir Thomas Lynch. However, Molesworth reported, 'having more the beast than the man in him he committed so many scandalous actions that he was rebuked by Sir Thomas Lynch. Remembering the rebuke but forgetting his preferment' (by Lynch), he published a 'most scandalous libel' against Sir Thomas, for which he was jailed for a year and fined £300. Molesworth said he had been too ill at the time to write to Their Lordships or the bishop of London about it, and because Gilbert's appeal might have reached London, he was enclosing a copy of the libel.

It was a piece of verse and a savage attack on Lynch, beginning: 'He that would murder when he pleased/And with the gout so oft diseased,' and going on to accuse him of having cheated orphans and kept 'robber men in awe'. It referred to Lynch's death by saying he 'grew mad, and soon as madly died'.

When the duke of Monmouth, Charles II's illegitimate son, went back to England from exile in Holland after his father's death, landing at Lyme Regis and proclaiming himself 'head and captain-general of the Protestant forces of the Kingdom', and later being crowned at Taunton, the man who led the Devonshire militia to put down the insurrection had been the young duke of Albemarle. He was in good standing with King James, and had reasons of his own for wanting the governorship of Jamaica. His fortune was being rapidly depleted by his own not inconsiderable efforts, backed by his wife, and he had recently become involved in a treasure hunt in the West Indies, forming a syndicate to buy the 200-ton *Bridgewater Merchant* and send her out to find the plate in a Spanish galleon which had sunk on the Silver Bank north of Hispaniola.

The salvage attempt had begun three years earlier when Captain William Phipps was sent out in a small frigate to recover the treasure reported to be in a Spanish wreck among the Bahamas. Faced with a mutinous crew he put into Port Royal and replaced them, and subsequently heard that Puerto Plata, on the north-east coast of Hispaniola, had been given that name because of a plate ship that sank nearby. He searched in vain for the wreck but, sure it existed, returned to England to find backers, Albemarle among them, for a further hunt.

The amount of treasure said to be involved was enormous (thirty-two tons of silver were eventually recovered: the *Bridgewater Merchant* brought in £200,000 in gold and silver, giving a profit of £10,000 for every £100 invested), and the duke was anxious to be nearer the scene of the salvage.

When James II agreed to his governorship, Albemarle – already one of the Lords of Trade – sent the Privy Council a list of proposals covering what he wished to do when he arrived in the island. High among them was an investigation of Sir Harry Morgan's case and, if it proved favourable, his reinstatement. The Privy Council hedged and told the duke to inquire when he arrived, and then report back to London.

In the meantime Molesworth carried on in Jamaica. He heard that two hundred men who had taken part in Monmouth's Rebellion were being transported to Jamaica to serve ten years – except that thirty had escaped while being taken to the ships in Weymouth. Slave riots had been difficult to put down; the Assembly, led by Roger Elletson, was being troublesome. By September he had dissolved it, telling the members: 'You have been so fickle and inconstant that nothing was to be depended on from you...'

Although the whole situation was far from satisfactory in the island itself, Molesworth was able to report some success against pirates: in February 1687, as Albemarle began his preparations for coming out, Molesworth described the *Ruby* frigate's arrival: 'Captain Spragge returned to Port Royal ... with Captain Banister and three of his consorts hanging at his yardarm, a spectacle of great satisfaction to all good people and of terror to the favourers of pirates, the manner of his punishment being that which will most discourage others, which was the reason why I empowered Captain Spragge to inflict it.'

The first political row of the year came when Byndloss, without making adequate inquiries to see who else was involved, accused Colonel Samuel Barry, the judge of the Admiralty Court, of buying slaves who had been put on shore by an interloper, the *Hawk*.

Colonel Barry had a good answer and wrote to the Lords of Trade: 'If Colonel Byndloss knew of any malpractice here, why did he not complain to the Governor here instead of sending home malicious letters? Had he given information when the ship was at Port Maria and the captain at Sir Henry Morgan's house close by, feasting on a fat guinea goat, then the Government could have made some use of his services.'

Their Lordships asked Byndloss to make a definite charge, which he did, but a few weeks later he was taken ill and died. The first of the group of men round Sir Harry to die and with Henry Archbold one of his oldest and closest friends, he left eight children, four of them sons. The eldest, Thomas, inherited his estate, and Sir Harry took over the responsibility for the family. He was himself far from fit, and Byndloss's death was a sad blow at a time when he was still hoping that the new governor would be able to restore him to public life. He knew that the young duke had been appointed governor in October 1686; now they were almost through the hurricane season of 1687, yet there was no sign of him arriving at Port Royal.

Five days before Christmas in 1687 a small convoy of five ships reached through the entrance of Port Royal and began tacking into the anchorage to end a three-month voyage from England. The lookouts watching from Fort Charles were accustomed to unusual arrivals but this convoy caused particular interest.

It was led by the *Assistance* frigate, returning after a long absence, and there were two merchant ships astern. In the middle was a type of vessel never before seen in the West Indies, a private yacht. She was bringing out her owner, Christopher Monck, the second duke of Albemarle, to his new post. The merchant ships carried five hundred tons of his possessions and stores and most of the hundred servants the King had allowed his new governor to take out to Jamaica.

The duke and duchess watched from the quarterdeck as Captain Lawrence Wright brought the *Assistance* into the great, almost land-locked harbour, and while the seamen waited ready to swarm aloft to furl the sails, the Albemarles had their first proper sight of the tropical island which was to be their new home.

As though Nature sensed that their arrival was a special occasion, the sun was bright and the clouds sparkling white and gently rounded. The distant mountains forming the island's backbone were powder blue and the long sandy beach forming the Palisadoes and ending at the Point was dazzling enough for the casual onlooker not to notice the row of gibbets set a few yards back from the water's edge. The rainy season had refreshed the island and the various greens of the trees and shrubs seemed particularly lush to people who for weeks had seen nothing but the almost harsh blue of the tropical sea and sky. The guns of the forts began the steady boom of the salute, and as soon as the little convoy had anchored the island's leaders came out in boats to welcome the duke and duchess, all of them curious for their first sight of one of the most famous (not to say notorious) couples in Restoration England.

The first to pay his respects was Hender Molesworth. It was an uncomfortable meeting for several reasons. First, the duke had decided to claim half the salary and perquisites from the date of his commission, which covered fifteen months by the time he arrived. Molesworth protested that he had been doing the work and carrying the responsibility for the governor, but the duke won – a victory which put £3000 in his pocket.

The second was one that could easily be understood by those who appreciated the irony of this lively if dissipated sprig of the new nobility getting the better of a man proud that he was one of the first governors from Jamaica's merchant class, even though he had not yet received the customary knighthood. Captain William Phipps was being very successful in raising silver from the wreck off Puerto Plata, and the duke was insisting that Molesworth put up a security of £100,000 to cover the tenths due to the King. Molesworth protested that he could not raise such a security and anyway it was not his place to. Furthermore, he said, he was returning to England the following May. The duke was unimpressed and Molesworth was told he could not leave the island until the bond was posted.

After an uncomfortable meeting when these points were discussed, Molesworth then had to tell the duke and duchess that the King's House was not yet ready; a house had been rented for them until the repairs were completed. Fortunately the Albemarles were in no hurry to go on shore: even anchored well away from the land they had encountered the mosquitoes and sandflies, and they knew that the coolest place would be on board the ship. They would land, Molesworth was told, in six days' time; in the meantime they would celebrate Christmas on board their yacht...

In the salutes, greetings and excited chatter at Port Royal, those first meeting the Albemarles did not notice a shadow over the couple, a shadow that accounted for the presence of Dr Hans Sloane in their suite. The duchess had kept pace with her husband in pursuing a life of gaiety. She had seen Albemarle House sold to pay debts, but neither she nor her husband had tried to economize. A shortage of money entailed not economies but a search for fresh sources, the latest being Captain Phipps' treasure hunt.

The duchess was causing her husband concern. The Lady Elizabeth Cavendish whom he had married in such bizarre circumstances had changed from a gay and vivacious girl to be, at twenty-seven, a spoiled and wilful woman whose erratic behaviour was now slowly but steadily turning into mental instability.

The duke had finally employed Dr Sloane to attend the duchess. It was usual to have a doctor in such an entourage, and Albemarle had chosen one of the cleverest available, a young man whose name and reputation would live long after his illustrious employer's had become a small footnote in history. Sloane had been looking forward to the visit to Jamaica because in addition to being a physician he was a naturalist and collector. He had read the few books published on the natural history of the West Indies and they were of little consequence. The main works on the subject were Bartolomé de la Casas' manuscripts. Written nearly 150 years earlier, they were still gathering dust on a shelf in Madrid, and would not be published for another two centuries.

In addition to Sloane's concern that the duchess was not responding to treatment – there had been no improvement during the long sea voyage – the duke, a few months past his thirty-fourth birthday, was beginning to show unmistakable symptoms of the effect of his way of life. In Sloane's words, he had 'a sanguine complexion, his face reddish and his eyes yellow, and accustomed by being at Court to sitting up late and often being merry'.

The duke and duchess finally completed the ceremonial of their arrival and with the official business over Albemarle passed the word for the man he most wanted to see – an old friend on whose behalf he had used all his influence in London. The man was, of course, Sir Harry Morgan, whom he had not seen for a dozen years. In those heady days of 1675, Sir Harry had been thirty-nine years old, tall and lean, black-bearded and bright-eyed, hard-drinking and lively company, and that was the man that the young duke, who had then been twenty-two years old, remembered as the *Jamaica Merchant* sailed from the Downs to take the new lieutenant-governor back to the island.

Now, when they finally met again twelve years later on board the duke's yacht in Port Royal at Christmas 1687, the Albemarles were startled to find that their friend had become paunchy and puffy-faced, the whites of his eyes an unhealthy yellow and his skin blotchy. His stomach bulged, so swollen that it defied all attempts by his tailor to conceal it. Dr Sloane listened carefully when Sir Harry said that despite the paunch he had no appetite for food and, sitting down whenever he could, grumbled that his legs were swollen. Even without an examination, Dr Sloane 'was afraid of beginning dropsie'.

For all that, Sir Harry was still a lively guest, drinking hard and telling a good yarn. He heard from the duke the story of making Hender Molesworth go halves with the governor's salary, and gave the new governor his version of the island's present situation. But he was disappointed when the duke told him that the Lords of Trade had not agreed to restore him to the Council, although the report they required would be a matter of form; it would simply take time.

The duke and duchess finally went on shore in Jamaica the day after Christmas and received an almost hysterical welcome, 'being entertained at public expense for three days'. The Albemarles' coach took them first to the Assembly, where the members waited, perspiring in the heat, the public gallery full with their glowing wives and families. They were greeted by the speaker, Samuel Bernard, an old enemy of Sir Harry's. He presented them with an address declaring that the duchess's arrival was an honour 'which the opulent kingdoms of Mexico and Peru could never arrive at; and even Columbus's ghost must be appeased for all the indignities he endured of the Spaniards, could he but know that his beloved soil was hallowed by such footsteps'.

The beloved soil soon startled everyone: three weeks after the Albemarles moved into their rented house the whole island was shaken by an earthquake which damaged several buildings but, the duke reported to the Lords of Trade, 'no great harm done that I can hear'.

Once the Albemarles moved on shore Sloane was able to indulge his hobby as a naturalist, travelling round the island to begin a collection which later became the nucleus of the British Museum, and writing notes which were to be a detailed account of his stay in the island and the only record of Sir Harry Morgan's last illness.

Wherever Sloane looked he could scarcely believe his eyes: scores of different orchids, hundreds of different ferns, tiny birds with iridescent feathers that could hover almost motionless, strange fruits and vegetables, unusual trees, seashells of startling beauty thrown up on the beach ... And he saw the remarkable progress of the new arrivals to the West Indies: the bananas first brought from the Canary Islands by the Spanish a hundred years earlier, the sugar cane, the oranges and lemons from Spain. A lush island where, it seemed, anything would grow; where seeds seemed to sprout overnight in a temperature that stayed comfortably close to eighty degrees most of the year. For Sloane it seemed hard to believe that the banana, orange, lemon and sugar cane were not native to the Caribbean.

While Sloane walked and rode through the island, magnifying glass, specimen box and notebook to hand, the duke went to work on Sir Henry's behalf. His first report to the Lords of Trade, written the day the *Assistance* anchored in Port Royal, said that the island's Council had recommended Sir Harry's readmission. Sir Harry himself was being forced to spend more and more time at home. His swelling legs made walking or standing painful, and he rested for much of each day in a hammock.

In his weakened state, Morgan found the nights hard to bear: all too often the wind dropped, leaving the house oppressively hot and humid, the air buzzing and whining with mosquitoes which always seemed to defy the smoking fires and smouldering tobacco leaf intended to drive them off. Sleep came only if he had drunk enough rum or brandy, yet his doctors told him to reduce his drinking. Dr Sloane, who was not attending him officially at this time, noted that if anything he was increasing his drinking.

However, at fifty-three a sick man wakes up in the dark hours and broods over the fact that he is not immortal. In the seventeenth century a man of that age knew that he had very few years left, particularly if he lived in the Tropics. Byndloss had died at fifty, Lynch at fifty-one, Charles II had died at fifty-five, as had Drake ...

The duke's letter recommending Sir Harry's restoration, although written before Christmas, did not reach London until the beginning of April. When they saw that not only did one of their former colleagues consider that Morgan should be restored to the Council but the Council itself favoured it, the Lords of Trade recommended to the Privy Council that he should be reinstated. The King agreed on 27 April, and although the news was brought to Jamaica in the next available ship, it did not arrive until the beginning of July.

By then Dr Sloane despaired of Morgan's life. Within a month or two of arriving in the island he had attempted to treat him, but Sir Harry was an impossible patient. Fortunately, Dr Sloane kept notes. He guessed Sir Harry's age and underestimated it by eight years. Describing him as 'lean, sallow-coloured, his eyes a little yellowish and belly jutting out or prominent', he wrote that Morgan,

complained to me of want of appetite for victuals, he had a kicking or roaching to vomit every morning and generally a small looseness attending him, and withal is much given to drinking and staying up late, which I supposed had been the cause of his present indisposition.

I was afraid of beginning dropsie and advised him to an easy vomit of Oxymel.Scill., with the help of a feather and thin water-gruel, fearing

Vin.Emet. might disorder him too much by putting him into a looseness or too great evacuation. After that I gave him some Madera wine in which roots of gentian, tops of centaury had been infused with Mich.Vomit.

It worked very easily and the bitter wine, taken every morning for some days, he recovered his stomach and continued very well for a considerable time.

By April the weather had changed: the cool winter nights were past and in May many of them were hot and uncomfortably humid for a man with a great belly and who, because he was an alcoholic, perspired freely at the slightest exertion. Dozing during the day to rest his legs meant he was less ready for sleep at nights, and the prospect of long, sleepless nights in turn led him to justify the hard liquor as being the only way of sleeping.

'Not being able to abstain from company,' noted Dr Sloane, 'he sat up late at night drinking too much, whereby he had a return of his first symptoms, but complained he could not make water.' He did not continue Dr Sloane's treatment for long although, the doctor noted, 'this course did very well with him, but making very little water and being much troubled with belchings and a cough in the night, he sent to another doctor, who, when he came, was of opinion that his disease was a timpany, and that the swellings of his belly came only from wind, according to Hippocrates, that he was not troubled with the beginning of a dropsie nor had a gravel (which is not unusual in this case and he had always been troubled with)'.

Sloane told the new doctor of post-mortem examinations which

had discovered the bellies of people dying of supposed timpanies to be distended with water and no more wind than is supposed to be the effect of phlegm and crude humours lying in the stomach and guts.

I desired him that he should put off talking of the theory and come to the practice, that we might very well agree in the medicine he should take, as it very often happens to physicians, who may disagree in the theory and yet agree in the practice.

I waited on Sir H. and told him of Dr Rose's and my opinion, which agreeing, he was satisfied therewith. We gave him all manner of diuretics and easy purges we could find in Jamaica ... advised him to eat juniper berries, used oil of scorpion with ling. Dialth. outwardly, by which he recovered again.

By the middle of June, with still no word from England, Morgan was ill enough to know that the time had come to bring in the attorneys and sign a document which began: 'I, Sr Henry Morgan Knt being sick in body but of sound mind and memory doe make and ordaine this my last will and testament ...'

The first beneficiary, receiving most of his estates (which totalled several thousand acres), was 'my very well and intirely beloved wife Dame Mary Elizabeth Morgan'. After her death the estates would pass to Charles Byndloss 'upon this express condition', that he and his heirs 'doe alter and change the name or surname of Byndloss and take upon him and them the name of Morgan and always go thereby'. If he had no sons, the estates would then go to 'the second son of Henry Archbold, son and heir of the present Henry Archbold Esqre', on the same condition, that he and his heirs took the surname Morgan. If neither Charles nor Henry had sons, the estates passed in succession to sons of Anna Byndloss and her two daughters. Young Morgan Byndloss would receive the Penkarne estate when he was twenty-one, while Elletson's son Richard would receive another estate called Arthur's Land.

Having disposed of the estates, he then dealt with the small bequests. Colonel Thomas Ballard would get 'my Greene saddle with the furniture thereunto belonging', while Roger Elletson had 'the choice of anyone of my horses, my blew saddle and furniture thereunto belonging, together with one case of pistolls tipped with silver'. To 'my well beloved sister Catherine Loyd [sic]' he left £60 a year which would be paid 'into the hands of my ever honest cozen Mr Thomas Morgan of Tredegar'. His godsons Henry Archbold and Richard Elletson and his nephew Thomas Byndloss were each left a silver-hilted sword and a mourning ring, while Thomas was to have 'another case of pistolls tipped with silver'.

Many people were left the customary mourning rings – among them the duke and duchess of Albemarle, his servants, Sir Francis and Lady Watson, the Ballards, Major John Peake (his secretary on the Panama expedition), 'my sister Byndloss and sister Archbold', and Dr John Longworth.

He chose as trustees Colonel Ballard, Henry Archbold, the eldest Byndloss son, and Roger Elleston, and he signed the will on 17 June 1688. A note at the end, signed by the duke of Albemarle and dated 14 September, said that two of the four witnesses – one had since died – had appeared before him and sworn that they had seen Sir Henry sign and seal the will.

At the beginning of July a ship came in with dispatches, and a delighted Albemarle read that the King had agreed to Sir Harry being reinstated in the Council. The duke called a meeting for 12 July, just as the island was preparing to vote for a new Assembly, and with considerable pomp and flourish announced the reinstatement. Sir Harry came by carriage from Lawrencefield to attend the meeting, and it was obvious to everyone present that the doctors were fighting a losing battle for his life. He returned to Lawrencefield with the satisfaction of knowing that after five years he was back on the Council and restored to favour, both at Court and in Jamaica.

There was just one more wish that he wanted fulfilled, and that was up to the island's freeholders, who would soon be voting for the members of the new Assembly. The issues facing the voters were, for once, fairly straight-forward, and the election was a struggle between Whigs led by Samuel Long and backed by the merchants, and Morgan's Tories, supported by the planters.

The election was an overwhelming victory for Morgan's group; indeed, most of the men Sir Harry had mentioned in his will were returned. The Assembly met on 20 July, elected Roger Elletson as speaker and adjourned until the next day, when the duke would attend as the governor.

As soon as the duke in full regalia had declared the Assembly in session, Elletson rose and, as speaker, presented him with an Address, which he read. It could have been intended as a justification of the political activities of Morgan's group over the past years but more likely it was a clumsy tribute to a man that Elletson and all the Assembly knew was dying.

Elletson began by referring to the time, ten years earlier, when Vaughan was governor and Morgan lieutenant-governor. When Vaughan left the island, Sir Henry Morgan succeeded him and 'with perfect loyalty to his Sovereign, justice to his Majesty's subjects, care and diligence for the general good of this his Majesty's island', continued until the arrival of the earl of Carlisle, 'into whose hands, with all duty, obedience and service, Sir Henry Morgan delivered the government'.

The earl's government was 'both profitable and pleasant, the island flourished, and the inhabitants thereof sat each under his own vine, in peace and quietness'. When the earl returned to England the government again devolved on Morgan.

[Morgan's] study and care was that there might be no murmuring, no complaining in our streets, no man in his property injured, or of his liberty restrained; his dispensations of favour and kindness were great and many, even to those who, true hornet like, lay buzzing about him during his government, but immediately upon the alteration [i.e. when Lynch arrived as Governor] stung him even unto death.

[Lynch] found this island in a happy and good condition; all men at least appeared as of one house, of one heart, and of one mind ... It was then the golden age; but as was sweet, so it proved short; for that method and current of affairs in Sir Henry Morgan's government were quickly changed, and several of those persons, who had the honour to bear their parts in the harmonious concert of his government, grew presently pale, peevish, envious and angry, as if they had been truly weary of well doing.

Sir Thomas Lynch was scarce warm in his chair of state before the goats were divided from the sheep, and esteemed the only creatures; before the island was upon the decay, and brought into such a hectic as it still languisheth ...

*   *   *

Elletson ended the Address with an attack on Hender Molesworth. His three years' government, he told the duke, were summed up in the island's circumstances when the duke arrived – 'no trade, no money, poor and miserable ...'

As the Assembly adjourned for the day Sir Harry Morgan, walking with a stick, hobbled to his carriage which took him back to Lawrencefield and a celebration of his final reinstatement. But no celebration could disguise the fact that it was now the hurricane season, and when the wind dropped away at night the heat and humidity were oppressive.

Like many once-active men, Morgan seems to have found that facing a long and lingering death was frightening in a way that he had never before experienced: his bravery in battle was a matter of legend but it required a vastly different kind of courage to face a death slowly advancing week by week, like the tide flooding over a sandy beach.

Sloane continued the notes describing his famous patient: 'On intemperance he fell again into a looseness threatening his life which by an opiate &c at night we stopped and he enjoyed his health for some time longer very well.' But it was a temporary recovery; Morgan was too old to change his ways:

> Falling after into his old course of life and not taking any advice to the contrary, his belly swelled so as not to be contained in his coat, on which I warned him of his very great danger because, he being very weak and subject to a looseness, there was no room for purging medicines, which seemed to be the greatest remedies for his dropsie threatening his life, seeing that diuretics did not produce the desired effect.

This warning did produce an immediate effect, but not the one that Sloane wanted:

> On this alarm he sent for three or four other physicians who, as I was told, said he had no dropsie because his legs did not swell, the reason of which was because he lay in a hammock with his legs up and used very little exercise.
>
> They advised him to a cataplasm of Ocroain of this country for his swelled belly and would have given him a vomit next morning but that it was an unlucky day, as indeed in all likelihood been to him if he had taken it, for he fell naturally by only the cataplasm into a very dangerous looseness, which had almost carried him off; so that the thoughts of this proceeding was put off.
>
> He changed soon after his physicians, and had first a black who gave him clysters of urine &c and plastered him all over with clay and water, and by it augmented his cough. So he left his black doctor and sent for

another, who promised him cure, but he languished and, his cough augmenting, died soon after.

Although they had known for so long that he had been ill, the people of Jamaica were stunned by the news on that Saturday morning, 25 August, that Sir Harry Morgan was dead. Many had seen him sailing a victorious squadron back into Port Royal after sacking some Spanish town on the Main; most had seen him lurching drunkenly but cheerfully from one tavern to another. Many hated him, many had grown rich as the result of his activities. But whatever their attitude, he was the man to whom they had always turned when an enemy threatened the island.

In the Tropics the burial is held within twenty-four hours of a person dying, and the duke of Albemarle ordered an immediate state funeral. Dr John Longworth, the former buccaneer chaplain, prepared St Peter's Church for the service in Port Royal; arrangements were made for the carriages to carry the mourners. Orders for salutes were given to Captain Lawrence Wright, commanding the *Assistance* which had brought out the Albemarles, and to the commanding officer of the *Drake*, another warship also anchored in the harbour. Captain Wright noted in his log: *'August, 1688. Saturday 25th. This day about eleven hours morn'g, Sir Harry Morgan died.'*

Early on Sunday morning the lead-lined coffin was carried from Lawrencefield round the eastern end of the harbour and along the arm of land ending in Port Royal. The procession passed through the gates of Fort Rupert – built by Morgan – and into Port Royal itself. At the King's House the coffin was carried inside so that mourners could pay their last respects.

By now Port Royal was unusually full of men and women, but they were not roistering and most wore signs of mourning. The governor had wisely proclaimed a general amnesty for twenty-four hours, so pirates – many of them former privateersmen – could slip in for the funeral. Wealthy planters and their wives in heavy mourning rubbed shoulders with officers of the militia in full uniform; owners of taverns within a few yards of where the coffin now rested paid their respects to the man who had spent many days and nights of his life drinking within their walls. Finally the duke and duchess arrived, Morgan's coffin was placed on a gun carriage and the funeral procession moved slowly to St Peter's Church. There Dr Longworth, no doubt reflecting on the days long past when he had followed Sir Harry in raids on the Main, conducted the service and then led the way to the cemetery on the Palisadoes nearby.

Later, Captain Wright noted in the *Assistance*'s log (little realizing that within four years the pages would be one of the few surviving mementos of the day) that after the service Sir Harry Morgan's body *'was carried to the Palisadoes & there buried. We fired two and twenty* [guns], *& after wee and the* Drake *had fired, all the merchantmen fired'*. It is significant that the ships fired one more gun than was laid down for a governor's salute.

Dr Sloane had little time for regrets that one of his patients had ignored his advice with such fatal results, because the duke was soon very ill. Sloane had already noted that Albemarle 'sometimes sat up too late and drank too freely, whereby he in a short time had in one of his legs a great pain'. Less than two months after the guns of Port Royal fired their salute at Morgan's funeral, they were firing again for the death of Christopher, the 2nd duke of Albemarle, at the age of thirty-five. As with Morgan, the major factor in his death had been alcoholism. His bowels were removed and at a special service buried beneath the altar of the church in Spanish Town; his body was preserved in pitch and sent back to England.

The duchess of Albemarle, now almost completely unbalanced, took her husband's body back to England. Lady Morgan remained at the Llanrumney estate, with the Archbolds as her neighbours, so that their four young sons were frequent visitors. With the Byndloss sons marrying, she soon became a great-aunt, dying eight years later in 1696.

The Albemarles, father and son, had been good friends of the Morgans, uncles and nephew: it was a grim coincidence that the son and the nephew died almost simultaneously in Jamaica, bringing to a close not just a personal association but an age in British history. Port Royal itself, which had grown and matured with Morgan, barely outlasted him.

Dinner in Port Royal

The cooling Trade winds had fallen away to leave the whole island of Jamaica hot and humid, a sprawling ridge of scorching rock in a mirror-smooth sea. The unusual high haze on this Tuesday morning in 1692 had turned the sun into a harsh white disc and was bleaching the blue from both sea and sky.

The people in the hot streets of Port Royal squinted against the glare, pulled down the brims of their wide hats and bonnets and shrugged their shoulders: the hurricane season had begun and they had to expect the temper-fraying heat and the long breathless days and nights. Wives nagged more frequently and many husbands were drunk earlier in the day, thankful for the excuse that the hot weather made them so dry.

Some people in Port Royal later claimed that from soon after dawn this day, 7 June, had an ominous air about it; the sort of day when things went wrong, a carving knife slipped and cut a finger or an unexpected creditor banged on the door, or a ship came in from England with bad news. Certainly thunderstorms seemed to threaten even though none had yet started billowing on the horizon, and in the pantries milk that was not yet even on the turn suddenly curdled while children behaved with such fractiousness that they seemed possessed of the devil.

The distant mountains forming the island's backbone were greyish-blue and fading into the haze and, if they were honest, knowledgeable sea captains whose ships were anchored in the great enclosed harbour shrugged their shoulders and admitted they were puzzled: there was no sign of the long and low swell waves breaking on the lengthy sand spit on which Port Royal was built and which they had long ago learned were the distant out-riders of a hurricane, nor were there high clouds overhead, the delicate mare's tails that often warn of an approaching storm. No weather lore accounted for the curious, almost ominous atmosphere, a point on which fishermen, planters and pundits for once agreed.

Yet the heat and dust, the heads throbbing from too much rum the night before, the aimless lurching of besotted seamen turned out of taverns or trollops' beds with the last of the night because their pockets were empty, were familiar to the people bustling about their business in Port Royal where the streets, narrow but many of them paved, were set out with almost geometrical precision.

The hucksters' shouts of unrepeatable bargains showed that all three markets were open, with customers selecting their fish and meat. Buyers pointed out the lobsters they wanted and a slave jerked them out of the crawl with his snare. In the taverns the potmen served the drinkers and the first of the canoes came over with fresh water from across the harbour.

On board the *Swan*, one of the two ships of war in the anchorage, the heavy yards had been sent down and the seamen were about to hoist out the guns and lower them into a barge ready to careen the ship, heeling her over so that her bottom could be scraped clean, one side at a time. It would be coated with a tar mixture in the endless fight to stop weed and barnacles growing and to keep out the teredo worms.

Some of the people in the streets were on their way to church – to satisfy the spiritual needs of the people in Port Royal alone there were a Protestant and a Presbyterian church, a Quakers' meeting house, 'a Romish Chapell ... and a Jew's Sinagog'. The Protestant church, St Peter's, was still the most magnificent: its buttressed tower stood four-square above the city with a clear view seaward along the southern coast and in sight of all five of the city's forts, particularly the nearest, Morgan's Fort, the largest and most important of Port Royal's defences. Sir Harry Morgan had paid for much of St Peter's, and he and his friends had not stinted: it was 'paved with marble, well adorned with cedar pews, and good marble steps and curiously paved work...'

It had been a fitting place one Sunday morning four years earlier for the state funeral of Sir Henry Morgan when wealthy planters and their wives had prayed in company with some of the Caribbean's most desperate pirates and their doxies, and honest citizens had looked at the politicians and feared for the island's safety now that Sir Harry had gone.

At the time of his death such a centre of wealth and debauchery was nevertheless well equipped to take care of itself in the event of an attack by the Spanish. It was ringed by five forts, the oldest of which was Fort Charles, mounting thirty-two guns (and which started life in 1657 as Fort Cromwell), while Fort James, named after the King's brother and successor, was hexagonal, built of stone and mounting twenty-six guns. Close to Charles was the twenty-six-gun fort named after Morgan, flanked by Morgan's Lines and almost next door to St Peter's church. One of the remaining forts, the fourteen-gun Carlisle, was 'begun and finished by the great care and diligence of Sir Henry Morgan', as a report from the governor had told the Lords of Trade.

Although he had now been dead four years, the name of Harry Morgan was far from forgotten: Port Royal's defences were more of a memorial to him than his tombstone, and whenever groups of men lapsed into drunken nostalgia they were still hard put to find words to describe to strangers those weeks of roistering that followed when Harry Morgan and his buccaneers returned from a raid, and how he would buy a great cask of wine and set it up in the street and insist that every passer-by join him in a toast. That had been 'Harry Morgan's way'; now it was past, and trade flourished only if men worked hard.

On this particular morning Dr Heath, who had replaced the militant Dr John Longworth as rector of St Peter's, had already read prayers, 'which I did every day since I was rector at Port Royal, to keep some show of religion among a most ungodly debauched people', and had gone on to a 'place hard by the church', as he later wrote euphemistically to a friend, 'where merchants used to meet'.

There he found John White, recently appointed president of the Council and now acting as governor of Jamaica until a new one arrived from England. 'This gentleman came into my company and engaged me to take a glass of wormwood wine with him, as whet before dinner.

'He being my very great friend, I stayed with him. Hereupon he lighted a pipe of tobacco, which he was pretty long in taking; and not being willing to leave him before it was out, this detained me from going to dinner at one Captain Ruden's...' White's tardiness with his pipe was to save Dr Heath's life.

In addition to the acting governor, the island's attorney-general, Simon Musgrove, was also visiting Port Royal, where some of the island's wealthiest inhabitants lived. Half an hour before noon one of the port's leading merchants, Mr John Uffgress, was in a tavern having a drink before his mid-day meal while Dr Trapham, described as 'a doctor of physick' and in fact the port's physician, was at his house with his wife and children. Captain Ruden was at his house with his family, waiting for Dr Heath to join them.

The worthy doctor, however, was still in a club at the other side of Port Royal watching the acting governor puffing his pipe. Dr Heath wrote:

Before that was out, I found the ground rolling and moving under my feet, upon which I said, 'Lord, sir, what is this?' He replied very composedly, being a very grave man: 'It is an earthquake, be not afraid, it will soon be over.'

But it increased, and we heard the church [St Peter's] and tower fall; upon which we ran to save ourselves. I quickly lost him, and made towards Morgan's Fort, which being a wide open place, I thought there to be securest from falling houses, but as I made towards it, I saw the earth open up and swallow a multitude of people, and the sea mounting in upon us over the fortifications.

One of the first houses to vanish into an enormous crack in the ground was Captain Ruden's. He and his family were never seen again.

Another eyewitness wrote:

> The earth suffered a trepidation or trembling, which in one minute's time was increased to that degree that several houses began to tumble down and, in a little time after, the church and tower [St Peter's], the ground opening in several places at once, swallowed up multitudes of people together, whole streets sinking under water with men, women and children in them; and those houses which but just now appeared the fairest and loftiest in these parts, and might vie with the finest buildings, were in a moment sunk down into the earth, and nothing to be seen of them ...

The writer, the captain of a ship, noted that the tidal waves tearing at the anchored ships drove several right into the town, a French prize ending up stranded in the market place. 'The burying place at the Palisadoes is quite destroyed, the dead bodies being washed out of their graves, their tombs beat to pieces, and they floating up and down,' he recorded. Sir Harry Morgan's tomb was among those that vanished.

In the meantime Dr Heath, not yet realizing how narrowly he had missed being crushed and buried in Captain Ruden's house, 'laid aside all thoughts of escaping, and resolved to make towards my own lodging, there to meet death in as good a posture as I could. From where I was, I was forced to cross, and run through two or three very narrow streets. The houses and walls fell on each side of me and some bricks came rolling over my shoes, but none hurt me'.

At the tavern, Mr Uffgress,

> felt the house shake and saw bricks begin to rise in the floor and at the same instant heard one in the street cry, 'an earthquake!' Immediately we ran out of the house, where we saw all people with lifted up hands begging God's assistance.
>
> We continued running up the streets whilst on either side of us we saw the houses, some swallowed up, others thrown on heaps; the sand in the streets rise like the waves of the sea, lifting up all persons that stood upon it and immediately dropping into pits; and at the same instant a flood of water breaking in and rolling those poor souls over and over; some catching hold of beams and rafters of houses, others were found in the sand that appeared when the water was drained away ...

Another man who escaped wrote later that Dr Trapham 'was miraculously saved by hanging by his hands upon the rack [mantelpiece] of a chimney, and one of his children about his neck, were both saved by a boat, but his wife and the rest of the children and family were lost'.

Uffgress tried to get to his house 'upon the ruins of the houses that were floating upon the water, but could not. At length I got a canoe and rowed upon the great sea towards my house, where I saw several men and women floating upon the wreck [of a ship] out to sea'. He rowed out and picked up as many as the canoe would hold and rowed back 'to where I thought my house stood, but could not hear of either my wife nor family'.

Next day he managed to find his wife among the survivors and she told him that 'when she felt the house shake, she ran out, and called all the house to do the same. She was no sooner out, but the sand lifted up, and her Negro woman grasping about her, they both dropped into the earth together, when at the very instant the water came in, rolled them over and over, till at length they caught hold of a beam, where they hung, till a boat came from a Spanish vessel and took them up'.

The rector of St Peter's, Dr Heath, had in the meantime found his house still standing and gone up to look out from the balcony. There he was seen by people in the street who 'cried out to me to come down and pray with them'. He went downstairs and joined them, whereupon:

Every one laid hold of my clothes and embraced me, that with their fears and kindness I was almost stifled.

I persuaded them at last to kneel down and make a large ring, which they did. I prayed with them near an hour, when I was almost spent with the heat of the sun and the exercise. They then brought me a chair; the earth working all the while with new motions, and trembling, like the rolling of the sea; insomuch that sometimes when I was at prayer I could hardly keep myself upon my knees.

He spent another half an hour 'setting before them their sins and heinous provocations, and seriously exhorting them to repentence'. After that he managed to board a ship in the harbour, where he found the acting governor safe but saw that 'the sea had entirely swallowed up the wharf, with all the goodly brick houses upon it, most of them as fine as those in Cheapside [in the City of London] and two entire streets beyond that...'

Another eyewitness described how, 'Several people were swallowed up by the earth, when the sea breaking in before the earth had closed, were washed up again and miraculously saved from perishing; others the earth received up to their necks and then closed upon them and squeezed them to death with their heads above ground, many of which the dogs ate. Multitudes of people floating up and down, having no burial...'

Several of the forts had been destroyed, including Fort Morgan. Fort James had sunk under twenty-five feet of water and Fort Carlisle under thirty-five; only Fort Charles remained. In the massive upheaval of the earth, followed by the tidal wave, about a third of Port Royal had submerged. More than two thousand people had perished and only one house in ten was left standing.

The earthquake affected the whole island and the capital, Spanish Town, was badly damaged, though escaping the tidal wave that hit Port Royal. The violent tremor had 'thrown down almost all the houses and churches, sugarworks, mills and bridges through the whole country', Dr Heath wrote. 'It tore the rocks and mountains, destroyed some whole plantations, and threw them into the sea.'

Port Royal, apart from some ten acres, vanished for nearly three hundred years, until a minor earthquake in 1965 led to the discovery in the sea of the walls of some of the buildings in the old sunken city, and within a short while divers were bringing up several of the articles of everyday life in use on Tuesday, 7 June 1692 – silver and pewter dishes and cutlery, silver shoe and belt buckles, a gold pocket watch with the maker's name still decipherable, dozens of clay pipes and hundreds of bottles, a brass oil lamp from the site of the synagogue.

The earthquake not only ended an age, happening with all the coincidence and improbability associated with Greek mythology, but it made a fitting end to the story of Sir Harry Morgan: for all practical purposes and certainly all historical, the port and town which he had done more than any single man to build, defend and make famous had disappeared at the same instant that his own grave vanished.

Notes

I wish to thank Señora Maria Elena Cardona for her assistance and for putting the resources and staff of the Biblioteca Regional del Caribe y Norte Sur in San Juan, Puerto Rico, at my disposal. Documents in the Public Record Office are used by permission of the Keeper of Public Records and material from the British Museum and Library is used by permission of the Trustees; material from Trinity College Library is quoted by permission of The Board of Trinity College, Dublin; and material from Cambridge University Library by permission of the Syndics of Cambridge University Library.

The full titles of sources are listed separately on pages 367–9 while the references given below have the main title abbreviated. They and the notes are given page by page and indicated by the first few words of a line, a key phrase or a specific description.

The following abbreviations are used: PRO (Public Record Office); CSP/WI (Calendar of State Papers, America and West Indies); CSP/C (Calendar of State Papers, Colonial Series); Acts/PC (Acts of the Privy Council, Colonial Series); Journals, Assembly (Journals of the Assembly of Jamaica); CCR (PRO, Commissioner of Customs Reports); Arch de Ind (Archivo General de las Indias, Seville, Spain).

The line print at the head of each chapter shows a Mexico City Piece of Eight, 1681, from the British Museum, both sides of which are reproduced at the foot of the second page of illustrations.

CHAPTER 1

Page

3 An ounce of gold: see Sutherland, *Gold*. The early gold used by the Egyptians was about 85 per cent fine (i.e. 85 per cent pure) but they later produced 95 per cent fine.

5 In an age: see Morales-Carrión, *Puerto Rico*.

7 San Salvador island: the identity of the actual island is still in dispute.

8 The naming of islands: on this voyage he visited Santa Cruz (today's St Croix) and, attacked by four Carib men and two women in a canoe, fought the first battle between men of the Old World and the New.

11 From tax records: see Sutherland, *Gold*, 132.

CHAPTER 2

12 'Her master with ten': the Spanish account is in the Arch de Ind 53–1–9, depositions taken 26 Nov – 9 Dec 1527. See Wright *Spanish Documents*.

13 Using Lucaya Islands: see Newton, *European Nations*, 51.

13 Four years later: see Haring. *Trade*, 26, which gives by far the best description of the sailing of the fleets and losses sustained.

Page

20 First port of call: if a slow passage left the galleons or *flota* short of water, the ships usually called at Dominica, by far the wettest of the Lesser Antilles islands, to refill their casks.

23 The Crown was: wood was plentiful, oak coming from the hills of Asturias and Galicia and pine from the south. Flax for sails and cordage was usually imported.

23 From the very early days: experiments in sheathing hulls with metal to keep out teredo worms began early: Pedrarias D'avila was ordered to sheath two caravels with lead. One, the *Santa Catalina* used 35 cwt, and the other 40 cwt. They sailed in 1514. See Arch de Ind 109-1-15, Valadollid, 7 Aug 1513. This may well have been the first time that ships were metal-sheathed below the waterline.

24 'Those of gentle birth': Haring, *Trade*, 103.

CHAPTER 3

27 An English priest: the account is given in Gage, *New Survey*.

28 The people who suffered: the taxes were calculated in the same way as the value added tax of the twentieth century and were equally as unwieldy.

28 At Potosí: see Crow, *Epic*, and Luis Galdames, *A History of Chile*, 1941.

28 Indies trade: see Haring, *Trade*, 214.

29 The smuggling: this went on in Spanish ships and was referred to as 'unregistered' cargo. Punishment was severe – ten years in the galleys – although smuggling bullion could mean perpetual banishment.

29 The total amount: BM Add 13964, f. 196; Add 13964, f. 405.

29 Spain found, looted: see Crow, *Epic*, 217, and Sutherland, *Gold*, 135.

30 Jean d'Argo's attack: although it is not known how much he captured, the remaining ships reached Seville with bullion worth 280 million maravedis.

CHAPTER 4

33 'Divine tobacco': *The Faerie Queene*, Bk III, c.v. xxxii.

CHAPTER 5

42 The Tropics: these judgements are based on twelve years' observation by the author.

43 For the merry: *Colonising*, ed. Harlow, 44.

43 The best picture: Colt Journal, in *Colonising*, 55-102.

45 Sir Henry was proud: prayers were held thrice daily, at 10 a.m., 4 p.m. and 8 p.m. The ship frequently averaged six and a half knots over a 24-hour period and on 1 June was making eight knots until forced to furl the topgallant.

45 By 23 June: the unreliability of clocks made it impossible to determine longitude with any accuracy.

46 Nevertheless he wrote: he complained, as does the twentieth-century visitor in the West Indies, of 'an abundance of small gnats by the sea shore', the tiny and vicious sandflies.

47 Sir Henry was looking: he visited the new plantation of Colonel Holdip, the first man to plant sugar, and admired his work.

CHAPTER 6

Page

50 The tobacco was so earthy: Richard Ligon, *A True and Exact Account of Barbados*, London 1657, page 28.

51 'If Newgate ...': quoted in Williams, *From Columbus*, 100.

52 The Earl of Warwick: he advised dropping any ideas that 'may disoblige the Parliament's case...' BM Sloane MSS 184, f. 124B.

52 'A restless spirit': Cundall, *Governors*, 21.

53 Prince Maurice's fate: more than ten years later depositions were being taken at Tortuga and St Kitts and sent back to London: see Historic Manuscript Commission, J. M. Heathcote MSS, L. 117, 134–9.

53 Capturing 500 ships: see Crow, *Epic*, 19.

54 Value of bullion: BM Add 13964, f. 196.

58 Natural ranches: hogs were so flourishing in Jamaica at this time, 1654, that the Spanish were killing 80,000 a year to send lard to Cartagena.

58 The governor to Colbert: Ogeron to Colbert, 20 July 1665, in Vaissière, *Saint-Dominque*, 18–19.

59 Unorganized rabble: du Tertre, *Histoire*, I. 415.

59 A particular relish: Burney, *History*, 49.

61 One of the buccaneers: Esquemeling, Paris edition of 1688, I. 22, published under the name Oexmelin.

CHAPTER 7

63 Edward and Thomas Morgan: see also Cruikshank, *Life*.

65 'The office of Judge Admiral': CSP/WI 1304, 25 February 1680.

66 'Hectors and knights': Firth, *Venables*, XXXIII.

67 Their worst men: Venables, *Narrative*, quoted in Southey, *History*, 4.

68 'This illand is': Whistler's journal, BM Sloane MSS, 3926.

68 'We shall not tie': Firth, *Cromwell*, I. 376.

72 'Resolved to attempt': Firth, *Venables*, 94.

CHAPTER 8

73 William Jackson: see Harlow, *Voyages*.

74 Settlers from New England: Southey, *History*, 11.

75 'The truth is': Carlyle, *Cromwell*, Speech V; Firth, *Cromwell*, II. 376.

CHAPTER 9

84 Giving up Jamaica: Acts/PC 1,302; House of Commons Journal VIII, 163.

84 'Foreign Plantations': the committee's name was usually 'Trade and Plantations', but it was often called 'of Trade' or 'of Plantations' depending on the subject involved.

87 One writer: Haring, *Trade*, 130–1.

88 New settlers: Acts/PC 522, 3 July 1661.

88 Newgate Prison: Acts/PC 527, 24 July 1661.

89 'Obtain and preserve': CSP/WI 278.

89 Renaming Port Royal: Ibid 275, 670.

CHAPTER 10

Page
91 'More Like a soldier': Morales-Carrión, *Puerto Rico*, 35.
91 Offered salt: Ibid, 39.
96 Mings' report: Mings to Windsor, 19 October 1662.
96 Pepys' diary: entry for 19 February 1663.
96 French commissions: CSP/WI 817.
97 Barry at Tortuga: Ibid 443, 474.
98 Mings sails: Ibid 521.

CHAPTER 11

101 The Old Standers: see CSP/WI 612.
101 After the Santiago raid: Rumbold to Fanshaw, 21 March 1663, HMC Heathcote
      MSS.
102 The King's proclamation: CSP/WI 443.
103 Bennet's draft: Ibid 739, 30 April 1664.
104 'Hated and cursed...': Ibid 774, Lynch to Bennet, 25 May 1664.

CHAPTER 12

105 Daughter's death: CSP/WI 1085, Modyford to Arlington (formerly Bennet),
      16 November 1664.
106 News of Jack: Ibid 1827, deposition of H. Wasey.
106 By now the King: Ibid, King to Modyford, 15 June 1664.
106 Searle's cargo: Ibid 789, Minutes of Council.
108 Privateers come in: Ibid 842, Modyford to Arlington, 12 April 1665.
108 'They are chiefly': Ibid 979, Modyford to Arlington, 20 April 1665.
110 On Marteen: Ibid 1264, Modyford to Albemarle, 21 August 1666.
112 Shipmates marooned: ammunition was a problem because English and Spanish
      shot sizes differed. Slow match could be made from the bark of the mangrove
      trees lining the coasts.

CHAPTER 13

117 Colonel E. Morgan's death: CSP/WI 1086, Colonel Cary's report on the
      expedition.
118 Statia privateers: Ibid 1264, Modyford to Albemarle, 21 August 1666.
118 The Spanish prizes: Ibid 1085, Modyford to Arlington, 16 November 1665.

CHAPTER 14

122 Beeston added: entry for 10 November.
123 It seems to be: CSP/WI 1138, Minutes of Council.
123 Their weak condition: Ibid 1264, Modyford to Albemarle, 21 August 1666.
124 Privateers alienated: Ibid 1132, Modyford to Albemarle, 1 March 1666.
125 'Meantime we are': Ibid 1213, Modyford to Albemarle, 16 June 1666.
126 Soldiers muttering: Ibid 1208, Modyford to Albemarle, 8 June 1666.
127 Attack on island: Ibid 1213, Modyford to Albemarle, 16 June 1666.
128 Wicked life: Esquemeling, 121.
129 Refuge for pirates: Esquemeling, 127.
129 Smith had sailed: CSP/WI 1264, Modyford to Albemarle, 21 August 1666.

Page

129 The Great Fire: Pepys describes it in his diary entry for 2 September. Altogether 13,000 houses and 87 churches were destroyed and nearly 400 acres devastated.

131 Report by Sanchez: this, 'A True Relation...', is given fully in Esquemeling, 122–6, and taken from the Spanish account.

132 The three Britons: CSP/WI 1851, Depositions of Richard Rawlinson, Richard Cree and Isaac Webber, 5 October 1688.

132 Major Smith had: in forwarding the depositions to London, Modyford pointed out to Albemarle in his dispatch of 5 October 1668 that Old Providence had only ever been occupied by the English, so Spain had committed 'a violation of the peace'.

CHAPTER 15

133 'I had no money': this seems a clear indication that many of the buccaneers were Dutch. See CSP/WI 1537, Modyford to Arlington, 30 July 1667.

135 'The Spaniards look': Ibid.

136 Morgan's commission: Ibid 1838, Information of Admiral Henry Morgan and officers, 7 September 1668.

137 The buccaneers had: Esquemeling, 59–61.

139 Ships at anchor: the cables were, of course, made of rope, and even modern synthetic ropes can chafe through in half an hour in similar circumstances.

140 Calling council: Esquemeling, 128.

CHAPTER 16

144 The governor's report: this is dealt with in Pezuela, *Historia de la Isla de Cuba*, II. 165–6.

146 Not all overjoyed: Leslie, *Jamaica*, 115–20.

147 'Hearts are great': Esquemeling, 136.

148 A young Scottish: Wafer, *New Voyage*, 41–3.

154 Report on raid: CSP/WI 1838, Report of Admiral Henry Morgan and his officers, Port Royal, 7 September 1668.

154 Total purchase: Leslie, *Jamaica*, 115–20, and Southey, *History*, 85.

154 London's exports: BM Sloane MSS 2902, f. 117.

154 Customs paid: PRO, Commissioners of Customs to Lords of Trade, 22 April 1678, CO 324/4, 58–9.

155 Duty on spirits: PRO, Plantation Registers, 1677–1730, PC 5/150, I.

155 'It is almost certain': CSP/WI 1850, Modyford to Albemarle, 1 October 1668.

155 News of Jack Modyford: Ibid 1859, Deposition of Francisco Martin, 12 September 1668.

156 Orders to Duke: Acts/PC, I, No. 751, 17 February 1668. Although they specified a fifth rate the *Oxford* was a sixth.

156 *Oxford*'s dimensions: see Anderson, *Lists*.

156 Fair quarter: CSP/WI, 1357, Minutes of Council, 10 December 1666.

CHAPTER 17

157 Cotton beds: du Tertre, *Histoire*, I. 508.

Page

158 Colt's advice: Colt Journal, in *Colonising*, 100–1.

161 Port Royal bread: from second part of John Taylor's history of his life and travels in America. A manuscript copy is in the Institute of Jamaica, Kingston: material is reproduced by permission.

163 Welcome guests: Leslie, *Jamaica*, 120–1.

163 Sailing in October: see CSP/WI 1863, Modyford's dispatch of 31 October 1668.

164 The surgeon's report: Ibid, Browne to Williamson, 9 November 1668.

166 Browne's account: this also gives the casualties and is in his letter to Williamson, 20 January 1669.

CHAPTER 18

167 Soares and Delander: CSP/WI 1894, Deposition of Captain Robert Delander.

168 'Hostile actions': Acts/PC No. 822, 18 December 1668.

168 Full satisfaction: CSP 1899, Memorandum of the Spanish Ambassador, 17 January 1669.

169 Lofty convent: Dampier, *Voyage* I. 72.

169 'While Morgan': Leslie, *Jamaica*, 121.

170 'Spied on English': Esquemeling, 146.

171 Neck of the flask: see Admiralty, W. Indies Pilot, vol. I, 1956 edition, page 216, Lago de Maracaibo, and edition of 1861, page 144, referring to Baja Seco Island.

173 The quicksands: see Admiralty, W. Indies Pilot, vol. I, 1861 edition, page 145, and 1956 edition, 201, 225.

175 Tormented prisoner: Esquemeling, 154.

CHAPTER 19

177 Admiral's letter: this is given fully in Esquemeling, 160.

181 The pilot's story: see Esquemeling, 166–8.

184 Don Alonso to prisoners: Esquemeling, 170.

CHAPTER 20

188 Pipe of wine: Leslie, *Jamaica*, 100–1.

189 'I always reproved': CSP/WI 103 (New Series), Narrative of Sir Thomas Modyford, 23 August 1669.

190 The patent refers: Record Office, Jamaica, Liber of Letters Patent, vol. 3, f. 227.

190 Campo's arrest: see Haring, *Trade*, 254; Linaje, *Norte*, vol. 2, chap. 5, paras 8, 9; Duro, *Armada*, V.171.

192 Signing letter: CSP/WI 114, Modyford to Arlington, 1 October 1669.

192 Charles's account: Ibid 144, Charles Modyford to Arlington, 22 January 1670.

194 Carstens and Captain Bernard: Ibid 172, Deposition of Cornelius Carstens.

194 Searle's arrival: Ibid 162, Modyford to Arlington, 15 March 1670.

195 Brethren incensed: Ibid 162, Modyford to Arlington, 15 March 1670.

196 'I could wish': Ibid 162, Sir James Modyford to Thomas Lynch, 18 March 1670.

196 *Amity* capture: deposition of William Lane, 5 May 1670.

197 Three ships sighted: Ibid 214, Council Minutes.

197 Pardal's challenge: Ibid 310. ii, but the original poster, sent to London later, is now missing from the PRO.

Page

199 Extraordinary alarm: Ibid 214, Council Minutes, 29 June 1670.

199 'With this resolution': Esquemeling, 174.

201 Morgan's orders: given fully in Council's Minutes, 29 June 1670.

201 'It is possible': CSP/WI 214, 6 July 1670, Modyford to Arlington and enclosing Council Minutes.

202 Browne bored: Ibid 227, Browne to Williamson, 7 August 1670.

203 Deliver documents: these included a copy of the Queen-Regent's *cédula*, the *San Nicolas*'s commission, Carsten's deposition, a report on Pardal's operations, his challenge, and the Council Minutes.

203 'The country abounds': Ibid 216, Modyford to Lord Ashley, no date.

204 Chilling words: Ibid 194, Arlington to Modyford, 12 June 1670.

205 Frank reply: Ibid 237, Modyford to Arlington, 20 August 1670.

CHAPTER 21

206 *Dolphin*'s broadside: Ibid 293, Browne to Williamson, 12 October 1670. Browne was writing from on board the *Satisfaction*.

206 Canvas poster: Ibid 319, Modyford to Arlington, 31 October 1670. A copy had earlier been sent to London.

207 Another storm: Southey, *History*, 99–100.

208 Browne's judgment: CSP/WI 293, Browne to Williamson, 12 October 1670.

209 Selling Jamaica: Ibid 284, Modyford to Arlington, 20 September 1670.

210 Ships and captains: Ibid 704. i, has list, while the names are also recorded in Jamaica, Journals of the House of Assembly, vol. I.

213 'Impossible for us': CSP/WI, Morgan to Modyford, 20 April 1671.

214 Council vote: Morgan's report to Modyford is in Ibid 504.

214 Lynch's family: see Cundall, *Governors*, 27.

216 Hack's chart: this chart, used as the dustjacket of this book, is BM Add MSS 5414, f. 25.

219 Horse or mule: Wafer, *New Voyage*, 46.

220 A few years later: Ibid 24.

222 Hold Chagres: Bartholomew Sharp, *Voyages*, 145.

223 'Wanted water': *Gentleman's Magazine*, 1740, vol. X, 457–8.

227 'Having this morning': Esquemeling, 195.

CHAPTER 22

234 This combat: Esquemeling, 200–1.

236 Don Juan's narrative: his report to Spain was intercepted and published in 1684 in Sharp's *Voyages*, 145, and is used throughout to describe the Spanish part in the battle.

243 Young Spanish woman: Esquemeling, 216.

243 Seven months after: CSP/WI 608, Browne to Williamson, 21 August 1671.

CHAPTER 23

248 In the past six: see Haring, *Trade*, 249–50; Duro, *Armada*, V. 310.

249 Exports from England: BM Sloane Add MSS 2902, f. 117.

250 Help Lynch: Cundall, *Governors*, 33.

Page
250 Old Providence: CSP/WI 484, Sir J. Modyford to Williamson, 18 April; 534, same to same, 18 May.
250 Morgan's report: Ibid, 543, Jamaica Council Minutes, 31 May 1671.
251 Lengthy document: Ibid 578, Modyford to Arlington, 7 June 1671.
252 Lynches as guests: see Cundall, *Governors*, 33.
253 First report: CSP/WI 580, Lynch to Arlington, 2 July 1671.
253 Browne's criticisms: Ibid 608, Browne to Williamson, 21 August 1671.
255 Six years in jail: see Haring, *Trade*, 12–15.
255 Dr Holme's case: CSP/WI Council Minutes, 21 September 1671.
257 Diarist noted: John Evelyn, entry for 18 August 1671.
257 Grandees of Spain: CSP/WI 683, Lynch to Arlington, 29 November 1671.
258 'The chief officer': Cundall, *Governors*, 35.
259 'To speak the truth': CSP/WI 697, Lynch to Arlington, 17 December 1671.
259 'Thirty-six years': see Cundall, *Governors*, 56.
260 'Not defend': CSP/WI 729, Lynch to Arlington, 13 January 1672.
260 Browne's complaint: Ibid 798, Browne to Williamson, 4 April 1672.
261 Bannister's letter: Ibid 789, Bannister to Arlington, 30 March 1672.

CHAPTER 24

262 'All may be lost': CSP/WI 887, Lynch to the King, 6 July 1672.
263 Petition rejected: Cundall, *Governors*, 29.
263 Without being charged: in *An Historical Account of the Rise and Growth of the West Indies Colonies* by Sir Thomas Dalby, London 1690, page 42.
264 Many people: CSP/Domestic, p. 451, from William Morgan, August 1672.
267 Assembly dissolved: Cundall, *Governors*, 46–7.
269 Biscayners: see Morales-Carrión, *Puerto Rico*, 54; Linaje, *Norte*, vol. 2, chap. 5.
269 The astronomer: Gadham, working from his office in Brick Court, Dean's Yard, Westminster, was extending the scope of his 1675 edition, which was to be called the *West India Almanack*. It was short on astronomical data but long on astrology.
270 He then looked: CSP/WI 1389, Lynch to Williamson, 20 November 1674.
270 New commissions: Cundall, *Governors*, 78–9.
273 Morgan's Council: CSP/WI 459, Council Minutes, 11 March.
274 Stores so exhausted: CSP/WI 521, Morgan to Williamson, 13 April 1675.
275 Gallop's profit: the ship would have fetched about £500. The total of £7,500 was 30,000 pieces of eight, compared with the 50,000 from Morgan's raid on Puerto Principe, and 250,000 from Maracaibo.
275 Sir Henry wasted: CSP/WI 521, Morgan to Williamson, 13 April 1675.
275 'Conduct of affairs': Ibid 566, Vaughan to Williamson, 18 May 1675.
276 One such man: a copy of the letter is in Ibid 657, Morgan to Edmunds, 25 August 1675.
276 Power of Attorney: the copy sent to London by Vaughan is in Ibid 638, d'Ogeron to Byndloss, 5 July 1675.
277 A heated reply: Ibid 673, Vaughan to Williamson, 20 September 1675.
278 Grow as rich: Cundall, *Governors*, 80.
278 Reply was bland: CSP/WI 807, Morgan to Williamson, 2 February 1676.
279 Vaughan ordered: see Cruikshank, *Life*, 236.
279 Captain Deane: CSP/WI 863, Vaughan to Williamson, 4 April 1676.
280 Questioning Barré: Ibid 1129, Examination of C. Barré.

Page

282 'But if His Majesty': Ibid 1129, Morgan to Coventry, 2 August 1676.

CHAPTER 25

283 A month later: CSP/WI, 1001, Lords of Trade to Vaughan, 28 July 1676.
283 Only reply: Ibid 1093, Vaughan to Lords of Trade, 30 October 1676.
284 John Byndloss: CSP/C 461, Journal of the Lords of Trade, 28–9 October 1677.
284 A resident: the letter is printed in *Interesting Tracts*, Jamaica 1800, page 105.
285 A series of events: Acts/PC, 23 March 1677.
286 Great pains: Acts/PC, 1 June 1677.
287 Letters of reprisal: Acts/PC, 4 July 1677.
287 No vessel comes: see Cundall, *Governors*, 81–2.
287 Ships sailing: PRO CO 324/4, 58–9.
287 Jamaica exports: BM Add MSS 8133c, f. 237.
287 Money bill: see Cundall, *Governors*, 81–2.
288 Piece the story: CSP/WI 243, Vaughan to Williamson, 14 May 1677.
288 Elephants' teeth: Acts/PC, 22 November 1676.
288 The bishop packs: Wafer, *Voyages*, 6 f.n.
288 Peter Beckford: CSP/WI 1007, Beckford to Williamson, 2 August 1676.
290 Repeat the request: Ibid 365, Journals, Assembly, 24 July 1677.
290 In the King's name: see Cundall, *Governors*, 84.
290 Whereupon: Journals, Assembly, 24 July 1677.
290 Lynch wrote: CSP/WI 383, Lynch to Williamson, 5 August 1677.
292 Commissions: Ibid 571, Warrant for Carlisle; 572, Commission for Morgan; 570 warrant for Carlisle 'to cause drums...'.
293 Largest landowner: Cundall, *Governors*, 85.
293 In Carlisle's first year: PRO, PC 5/150, 1, Plantation Register.

CHAPTER 26

294 Island's defences: CSP/WI 654, Minutes of a Council of War, 5 April 1678.
295 Morgan's report: Ibid 692, Council Minutes, 25 April 1678.
296 An embargo: Ibid, Council Minutes, 31 May 1678.
296 Attack Curaçao: Ibid 718, Relation to T. Wigfall, 1 June 1678.
297 Wigfall's reward: Ibid 725, Council Minutes, 7 June 1678.
297 Carlisle's gout: Ibid 770, Carlisle to Coventry, 21 July 1678.
298 So dissatisfied: Ibid 794, Carlisle to Coventry, 11 September 1678.
299 Mounting guns: BM Add MSS 17019, f. 37.
301 'The French': CSP/WI 869, Carlisle to Coventry, 26 January 1679.
301 'My kindness': Ibid 943, Carlisle to Coventry, 26 March 1679.
301 A new hearing: Acts/PC, 10 October 1679.
302 'No malice': CSP/WI 1304, Morgan to Lords of Trade, 24 February 1680.
303 Requested liberty: Acts/PC, vol. 2, 30 June 1680.
303 £2000 security: Acts/PC, vol. 2, 21 July 1680.
305 'They admired': CSP/WI 1049, Carlisle to Coventry, 13 August 1679.
306 The Assembly asked: Ibid 1097, Journals, Assembly, 21 August 1679.
306 Sir Henry wrote it: Ibid 1101, Report of a Committee of the Council and Assembly, 23 August 1679.
307 Present juncture: Ibid 1105, Address of the General Assembly, 28 August 1679.
307 'Warm and nettled': Ibid 1107, Carlisle to Coventry, 30 August 1679.

Page

CHAPTER 27

CHAPTER 28

Page

      meant verse dedicated to Morgan and which ended: 'Great Morgan's fame shall last as long as there / Is beat of drum or any sound of war.'

335 Sold himself: this statement, published as part of a libel statement, puts paid to the tale that Morgan went out as an indentured servant.

335 Piratical English: CSP/WI 67, Molesworth to Sunderland, 16 March 1683.

336 Charles Swan: he wrote of his wife that he hoped to do things that 'would make her a lady; but now I cannot tell but it may bring me to a halter'. (CSP/WI 87, Charles Swan to Captain John Wise, 4 March 1685.) He was writing from Panama and a few months later was killed in the Philippines.

336 Parson jailed: Cundall, *Governors*, 99.

338 Barry's answer: CSP/WI 1171, Statement of Colonel Barry, 3 March 1687.

338 Byndloss's charge: Ibid 1301, Byndloss to Lords of Trade, 12 August 1687.

341 'Opulent Kingdoms': Journals, Assembly, I. 105.

341 Writing notes: Sloane, *Voyage*, was published in 1707, by which time most of the work on his collection had been completed.

343 Morgan's will: Records Office, Jamaica, Liber of Wills, 6, f. 8. signed 17 June 1668; entered 14 September 1688. In it, Henry Archbold's name is variously spelled 'Archbould' and 'Archbold'.

346 Sloane's treatment: see Sloane, *Voyage*, vol. I. pp. xcviii–cxix.

348 Lady Morgan: when she died she was buried at Spanish Town.

CHAPTER 29

350 Sir Henry's diligence: the report was by the Fort's namesake, Lord Carlisle, CSP/WI 770, Carlisle to Coventry, 21 July 1678.

349–53 The best description of the earthquake, with a drawing, is given in *A True and Perfect Relation of that most sad and terrible Earthquake, at Port Royal in Jamaica . . .*, published by R. Smith in 1692. (BM 719. m. 17.) The letter from which the broadsheet was written was dated 30 June, just three weeks after the earthquake.

354 The results of the modern diving on the old sunken city are well described in Marx, *Port Royal*, which also gives photographs of many of the articles.

Bibliography

The following are the full titles of documents and volumes referred to in the Notes and Bibliography as well as many books consulted in the course of research or which make interesting further reading:

Journals of the House of Lords, vols VI, VII, X.
Journals of the House of Commons, vols III, VI.

PUBLIC RECORD OFFICE

Acts of the Privy Council, Colonial Series, 1613–80, edited by W. L. Grant and J. Munro, 6 vols, HMSO, 1908–12.
Journals of the Assembly of Jamaica, 1663–1826, 15 vols, Jamaica, 1811–29.
Calendar of State Papers, Colonial Series, 1574–1660; North America and West Indies 1661–1736; America and West Indies Addenda 1658–63, edited by W. N. Sainsbury, J. W. Fortescue and C. Headlam, London, 1860–1924.
Commissioner of Customs Reports, CO 324/4, 33/13.
Plantation Register 1677–1730, PC 5/150J.

BRITISH LIBRARY

'A Journal kept by Colonel William Beeston from his first coming to Jamaica'.
Sloane MS 2902 f. 117; 3926 (Whistler Diary).
Egerton MSS 2395 ff. 503–509B.
Add MSS 13964 ff. 196, 405; 5414 f. 25 (Hack chart); 79019 f. 37; 719 m. 17.

TRINITY COLLEGE, Dublin

MSS (G4, 15) No. 736.

CAMBRIDGE UNIVERSITY LIBRARY

MSS Mm. 3, 9 (Sir Henry Colt's Journal and letter to son George).

GENERAL BIBLIOGRAPHY

The Governors of Jamaica in the 17th Century, Frank Cundall, W. India Committee, London, 1936.

The West Indies and Spanish Main, Anthony Trollope, London, 1859.

The Buccaneers of America, John Esquemeling, London, 1684–5 (Broadway Translations reprint, London, n.d.).

Chronological History of the West Indies, 3 vols, Thomas Southey, London, 1827 (Reprinted Cass, 1968).

The Annals of Jamaica, G. W. Bridges, 2 vols, London, 1827–8.

The History, Civil and Commercial, of the British Colonies in the West Indies, B. Edwards, London, 1819.

Trade and Navigation between Spain and the West Indies in the Time of the Hapsburgs, C. H. Haring, Harvard University Press, 1918.

The French Struggle for the West Indies, 1665–1713, Nellis M. Crouse, New York, 1943.

Spanish Documents Concerning English Voyages to the Caribbean 1527–68, Hakluyt Society, 2nd Series, LXII.

A Description of the Island of Jamaica, Richard Blome, London, 1672.

The Life of Sir Henry Morgan, with an account of the English Settlement of the Island of Jamaica, 1655–1688, E. A. Cruikshank, Macmillan London and Basingstoke, and Toronto, 1935.

The Present State of Jamaica, Thomas Malthus, London, 1683.

The Voyages and Adventures of Capt. Barth Sharp and others in the South Seas, by 'P.A.', London, 1684.

Gentleman's Magazine, August, September 1740; February, March, 1832, articles by Charles E. Long.

A New History of Jamaica, Charles Leslie, London, 1740.

The Voyages of Captain William Jackson, 1642–5, edited V. T. Harlow.

A History of Jamaica, 3 vols, Edward Long, London, 1774.

Colonising Expeditions to the West Indies and Guiana 1623–67, edited V. T. Harlow, Hakluyt Society, London, 1925.

English Historical Review, XX, pp. 315 *et seq.*, article by F. A. Kirkpatrick, 'The First Recorded English Voyage to the West Indies'.

Lists of Men of War 1650–1700, Pt 1, English Ships 1649–1702, compiled by R. C. Anderson, Society of Nautical Research, London, 1966.

The Great Buccaneer, Philip Lindsay, London, 1950.

Puerto Rico and the Non-Hispanic Caribbean, Arturo Morales-Carrión, University of Puerto Rico, 1952.

Gold, C. H. V. Sutherland, London, 1959.

The English Conquest of Jamaica ... What happened in 1655–6, Julián de Castilla, translated and edited by Irene A. Wright, Campden Society Misc., London, 1923.

A Voyage to the Islands of Madeira ... Jamaica, Sir Hans Sloane, London, 1707.

The Cavaliers and Roundheads of Barbados 1650–2, N. D. Davis, Georgetown, Guiana, 1887.

A New Voyage and Description of the Isthmus of America, Lionel Wafer, Hakluyt Society, London, 1934, Series 2, LXXIII.

The Epic of Latin America, J. A. Crow, New York, 1952.

A New Survey of the West Indies, Thomas Gage, London, 1655.

A New Voyage Round the World, 1697, William Dampier (reprinted London, 1927).

The Narrative of General Venables, with an appendix of papers relating to the Expedition to the West Indies and the Conquest of Jamaica 1654–5, London, 1900 (edited C. A. Firth for Royal Historical Society).

War and Trade in the West Indies, Richard Pares, Oxford, 1936.

The Western Design, S. A. G. Taylor, Institute of Jamaica and Jamaica Historical Society, Kingston, 1965.

From Columbus to Castro: the History of the Caribbean 1492–1969, E. Williams, London, 1970.

The Early Spanish Main, C. O. Sauer, Los Angeles, 1966.

The European Nations in the West Indies 1493–1688, A. P. Newton, London, 1933.

Cromwell, C. A. Firth, London, 1934.

The Last Days of the Protectorate, C. A. Firth, London, 1909.

A History of the Buccaneers of America, J. Burney, London, 1816.

Port Royal Rediscovered, Robert F. Marx, London, 1973.

Norte de la Contratación de las Indias Occidentales, Joseph de Veitia de Linaje, Seville, 1672 and Buenos Aires, 1945.

Armada Española..., C. Fernández Duro, 9 vols, Madrid, 1895–1903.

Historia Maritima Militar de España, Adolfo Navarette, Madrid, 1901.

Disquisiciones Naúticas, C. Fernández Duro, 6 vols, Madrid, 1867–81.

Saint-Domingue 1629–1789, P. de Vaissière, Paris, 1909.

Histoire de l'Isle Espagnole ou de Saint-Domingue, Père P.-F.-X. Charlevoix, 2 vols, Paris, 1730–1.

Nouveau Voyage aux Isles de l'Amérique, Père Labat, 6 vols, Paris, 1722.

Histoire Générale des Antilles, Père J.-B. du Tertre, 3 vols, Paris, 1667–71.

Index

NOTE: Ships are listed alphabetically under 'Ships'. San, Sainte and Saint are treated as the same word. References to Spanish names are usually listed under the penultimate name (e.g. Manuel Rivera Pardal is indexed under Rivera) but usually also cross-referenced under the last name.